AMERICA ASCENDANT

AMERICA ASCENDANT

The Rise of American Exceptionalism

DENNIS M. SPRAGG

Potomac Books

An imprint of the University of Nebraska Press

All rights reserved. Potomac Books is an imprint of
the University of Nebraska Press.
Manufactured in the United States of America.

∞

Library of Congress Cataloging-in-Publication Data
Names: Spragg, Dennis M., author.
Title: America ascendant: the rise of American
exceptionalism / Dennis M. Spragg.
Other titles: Rise of American exceptionalism
Description: Lincoln NE: Potomac Books, an imprint
of the University of Nebraska Press, [2019] | Includes
bibliographical references and index.
Identifiers: LCCN 2019005294
ISBN 9781640121430 (cloth: alk. paper)
ISBN 9781640122628 (epub)
ISBN 9781640122635 (mobi)
ISBN 9781640122642 (pdf)
Subjects: LCSH: World War, 1939–1945—United States—
Propaganda. | Exceptionalism—United States—History. |
World War, 1939-1945—United States—Mass media and
the war. | Government and the press—United States—
History—20th century. | Press and politics—United
States—History—20th century. | Political culture—United
States—History—20th century.
Classification: LCC D810.P7 U48 2019 |
DDC 940.53/73—dc23
LC record available at https://lccn.loc.gov/2019005294

Set in Minion Pro by Mikala R. Kolander.

In memory of Charles Krauthammer,
an exceptional American

Champion of rational thinking, intellectual honesty,
principled debate, courtesy, and wit

1. Pres. Abraham Lincoln. Portrait by George Peter Alexander Healy, 1869.
White House Collection, White House Historical Association, Washington DC.

Fellow-citizens, we cannot escape history. We of this Congress and this administration, will be remembered in spite of ourselves. No personal significance, or insignificance, can spare one or another of us. The fiery trial through which we pass, will light us down, in honor or dishonor, to the latest generation. We say we are for the Union. The world will not forget that we say this. We know how to save the Union. The world knows we do know how to save it. We—even we here—hold the power, and bear the responsibility. In giving freedom to the slave, we assure freedom to the free—honorable alike in what we give, and what we preserve. We shall nobly save, or meanly lose, the last best hope of earth. Other means may succeed; this could not fail. The way is plain, peaceful, generous, just—a way which, if followed, the world will forever applaud, and God must forever bless.

—Pres. ABRAHAM LINCOLN, December 1, 1862

CONTENTS

ILLUSTRATIONS

PROLOGUE

The United States of America is an exceptional nation that uniquely transcends region, race, and religion. Dictionaries define the word *exceptional* as (a) forming an exception: rare; (b) better than average: superior, and (c) deviating from the norm, such as having above average intelligence. Historians have used variations of all three definitions to explain how thirteen British North American colonies became an independent nation that developed into a global superpower. Attempts to define American exceptionalism differ by era, and national leaders have engaged in a robust debate over the meaning of America for most of the nation's history.

Nineteenth-century and early twentieth-century political discourse was a contest between expansionism versus morality. The main themes were "manifest destiny" and the question of slavery. The competing ideals were well defined and widely argued; for example, Hamilton federalism versus Jeffersonian republicanism; the abolitionist North versus the slave South; and Wilsonian progressivism versus Lodge pragmatism. It took the greatest challenge in American history and skilled leadership to cause an intersection of the competing impulses to unify the nation and define American exceptionalism.

Franklin Delano Roosevelt, aided by exceptional bipartisan statesmen and soldiers, changed the dynamic of competing American visions by replacing expansionism as a national imperative and replacing it with interventionism, which he defined in the Atlantic Charter as a moral responsibility. Interventionism became victory and then internationalism with the founding of the United Nations. America conceived and led far-reaching global relief, economic aid, and security arrangements that have lasted into the twenty-first century.

Two exceptional generations of Americans directed and fought World War II. An extraordinary bipartisan government alliance with industrial and media leaders, all of whom were born in the late nineteenth century, had the imagination and reason to organize and communicate on an unprecedented scale. Roosevelt's Office of War Information, Hollywood, and the broadcasting industry capably *defined* American exceptionalism at home and abroad. Millions of exceptional Americans born in the twentieth century did not hesitate to do what was necessary to save the world. They unselfishly *proved* American exceptionalism on the battlefield, upholding and advancing American values.

The alliance between government and media, including the Office of War Information, Hollywood, and broadcasters, defined and communicated the convergence of national interest with moral imperative. As young Americans proved exceptionalism on battlefields in every corner of the earth, they and their fellow Americans, motivated by the ideas and ideals of their forebears and leaders communicated to them by the alliance, went on to build an enlightened postwar world.

The exceptional generations did not simply achieve victory in a global war of survival, but they did so to create a better world without the motivation of territorial conquest. What they achieved *after the war* and how the history of America empowered them to be exceptional is as important as their service. They need not be America's most exceptional generations in the decades and centuries to follow. There will certainly be others who will carry the torch.

The twenty-first-century descendants of the "exceptional generations" have diverse and inaccurate ideas about what American exceptionalism is. Polarized political discourse has upset the equilibrium won by the wartime generations. The Vietnam War, Watergate, and the personal imperfections of self-absorbed and unorthodox politicians have clouded the memory and awareness of Americans about where they came from, why they are exceptional, what exceptionalism really is, and how they can apply exceptionalism to continue building a better nation and world. This includes the constructive role of the media and its relationship to sound governance.

The modern American media, political establishment, and special interest groups have divided themselves among red and blue states, race, gender, and lifestyle. Amazing technologies are isolating Americans rather than bringing them together. As media have fragmented among confusing options and voices, the dependable world of Walter Cronkite has devolved into a Tower of Babel. News has become commentary, as journalism has descended into partisan argument. As universities have become racially diverse but intellectually segregated as leftist bastions, false traditionalist prophets have appeared in response, preaching long-discredited doctrines of isolation and intolerance. Citizens caught in the middle yearn for a renaissance of civility and mourn the absence of civics in revisionist classrooms. Generations that have come of age during and after the pivotal Vietnam War era, devoid of civics and history, might consider the Nicomachean Ethics espoused by Aristotle, that earlier generations of conscientious Americans well understood: *in medio stat virtus . . .* virtue stands in the middle, or, good practice lies in the middle path.

What twenty-first-century Americans and the exceptional generations have in common with their forebearers is liberty, equal justice, and a respect for human dignity. With the momentous achievements of victory and global leadership came the blessings of great wealth and power but also an important duty. American leaders have not always appreciated these blessings or acted as responsible stewards of their trust. Although the nation has always continued along a progressive and ascending trajectory, mistakes and missed opportunities have bred cynicism among the intellectual class, political elite, and media that polarizes twenty-first-century American discourse.

America's founders had an astonishingly different vision for their nation and humanity than the kingdoms of their time and the technologically advanced nation-state, corporate, and academic dictatorships of today. Their experiment in liberal mercantile democracy has evolved, but their Constitution and Bill of Rights remain as milestones in the march of human progress, liberty, and rational thinking from the first tribes to the classical Greek and Roman republics, the English Magna Carta, and the European Renaissance. America is still an enlightened concept as well as an exceptional nation.

With struggle and sacrifice, mid-twentieth-century America found a mature equilibrium that allowed it to create a new world order and cleanse its sins. America liberated more people from tyranny and poverty than any nation in history, rejected territorial conquest, was magnanimous and generous, fought a war of national and cultural survival against fascism with no quarter asked or given, but also had the wisdom to fight a cold war against communism with restraint and invested in the planet by rebuilding it while supporting self-determination.

Many pundits and politicians claim American exceptionalism is a "dangerous myth," and that there has never been anything exceptional about America. Cynics seek to expunge history with virtuous revisionist manifestos, erasing evidence and dismantling monuments. The truth of America is both inspiring and intermittently problematic, but it stands on its own historic merit. Americans cannot deny, polish or forget their heritage if the United States is to continue moving forward toward its inexorable purpose.

American exceptionalism is not the manifest destiny of the nineteenth century, the ambitious aftermath of the Spanish-American War, or Woodrow Wilson's zealotry. America never was and is not an imperialist power. Americans have long rejected imperial privilege and have either at their best embraced global leadership and responsibility or at their worst retreated into isolation and protectionism.

The United States once came to a rendezvous with destiny and forever changed the course of human history. This is the story of how an ascendant America came to define itself and be an exceptional nation.

> A knowledge of history is important to the defense of our cause.... This enables us to rebut falsehoods and place truths in proper perspective.—Maj. Gen. Vernon A. Walters

ABBREVIATIONS

AAF	Army Air Forces
AAFTC	Army Air Forces Training Command
ABAEF	American Band of the Allied Expeditionary Force
ABC	American Broadcasting Company
ABSIE	American Broadcasting Station in Europe (Voice of America)
AEFP	Allied Expeditionary Forces Programme (of the BBC)
AFHQ	Allied Force Headquarters, Mediterranean and North Africa
AFL	American Federation of Labor
AFM	American Federation of Musicians
AFN	American Forces Network
AFRA	American Federation of Radio Artists
AFRS	Armed Forces Radio Service
AFRTS	Armed Forces Radio and Television Service
AG-AUS	Adjutant General, Army of the United States
AGWAR	Adjutant General, War Department
ANZUS	Australia, New Zealand, and United States Security Treaty
ATC	Air Transport Command (Army Air Forces)
ATIS	Allied Translator and Interpreter Section
AUS	Army of the United States
AVIANCA	Aerovías Nacionales de Columbia
BBC	British Broadcasting Corporation
BMP	Bureau of Motion Pictures (Office of War Information)
BPR	Bureau of Public Affairs (War Department)

BSC	British Security Co-ordination
CAB	Civil Aeronautics Board
CBI	China-Burma-India Theatre of Operations
CBS	Columbia Broadcasting System
CCC	Civilian Conservation Corps
CIA	Central Intelligence Agency
CIG	Central Intelligence Group
COMZ	Communications Zone, U.S. Army in Europe
COSSAC	Chief of Staff to the Supreme Allied Commander
CPI	Committee on Public Information (World War I)
CPO	Chief Petty Officer (Navy)
CSU	Conference of Studio Unions
DAR	Daughters of the American Revolution
DBST	Double British Summer Time
ENSA	Entertainments National Service Organization (United Kingdom)
ERP	European Recovery Plan (Marshall Plan)
ETO	European Theatre of Operations
ETOUSA	U.S. Army in Europe
FBI	Federal Bureau of Investigation
FCC	Federal Communications Commission
FEAF	Far East Air Forces (United States)
FEN	Far East Network (Armed Forces Radio Service)
FFI	French Forces of the Interior (La Résistance)
FMPU	Army Air Forces First Motion Picture Unit
GM	General Motors Corporation
HQ	headquarters
HUAC	House Un-American Activities Committee
IAEA	International Atomic Energy Agency
IATSE	International Alliance of Theatrical Stage Employees
IBRD	International Bank for Reconstruction and Development
ICBM	intercontinental ballistic missile
IJN	Imperial Japanese Navy
IMF	International Monetary Fund
IMT	International Military Tribunal (Germany)

IMTFE	International Military Tribunal for the Far East
LATI	Linee Aeree Transcontinentali
LCVP	landing craft vehicle personnel (Higgins Boat)
LVT	Landing Vehicle Tracked (Amtrak)
MOI	Ministry of Information (United Kingdom)
MPA	Motion Picture Alliance for the Preservation of American Ideals
NAACP	National Association for the Advancement of Colored People
NAB	National Association of Broadcasters
NACA	National Advisory Committee for Aeronautics
NAMPI	National Association of the Motion Picture Industry
NAS	Naval Air Station
NASA	National Aeronautics and Space Administration
NATO	North Atlantic Treaty Organization
NATS	Naval Air Transport Service
NBC	National Broadcasting Company
NHK	Nippon Hōsō Kyōkai
NLRB	National Labor Relations Board
OCD	Office of Civil Defense
OCIAA	Office of the Coordinator of Inter-American Affairs
OCOI	Office of the Coordinator of Information
OFF	Office of Facts and Figures
OGR	Office of Government Reports
OKW	Oberkommando die Wehrmacht
OPEC	Organization of the Petroleum Exporting Countries
OSS	Office of Strategic Services
OWI	Office of War Information
PCE	patrol craft escort
PRC	People's Republic of China
PRD	Public Relations Division (SHAEF)
PTO	Pacific Theatre of Operations
PTT	Postes, Télégraphes et Téléphones
PVA	People's Volunteer Army (China)
PWA	Public Works Administration
PWB	Psychological Warfare Branch (OWI)

PWD	Psychological Warfare Division (SHAEF)
PWE	Psychological Warfare Executive (United Kingdom)
RAF	Royal Air Force
RCA	Radio Corporation of America
RFE	Radio Free Europe
RIAS	Radio in the American Sector (Berlin)
RL	Radio Liberty
RPU	Army Air Forces Radio production units
SCADTA	Sociedad Colombio-Alemana de Transportes Aéreos (Colombian-German Air Transport Company)
SCAP	Supreme Commander, Allied Powers
SDI	Strategic Defense Initiative
SEALS	Sea, Air, and Land Teams (U.S. Navy)
SEATO	Southeast Asia Treaty Organization
SEC	Securities and Exchange Commission
SHAEF	Supreme Headquarters, Allied Expeditionary Force
SLBM	submarine-launched ballistic missile
SOE	Special Operations Executive
SPAR	Semper Paratus Always Ready (U.S. Coast Guard)
SSD	Special Services Division of the War Department
SSU	Strategic Serves Unit
TVA	Tennessee Valley Authority
TWA	Transcontinental and Western Airlines, later Trans World Airlines
UN	United Nations
USAF	U.S. Air Force
USAFFE	U.S. Air Forces in the Far East
USIA	U.S. Information Agency
USN	U.S. Navy
USNR	U.S. Navy Reserve
USO	United Service Organizations
USSTAF	U.S. Strategic and Tactical Air Forces in Europe
USV	U.S. volunteer
VARIG	Viação Aérea Rio-Grandense (Rio Grandean Airways)

VASP	Viação Aérea São Paulo (São Paulo Airways)
VOA	Voice of America
WAAC	Women's Auxiliary Army Corps
WAC	Women's Army Corps
WASP	Women Air Service Pilots
WAVE	Women Accepted for Voluntary Emergency Service (U.S. Navy)
WIB	War Industries Board (World War I)
WLPB	War Labor Policies Board (World War I)
WMC	War Manpower Commission
WPA	Works Progress Administration
YMCA	Young Men's Christian Association
YWCA	Young Women's Christian Association

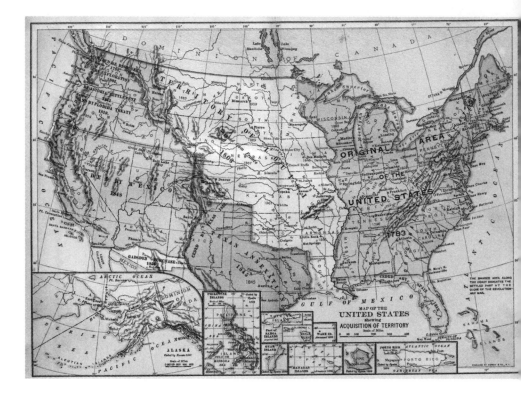

2. Map of the United States showing territorial expansion.
From William Shepard's *Historical Atlas* (New York: Henry Holt, 1911).
Perry-Castaneda Library Map Collection, University of Texas Libraries,
University of Texas at Austin.

PART I

Manifest Destiny

This is the time of all others when Democracy should prove its purity and its spiritual power to prevail. It is surely the manifest destiny of the United States to lead in the attempt to make this spirit prevail.

Pres. THOMAS WOODROW WILSON, December 7, 1920

3. Pres. Thomas Woodrow Wilson. Official White House portrait by F. Graham Cootes, 1938. White House Historical Association, Washington DC.

ONE

From Sea to Shining Sea

The Blessings of Freedom

On July 4, 1776, at Philadelphia, Pennsylvania, the fifty-six delegates to the Continental Congress, standing for thirteen colonies, pledged their lives and fortunes by signing a Declaration of
Independence from Great Britain. This was an exceptional decision, and the colonial representatives were taking a grave risk.
The delegates were committing high treason and would pay with
their heads if their cause faltered. And as it happened, some did
lose their lives, and many more lost their fortunes. Their unprecedented declaration had come over a year after the outbreak of
hostilities in the Province of Massachusetts Bay on April 19, 1775.[1]

On the extraordinary morning of October 19, 1781, Brig. Gen.
Charles O'Hara surrendered besieged British forces at Yorktown,
Virginia, to Gen. George Washington, commander of the Conti-
nental Army, Gen. Comte de Rochambeau, and Adm. Comte de
Barras of France. O'Hara represented British commanding general
Lord George Cornwallis, who, pleading illness, refused to attend
the ceremony. Perhaps confusing the elegant Rochambeau for
Washington, O'Hara awkwardly offered his sword to the French
commander, who graciously declined in deference to the American commander. As he sat astride Nelson, his favorite mount,
Washington directed his deputy, Maj. Gen. Benjamin Lincoln, to
accept O'Hara's sword. O'Hara had marched the British forces,
including many German mercenaries, out of Yorktown between
two lines of allied troops, the French on one side and the Americans on the other. The French and American lines stretched for
more than a mile.[2]

The repercussions and recriminations in London were immediate. Bogged down in expensive struggles in other realms, an exhausted Parliament passed a resolution in March 1782 to end the costly war with the American colonies. The Treaty of Paris formally ended the American Revolutionary War in September 1783.[3]

The Constitution of the United States was ratified June 21, 1788. There are twenty-seven amendments to the Constitution, and the first ten amendments are known collectively as the Bill of Rights.[4] The Constitution replaced the Articles of Confederation and Perpetual Union that the newly independent thirteen states ratified in early 1781. The Articles of Confederation incapacitated the new nation by limiting the role of a central government. The Articles did not bring unity, effectively fund a national government, or support national defense.[5] Deliberations toward a new constitution convened May 25, 1787, in Philadelphia. Following lengthy and raucous debate for over a year among disparate state delegations and then ratification by eleven of the thirteen states, the Continental Congress voted on September 13, 1788, to implement the Constitution.[6] A new federal government met on March 4, 1789, and George Washington became president on April 30. Two holdouts, North Carolina and Rhode Island, later ratified the Constitution.

The frail Benjamin Franklin was too weak to stand and asked James Wilson to read his closing comments at the convention to the delegates, in which he said, in part,

> I confess that there are several parts of this constitution which I do not at present approve, but I am not sure I shall never approve them: For having lived long, I have experienced many instances of being obliged by better information, or fuller consideration, to change opinions even on important subjects, which I once thought right, but found to be otherwise. It is therefore that the older I grow, the more apt I am to doubt my own judgment, and to pay more respect to the judgment of others . . . sir, I agree to this Constitution with all its faults, if they are such; because I think a general Government necessary for us, and there is no form of Government but what may be a blessing to the people if well administered, and

believe farther that this is likely to be well administered for a course of years, and can only end in Despotism, as other forms have done before it, when the people shall become so corrupted as to need despotic Government, being incapable of any other. I doubt too whether any other Convention we can obtain, may be able to make a better Constitution. . . . It therefore astonishes me, Sir, to find this system approaching so near to perfection as it does; and I think it will astonish our enemies, who are waiting with confidence to hear that our councils are confounded like those of the Builders of Babel; and that our States are on the point of separation, only to meet hereafter for the purpose of cutting one another's throats. Thus, I consent, Sir, to this Constitution because I expect no better, and because I am not sure, that it is not the best.[7]

Franklin and his colleagues thus embarked upon the creation of a truly revolutionary experiment in human freedom and expression, grounded upon English common law, property rights, individual freedoms, capitalism, and Judeo-Christian values. The provident Constitution embodied this unprecedented combination of core principle. The fragile new nation was unique in human history and destined to be exceptional.[8]

His countrymen and the national media revered and glorified Gen. George Washington at the time of his inauguration.[9] By the end of his first term writers were attacking Washington's domestic and foreign policies. During his second term media attacks became personal and questioned the president's integrity, republican principles, and even his military reputation. Revolutionary unity had disappeared. A new type of rough-and-tumble American political and media dynamic had appeared. The nature of this new atmosphere would evolve but continue throughout the history of the United States, where the First Amendment to the 1789 Constitution enshrined freedom of speech.

The media included no more than 50 newspapers in 1776. By 1800 there were 250, because new regulations made it less expensive to circulate newspapers through the postal system.[10] Aggressive editors criticized the "monarchial style" and "aristocratic behavior" of the Washington administration. Reluctant to attack Washington directly, editors aimed considerable criticism at his lieutenants, particularly Treasury Secretary Alexander Hamilton.

In a letter to New York representative James Madison, Secretary of State Thomas Jefferson wrote, "the President, tho' an honest man himself, may be circumvented by snares and artifices, and is in fact surrounded by men who wish to clothe the Executive with more than constitutional power."[11] Allied with Jefferson against the Federalist economic policy of Hamilton, Madison organized the opposition Democratic-Republican Party, which he centered around Jefferson. Opposition newspapers gave the new party an opportunity to frame the debate in terms of "republicanism" versus "aristocracy."

In April 1793 Washington proclaimed that the United States would remain neutral in a quarrel between revolutionary France and Great Britain. The media and the new political opposition were pro-French, and they denounced Washington's decision. The president ratified a document formally titled "Treaty of Amity Commerce and Navigation Between His Britannic Majesty and the United States of America" in August 1795. The document was better known as the Jay Treaty because special envoy John Jay, chief justice of the Supreme Court, negotiated it. Washington wanted to avoid war over justified claims that the British government was refusing to open its ports to American shipping.[12] Jay signed the document on November 19, 1794. It took four months to reach the president on March 7, 1795, when Congress had adjourned. The media were stymied by secrecy, and rampant newspaper speculation stirred public agitation. The Senate met in special session on June 8, 1795, to consider the treaty. Members objected particularly to Article XII, which limited commercial access to the British West Indies to ships of seventy tons or less. The Senate approved the treaty subject to the suspension of Article XII. Washington concluded that the partial approval implied final consent. Newspapers were outraged, and riots ensued with public bonfires of the Union Jack. An appalled Washington urged his advisers to fight back against the "poison" of political and media opponents.[13]

After Washington ratified the Jay Treaty unconditionally, protests continued. The House of Representatives demanded the president send documents related to the treaty. In an early example of what today is known as executive privilege, Washington refused, insisting that the House had no constitutional authority to determine treaties. In May 1796 the president expressed the hope that his action would offer the United States peace and the time to become a prosperous nation.[14]

Born out of wedlock on the island of Nevis in the West Indies, Alexander Hamilton served as a decorated combat officer and Washington's military aide de camp during the Revolution. He founded the new nation's financial system as its first Treasury secretary and was a key advocate for the Constitution of the United States. Hamilton, John Jay, and James Madison published eighty-five articles essays using the pseudonym "Publius," which are now known as the *Federalist Papers*.[15] Hamilton's commentaries were provocative, rational, and influential. Hamilton believed that is was the "manifest destiny" of the original colonies to become a continental nation by expanding to the Pacific Ocean. He also predicted that the United States would become the dominant hemispheric power.[16]

Arguing for a strong central government, Hamilton followed British financial practices, advocating capitalism, common interests, and a strong American navy. He helped to create an American sense of identity by developing key institutions during the vital first presidency of national hero George Washington. Hamilton believed that the United States could become a great empire. He supported the annexation of all territories east of the Mississippi, including Florida. In *Federalist 11*, Hamilton argued that geography, abundant natural resources, and the national interest favored the creation of "one great American system, superior to the control of all transatlantic force or influence, and able to dictate the terms of the connection between the old and the new world."[17]

During the Washington administration, the political class and media of the new nation divided between the competing visions of the Democratic-Republicans and the Federalists. The Democratic-

4. Alexander Hamilton, secretary of the Treasury, 1789–1795.
Portrait by Alexander Trumbull, 1806. National Portrait Gallery,
Smithsonian Institution, Washington DC (NPG.79.216).

Republicans, led by Jefferson, represented southern agrarian and slave-ownership interests and favored close relations with France. The Federalists, led by Hamilton and including Washington's vice president and presidential successor, John Adams, represented northern commercial interests and favored close relations with Britain. The parties agreed the nation should expand and that the federal government needed the necessary power to control diplomacy and the military. Jefferson prevailed in the important election of 1800, which led to the disappearance of Hamilton's Federalist Party. Jefferson appointed James Madison as his secretary of state.[18]

The February 6, 1778, Treaty of Alliance between the United States and France promised mutual military support to endure in perpetuity.[19] This open-ended marriage bothered Hamilton and the Federalists. On January 21, 1793, the citizens of the revolutionary French Republic executed King Louis XVI. Hamilton wanted to nullify the treaty, since it was with the deposed monarchy. Washington sided with Secretary of State Jefferson and kept the treaty in effect.[20] On April 22, Washington proclaimed American neutrality when the new French Republic declared war on Britain. Jefferson resigned as secretary of state on December 31. The formal Neutrality Act followed in 1794, which prompted a bitter media and pamphlet war between Hamilton, writing as "Pacificus," and Madison, replying as "Helvidius."[21]

The United States delayed payment of Revolutionary War debt to France. The French Republic retaliated by seizing American merchant vessels in the West Indies. In reply Congress canceled the treaty of 1778 and authorized attacks on French vessels on July 7, 1798. An undeclared war followed. With tacit support from the British and showing surprising professional fighting ability, the new American Navy destroyed French West Indies trade. Between 1801 and 1805 the fledgling navy and the Marine Corps would again show their ability "to the shores of Tripoli" in the first of two wars with Barbary Pirates in Africa.[22]

President Adams had to deal with pro-French Democratic-Republicans and anti-French members of his own party. He sought a diplomatic solution with France, which enraged Federalists.

France ceded Louisiana to Spain in the 1763 Treaty of Paris, which combined the vast Louisiana land mass with Spanish Florida. The deal blocked any potential expansion of the United States at the Mississippi River. At the same time, Scots-Irish Americans were pouring across the Appalachian Mountains into the Ohio and Tennessee River valleys, and the economic development of lands west of the Appalachians needed access to the Mississippi River.[23]

Upon the discovery of French agents conducting military surveys to determine how best to defend Louisiana, the Federalist-dominated Congress passed and Pres. John Adams signed the Alien and Sedition Acts in 1798. The acts were four individual bills that set off a political and media firestorm and affected the presidential election of 1800. Democratic-Republican and media critics argued the acts suppressed opponents of the Adams administration.[24]

Public opinion was raw following the Whiskey Rebellion, when Democratic-Republican officials in some states refused to enforce the 1791 whiskey tax. The French Revolution inspired other Democratic-Republican politicians and media to call for secession. In acting to keep order, Adams and the Federalists set themselves up for electoral defeat.[25] Following his victory over Adams in the 1800 election, Thomas Jefferson repealed three of the four acts. The Alien Enemies Act is still in effect as Chapter 3, Sections 21–24 of Title 50 of the United States Code.[26]

Meanwhile Napoléon Bonaparte orchestrated the Coup of 18 Brumaire on November 9, 1799, and became first counsel of the French Republic.[27] Adams authorized a commission to negotiate with France a formal end of the 1778 Treaty of Alliance, confirmation of American neutrality, an agreement for shipping loss compensation, and to end the undeclared naval war. One of the commissioners was Virginian John Marshall, who became chief justice of the Supreme Court in 1801. What Adams did not know was that Napoléon wanted to reestablish a North American empire. The Adams commission did not arrive in Paris until March 1800. By then, France was negotiating the transfer of Louisiana from Spain. On September 30, 1800, the United States and France signed the Convention of 1800 (or Treaty of Mortefontaine), ending the undeclared naval war and the 1778 Treaty of Alliance. Shipping loss compensation remained unresolved.[28] Spain transferred Louisiana to France in the 1801 Treaty of Aranjuez. Napoléon sent troops to the West Indies to restore the production of sugar and to use New Orleans as a strategic base. Then many of the French troops died of yellow fever, a slave rebellion seized control of Haiti, and renewed hostilities with Great Britain were likely.

Adroitly understanding the French position, Jefferson dispatched James Madison to join ambassador Robert Livingstone in Paris to buy Louisiana.[29] Negotiations moved swiftly. The United States agreed to pay $11.5 million and assume the shipping loss claims of American citizens against France of $3.75 million. In exchange, the United States bought the vast Louisiana domain of 830,000 square miles, stretching from the Gulf of Mexico to Canada and from the Mississippi River to the Rocky Mountains. Jefferson had pulled off the biggest land deal in history, paying exactly 4 cents per acre.[30]

On December 20, 1803, a French honor guard lowered the French tricolor in the Place d'Armes, and an American honor guard raised the American flag. As sophisticated French and Spanish residents wept in disbelief, William Claiborne and Gen. James Wilkinson, the new territorial commissioners, assured all residents that the United States would respect their property, rights, and Catholic religion. Celebratory salvos boomed from dozens of cannons as proud Americans shouted "Huzzah!"[31]

Hamilton supported Jefferson's astute and epic purchase of Louisiana, which fit perfectly with Hamilton's vision of continental expansion.[32] Rich in natural resources with endless forests and grazing lands, the vast Louisiana realm made America wealthy. The president announced, "The fertility of the country, its climate and extent, promise in due season important aids to our treasury, an ample provision for our posterity, and a wide-spread field for the blessings of freedom."[33]

Jefferson commissioned Capt. Meriwether Lewis, Lt. William Clark, and their Corps of Discovery expedition to explore the lands northwest from St. Louis, along the muddy Missouri River, among the many unfamiliar indigenous nations, and to discover a practical route from the mysterious Rocky Mountains to the Pacific Ocean. This exceptional undertaking into the vast unknown, guided by the Lemhi Shoshone woman Sacagawea from North Dakota to the Pacific Ocean, also sought trade with the tribes and scientific study. The trek was no less daunting in its time than men traveling to the moon.

Aaron Burr of New York served as vice president during Jefferson's first term, but Jefferson never trusted him. Burr had been Jefferson's presidential opponent, and their uneasy relationship led in part to a change in the vice presidential election process.[34] When Burr realized that Jefferson would decline to run with him in the 1804 election, he ran and lost the election for governor of New York. Alexander Hamilton opposed Burr, who he believed was involved in a secession movement. A letter in which Hamilton described Burr as a "dangerous man" came to Burr's attention. After several exchanges of letters, Burr demanded that Hamilton either recant or deny the accusations, which Hamilton did not. Burr then challenged Hamilton to a duel. The foes met at Weehawken, New Jersey, at 7:00 a.m. on July 11, 1804, and Burr fatally wounded Hamilton.[35]

For generations slaves were an integral element of trade between black African nations, slave traders, the New World, and Europe. About 6 percent of the 12 million Africans forced to the Western Hemisphere came to British North America. Following independence, northern states gradually abolished slavery, and the progressive Northwest Ordinance outlawed it.[36] The United States and Britain banned the importation of slaves in 1808, and Britain outlawed slavery throughout the Empire in 1833. Although crop and climate conditions in the upper southern states made slavery impractical, owners and traders cruelly separated and transplanted slave families to the Deep South, where a lucrative cotton economy made slavery profitable.[37]

The United States fought a second war with Great Britain between June 1812 and February 1815. The Treaty of Ghent, signed December 24, 1814, ended the conflict with a status quo ante bellum (a draw). News of the peace did not arrive before British forces invaded Louisiana in January 1815. Gen. Andrew Jackson and his odd army of regulars, militia, civilians, slaves, indigenous peoples, and Jean Laffite's pirates dramatically defeated the finest army in the world at the Battle of New Orleans. After the war the United States adopted a policy of political isolation from Europe and economic accommodation with Britain and British North America (Canada).[38]

In his December 2, 1823, State of the Union address, President James Monroe outlined a hemispheric foreign policy that came to be known as the Monroe Doctrine. Mainly written by Secretary of State John Quincy Adams, the policy opposed European colonialism in the Western Hemisphere, although the United States recognized existing European colonies. In exchange, the United States pledged not to interfere with the internal affairs of European nations.[39] Simon Bolivar and other Latin American nationalists welcomed Monroe's pledge, although they did not view the doctrine as a hemispheric alliance. The United States, founded upon English Common Law and British tradition, was developing along different lines than its southern hemispheric neighbors. At the turn of the nineteenth century, the free-born population of the infant United States was primarily of northern European heritage, as contrasted with the diversity of minority European, slave, and majority indigenous and assimilated mixed-race populations of the Americas.

The Northwest Territory, including Ohio, Michigan, Indiana, Illinois, and Wisconsin, was rich in timber, furs, minerals, and fertile land. The Appalachian Mountains blocked transportation to the interior. It took four weeks to travel from New York to Detroit, and the rivers of the interior flowed west into the Mississippi Basin and south to New Orleans. Westward expansion to the Great Lakes had to pass through the Iroquois (Haudenosaunee) Confederacy of Cayuga, Mohawk, Oneida, Onondaga, Seneca, and Tuscarora nations. The Confederacy had hitherto blocked the French and contained the British. During the American Revolution the nations divided their loyalties, and the Colonials defeated the pro-British members. The six nations signed the Treaty of Canandaigua with Pres. George Washington on November 11, 1794, which has continued to affirm perpetual Haudenosaunee land rights to the present day.

The idea of a Mohawk Valley canal appeared during the 1780s. Beginning in 1807, flour merchant Jesse Hawley began authoring essays describing a Mohawk Valley canal system, and his ideas caught the attention of New York City mayor Dewitt Clinton. When Clinton became governor of New York, he launched a canal project, and construction began in 1817. Critics called the project "Clinton's Folly" and "Clinton's ditch." Free labor, including many Irish immigrants, built a water highway between the Hudson River and Lake Erie that Clinton opened on October 28, 1825.[40] There is an elevation difference of 565 feet between the eastern and western terminuses, so the Erie Canal had thirty-four numbered locks to lift and lower boats and barges. The important waterway was an unprecedented engineering feat that revolutionized the shipment of goods from the Great Lakes to the Atlantic Ocean. It is the best early example of American ingenuity.[41]

As the result of the bitter and tumultuous election of 1828, populist Gen. Andrew Jackson of Tennessee became president of the United States. The intensely charged election was even more controversial because of personal attacks against Jackson's wife Rachel by supporters of incumbent president John Quincy Adams.[42] The stress led to her death three weeks after her husband's victory. Jackson never forgave the Adams supporters, saying "may God forgive her murders; I never can."[43] A fierce partisan, Jackson is among the most colorful and controversial of American presidents, both admired and criticized by historians. His reputation suffered as historians came to see his military campaigns against indigenous nations as genocide. His unrepentant ownership of slaves also complicates his legacy. In his lifetime and for many generations thereafter, Jackson was one of the most admired figures in American history.[44] When the United States won independence, the Southeastern Chickasaw, Choctaw, Muscogee-Creek, Seminole, and Cherokee nations were well established and autonomous. Thomas Jefferson believed that the tribal nations of North America were the intellectual equals of European Americans, and his government tried to peacefully absorb the nations, so long as they adopted American values and assimilated into a new hybrid culture. Jackson fought with and against many of the nations in the years before he became president. Indigenous warriors were at his side at the Battle of New Orleans. However, his attitude toward the nations could be brutal. In 1818 he took it upon his own authority to invade Florida and provoke the Seminole Wars.[45] Jackson came to believe there was no place for the Southeastern nations east of the Mississippi and moved to transfer land west of the Mississippi to them. He thus put into motion the notorious Indian Removal Act of 1830 and forcibly removed the nations from their ancestral homes in the southeastern United States along the Trail of Tears.[46]

A More Perfect Union

Before his death Jackson supported the annexation of Texas following the 1836 Anglo Texan Revolution against Pres. Gen. Antonio Lopez de Santa Anna, "the Napoléon of the West," who had usurped the Mexican Constitution of 1824. Jackson's successor, Martin Van Buren, believed the annexation of Texas was a liability that would arouse antislave opposition and trigger a war with Mexico.[47] On March 6, 1836, after a costly thirteen-day siege, an infuriated Santa Anna infamously put to the sword all the Texan defenders of the Alamo Presidio in San Antonio commanded by Col. William Barrett Travis. The garrison included American legends Davy Crockett and Jim Bowie. Like Jackson at New Orleans, Travis fought from behind fixed emplacements. Santa Anna was unaware of British military doctrine (since New Orleans) that massed infantry could not directly assault American riflemen behind breastworks without an unacceptable cost. The marksmen from Tennessee and Kentucky did not miss. Sharpshooters killed hundreds of smartly attired and disciplined Mexican troops before they overwhelmed the doomed garrison.[48] Travis bought the Texans precious time. On April 21, 1836, in a battle that lasted only eighteen minutes, Gen. Sam Houston and the Texan Army engaged and defeated leading elements of the Mexican Army at San Jacinto. The next day Houston captured a humiliated Santa

Anna, disguised as a soldier, and forced Caudillo Maximo to sign a treaty that withdrew sizeable remaining Mexican forces from Texas, which declared itself to be an independent country.[49]

Northwest Territory icon Gen. William Henry Harrison defeated Van Buren in the 1840 election but fell ill and died after only one month in office. John Tyler of Virginia succeeded the hero of Tippecanoe, who defeated the eloquent Shawnee leader Tecumseh's formidable tribal confederation. Tyler, an expansionist, conducted sensitive negotiations with Houston to bring Texas into the union. The controversial Tyler also switched parties from Whig to Democratic-Republican.[50]

On December 29, 1845, Tyler's successor James K. Polk signed legislation making the former Lone Star Republic the twenty-eighth state of the Union. Secretary of State Daniel Webster of Massachusetts resigned. Henry Clay, "the great compromiser," also opposed Texas annexation.[51] Clay, Webster and John C. Calhoun were the "great triumvirate" that put together the Missouri Compromise of 1820, the Compromise Tariff of 1833, and the Compromise of 1850. Clay was known as the champion of western interests; Webster, northern (free) interests; and Calhoun, southern (slave) interests.[52]

During 1846 Polk negotiated the Oregon Treaty with Great Britain. As early as 1818 the United States and Britain agreed to fix the border between the United States and Canada along the forty-ninth parallel from Minnesota Territory west to the Rocky Mountains. While the United States proposed to extend the border to the Pacific Ocean, Britain wanted it drawn west to the Columbia River and from there to the western coast. Inexorable American immigration along the Oregon Trail into the territory created an emotional issue in Congress and the slogan "Fifty-four forty or fight," indicating the line of latitude preferred for the border. The parties settled the competing claims of Russia and Spain and peacefully agreed to a compromise settling on the forty-ninth parallel border but giving all of Vancouver Island to Canada.[53]

Following the annexation of Texas, relations between the United States and Mexico deteriorated because the border with Mexico had never been formally fixed. The border according to Texas was the Rio Grande. Mexico considered the Rio Nueces to be the border. Polk ordered Gen. Zachary Taylor to garrison the southern border of Texas along the Rio Grande, which Mexico regarded as a violation of its sovereignty. Mexican forces attacked an American outpost in the disputed territory, and war broke out. The Americans quickly occupied Santa Fe de Nuevo Mexico along the upper Rio Grande and the province of Alto California. On March 9, 1847, American forces made an amphibious landing from the Gulf of Mexico at Veracruz. The ensuing campaign resembled the advance of Hernán Cortés and his Conquistadors from Veracruz to the Aztec capital of Tenochtitlán in 1591–92. U.S. forces commanded by Gen. Winfield Scott entered Mexico City on September 14, 1847, and raised the Stars and Stripes over the Halls of Montezuma. On February 2, 1848, the Treaty of Guadeloupe Hidalgo ended the war. Mexico ceded Alto California and Santa Fe Nuevo Mexico to the United States in exchange for a $15 million lump sum payment and the assumption by the United States of $3.25 million in Mexican debt owed to American citizens. Mexico acknowledged the loss of Texas and accepted the Rio Grande border.[54] There was nothing dishonorable about the war and outcome from the American point of view. Mexico all but assured war by declaring American annexation of Texas to be unacceptable. For Mexico, losing half of its original territory was a humiliating disaster that Mexican patriots would never forgive or forget. The vigorous and confident United States won continental expansion but at a steep price in casualties, money, and virtue. Strongly resisted by anti-expansion northern abolitionists, the war accelerated the bitter debates that led to the American Civil War.

Tensions between the United States and Mexico complicated efforts to survey a practical southern route for a transcontinental railroad. James Gadsden, the American ambassador to Mexico, negotiated a treaty to pay Mexico $10 million for 29,670 square miles of territory that later became part of Arizona and New Mexico. The Senate ratified the Gadsden Purchase on April 25, 1854.[55]

President Polk was a firm believer in the concept of manifest destiny as foreseen by Alexander Hamilton. There were three tenants to this vision: the special virtues of the American people and their institutions; the mission of the United States to redeem and remake the west in the Jeffersonian image of agrarian America; and a divine destiny to carry out this essential duty.[56] The theme of virtue became identified as American exceptionalism. Puritan founder John Winthrop's famous 1630 "City upon a Hill" sermon suggested this, when he called for a virtuous community that would be a "shining example" to the Old World. In his provocative 1776 pamphlet *Common Sense*, Thomas Paine argued that "we have it in our power to begin the world over again. A situation similar to the present hath not happened since the days of Noah until now. The birthday of a new world is at hand." Thus, the westward expansion of the United States continued beyond North America. A lucrative China trade meant that fast Yankee Clipper ships needed a network of ports across the Pacific Ocean. When Commodore Matthew Perry sailed to Japan in 1853, his primary motivation was to strengthen America's trading position and diplomacy with China. As the United States opened consulates across the Pacific, American planters and whaling interests settled in Hawaii, leading to the annexation of the islands in 1898.[57]

Democrats tended to favor territorial expansion, while the Whigs saw America's moral mission as only one of democratic example. By 1843 former president John Quincy Adams and other prominent leaders had repudiated continental consolidation because the annexation of Texas meant the expansion of slavery. In fact, although he preferred peaceful coexistence within a greater Mexico, Stephen Fuller Austin, the founder of the Republic of Texas in 1825, split with emancipated Mexico over slavery. According to historian Frederick Merck, "manifest destiny . . . lacked national, sectional or party following commensurate with its magnitude."[58]

Influential journalist John L. O'Sullivan was an advocate of Jacksonian democracy. In an 1839 essay he predicted a "divine destiny" for the United States that was not explicitly territorial. In 1845 O'Sullivan wrote another essay, where he first used the phrase "manifest destiny" to urge the annexation of Texas.[59] He again invoked the specific phrase in a December 27, 1845, article in the *New York Morning News*, asserting that the United States had the right to claim "the whole of Oregon . . . by the right of our manifest destiny to possess the whole of the continent which Providence has given us for the development of the great experiment of liberty and federated self-government entrusted to us."[60]

On January 3, 1846, Rep. Robert Winthrop of Massachusetts rose to ridicule the concept on the House floor, saying "I suppose the right of a manifest destiny to spread will not be admitted to exist in any nation except the universal Yankee nation." Winthrop was among many critics who suggested that advocates were citing "divine providence" to justify actions motivated, from their perspective, by chauvinism and self-interest.

Among the most profound and lasting results of expansionism was the European settlement and development of rich midwestern farmlands. New immigrants from Germany, Scandinavia, and eastern Europe joined pioneers from eastern families as farms and communities sprouted up west of the Mississippi River and into the Dakotas. The Homestead Act of 1862 encouraged 600,000 families to settle the west by giving them land almost for free, which they had to live on for five years. The homesteaders faced great physical problems, including attacks by hostile indigenous tribes, plagues of insects, and harsh winter weather. Rapid changes in railroad transportation and other tools rewarded those who persevered, easing some of the hardships. Eventually the government gave away more than 270 million acres of public land (10 percent of the United States) to 1.6 million homesteaders.[61]

It was inevitable and tragic that the relentless westward push of American European civilization would displace and harm the native peoples. During the early generations of contact with Europeans, disease had wiped out entire indigenous populations, who had no immunity to common European infirmities. Expansionism marginalized the surviving indigenous peoples. At every step agrarian eastern nations and nomadic western nations were deceived, cheated, resettled, and murdered. Americans of moral disposition were ashamed and repentant but powerless to stop the inevitable. The media fueled the march west by misrepresenting facts, creating legends, exhorting settlement, justifying extermination, and abetting the eventual captivity of the remaining indigenous nations.

Until a reckoning between North and South occurred, manifest destiny offered nothing to enslaved Africans. During the antebellum era, southern planters continued to grow tobacco and rice as they had in colonial days. The creation of a mechanical cotton gin by Eli Whitney in 1793 revolutionized the production of cotton, which was heretofore not grown as a commodity crop in the United States. By the 1850s, the hot and humid American Deep South supplied 80 percent of the world's cotton, with most of the slaves in America producing two billion pounds of cotton per year. The hybrid *Gossypium barbadense* or Petit Gulf cotton is an easily grown, stored, and transported staple crop that defined the conviction of southern politicians and planters. Slaves cleared forests and cultivated the lucrative crop for white planters from Georgia to Texas. This was a far different America than Jefferson's vision of white yeoman farmers that was simultaneously taking root in the north and west.[62]

For decades white American politicians and scholars, including Jefferson, agonized over the cultural ramifications of abolishing slavery. The black slave population of the United States surged from four hundred thousand in 1808, when Congress banned the importation of slaves, to about four million by 1861.[63] Southern authorities were terrified. Among the most militant were the state legislatures in South Carolina and Mississippi, where most of the population was black.[64]

In 1858 South Carolina senator (and former governor) James Henry Hammond confidently proclaimed on the Senate floor that the North could never threaten the South because "cotton is king." But cotton with slavery was a one-dimensional economic trap. As the Industrial Revolution advanced in the North, the South became dependent for food, resources, and financing. Its rail transportation infrastructure was inadequate, and the North could blockade its ports in the event of war. The proud and prejudiced South was vulnerable.[65]

Southern representatives tried to expand slavery to new states and territories, leading to a series of compromises with the polarized North. The discovery of gold by James W. Marshall at Sutter's Mill near Coloma in 1848 lured about 300,000 prospectors to California and intensified the issue, as all the western territories were potentially new free states. The pivotal and potentially powerful California joined the Union on September 9, 1850, as a free state in the Compromise of 1850, consisting of five laws that resolved the status of the territories won from Mexico. Henry Clay's bargain, supported by Daniel Webster and opposed by John C. Calhoun, confirmed Texas as a slave state but ensured that slavery did not spread west to the Pacific.[66]

In his influential treatise *Democracy in America*, Alexis de Tocqueville observed that "the colonies in which there were no slaves became more populous and richer than those in which slavery flourished."[67]

By 1860 the southern states had a population of twelve million, including four million slaves. The northern states had a population of nineteen million and virtually no slaves.[68] In a series of "three-fifths" legislative acts that enshrined disproportionate southern political power in the Constitution, slaves counted in the calculation of how many representatives a state held in Congress (three-fifths of a free person). In the 1857 Dred Scott case, the Supreme Court held that a slave did not become free when transported to a free state, but that the slave remained the property of his or her owner. People of African descent imported into the United States as slaves, and their descendants, could never be citizens.[69]

As western territories populated by immigrant homesteaders lined up to become new free states, tensions gave way to violence in "bloody" Kansas, only admitted in 1861 and following the election of 1860. Abolitionist activist John Brown tried to incite an armed slave revolt by seizing the U.S. arsenal at Harpers Ferry, Virginia, on October 16, 1859. Brown had invited fellow activists Harriet Tubman and Frederick Douglass to join him, but Tubman was ill and Douglass wisely declined. When Brown occupied Harpers Ferry, an alert sounded. Under the command of Col. Robert E. Lee of the army's Second Cavalry Regiment, Lt. J. E. B. Stuart and a company of U.S. Marines attacked and subdued Brown's group when they refused to surrender. The United States tried Brown for treason and executed him by hanging on December 2.[70]

The question of slavery passed the point of no return with the election of westerner and Republican Abraham Lincoln of Illinois on November 6, 1860. Lincoln defeated a Democratic party divided between northern candidate Stephen A. Douglas and southern candidate John C. Breckinridge. There was also a fourth candidate, John Bell of the Constitutional Union Party.[71] Lincoln had not even appeared on the ballots in ten southern slave states. Lincoln won the Electoral College 180–123 but only carried 39 percent of the popular vote. In the months leading to the inauguration, seven southern states seceded from the Union to form the Confederate States of America. Four more southern states seceded after Lincoln's inauguration.

Cataclysm came on April 12, 1861, when Confederate artillery opened fire on the federal garrison at Fort Sumter, South Carolina. Although later generations rationalized the war as a noble battle to protect states' rights and the southern way of life, in 1861 slavery *was* the southern way of life. Confederate leaders explicitly announced that the protection of slavery and the cotton economy was their reason to secede and wage war. Although most Confederate soldiers were people of modest means who did not own slaves, still almost one-third of all white southern families owned slaves. Slave labor and fertile soil enabled Deep South capitalism.[72]

In 1857 Mexico fell into one of its own series of civil wars, pitting the forces of liberal reformist Benito Juárez, who admired Abraham Lincoln, against conservatives led by Félix Zuloaga. The United States recognized the Juárez government in 1859. In 1862 Emperor Napoléon II maneuvered to set up a French-sponsored monarchy in Mexico, installing Maximillian of Hapsburg, the archduke of Austria, as emperor of Mexico. Napoléon's reasoning was that the United States, embroiled in its Civil War, could not stop this violation of the Monroe Doctrine. Secretary of State William Henry Seward had no desire to challenge France and open the door to French aid to the Confederacy. During the French invasion Juárez led a popular national insurgency. After the end of the American Civil War, Seward was free to give support to Juárez. Napoléon withdrew French troops, and the insurgents captured and executed the ill-fated Maximillian.[73]

In a fatal miscalculation, the Confederates banned cotton exports to force British diplomatic recognition. Britain and Europe simply developed other sources for cotton, Egypt and India. By the time the Confederates realized their error, a federal blockade forced the Confederacy to rely on smugglers. Cotton exports to Europe dropped to almost none in 1862, and the southern economy collapsed.[74]

Following the bloodiest day in American history at the battle of Antietam, Lincoln signed an executive order on September 22, 1862, and then an Emancipation Proclamation on January 1, 1863. Bypassing Congress, he changed the status of persons held as slaves in the Confederate-controlled territories from slave to free. On April 8, 1864, the Senate passed the 13th Amendment to the Constitution, abolishing slavery except as punishment for a crime. The House passed the amendment on January 31, 1865. The Supreme Court found secession to be unconstitutional in *Texas v. White* (74 U.S. 700 [1868]).[75]

On November 19, 1863, Lincoln brilliantly summed up his war aims and vision for "a more perfect Union" and national reconciliation in an address dedicating the Soldier's Cemetery at Gettysburg, Pennsylvania, the site of the war's pivotal battle. Lincoln's succinct remarks followed a two-hour oration by former senator and Secretary of State Edward Everett.[76]

While the viewpoint of the enemy Confederate media was naturally negative toward the despised Lincoln, it is illustrative to remember how divided and often defeatist the northern media were during the war. The northern media callously smeared Abraham Lincoln. In 1864 the northern Democrats ran Gen. George McClellan for president against Lincoln on an appeasement platform, promising to end the war with an armistice in which the southern states would keep slavery.

The fortunes of war changed when Lincoln allowed Gen. Ulysses Grant and his lieutenants from the Union's western Armies of the

Cumberland and Tennessee, including Gen. William Tecumseh Sherman, to wage total war and implement a scorched earth policy. Grant knew from bitter experience at Shiloh and Vicksburg that the enemy could not survive a brutal war of attrition. He was not hesitant, as had been Lincoln's inept Army of the Potomac commanders, including the ambitious Democrat McClellan. It was only a matter of time before the chivalrous Gen. Robert E. Lee, commander of the Army of Northern Virginia, and his gallant field commanders ran out of food, clothing, and ammunition. The mythical serene and civilized plantation Dixie of Margaret Mitchell's *Gone with the Wind* disappeared at Appomattox Courthouse on the afternoon of April 9, 1865.

Deranged southern sympathizer and actor John Wilkes Booth assassinated Lincoln on April 14 at Ford's Theatre in Washington DC. The critical media deified the slain president as a martyr and the beloved savior of the Union, which, in fact, he was.

Some 620,000 Americans lost their lives. The 1861–1865 war remains America's most costly conflict, rivaled only by World War II. Taken as a percentage of America's twenty-first-century population, the shocking toll is equivalent to six million lives. These Americans paid reparations for America's original sin of slavery on the bloody battlefields of Shiloh, Antietam, and Gettysburg.

The excesses of Reconstruction destroyed Lincoln's vision for a peaceful reconciliation between the states. Bureaucratic incompetence and opportunistic carpetbaggers embittered white southerners and abandoned the freed blacks. Many disgruntled whites joined violent, racist, anti-Catholic and anti-Jewish vigilante groups such as the Ku Klux Klan. Legislated and legalized racial discrimination, institutionalized segregation, and Jim Crow laws that denied voting rights to newly emancipated African American citizens would follow well into the next century. The South would remain disadvantaged until World War II. Rationalizing defeat, generations of Confederate descendants perpetuated the myth of the Confederacy as the "noble cause."

The American Civil War and emancipation transformed the historic dependence of global trade on slave labor and thus the world economic order. From this point forward, politicians, plant-ers, manufacturers and merchants had to reform capitalism with free and fair labor or face the consequences of new movements such as socialism.[77]

Popular prewar stage productions known as minstrel shows grew in popularity during Reconstruction and well into the next century with vaudeville. The popular and pleasant songs of the prolific Stephen Collins Foster immortalized a mythical genteel south and were respectful of traditional African American spir-itual musical tradition. The darker side of the popular traveling productions was the negative portrayal of African American cit-izens as comic inferiors and the use of "blackface" makeup by white performers to imitate blacks. The effect of the shows was to perpetuate stereotypes, institutional racism, and discrimination.

Westward the Course of Empire

In 1725 Tsar Peter the Great sent Vitus Bering and Alexei Chirikov to explore Alaska and the Pacific coast. In 1856, when Russia lost the Crimean War, the imperial government in St. Petersburg lacked the financial resources and will to continue supporting a toehold along the Pacific coast of North America. Russia offered to sell Alaska to the United States in 1859. The American Civil War delayed the transaction, but following the war Seward resumed negotia-tions. On March 30, 1867, the United States agreed to buy Alaska for $7.2 million, and it became American territory on October 18. Media and political skeptics sarcastically called the purchase of Alaska "Seward's Folly." However, the discovery of gold in the Yukon in 1896, making Alaska the gateway to the Klondike, vin-dicated Seward.[78]

On May 10, 1869, Amasa Leland Stanford, the president of the Central Pacific Railroad Company of California, drove a ceremo-nial "last spike" into the tracks at Promontory Summit, Utah Ter-ritory, marking the completion of a transcontinental railroad. The Union Pacific Railroad's free Irish immigrant laborers and others had built west from Omaha, Nebraska, and the Central Pacific's free Chinese immigrant laborers and others had built east from

Sacramento, California. The dream of Hamilton and a presidential priority of Abraham Lincoln to span the continent had become a reality.[79] The men who financed, designed, and built lines east and west had created an engineering marvel, and "there was nothing like it in the world." America was finally a truly transcontinental nation, "from sea to shining sea." Lincoln's foresight and faith in the exceptional Gen. Grenville Dodge of Council Bluffs, Iowa, chief engineer of the Union Pacific, was well placed. Dodge succeeded despite a multitude of competing business interests, intrigues, and setbacks. In 1859, when Lincoln was an Illinois politician and railroad attorney, he met Dodge in Iowa. Lincoln's first words were "Dodge, what is the best route for a Pacific railroad to the west?" Dodge convinced Lincoln to follow a Platte River Valley route and found a way through the Black Hills, Wyoming, and Utah. The president was the most ardent supporter of the transcontinental railroad, which he saw a strategic necessity, and Dodge was his man.[80] The establishment of the transcontinental railroad and new settlements attracted thousands of Americans of European descent to the frontier. Improved communications and reduced travel times hinted at a prosperous future for the farmers and ranchers who were rapidly populating the west. The days when mountain men and fur trappers risked their lives to explore, trap, and trade were over.

The nation celebrated its centennial but had suffered an economic depression in 1873. President Ulysses Grant needed an economic stimulus package. The discovery of gold in the Black Hills in South Dakota, lands that were sacred to the Lakota people, was helpful. The United States ordered the Lakota nation to surrender the Black Hills so that prospectors could exploit the mineral wealth of the region. The tribal leaders refused, and the army moved to enforce the eviction. The resulting annihilation of Lt. Col. George Armstrong Custer and much of his command at Little Bighorn, Montana Territory, on June 25, 1876, shocked Americans. After the disaster the national media glorified the impetuous and incompetent Custer. The thirty-six-year-old "boy general" of Civil War fame divided his Seventh Cavalry Regiment command of 647 men into

5. Gen. Grenville M. Dodge at the ceremony for the driving of the Golden Spike and completion of the first transcontinental railroad at Promontory Summit, Utah, on May 10, 1869. Samuel S. Montague of the Central Pacific Railroad (*center left*) shakes hands with Dodge of the Union Pacific Railroad (*center right*). Yale Collection of Western Americana, Beinecke Rare Book and Manuscript Library, Yale University, New Haven CT.

three columns. Against orders, he led 268 troopers and Crow and Pawnee scouts to their deaths by attacking at least 2,000 armed and motivated Lakota Sioux and Northern Cheyenne warriors, led by Hunkpapa leader Sitting Bull (Tȟatȟáŋka Íyotake), who outnumbered the five companies of cavalrymen 9–1. The Little Bighorn was one of a series of climatic battles fought in the Dakota, Montana, and Wyoming Territories known variously as the Great Sioux War of 1876 and the Black Hills War. Other engagements included the Battles of Powder River, Warbonnet Creek, Rosebud, Slim Buttes, Cedar Creek, and Wolf Mountain.[81] Little Bighorn was the greatest allied tribal triumph since the arrival of Europeans to North America. It was a pyrrhic victory that was avoidable from the American military perspective and that came too late to stop the inevitable. Wounded Knee and the twilight of the indigenous cultures were at hand.

Reviewing the results of the 1890 United States Census, historian Frederick Jackson Turner announced in 1893 that rapid western settlement meant "there can hardly be said to be a frontier line."[82] In the quarter century since the end of the Civil War, new European immigrants made the West America's most culturally diverse region. Although most western residents lived in new cities and towns, over three million agrarian families were working the land. The 1890 census also showed that the indigenous population of the United States was 248,253 down from the 400,764 people found in the 1850 census.[83] During the first half of the nineteenth century, German and Irish immigrants swarmed into America. Toward the close of the century, the nation experienced a new wave of immigration from Italy. The Catholic population of the United States was increasing exponentially. America was also about to absorb a new wave of immigrants from eastern Europe, including more Catholics from Poland and Austro-Hungarian nations. A sizable number of Jewish immigrants from eastern Europe and Imperial Russia joined the steady flow of people entering the United States. The new European citizens would soon produce a generation of leaders who would affect the prosperity, progress, and perspective of the United States.[84]

In June 1894 the American Railway Union struck the Pullman Palace Car Company, and railway workers nationwide refused to handle Pullman cars. Some 125,000 railroad workers shut down twenty-nine railroads and paralyzed the nation. Riots and sabotage followed.[85] A federal court invoked the Sherman Anti-Trust Act of 1890, but workers ignored the order. Democratic Pres. Grover Cleveland ordered the U.S. Army and federal marshals to end the strike, citing disruption to the U.S. mail. Southern and western Democrats and Populists denounced Cleveland's intervention.[86]

The most serious incidents of the strike occurred in and around Chicago, headquarters of the Pullman Company and the nation's central railway hub. The American Federation of Labor did not support the strike. President Cleveland's intervention infuriated

Illinois governor John P. Altgeld. Media coverage was mostly negative toward the strikers. Editors denounced immigrant workers,
anarchy, and defiance of the law. The government arrested Eugene
V. Debs, president of the American Railway Union, and sentenced
him to six months in prison. Debs became an advocate of socialism and ran for president five times as head of the Socialist Party
of America. In a gesture of conciliation hailed by Samuel Gompers, president of the American Federation of Labor, Cleveland and
Congress made Labor Day a federal holiday.[87]

The economic turmoil also encouraged the formation of the
People's Party, or Populists. This leftist movement was critical of
the banking system and railroads and drew support from angry
southern and western farmers. The party existed from 1891 until
1919, although its largest influence was between 1892 and 1896. The
People's Party carried four states in the 1892 presidential election
won by Cleveland.[88]

In 1896 the Democrats nominated gifted orator William Jennings Bryan for president. Bryan favored much of the populist
agenda and generated great excitement with his "Cross of Gold"
speech. Bryan had an opportunity to win the election if the Populists threw their support behind him, which, after serious debate
among themselves, they did. But in the end Bryan lost to Republican William McKinley, who defeated him again in a 1900 rematch.[89]

In 1890 an American naval officer, Capt. Alfred Thayer Mahan,
wrote *The Influence of Sea Power upon History, 1660–1783*. It was
his strong belief that the United States and Great Britain had common security interests.[90] In an 1890 article that appeared in *Atlantic Monthly*, Mahan proposed that the United States should come
to a "cordial understanding" with Britain because "we share a sim-
ilarity of character and ideas" that would ultimately yield "cooperation beneficial to both."[91] Mahan went further in an 1894 *North
American Review* article, "The Possibilities of an Anglo-American
Reunion," in which he states, "To Great Britain and the United
States . . . is entrusted a maritime interest in the broadest sense of
the word, which demands, as one of the conditions of its exercise
and its safety, the organized force adequate to control the gen-

eral course of events at sea."[92] Mahan advocated the annexation of Hawaii and the Philippine Islands. He felt that the world was shrinking and that an isolated America was vulnerable, explaining, "though distant, our shores can be reached."[93] He also recommended the construction of a canal across Central America to assert American control of the Caribbean Sea and to enable the rapid movement of ships between the Atlantic and Pacific. It was therefore inevitable that Mahan came to the attention of the assistant secretary of the navy and the future president Theodore Roosevelt. The men corresponded regularly, and Mahan had a considerable influence on Roosevelt's thinking.

The first transcontinental single-wire telegraph began service on October 24, 1861, and offered near instantaneous communication using the Morse Code between the East and West Coasts of the United States. By comparison, messages carried by daring Pony Express riders took many days. The invention of American artist Samuel Morse was a quantum leap in linking a continental nation, despite interruptions caused by harsh weather, irritated indigenous peoples, and the Civil War. The Commercial Cable Company of New York became one of the world's leading technology companies, controlling five of the sixteen undersea cables that sent telegrams across the Atlantic Ocean. The company also ran one of two new cables across the Pacific Ocean. The undersea cables meant that messages could be sent to and from the United States in minutes rather than weeks or months.

The capitalist and liberal democratic America enabled inventors and entrepreneurs who changed the course of human history. Small groups of pioneers developed audio and visual technology invented and inspired by the prolific inventor and businessman Thomas Alva Edison of Menlo Park, New Jersey, including audio recording and the phonograph, the motion picture camera, the light bulb, and batteries. In addition to making the modern industrialized world possible, Edison made modern mass communication possible. Meanwhile Orville and Wilbur Wright of Dayton, Ohio, would take to powered flight on December 17, 1903, on the Outer Banks of North Carolina at Kill Devil Hills. Henry Ford of

Dearborn, Michigan, was perfecting the manufacture of powered horseless carriages, which would become known as automobiles. Cities and towns were becoming lit by electricity, and speaking "ahoy ahoy" into his invention, Canadian-born Alexander Graham Bell revolutionized communications with the telephone.

As of 1898 Spain continued to keep its colonies of Cuba, Puerto Rico, Guam, and the Philippine Islands. Revolts were long simmering in Cuba. Leading American newspaper publishers including Joseph Pulitzer and William Randolph Hearst engaged in what came to be known as "yellow journalism" to press the cause of Cuban independence, and they made a significant impact upon the American people. President McKinley was inclined to avoid a confrontation with Spain. Then, on the evening of February 15, 1898, the American battleship USS *Maine* mysteriously exploded in Havana harbor, killing most of the crew. As a naval board of inquiry tried to investigate, the media pushed inflammatory articles blaming a deliberate Spanish attack or act of sabotage, and "Remember the Maine!" became a national rallying cry. The naval board of inquiry concluded in 1898 that an external explosion caused by a mine destroyed the *Maine*. After raising the wreck from the harbor, a 1911 study suggested that an internal explosion caused the loss of the ship and most of its crew. Another study, commissioned in 1974 by Adm. Hyman Rickover, confirmed the 1911 finding. The powder magazine was too close to the boiler, and heat caused the magazine to explode. The cause was a design flaw and not Spain.[94]

The facts did not matter. After the United States and Spain exchanged threats and demands, Congress declared war on April 25, 1898. The United States demanded that Spain surrender Cuba. When Spain did not reply quickly, a ten-week confrontation ensued, in which American naval power was decisive. Expeditionary forces landed in Cuba to support a Cuban rebellion against a Spanish garrison wasted by yellow fever. The Armada Española prepared to engage the U.S. Navy, but the more modern American squadrons outgunned them. Before dawn on the morning of May 1, 1898, the American Asiatic Squadron commanded by Commodore George Dewey slipped unmolested into Manila Bay, past the big naval guns of fortified Corregidor Island, and into the mined Boca Grande passage below the Bataan peninsula. At dawn, Dewey formed a "perfect line of battle" and headed directly toward the ships of Contralmirante Particio Montojo y Pastrón. At 5:41 a.m. and within five thousand yards of the Spaniards, Dewey turned to Capt. Charles Vernon Gridley on the bridge of his flagship *Olympia* and said calmly, "You may fire when you are ready, Gridley." Over the next several hours the Americans methodically blew the Spanish fleet out of the water. At sunset crowds gathering along the Manila waterfront gazed at the now anchored and lit American warships following the capitulation of Admiral Montojo and the scuttling of the Spanish ships that had not already been destroyed by the American attack. The band of the *Olympia* played "La Paloma" and other Spanish melodies.[95]

The proud Contralmirante Don Pascual Cevera y Topete sailed from Cadiz on April 8 in anticipation of war, with instructions to defend Puerto Rico. He was sailing toward a rendezvous with Commodore Winfield Scott Schley's battleships. The Spanish fleet was trapped, blockaded, and destroyed at Santiago de Cuba when Admiral Cevera tried to maneuver out of the harbor.[96] At the Battle of San Juan or Kettle Hill on the San Juan Heights, the First Volunteer Regiment "Rough Riders" led by Col. Theodore Roosevelt famously stormed Spanish positions along with the Third Cavalry Regiment in support of the Tenth Cavalry, the legendary African American Buffalo Soldiers. In 2001 Roosevelt posthumously won the Medal of Honor for his gallantry. As Lt. John J. Pershing, a Tenth Cavalry officer, recalled, "The entire command moved forward as coolly as though the buzzing of bullets was the humming of bees. White regiments, black regiments, regulars and Rough Riders, representing the young manhood of north and south, fought shoulder to shoulder, unmindful of race or color, unmindful of whether commanded by ex-Confederate or not, and mindful of only their common duties as Americans."[97]

Many of the Cuban insurgents were poor blacks. When the Spanish garrison at Santiago de Cuba surrendered, the Americans barred the insurgents from the ceremony ostensibly because the prejudiced Spanish officers wanted to preserve their honor by only surrendering to the prejudiced American officers who also held the rebel army in disdain. Following liberation, the U.S. military occupied Cuba until 1902 to keep order until the island became, as promised, an independent nation.

The United States honored its policy of Cuban independence with fidelity to the principles of Cuban patriot José Martí. After communist dictator Fidel Alejandro Castro Ruz seized power in 1959, he and his disciples used the slight by the Spanish and Americans at the surrender ceremony, and the four-year U.S. occupation, to falsely portray the American intervention and the truth about the birth of the independent Cuban republic to justify their communist regime. History may have been different if the Americans had not slighted the Cuban insurgents in 1898.[98]

There was a significant humanitarian outcome of the Spanish-American War. The exceptional Maj. Walter Reed of the U.S. Army Medical Corps discovered the causes of yellow fever, which led to the eradication of the dreaded disease. Reed, Maj. William Gorgas, and the pioneering studies of Cuban physician Carlos Juan Finlay proved that mosquitoes spread yellow fever. Several volunteers lost their lives in the effort. Their yeoman effort made it possible for the United States to build and complete the Panama Canal.[99]

The United States gained control of Puerto Rico, Guam, and the Philippine Islands and took temporary custody of Cuba. The United States paid Spain $20 million for the Philippine Islands to reimburse Spanish citizens for the loss of property. The quick defeat and loss of its remaining colonies was a deep psychological shock to Spain and the second time within one hundred years that the United States had expanded at Spanish expense.

The brief conflict between the United States and Spain was the culmination of a centuries-long battle for dominance in the Western Hemisphere between growing American influence based upon English governance, common law, and individual freedoms—versus a fading Spanish Empire and proud tradition. Most of the caudillismo nations were a patriarchic amalgamation of Hispanic, indigenous, and former slave peoples. They resented the dynamic cultural, economic, and political juggernaut from the north.

In 1842 Secretary of State Daniel Webster sent a letter to agents of the island nation of Hawaii affirming American support and opposition to the annexation of the islands by any European power. After 1849, when Hawaii and the United States concluded a treaty of friendship, Hawaii steadily integrated with the United States as a source of sugar cane production and as a strategic provisioning station for American whaling ships. Protestant missionaries evangelized the Hawaiian people, and American sugar plantation owners came into control of the Hawaiian economy and politics. In 1893, when Queen Liliuokalani moved to set up a stronger monarchy, Americans led by Samuel Dole deposed her. The planters believed their coup d'état would remove the threat of a harsh sugar tariff and encourage American annexation. President Benjamin Harrison ordered sailors from the uss *Boston* to surround the royal palace. When Dole sent a delegation to Washington DC in 1894 to secure annexation, the new president, Grover Cleveland, tried to restore the queen. Dole then declared Hawaii to be an independent republic. Swept along by Spanish-American War nationalism, President William McKinley approved the annexation of Hawaii in 1898, and Dole became the first territorial governor.

The United States had reached the zenith of its territorial expansion. The rapid development of the republic had been exceptional, though there was still no consensus about what exceptionalism meant or, other than manifest destiny, what the essential purpose of the dynamic nation was. A steady flow of legal, skilled, and motivated immigrants was readily assimilating into the dynamic new society. The exceptional adolescent was about to step onto the world stage, grounded by core founding principles and unique advantages of English common law, property rights, individual rights, capitalism and free markets, Judeo-Christian values, and religious freedom. The Protestant values of the founders gave Americans the freedom *to* worship as well as freedom *from* worship, since a state-imposed religious hierarchy did not control them.[100]

European elites cynically relished the calamity of the American Civil War as confirmation that the democratic experiment "of the people, by the people and for the people" was a failure. To their

Fig. 6. *Westward, the Course of Empire Takes Its Way.* 1861. Painted mural by Emanuel Gottlieb Leutze symbolizing manifest destiny, displayed behind the western staircase of the House of Representatives chamber in the U.S. Capitol Building. Courtesy Architect of the United States Capitol and the Smithsonian Institution, Washington DC.

surprise, the restored Union survived to build, invent, and push its way to the brink of international leadership in only three decades.

A handsome mural titled *Westward, the Course of Empire Takes Its Way* hangs in the west stairway of the House wing in the U.S. Capitol. Emanuel Gottlieb Leutze, an American painter born in Germany, painted it in 1861 and 1862 during the Civil War. Leutze is known for his paintings of American history, including his famous 1851 work, *Washington Crossing the Delaware.* The stirring work of art captures the remarkable miracle that was nineteenth-century America and, particularly, westward expansion.

TWO

Gospel of Americanism

Bully Pulpit

In the United States a vigorous new debate raged among intellectuals, clerics, and the political establishment over the wisdom, cost, and morality of expansionism. America also found itself fighting a four-year insurrection with Philippine nationalists who had wanted independence from Spain and did not accept American occupation. The United States disestablished the Catholic Church as a state religion, introduced English as a language to unify the islands, and forcibly put down the insurrection at the cost of four thousand casualties. The Americans had lost only four hundred casualties in the Spanish-American War. In 1902 Congress passed the Philippine Organic Act, creating a Philippine representative assembly. In 1916 the Philippine Autonomy Act made a formal declaration that the United States was committed to the full independence of the Philippine Commonwealth. Although Americans were never comfortable as an occupier, in terms of education and infrastructure, the United States did more in fifty years to aid Philippine development than Spain did in five hundred years.

Occupation of the Philippines and Guam positioned the United States to take a greater role in Asian and trans-Pacific commerce and governance, as well as the proclamation of an "Open Door Policy" for China. This did not escape the attention of Japan, where Emperor Meiji the Great had swiftly moved Japan from an isolated feudal state to a capitalist power fueled by a remarkable Japanese industrial revolution.

Territorial and then commonwealth status succeeded the military occupation of Puerto Rico. As in the Philippines, the Americans emphasized infrastructure, public education, and the English language. Unlike in the Philippines with its many dialects, Spanish was the single language in Puerto Rico, and it remained.

On September 6, 1901, anarchist Leon Czolgsz shot President McKinley on the grounds of the Pan-American Exposition at the Temple of Music in Buffalo, New York. McKinley died eight days later. Just after 3:00 p.m. on September 14, Theodore Roosevelt took the oath of office as president. Republican political leader Mark Hanna said, "that damned cowboy is president now."[1] After the uss *Maine* exploded in Havana harbor in 1898, without approval Undersecretary of the Navy Roosevelt had ordered naval squadrons to prepare for war. This meant that Commodore Dewey's Asiatic Squadron was up to steam and in position to surprise and defeat the Armada Española at Manila Bay. Determined to see battle, Roosevelt resigned from his post and with Col. Leonard Wood formed the First U.S. Volunteer Cavalry Regiment, or the "Rough Riders." Since the colorful Roosevelt was the "gift that kept on giving" for the media, it was no surprise that the First usv and their exploits in Cuba were the toast of the national newspapers and popular magazines. Not everyone admired the new president. America's most popular writer, commentator, traveler, riverboat hand and wit Samuel Clemens, known as Mark Twain, despised Roosevelt and excoriated him at every opportunity.[2]

Roosevelt returned home to run for governor of New York on the condition that he would try not to make war with the Republican establishment. Winning by a close margin, he proposed a "Square Deal" to establish "honesty in public affairs, equitable sharing of privilege and responsibility and subordination of party and local concerns to the state at large." The new governor held two press conferences every day to connect to the people, and to the irritation of the establishment and New York Republican leader Thomas Platt, he rudely upended the patronage system of state government appointments. The media could not get enough of his battles with the establishment and played them to the hilt.[3] Eager to be rid of Roosevelt in Albany, Platt and the New York Republi-

Fig. 7. Pres. Theodore Roosevelt (standing on the 12-in. gun turret) addresses officers and crewmen on the afterdeck of the uss *Connecticut* (Battleship 18) at Hampton Roads, Virginia, upon its return from the Atlantic Fleet's cruise around the world, February 22, 1909. Collection of Lt. Comm. Richard Wainwright Jr., usn, 1926. Courtesy U.S. Naval History and Heritage Command, Washington dc.

can establishment maneuvered to get him on the 1900 ballot with McKinley. Campaign manager Mark Hanna loathed Roosevelt, but Platt prevailed.[4] As president, Roosevelt lived up to his media hype. He famously invited renown black educator and scientist Brooker T. Washington to dinner at the White House, infuriating the segregated South.[5] Addressing the question of capital versus labor, Roosevelt took proactive steps as a "trust buster" to regulate corporate trusts, bringing forty-four antitrust suits as compared to eighteen by his three predecessors combined; mediated a coal strike rather than calling out troops; prosecuted corrupt officials; regulated the railroads; passed a pure Food and Drug Act; and was an advocate for child labor laws. In addition to mediating the Russo-Japanese war, he is well known for creating national parks and wildlife preserves and for emphasizing conservation of natural resources despite considerable opposition. He gave logging and mining interests heartburn. Roosevelt was a zealous advocate for the elimination of the outrageous bird plume trade in Florida. Poachers and profiteers hated him.[6]

Roosevelt's most prestigious and far-sighted, if controversial, achievement was the construction and opening of the Panama Canal. Denounced as an imperialist, war monger, and even a lunatic, Roosevelt was determined to build a canal across the isthmus to link the Atlantic and Pacific. In 1903 Roosevelt mediated a dispute between European powers and Venezuela over repayment of delinquent loans. He averted a naval blockade, but this led him to issue a "Roosevelt Corollary" to the Monroe Doctrine. He was famously quoted from a Chicago speech: "There is an old homey adage which runs, speak softly and carry a big stick, you will go far . . . the American nation will speak softly and yet build and keep at a pitch of the highest training, a thoroughly efficient Navy; the Monroe Doctrine will go far."[7]

Congress approved a Panama Canal plan, but Colombia rejected it, and Panamanians rebelled. When American warships supported the Panamanians, the media coined the term "gunboat diplomacy." Panama seceded from Colombia, Roosevelt recognized the new sovereign nation, and Panama and the United States signed a deal that divided Panama with an American-run Canal Zone in the middle, to administer the new waterway construction and then the operational canal. Critics denounced Roosevelt when the United States bought out the rights and equipment of the defunct French Panama Canal Companies. Recriminations thundered in the halls of Congress and in the media, but construction of the canal started.[8] The *New York Times* was among the media that denounced the machinations that created Panama and launched the canal project, calling construction an act of "dishonorable intrigue and aggression." Forty years later, the same publication would be among commentators relieved that the United States could move its navy between oceans during World War II.

Walter Reed's yellow fever cure and American medical personnel made it possible to build the canal and support proper health conditions in Panama for the Americans and up to seventy-five thousand Afro-Caribbean and other canal workers. On November 6, 1906, Roosevelt traveled to Panama to inspect his audacious project. In one of the most effective photo opportunities of all time, the media caught the president working the controls of a huge Bucyrus Erie steam shovel, which boosted the morale of the canal workers. Roosevelt continued on to Puerto Rico, where he recommended that Puerto Ricans become citizens of the United States.[9]

Roosevelt had an adroit appreciation for the media and developed close relationships with publishers, editors, and writers. He had been a writer and editor and loved intellectual discussions. However, Roosevelt had no use for the scandal mongers that he called "muckrakers." In all, he enjoyed a very favorable but not compliant media and made maximum use of his self-described "bully pulpit" as president. Popular magazines lionized him and eagerly published stories about the sickly Roosevelt's formative years and his transition into a virile South Dakota cowboy, hunter, and wilderness advocate. After a story surfaced in a 1902 *Washington Post* political cartoon depicting Roosevelt humanely sparing a black bear cub during a Mississippi hunt, toymakers Morris Mitchcom and Richard Steiff immortalized him with the "teddy bear."[10]

Democrat Alton Brooks Parker ran against Roosevelt in 1904. The Democrats charged him with campaign corruption and illegal corporate donations. Roosevelt won 56 percent of the popular vote and an Electoral College margin of 336–140. He won all the northern and western states, and as usual, the Democrats swept the South. Before the inauguration, Roosevelt declared that he would not seek reelection in 1908.[11]

In 1906 Roosevelt was the first head of state to receive the Nobel Peace Prize for negotiating the Treaty of Portsmouth (Maine) and peace in the Russo-Japanese war of 1904–1905. He also resolved a dispute with Mexico by resorting to arbitration. Scandinavian leftists, who detested the American president as a "military mad" imperialist, bitterly opposed the honor.[12]

From December 1907 to February 1919 a U.S. Navy battle fleet completed a journey around the world. Its mission was to make courtesy calls and to display American naval power to the world. The navy painted the hulls of the ships white and gave the armada the nickname "The Great White Fleet." The cruise gave the fleet practical long-distance operational experience and influenced capital ship design. When Roosevelt met the returning sailors, he said, "Other nations may do what you've done, but they'll have to follow you."[13] Impulsive imperialist or vigorous visionary, Roosevelt and America stood astride the world.[14]

In 1907 San Francisco started segregating schools, whether immigrant Japanese children were newcomers or from citizen families. Roosevelt and the government of Japan were outraged. Roosevelt admired Japan's national character, navy, and military strength, and he feared a racial war. The federal government did not control local school boards, so Roosevelt summoned San Francisco mayor Eugene E. Schmitz to the White House, where he agreed to readmit Japanese children so long as they could speak some English. In 1908, the United States passed a new immigration law and made a "gentleman's agreement" with Japan that set limits on Japanese immigration.[15]

When Roosevelt made good on his belief in term limits, his friend and chosen successor, Secretary of War William Howard Taft, defeated three-time Democratic challenger William Jennings Bryan, who remained popular with liberals and populists. Bryan was able to pick off three western states and carry more counties than recent Democratic presidential candidates.[16]

Taft was deliberate, thoughtful, measured, and rotund. Taft's physical appearance was ideal for cartoonists if his steady and professional manner appeared boring. In part to help his successor, Roosevelt went about as far away as he could, on safari to Africa and touring Europe. He did, however, meet with heads of state in Europe. During his first year in office, Taft became embroiled in tricky tariff issues and ended up alienating all sides. Roosevelt came home and became disenchanted with Taft, particularly over relaxation of conservation efforts. In 1910 Roosevelt broke with Taft when he advocated a "New Nationalism," emphasizing labor over capital interests. The Republicans began to split. The Democrats took the House in the 1910 midterm election. Roosevelt impulsively contested the Republican nomination for 1912, but the party establishment and rules insured that Taft was their nominee. Roosevelt ran as a progressive or "Bull Moose" third-party candidate against Taft and Democrat Woodrow Wilson. His insurmountable challenge was the South. He won 27.4 percent of the electorate, and Taft won 23.2 percent of the electorate, or 50.6 percent of the popular vote. However, they divided the northern and western states, leaving Wilson with a plurality and a massive electoral college win of forty states and 435 electoral votes. Republican progressive expansionism imploded, and Democratic progressive moralism ascended.[17]

On August 15, 1914, the steamship ss *Ancon* made the first official transit of the Panama Canal. The United States completed the technological marvel and strategic asset at a cost of about $375 million, under the original budget estimate of 1907. Gen. George Washington Goethals, chief engineer of the project from 1907 to 1914, said graciously but with conviction, "The real builder of the Panama Canal was Theodore Roosevelt."[18]

Pres. Woodrow Wilson appointed William Jennings Bryan as secretary of state. Less than two months before the opening of the canal to traffic, Bryan entered into treaty negotiations for the settlement of claims from Colombia relating to the events surrounding the independence of Panama and the construction of the Panama Canal. Bryan's timing could not have been worse. He was signing a treaty at Wilson's direction that expressed "sincere regret for the conduct of the United States" in 1903 when President Roosevelt rejected the Colombian Congress's demand for a $5 million surcharge on the transfer of its land rights in Panama and encouraging the Panamanian Revolution. Bryan proposed to pay a compensatory $25 million. This was a clear insult to what Colonel Roosevelt felt was the most glorious achievement of his presidency. An incensed Roosevelt pointed out to the media that Panama had been trying to secede from Colombia for over fifty years before 1903. Although recovering from the ill effects of a well-publicized and dangerous expedition into the South American rainforests that nearly killed him, the former president had regained much of his stamina. In a June 24 statement Roosevelt issued a razor-sharp and detailed rebuttal to Wilson and Bryan. He considered the payment to Colombia "blackmail."[19]

On June 28 Serbian nationalist Gavrilo Princip shot and fatally wounded Archduke Franz Ferdinand of Austria-Hungary, heir to the Hapsburg dynasty, and his pregnant wife Sophie in Sarajevo, Bosnia. Within one week all the intermarried monarchial cousins and nation-states of Europe aggregated themselves into two opposing sides, the Central Powers of Austria-Hungary, Germany, and the allied Ottoman Empire versus the Entente Powers of Russia, Britain, and France. Back in the United States, President Wilson had called a special session of Congress to pass the Revenue Act of 1913, imposing a federal income tax to raise revenue lost from the removal of tariffs. The president encouraged passage of the Federal Reserve Act and the creation of a central banking system. When Europe blundered into war, Wilson declared neutrality.

Wilson was reelected in 1916 by a narrow margin against a reunified Republican Party and a unique candidate, Charles Evans Hughes, who was a Supreme Court justice. Wilson won 49.2 percent of the popular vote and 277 Electoral College votes to 46.1 percent of the popular vote and 254 Electoral College votes for Hughes. Wilson held the western states and the reliable former Confederate states. If Hughes had carried California, as Republicans and Roosevelt's Bull Moose had done for many elections, he would have had 267 total Electoral College votes and a victory.[20]

On January 25, 1915, Alexander Graham Bell made the first ceremonial transcontinental telephone call, although engineers completed and tested the voice connection in July 1914 for the Panama-Pacific Exposition in San Francisco. Popular music had started to come into its own with the widespread acceptance and purchase of Edison's "talking machines" or gramophones (record players). First cylinders and later discs began to affordably appear in homes across the nation. Magazines and newspapers publicized the lives of entertainers, musicians, and theatrical players. The new medium of silent motion pictures was becoming established in public places. Early pioneers including D. W. Griffith put their filming businesses in the promising climate of Southern California.

Filmmaker Griffith coproduced and directed *The Birth of a Nation* starring Lillian Gish. The 1915 film is three hours long and the most ambitious project of its era. It was a major commercial success that depicts the relationship of two families during the Civil War and Reconstruction, and it dramatizes the assassination of Abraham Lincoln. The film portrays the Ku Klux Klan during Reconstruction as heroes saving white women from black men played by white men in blackface. Composer Joseph Carl Breil created a three-hour musical score that the production company distributed to theaters for live performances to go with the silent film. The film debuted amid understandably strong protests, particularly from the National Association for the Advancement of Colored People (NAACP). Despite the controversy audiences flocked to see what all the fuss was about. The film rewrote history. For example, it begins with President Lincoln calling up conscripts but does not mention that South Carolina started the war by bombarding Fort Sumter. Creative license aside, this was the first film to make a powerful impact in the United States. *The Birth of a Nation* was the first motion picture seen at the White House by a president.[21]

Thomas Woodrow Wilson was born in Staunton, Virginia, on December 28, 1856, to a slaveholding Scots-Irish family. He spent his formative years in Augusta, Georgia, and Columbia, South Carolina. Wilson's father was a leading Southern Presbyterian and among the founders of the Presbyterian Church in the Confederate States of America. Wilson earned a PhD. in political science from Johns Hopkins University before his tenure at Princeton University and service as governor of New Jersey. As the first southerner elected president since Zachary Taylor in 1848, Wilson agreed with the revisionist view of the Confederacy that downplayed slavery and argued that the War Between the States was a struggle to preserve the southern and Jeffersonian agrarian way of life against northern subjugation.[22]

Following the 1916 election, Wilson had his hands full maintaining neutrality in the European war, and another chapter in the tumultuous history of Mexico distracted him. The regime of General José de la Cruz Porfirio Díaz Mori seized power in 1876. Diaz modernized Mexico, although his policies helped landowners, the upper class, and foreign investors. By 1910 Americans owned most of Mexican industry and infrastructure. Diaz caused a political crisis when he declared himself the winner of an eighth term of office in 1910 at the age of eighty. Massive election fraud had allowed Diaz to keep office.[23]

Before the election Diaz jailed his opponent, Francisco Ignacio Madero González. Following his escape from prison, Madero issued the manifesto "Plan de San Luis Potosi" to nullify the election and remove Diaz by force. The Federal Army suffered setbacks, and Diaz went into exile on May 31, 1911. Madero, "el caudillo de la Revolución," won the presidency on October 15 with 90 percent of the vote. In February 1913 a military coup d'état led by Gen. Victoriano Huerta arrested Madero, and he was assassinated on February 22.[24] In turn, Venustianio Carraza Garza overthrew Huerta in July 1914 and formed the Constitutional Party. Carraza was a mainstream leader who wished to restore peace and order. He opposed peasant leader Emiliano Zapata and revolutionary general Francisco "Pancho" Villa. A revolutionary general from the state of Chihuahua, Villa was a landowner, the commander of Division del Norte, and a member of the Constitutionalist Party. He played a decisive role in the ouster of Huerta and then fought against Carranza. At the Second Battle of Agua Prieta on November 1, 1915, Carranza's forces defeated Villa's Division del Norte. Villa then became a guerilla leader and raided Mexican and American pueblos on both sides of the border. The United States dispatched Gen. John J. Pershing on a punitive expedition to capture Villa during 1916. The incursion ended with the entry of the United States into World War I and without apprehending Villa.

On April 9, 1914, at Tampico, Tamaulipas, soldiers loyal to Huerta arrested nine unarmed American sailors. There was a sizable settlement of Americans connected with the petroleum industry living in Tampico and around the oil fields of Mexico's Gulf Coast. The minor incident was only a misunderstanding, but tensions escalated. Meanwhile, an advance of Carranza forces to within ten miles of Tampico threatened the local Huerta forces. With protection of the American residents and the sizable American petroleum investment as his rationale, and without warning Mexico, Wilson ordered the U.S. Navy to land Marines at the port of Veracruz on April 21, 1914. On the very same day, the German steamer ss *Yprianga* entered the harbor with arms and munitions for the Huerta junta, and the American Marines detained the steamer.[25] Wilson believed that confronting Huerta was a moral responsibility.[26]

President Taft had banned all weapons and ammunition sales from the United States to Mexico. That embargo forced Huerta to seek weapons and ammunition from European and Asian sources. American authorities had already intercepted several sizable and illicit arms shipments from the United States.[27] Though the first landing at Veracruz was unopposed, a battle ensued when the Americans spread out to set up a perimeter and occupy the city on April 22. The Americans withdrew on November 23 after the overthrow of Huerta. Opinion across Latin America concerning the occupation was negative, and Mexico expelled American citizens to refugee camps in California, Louisiana, and Texas. Wilson considered occupying the Tampico oil fields in 1917 but held off when Carranza threatened to set them ablaze.[28]

On January 16, 1917, British cryptographers intercepted a message from German foreign secretary Arthur Zimmerman to the German minister in Mexico, Heinrich von Eckhardt. In the message Germany audaciously promised Mexico the return of all the lands lost during the Mexican-American War, including Texas, New Mexico, and Arizona, in exchange for coming into World War I on the German side.

Carranza briefly considered entering the proposed alliance. His generals studied scenarios for "Reconquista," which was long a dream of Mexican patriots, but they concluded that recapturing territory from the United States was not realistic. Carranza also realized that aid from Germany for such a war could not reach

Mexico because of likely naval blockades by Great Britain and the United States. Mexico diplomatically declined the German offer and worked out an understanding with the United States about the strategic and productive oil fields. On August 31, 1917, the Wilson administration officially recognized the Carranza government, and in exchange Mexico stayed neutral during the rest of World War I.[29]

The Zimmerman telegram had a decidedly more dramatic effect among American politicians, media, and public. Revelation of the contents enraged Americans and hastened the entry of the United States into the war.[30]

Because the British had cut German access to British transatlantic cables at the start of the war, Germany had to send messages in code via the neutral American-owned cable, which Wilson had allowed as a good will gesture. When the British intercepted the Zimmerman telegram, they did not release it, because doing so would prove that they were listening to the American cable. Germany believed that American entry into the war was a fait accompli, and they sealed the deal when Ambassador Johann von Bernstorf informed the Wilson administration that Germany was resuming unrestricted submarine warfare on February 1. The United States broke off diplomatic relations with Germany on February 3. The British turned over the telegram to the United States on February 19, and Wilson released it to the media on February 28. The Zimmermann telegram exposed differences of opinion in the United States. Public opinion was anti-German and anti-Mexican, but Americans of German and Irish heritage remained anti-British. Because the British announced that they intercepted the message in Mexico, many Americans thought that it was a forgery. The Hearst Newspaper Syndicate promoted this point of view, as did German and Mexican diplomats.[31] Zimmerman held a press conference on March 3 and said, to an American journalist, "I cannot deny it. It is true." On March 29 Zimmerman gave a speech in the Reichstag and admitted the telegram was genuine. Zimmerman explained that the offer was that Germany would fund a Mexican war with the United States only if America had already entered the war against Germany. The resumption of unrestricted submarine warfare against American-flagged shipping using the language "ruthless employment of our submarines" was reason enough for the United States to enter the war, but the Zimmerman telegram was further justification to do so.

When World War I began in 1914, Wilson told the Senate and the American people that the United States "must be impartial in thought as well as action." He made several offers to mediate the conflict, which the belligerents ignored. Germany challenged his studied neutrality when it declared the seas around Great Britain to be a war zone. The major test of American neutrality came on May 7, 1915, when the Kaiserliche Marine Unterseeboot U-20 torpedoed and sank the big Cunard liner RMS *Lusitania* eleven miles southwest of Kinsale, Ireland, with the loss of 1,198 lives, including 128 Americans. Germany defended the sinking by claiming that the liner was carrying munitions or contraband of war in addition to passengers, and thus it was a military target. However, international law required that the submarine captain had to send a warning and allow the passengers and crew to get into lifeboats before an attack. The U-20 sent no such warning. Wilson got into trouble with his first statement about the sinking, when he said, "there is such a thing as a man being too proud to fight. There is such a thing as a nation being so right that it does not need to convince others by force that it is right."[32] Believing that Wilson was moving toward belligerency, the strongly antiwar secretary of state Bryan resigned, and Robert Lansing, an advocate of "benevolent neutrality," replaced him. In his memoirs Lansing recalled that following the sinking of the RMS *Lusitania* he came to believe that "we would ultimately become the ally of Britain." In May 1916 Wilson made a plea for postwar peace that offered American participation in a global peace organization. He never wavered from his conviction that the war was the result of corrupt European power politics, which he wanted nothing to do with. Critics, including Roosevelt, said Wilson's statements and policy were equivocation and cowardice.

Even after acknowledging the Zimmermann telegram, Wilson said, "we are the sincere friends of the German people and earnestly desire to remain at peace with them. We shall not believe they are hostile to us unless or until we are obliged to believe it." When Germany then sank several American ships, events checkmated the cautious Wilson. On April 2, 1917, he delivered his War Message to a special session of Congress, declaring that Germany had made his "armed neutrality" policy untenable. He asked Congress to "make the world safe for democracy" by declaring Germany's policy an act of war and, in turn, to declare war on Germany.[33]

Over There

On April 4, 1917, the United States declared war on Germany with a strong bipartisan mandate and scattered opposition from the rural South and German enclaves across the country. Wilson stopped short of a formal alliance with Great Britain and France. He declared that the United States was an "associated" power, or only an informal ally.[34] The United States instituted a wartime draft, the Selective Service Act of 1917, which Wilson signed into law on May 18. Wilson faced the manpower challenge of bringing together northern and western farmers and workers descended from the first British and German colonial settlers, decedents of Scots-Irish and Irish immigrants, more recent German immigrants, Scandinavians, grandsons of the Confederacy, and particularly the newer Italian and eastern European immigrants. Another dilemma was what to do about young blacks. While the subject of race and Jim Crow remained taboo, African Americans saw an opportunity to contribute to the war effort and make their mark.

The tools available to the Wilson administration to communicate and motivate were unlike those available to any earlier government, but this was an expansive national undertaking, and no one knew how to manage it. Wilson was not predisposed to invite Republicans into a coalition war cabinet. Of greater concern and danger to Wilson was the steadfast and consistent opposition he received throughout his presidency from Senate Republican icon Henry Cabot Lodge of Massachusetts. Lodge earned his PhD in history from Harvard and embodied principled intellectual opposition to Wilson. An advocate for an earlier mobilization and entry into the war on the side of the Entente Powers, Lodge was the powerful chairman of the Senate Committee on Foreign Relations and the Republican Conference. Though he discouraged Roosevelt from running as a third-party candidate in 1912, Lodge was of the Roosevelt worldview. He ardently favored the Spanish-American War and annexation of the Philippines. He supported the Immigration Act of 1917 that curtailed the steady flood of eastern and southern European newcomers but also sponsored the unsuccessful Lodge Bill that tried to protect African American voting rights. Lodge was a formidable foe.[35]

Among the many boards and agencies that Wilson's government formed to mobilize was the War Industries Board, so that military leaders could coordinate their needs with industrial managers. Chaired by financier Bernard Baruch, the WIB had teeth because it could regulate, and it had centralized purchasing power. Unavoidably the boards and agencies received help from many Republicans. Former president Taft headed the National War Labor Board. Harvard law professor Felix Frankfurter chaired the War Labor Policies Board, on which served Roosevelt's younger cousin, Undersecretary of the Navy Franklin Delano Roosevelt.

Of all the Republicans who helped, none was more essential than Herbert Clark Hoover. Among the first class to graduate from Stanford and a respected mining engineer, Hoover was a financier living in London at the outbreak of the war. Hoover engineered the return of over 100,000 Americans from Europe. He then organized the shipment of food to millions of hungry Europeans on both sides. Wilson put Hoover in charge of American food activities. Hoover had to accelerate crop production and upgrade inadequate railroad assets, which meant government intervention in the markets and price fixing.[36] Government advertising urged Americans to conserve fuel and save food, including going "meatless" at least one day each week. Hoover succeeded. America doubled its food production and shipments to Europe.[37]

The Wilson administration immersed itself in the first governmental attempt to coordinate or control information to explain the war aims of the United States. The public sacrifice and rare atmosphere of political good will inspired Wilson. He had worked hard to court support from many journalists and believed the media would join him to explain American war aims to the nation and the world. To "carry the gospel of Americanism" at home and abroad, the president set up the Committee of Public Information, which became the most controversial of his wartime agencies and boards. While other agencies and boards dealt with the physical aspects of successfully waging war, the CPI tried to deal with the psychological aspects of successfully waging war. Secretary of War Newton D. Baker later called it "mobilizing the mind of the world so far as American participation in the war is concerned." Baker went on to say that the CPI had intended to "expose information" rather than "impose strict censorship," which was "common for nations going to war."[38]

Wilson appointed progressive Denver journalist George Creel to run the CPI. This would not be the last time that a president selected a journalist to run a wartime information agency, but it was the first time that public opinion was a major consideration in wartime planning. The American people were intelligent and not all on board with declaring war, so they needed to be convinced. Creel later wrote that "the trial of strength was not only between massed bodies of armed men but between opposed ideals, and moral verdicts took on all the value of military decision. . . . The CPI was called into existence to make this fight for the verdict of mankind, the voice created to please the justice of America's cause before the jury of public opinion."[39] Creel noted that "we opened up the activities of the government to the inspection of the citizenship. A voluntary censorship agreement safeguarded military information of obvious value to the enemy, but in all else the rights of the press were recognized and furthered."[40] To "win the war by the pen as well as by the sword" and with a large budget, Creel brought in advertisers, publicists, and historians to create pamphlets and articles outlining "America's reasons for entering the war, the meaning of America, the nature of our free institutions, and our war aims" versus the "misrepresentations and barbarities" of the German government. Creel's team included some of the most respected writers and journalists in America, including Ray Stannard Baker, Edna Ferber, William Dean Howells, Ida Tarbell, Booth Tarkington, William Allen White, and Owen Wister.[41] Press agent Edward Bernays joined the CPI Bureau of Latin American Affairs. Bernays described his work as "psychological warfare," recognizing the importance of tapping less into what the people thought than into what they felt. A nephew of Sigmund Freud, Bernays went on to become a public relations giant.[42]

The CPI spread a Speakers Division across the country for public meetings to give the latest war information and to describe military battle progress at "war conferences." Some 75,000 additional volunteers spoke on topics ranging from morality to food conservation at theaters during the four minutes' time it took projectionists to change reels.[43] Artists contributed many colorful posters and window cards focused on romantic notions supporting the cause. Later the themes turned darker and pointedly anti-German. One poster was James Montgomery Flagg's legendary Uncle Sam saying, "I want YOU for the U.S. Army!"

The CPI produced motion pictures in cooperation with the young motion picture industry. They made many documentaries and feature films with negative portrayals of the enemy that resulted in widespread verbal prejudice, property damage, and physical attacks against German Americans. Lon Chaney appeared in *The Kaiser, The Beast of Berlin*. D. W Griffith produced an epic *Hearts of the World* starring Lillian Gish, about young lovers in France who are torn apart by war and reunited by killing a sadistic German rapist. Erich von Stroheim played a brutal enemy soldier who tries to rape a nurse before throwing a baby out of a window in *The Heart of Humanity*.[44] Creel noted that "every conceivable means was used to reach the foreign mind with America's message." Overseas the CPI set up small information offices in allied and neutral countries around the world. The speeches of Woodrow Wilson appeared everywhere along with stories about American life. It was the first time in history that any head of state commanded such widespread circulation.[45]

On June 15, 1917, Congress passed the Espionage Act, which Wilson had asked for in his December 7, 1915, State of the Union address.[46] The legislation moved slowly, even after the declaration of war. Although there was consensus about the parts of the act that dealt with spies and saboteurs, Wilson met a firestorm of protest about censorship language from all sides; the media, Democratic liberals, progressive and conservative Republicans. After weeks of debate the Senate removed the provisions by a 39–38 vote. Wilson insisted the provisions were necessary but signed the act without them. But Congress left in a provision that silenced citizens who opposed the war and another blocking distribution of opposition material through the post office.[47] The 1917 Espionage Act revived the First Amendment debate from Jefferson and Madison about the Sedition Act of 1798. During the Civil War Lincoln suspended habeas corpus several times, imposed martial law, and punished critics. When Wilson asked for the 1917 Espionage Act, he was asking for the authority Adams and Lincoln had enjoyed during similar emergencies. Many publishers and pundits argued against the act. Much of what Congress removed to pass the Espionage Act of 1917 was inserted into the Sedition Act of 1918, passed on May 16, 1918, which prohibited "disloyal, profane, scurrilous or abusive language about the form of government of the United States, or its military or naval forces or the uniforms or the flag thereof" and any language to cast upon them "contempt, scorn, contumely or disrepute."[48]

By its very existence and mission, the CPI avoided becoming seen as a censorship enforcer. Creel faithfully followed the guidance of the president, and without the censorship provisions, the CPI was able to do its wartime work without much media criticism. A byproduct of CPI literature and presentations was a widespread rejection of German American heritage by the public at large, as well as Americans of German descent. Hamburgers became "liberty steaks," and sauerkraut became "liberty cabbage." Families of German ancestry anglicized their names. Authorities suspended German operas and symphonies for the duration of the war. There was also ugly bigotry and acts of violence by perpetrators who months before had expressed no concern about their neighbors of German ancestry. Wilson urged for calm, expressing his "confidence in the entire integrity and loyalty of the great body of our fellow citizens of German blood."[49]

On January 8, 1918, Wilson delivered a speech on war aims and peace terms to the U.S. Congress that included a set of principles that came to be known as the Fourteen Points. He addressed the causes of the world war, calling for the abolition of secret treaties, an arms reduction, adjustments in colonial claims, and freedom of the seas. He wanted to see economic barriers removed, self-determination for national minorities, and a world peace organization or a League of Nations. Russian Bolshevik leader Vladimir Lenin called it "a landmark of enlightenment in international relations."[50]

There were three prominent figures of popular entertainment who had major influences on American culture during World War I. In 1910 James Reese Europe organized the Clef Club, a society for African Americans employed in the music business. His Society Orchestra, performing ragtime, jazz, and symphonic compositions including legendary musicians Noble Sissle and Eubie Blake, made phonograph records for the Victor recording company and performed at Carnegie Hall. As musical director for dancers Vernon and Irene Castle, he introduced and popularized the classic foxtrot using his composition "Castle Walk." When the United States declared war on Germany, Europe and Sissle secured commissions in the New York National Guard. They formed the regimental band for the 369th Infantry Regiment, known as the Harlem Hellfighters. Lieutenant Europe was the concertmaster and Lieutenant Sissle the drum major and violinist. The regiment and band were among the first American troops to arrive in France. The band became the most famous military band of World War I, performing ragtime and popular wartime tunes such as "Mademoiselle from Armentieres." Europe's popularity and projection of a genuine American art form was the genesis of the strong French affinity for the jazz idiom and African American performers.[51] Upon their triumphant return from France, including leading white and black troops on a rousing February 1919 Victory Parade in New York City, Europe and the band stayed together for public appearances and concert performances.[52]

In May 1919 Europe embarked on a national tour and was appearing at Mechanics Hall in Boston. During intermission the disciplinarian Europe had a talk with drummers Steven and Herbert Wright to straighten out their behavior. Without warning or clear cause, an agitated Herbert Wright stabbed Europe in the neck with a penknife. The wound appeared superficial, but it had severed Europe's jugular vein. Europe was honored with a public funeral procession in New York City and burial with full military honors at Arlington National Cemetery.[53] Decades later Eubie Blake would remember, "People don't realize yet today what we lost when we lost Jim Europe. He was the savior of Negro musicians and in a class with Booker T. Washington and Martin Luther King, Jr."[54]

George Michael Cohan was a colossus of the American theater. The prolific entertainer, playwright, and composer of popular musical, comedic, and dramatic plays composed over three hundred songs in his lifetime, including "Give My Regards to Broadway," "Yankee Doodle Dandy," and "You're a Grand Old Flag." Known as "the man who owned Broadway," Cohan was a successful theater owner and music publisher by 1917, when he lent his efforts to the war effort with enthusiasm. Cohan's composition "Over There" became the virtual theme song of America's participation in World War I, and his many exuberant productions were quintessential expressions of unabashed patriotism.

In 1911 the young American immigrant songwriter from Russia Irving Berlin (Israel Isidore Baline) composed and published the most recognizable ragtime tune of its day and his first major success, "Alexander's Ragtime Band," which sparked an international dance craze and catapulted him to a long and memorable career as one of America's most prolific and beloved composers of music and lyrics. The prolific Berlin agreed with Cohan that the entertainment industry should get behind the war effort. Berlin enlisted in the army. Stationed at Camp Upton, New York, with the 152nd Depot Brigade, he composed the all-soldier musical revue *Yip, Yip, Yaphank*. A tune that he wrote for the show but did not use was "God Bless America," which he would introduce twenty years later.

The young film industry had gravitated to California for better weather and the space to produce. When America entered the war, Hollywood began to produce pro-war feature films, serials, and short subjects. Films like *Beast of Berlin* were so effective that audiences emotionally reacted. In Davenport, Iowa, a man jumped up and shot at the image of German villain Eric von Stroheim on the screen with a revolver.[55] William A. Brady of the National Association of the Motion Picture Industry (NAMPI) worked closely with the CPI. He told Wilson, "You have the undivided conscientious and patriotic support of the entire film industry in America. I have the honor to be your obedient servant."[56] In May 1918 director Cecil B. De Mille told a Motion Picture War Relief Association meeting in Los Angeles, "The motion picture is the most powerful propaganda and sends a message through the camera which can't be changed by any crafty diplomat."[57]

The greatest contribution of Hollywood to the war effort was lending famous silent film stars to parades and rallies for war relief, war bonds, and appearances at military camps. The CPI also enlisted the film studios to create public relations shorts to sell war bonds. "Liberty Loans" were the World War I war bond campaigns. Charles Chaplin, Lillian Gish, Douglas Fairbanks, Mary Pickford, and many other celebrities pitched Liberty Loans on film, and they all made many personal appearances for war bonds and the other wartime causes.[58] Notwithstanding the presence of the CPI, the effort did not involve a comprehensive involvement or partnership between media and government. The collaboration narrowly focused on justifying war aims by villainizing Germany and raising money for war bonds and war relief.

The Wilson administration did not address issues including assimilation of recent southern and eastern European immigrants into conscripted armed forces or the extremely sensitive question of arming black troops as combat solders, as advocated by Gen. John J. Pershing, or pigeonholing them as stevedores, as favored by most white officers, southern politicians, and their segregationist commander-in-chief. Segregation and prejudice did not stop troops of color and many ethnicities from sacrificing their lives for the United States on Flanders Fields.

In addition to Mexico, Wilson intervened in unstable Haiti, the Dominican Republic, Cuba, and Panama between 1914 and 1918 to keep order in support of economic interests. He kept marines in Nicaragua during the entire period. The president commented with typical Wilsonian certainty, "I am going to teach the South American republics to elect good men."[59]

By August 1918 one million American troops were in France under the command of General Pershing, and as hoped, they tipped the balance of the war in favor of the Allies. On September 29, the powerful chief of the German high command, Gen. Erich Ludendorff, informed Kaiser Wilhelm II that he could not hold the front and that Germany should at once seek a cease fire. Ludendorff recommended that Wilson's Fourteen Points were the most favorable deal that Germany could obtain as a way of ending the war. On October 5 Germany sent Wilson a message asking to negotiate an armistice based upon the Fourteen Points. As a precondition for negotiations, Wilson replied that Germany must retreat from occupied territories and end submarine warfare, and that Kaiser Wilhelm II must abdicate. The problem was that the Entente Powers strongly felt that they, and not a third party, were the proper authority to set terms. Meanwhile, amidst desertion and revolt by elements of the German Army and Navy, and then riots in Berlin, a constitutional crisis erupted, and Kaiser Wilhelm II abdicated on November 9.

A German delegation arrived in France on November 8 and was taken aboard the private train of Allied supreme commander Marshal Ferdinand Foch to a railway siding in the forest of Compiègne. The Germans were handed a list of Allied demands and were given seventy-two hours to agree. The armistice terms demanded complete German demilitarization in exchange for no firm commitments of any kind. There was no negotiation, although the Germans protested the unconditional, harsh, and humiliating Allied terms. They had no choice but to sign the armistice at 5:00 a.m.

on November 11, and the cease-fire took effect "on the eleventh hour of the eleventh day of the eleventh month."

Hall of Mirrors

When Woodrow Wilson stood on the deck of the ss *George Washington* on December 13, 1918, about to disembark in France to a magnificent hero's welcome, he headed straight into a political swamp that was masquerading as the postwar peace conference. Initially Wilson would win accommodation on the issues and preliminary agreement about setting up the League of Nations. He would optimistically return to the United States on February 14, 1919, believing that his vision for peace was in hand. His nemesis Henry Cabot Lodge favored the League of Nations with reservations. Lodge objected to Article X of the Covenant of the League of Nations, which obliged all signatory nations to repel aggression of any kind if ordered to do so by the league.

On August 12, 1918, Lodge warned in the Senate speech: "The United States is the world's best hope, but if you fetter her in the interests and quarrels of other nations, if you tangle her in the intrigues of Europe, you will destroy her powerful good, and endanger her very existence. Leave her to march freely through the centuries to come, as in the years that have gone. Strong, generous, and confident, she has nobly served mankind. Beware how you trifle with your marvelous inheritance; this great land of ordered liberty. For if we stumble and fall, freedom and civilization everywhere will go down in ruin."[60]

In the 1918 midterm elections, the Republicans had gained a two-vote majority in the Senate, so Wilson would have to deal with Lodge to pass any treaty. The 1918 national election was the third one in which the popular vote and not state legislatures elected U.S. senators. The four-seat gain by Republicans from forty-four to forty-eight seats had a profound impact on the course of events. The buoyant Wilson who arrived in France on December 13 did not yet have the support of Congress, or even some of the Democrats.[61]

On October 18, 1918, former president Roosevelt urged Republican senators to reject the Fourteen Points, commenting "such a peace would represent not the unconditional surrender of Germany but the conditional surrender of the United States."[62] Colonel Roosevelt would not join the coming debate because on January 6, 1919, he peacefully died in his sleep at his Oyster Bay, New York, home. From Europe, Wilson released a gracious tribute to his longtime rival.

Europe was in bad shape. Empires had fallen, and revolutions had created many new countries. Communism seized Russia and threatened Germany. People were hungry. Europe already owed the United States more than it could pay, but only a large measure of added aid could save the continent from bankruptcy and starvation. In this charged atmosphere Wilson met French prime minister Georges Clemenceau, British prime minister David Lloyd George, and Italian prime minister Vittorio Orlando, each with their own set of priorities and each in their own way cunning and ruthless.[63]

From the opening of the conference on January 18, 1919, Clemenceau dominated the proceedings as chair. His hatred for Germany and desire for onerous reparations was obvious. When Wilson sought magnanimous arrangements, the French convinced themselves that he was not on their side. The American representatives at the conference with Wilson included Samuel Gompers (labor), Bernard Baruch (economics), Herbert Hoover (food), and Secretary of State Lansing's nephew, John Foster Dulles (banking).When the day came to debate the League of Nations, Wilson gave a stirring speech and said that he "spoke for America," and the delegates voted to create a commission to write a constitution for the league. The European diplomats believed that Wilson was a gifted orator but, as recalled by French diplomat Paul Cambon, that "he was out of touch with the world, giving confidence to no one, unversed in European politics and devoted to the pursuit of theories which had little relation to the emergencies of the hour."[64] On February 3 Wilson opened the first meeting of the Commission on the League of Nations. The commission crafted a covenant with thirteen articles of governance and organization and ten supplementary documents. Article X of the League Covenant defined collective security, which opponents in Congress

would later see as a surrender of sovereignty. The commission settled on twenty-seven Articles of the Covenant. Presumably need-
ing to attend to governing at home, Wilson sailed home with the
intention of returning to negotiate a treaty. He left business in
Versailles in the hands of his trusted aide, Col. Edward M. House.

Russia did not attend the conference but was on the minds of
everyone. Before leaving, Wilson sent William Bullitt, a twenty-
eight-year-old member of the American delegation, on a fact-
finding mission, accompanied by journalist Lincoln Steffens, a
Marxist sympathizer. Bullitt thought he had a mandate from Wilson, House, and British PM Lloyd George to negotiate peace terms
with the Bolsheviks.[65]

On February 26 the president hosted a dinner for members of
the congressional Foreign Relations Committees. Following dinner, Wilson described the conference and answered questions until
midnight. Lodge recalled that "we went away as wise as we came
in."[66] Two days later, Lodge obliterated the Covenant of the League
of Nations article by article in a Senate speech. Lodge hoped to
separate the League of Nations decision from a treaty of peace. He
circulated a letter pledging opposition that thirty-seven Republican senators signed. Wilson was in trouble, but the undeterred
president set sail back to France on March 4 after achieving nothing at home. Upon returning to France on March 13, Wilson discovered that while he was away, House had taken it upon himself
to negotiate changes to the covenant, including concessions to
France. On April 3 Wilson fell ill. He was diagnosed with Spanish
influenza, but further examination has suggested encephalitis or a
small stroke. Regardless of the precise cause or causes, Wilson suffered a viral infection that had neurological implications. American advisers sensed that the conference had changed, and that the
Europeans were working behind the scenes to discredit Wilson.
To preserve the League of Nations, Wilson began to compromise
and agree to many changes to the other thirteen points. This was
out of character with his prior consistency about all the points.[67]

The conference began to unravel. In late April Italy completely
withdrew, denouncing "Wilsonian peace." Japan had introduced a

motion for an amendment adding racial equity to religious equity in the covenant. This was unacceptable to Britain and potentially controversial in the United States. It was also unacceptable to Wilson, who did not consider the white and black races to be fundamentally equal. The Japanese raised the question to gain control of Shandong Province in Eastern China. Japan demanded Shandong in exchange for withdrawing the racial equity amendment. To the horror of the American delegation, Wilson accepted the Japanese demand rather than risk the dissolution of the conference and end of the covenant. With the acceptance of these terms, the treaty and the league were intact. Reaction in China was predictably negative. On May 4 students rioted in Peking's Tiananmen Square. In Hunan a young newspaper editor named Mao Zedong (romanized then as Mao Tse-tung) editorialized, "we are awakened . . . the world is ours, the state is ours, the society is ours."[68]

There were four more months of negotiations. Italy returned to the table. On Wednesday, May 7, the world awaited a ceremony for presentation of the draft Treaty of Versailles to the German delegation at the Galerie des Glaces or Hall of Mirrors in the ornate Trianon Palace Hotel. Twenty-five years later, the same edifice became the headquarters of a different allied coalition in another war. The ceremony was awkward. Chairman Clemenceau coldly announced the harsh terms, contained in 440 articles and 15 sections, beginning with establishment of the League of Nations.[69] Neither Wilson, Clemenceau, Lloyd George, Orlando, or anyone else present could foresee that within twenty years their misguided dictate would result in another and more horrific war.[70]

In Moscow Bullitt and Steffens met Lenin, were impressed, and thought they had a deal for a cease-fire between the Bolsheviks and Allies, who were supporting the White Russians. A stunned and bitter Bullitt returned to discover that neither Wilson nor Lloyd George were interested.[71] Wilson put no faith in Lenin's offer and ignored Bullitt, who quit.

Wilson hesitantly joined the European powers to intervene in Russia. He sent an American Expeditionary Force to occupy Vladivostok and maintain the Trans-Siberian Railway. Another

American force confronted the Red Army at Archangel.[72] Diplomatic relations between the United States and the Soviet Union (the USSR) did not begin until President Franklin D. Roosevelt recognized the USSR in 1933.[73]

Viewing Wilson, John Maynard Keynes stated, "this blind and brave Don Quixote was entering a cavern where the swift and glittering blade was in the hands of the adversary." Although Keynes and others did not believe that the problems with the treaty were Wilson's fault, many believed that the clever Allies had outfoxed him. The German government of Philipp Schiedemann fell, and a new government organized by Gustav Bauer signaled its acceptance. Kriegsmarine crews scuttled their interred ships rather than turn them over to Britain and France. On Saturday, June 28, in the Galerie des Glaces, Germany, the Allies and the United States signed the Treaty of Versailles, which Wilson considered a victory for mankind.[74]

Wilson arrived home on July 8. The United States was experiencing postwar inflation and a deadly flu epidemic. There were serious race riots, north and south, as disillusioned black veterans came home and realized that racism still existed. In some cities whites ignited the violence, looting, and arson. During the "red summer," Secretary of War Newton D. Baker called in troops to quell the disturbances. For the first time more Americans lived in cities than in rural towns and on farms. A recession lasted to 1921.[75]

There was never any doubt about where Lodge stood concerning the Treaty of Versailles. The Republicans controlled both houses of Congress, although their Senate majority was thin. There were fifteen Republicans solidly against the treaty under any circumstances. Thirty-four had reservations. If Wilson made concessions, some of the thirty-four might vote yes. Wilson was counting on all forty Democrats to vote yes. Lodge believed that there were a few Democrats who would vote no. Battling for the necessary two-thirds majority, Wilson and Lodge had to work the undecideds.[76] Wilson wanted to fast-track the treaty through the Senate with a simple up or down vote. The Republicans were in no rush. On July 10, when Wilson entered the Senate to present the

Fig. 8. Sen. Henry Cabot Lodge. Portrait by John Singer Sargent, 1890. National Portrait Gallery, Smithsonian Institution, Washington DC (NPG.67.58).

treaty, he received a standing ovation from the Democrats while the Republicans withheld applause. As Wilson then went about meeting with senators, he argued that neither he nor they had "the moral right to modify any Article unless every other country should be granted the same privilege." During August Lodge called sixty witnesses to testify about the treaty.[77] Although separation of powers did not compel him to do so, Wilson invited the Foreign Relations Committee to the White House on August 19 to testify himself. The president was prepared, and he answered every question. The problem was that he changed no minds. Wilson was experiencing a noticeable mental decline. He could not recall actions, events, and details, and he appeared confused. When the meeting ended, the courtly president invited the committee for a pleasant lunch. As days went by following the interview and luncheon, Democrat leaders realized that the treaty was floundering. Allies urged the principled president to accept "interpretive reservations" in the treaty language.

Wilson decided to make his case directly with the people. A four-week national tour would take the president to most of the states west of the Mississippi to plead his case. Wilson was horrified at the thoughts that he might have taken the nation to war without winning real peace and that the young men he sent to death in the trenches had died in vain. His personal physician was worried about Wilson's health and urged him not to go on the tour. But the president was determined and set off on this mission on September 3, accompanied by a large contingent of media that would report in print, photographs, and the new newsreel films on his attempt to win popular support.[78]

As Wilson gave convincing addresses to Republican audiences from Columbus to Des Moines, he kept experiencing headaches. The national media were abuzz with the news that Wilson was flipping opinion in the midwestern states from no to yes. Meanwhile, as Wilson continued to Seattle and Portland, the disgruntled Bullitt testified against the treaty on Capitol Hill, and it appeared Wilson was going to have to fire Lansing. By the time Wilson reached California, he was nearing the point of complete exhaustion. Henry Chandler, the Republican publisher of the *Los Angeles Times*, endorsed Wilson's effort. After a triumphant visit to California, the national media concluded that Wilson had moved national opinion to pro–League of Nations. After strenuous visits to Salt Lake City and Denver and stops in smaller Colorado communities, the asthmatic Wilson had a physical breakdown so complete and severe that presidential physician Admiral (Dr.) Cary T. Grayson canceled the rest of the tour. This was the moment that Edith Wilson realized that her husband's crusade was over and that she would have to carry on for him, a decision that would have controversial ramifications.

From Wichita the White House released the cancellation announcement. A shroud of secrecy descended upon returning to Washington, which only aroused suspicion. Wilson was gravely ill. On October 2 the already weakened president suffered what medical experts diagnosed as a thrombosis or ischemic stroke, a clot in an artery of his brain. There was no rupture. Wilson could think and speak. The White House told no one. At the advice of pioneering neurologist Francis X. Dercum and Dr. Grayson, Edith Bolling Wilson became the president's voice, eyes, and ears. For all intents and purposes, Woodrow Wilson, the man in control of his mind, body, and spirit, was gone.[79] To protect her husband, Edith assumed the legitimate constitutional duty of Vice President Thomas Marshall to temporarily replace the incapacitated president, and if not legally, she was, in effect, the first female president of the United States. Within days the media reported rumors that Wilson had suffered a cerebral hemorrhage, which Dr. Grayson denied. However, Edith, Dr. Grayson, and private secretary Joseph Patrick Tumulty decided to secretly inform Vice President Marshall, who wondered why he had not taken over as temporary president. It would not be until the end of October that the triumvirate allowed anyone to see and speak with the president. In a carefully managed interview Attorney General A. Mitchell Palmer met with Wilson. Palmer reported to the media that the president was alert and attentive; physically weak but mentally sharp.

During 1919 the United States ratified Prohibition as the Eighteenth Amendment to the Constitution. Congress passed the Volstead Act to implement the measure. The convalescing president, or more precisely, Edith and Tumulty, vetoed it, and the House and Senate both overrode their veto. The United States and the world also suffered a flu pandemic. The Spanish Flu of 1918–1920 killed 5 percent of the world's population. In the United States the flu tended to kill young adults rather than children and the elderly. Twenty-eight percent of the population of the United States became infected, and between 500,000 and 675,000 people died.[80]

Wilson's allies felt acceptance of Republican reservations would save the treaty and the league. Herbert Hoover wrote that "the (reservations) do not seem to imperil the great principle of the League of Nations" and that Wilson should accept at once. Lodge wrote out fifty language edits to the treaty that would guarantee Senate approval, which intermediaries delivered to Tumulty. We will never know if Wilson ever saw the Lodge compromise. Most Democrats favored a ratified treaty in any form, but Wilson would not budge an inch. Lodge made a formal proposal for a modified treaty, and Democratic minority leader Gilbert Hitchcock of Nebraska went to the White House to discuss it at length with Wilson himself and not the intermediaries. Wilson said no.[81] On November 19 the Democrats caucused and decided to unite against the Lodge resolution in fidelity to Wilson. That afternoon the Senate defeated the Lodge resolution of ratification by a vote of 55–39, with 42 Democrats and 13 Republicans voting no. Sen. Oscar Underwood (D-AL) then introduced the treaty exactly as Wilson brought it home from France, and the vote was 53–38 against.

On February 11, 1920, Secretary of State Lansing resigned at Wilson's invitation, and he issued a statement detailing his final correspondence with Wilson. It was a bombshell that led many newspaper editorial boards to question Wilson's competence. Several days earlier urologist Hugh H. H. Young of Johns Hopkins, a member of Wilson's medical team, divulged details of the president's cerebral thrombosis. Although Young stressed that Wilson's mind was sound, the story, coupled with Lansing's dismissal, suggested a White House cover-up.

Friends and supporters privately urged Edith Wilson to convince her husband to offer a compromise. The media and public opinion favored acceptance with the Lodge reservations. At that very moment there was an influenza outbreak in Washington that infected Wilson. On February 29, 1920, fifteen Democratic leaders huddled with Tumulty. The party elders agreed that the president should accept the Lodge reservations. Wilson again rejected their advice. He wrote a 1,400-word final letter to leader Hitchcock, and the White House released copies to the media. Wilson encouraged treaty supporters and opponents to again vote no against the compromise treaty with reservations.

Major national newspapers urged approval and lamented Wilson's inflexibility. The *New York World* editorialized, "these reservations at their worst are merely an expression of opinion on the part of a temporary majority of the Senate" and that what "a reactionary Senate under the leadership of Henry Cabot Lodge does a progressive Senate under enlightened leadership can undo."[82]

On March 19 the Senate voted on the treaty with Lodge's final language. The vote was 49–35 with 12 senators absent. The rules paired the absent votes on a 2–1 basis because of the two-thirds requirement to pass. The treaty lost by 7 votes. An almost equal number of Democrats voted yes as did not. The United States had neither ratified the treaty or joined the League of Nations, which came into existence on January 10, 1920, and never became an effective peacekeeping organization.[83]

A quip that defines the famous American columnist and wit of stage, radio, and screen, Will Rogers of Oklahoma, is that he never met a man he didn't like. But Rogers did not particularly like Woodrow Wilson and many other politicians. Rogers was the first comedian to tell a joke about a president who was in the audience. At a May 30, 1916, performance starring George M. Cohan, Rogers's target was Wilson, who laughed heartily. It was a rare moment of humor for the now-debilitated president whose vision of moral ideological purpose had floundered.[84]

America's robust advance through the Industrial Revolution and World War I had come with social costs, the rise of the extraordinarily wealthy "robber barons" and notorious business trusts. Yet something surprising happened. The likes of Andrew Carnegie, John Pierpont Morgan, and John D. Rockefeller became philanthropists and gave back to their fellow Americans. Philanthropy became a strong, enduring and meaningful part of the national fabric, inspiring giving, sharing, and even volunteerism by many citizens to social welfare, the arts, and the environment, and spawning many community and religious organizations committed to the common good, charity, shared values, human dignity, and progress in an unprecedented manner.

THREE

Arsenal of Democracy

New Deal

During the summer of 1920 the Republicans nominated long shot Ohio Senator Warren G. Harding for president and Massachusetts Governor Calvin Coolidge for vice president. The Democrats nominated Gov. James Cox, also of Ohio, for president and Franklin D Roosevelt, of New York, undersecretary of the navy for vice president. Socialist Eugene Debs, jailed during the war and campaigning from a federal prison, received 3 percent of the national presidential vote. Harding trounced Cox with 60.3 percent of the popular vote and 404 Electoral College votes.[1] The 1920 presidential election was the first in which women had the right to vote, since Congress and the states had ratified the Nineteenth Amendment.[2]

Americans favored global disarmament. In November 1921 the United States announced the Washington Naval Conference, chaired by Charles Evans Hughes, now secretary of state. It was clear that Britain and the United States would never go to war against one another. The issue was Japan, and there was division among Imperial Navy officers about what to do. Japanese naval doctrine held that Japan needed a fleet at least 70 percent the size of the U.S. fleet to win a war. Chief delegate Kato Tōmosaburō preferred treaty limits to the prospect of an expensive arms race in which the United States would outproduce Japan. His chief naval aide and the president of the Naval War College, Katō Kanji, disagreed. Many younger officers wanted a large navy that would engage and defeat America on a 1–1 basis. An exception was Isoroku Yamamoto, studying at Harvard and serving as a naval attaché in Washington, who opposed an arms race.Tōmosaburō prevailed, but the decision would remain bitterly controversial in Japan.[3]

The Washington Naval Treaty prohibited Britain, Japan, and the United States from building any new naval bases or fortifications in the Pacific Ocean area. This meant that Britain could not upgrade Singapore and the United States could not upgrade Hawaii or the Philippines, which was a big win for Japan in case of any future war. This restriction secured Japanese approval for warship limits.[4] The great powers respected the treaty limits, which the 1930 London Naval Treaty extended, although heated debate continued in Japan. The pro-treaty faction was comfortable that the agreement restricted American production in a 5:3 ratio with Japan.[5] Then, suddenly, on December 29, 1934, with a militarist faction dominant, Japan gave formal notice that it was ending the treaty when it expired in 1936. The implications were obvious.

Ace pilot Col. William L. "Billy" Mitchell returned from World War I convinced that air power would become a decisive weapon of modern warfare. As Army Air Service assistant chief of staff, Mitchell advocated for an independent air force. He believed that surface fleets were obsolete and vulnerable to air attack and tried to prove so with several highly publicized and controversial aerial bombing demonstrations that bombed and sank target ships at sea in 1921 and 1923. Although the resentful military establishment questionably court-martialed the outspoken Mitchell for insubordination, events soon vindicated him.[6]

Commerce Secretary Herbert Hoover was a standout among the Harding cabinet. Following World War I, he continued his yeoman responsibility directing human relief efforts to feed Europe. Returning home, Hoover focused on technology. He championed the 1926 Air Commerce Act creating the Bureau of Aeronautics to regulate commercial and general aviation. He also took the lead toward regulating communications and the new radio industry with the Federal Radio Act of 1927 and the establishment of the Federal Radio Commission.

The Harding presidency ended prematurely and under a cloud

of scandal. On August 2, 1923, Harding died of a heart attack in San Francisco, and his death was nationally mourned. Harding had appointed many associates from Ohio to his administration. After his death authorities and the media found some of them caught up in scandal and illicit activity. The biggest of the scandals was Teapot Dome, a shady oil lease deal involving bribes and kickbacks. It also eventually came out that Harding was a philanderer. Teapot Dome cost Secretary of the Interior Albert B. Fall and Attorney General Harry M. Daugherty their jobs and resulted in their prosecution.[7]

The Harding Administration is a contradiction, with the ethical and effective Hughes and Hoover on one hand and the corrupt Fall and Daugherty on the other. Harding appointed former president William Howard Taft as chief justice of the Supreme Court, the only person to have ever served both as president and a justice. The unexceptional Harding thus bears responsibility for both achievement and disgrace.[8] President Calvin Coolidge restored integrity and public confidence in the wake of the Harding scandals and won election in his own right in 1924 by a comfortable margin over Democrat John W. Davis of West Virginia. As president, the ethical and efficient Coolidge became legendary for his public reticence, becoming known as "silent Cal." During the 1924 campaign, he started giving the first presidential talks over radio. The exceptional Coolidge vowed to serve only one full term and successfully did so.

On the afternoon of February 12, 1924, in New York's Aeolian Hall, a rotund thirty-four-year-old bandleader from Denver called his Palais Royal Orchestra to order. Many important musicians were present, including Fritz Kreisler, Sergei Rachmaninoff, John Philip Sousa, Igor Stravinsky, and Leopold Stokowski, to hear popular maestro Paul Whiteman's "An Experiment in Modern Music." The second-to-last piece before Elgar's "Pomp and Circumstance March No. 1" was a new jazz concerto by George Gershwin, arranged by Ferde Grofé, with the composer present to play the piano. The exhausted audience was ready to leave until they heard the clarinet glissando that opened "Rhapsody in Blue." Grofé, Whiteman's pianist and chief arranger, continued to tweak the new composition in dozens of performances and with a best-selling Victor record during the 1920s. He wrote a new orchestration in 1926 and published another for full symphony orchestras in 1942. "Rhapsody in Blue" established Gershwin as a serious composer and became one of America's most recognizable and popular concert works.[9]

At 10:22 p.m. on May 21, 1927, an exhausted twenty-five-year-old American aviator and army reserve officer named Charles Augustus Lindbergh landed his airplane *Spirit of St. Louis* at Le Bourget Aerodrome in Paris, where 150,000 thrilled French men and women anxiously awaited his arrival. The crowd stormed the Ryan Aeronautical monoplane, dragged out the confused pilot, and carried him around the field. Lindbergh had just completed a 33½ hour flight from Roosevelt Field, New York, on dead reckoning, becoming the first man to fly the Atlantic Ocean by himself. Europe celebrated "Lucky Lindy," and massive crowds welcomed him home along with his damaged but intact *Spirit of St. Louis*. Lindbergh became *Time* magazine's first "man of the year" on January 2, 1928. Congress awarded him the Medal of Honor. He toured the United States and made a "goodwill tour" of Latin America.

Lindbergh went on to consult, survey, and develop routes for Pan American Airways (Pan Am) and Transcontinental and Western Airlines (TWA). He and his wife, Anne Morrow Lindbergh, remained in the public eye, particularly after the notorious kidnapping and murder of their twenty-month-old child, Charles, from their East Amwell, New Jersey, home on March 1, 1932. The "crime of the century" and resulting trial, conviction, and execution by electrocution of suspected German immigrant carpenter Bruno Richard Hauptmann was controversial and ugly and drew sensational media attention.[10]

Herbert Hoover won the 1928 election in a landslide over Democrat Al Smith, the governor of New York, the first Catholic candidate for president. The highly respected Hoover became the first president who was born west of the Mississippi River. The honeymoon did not last for the brilliant humanitarian. Everything changed on October 24, 1929, when the stock market collapsed. A firm believer in balanced budgets, Hoover instinctively addressed the economic crisis though local, state, and private sector solutions. He tried to raise agricultural tariffs in 1930 to protect farmers, but Congress added other industries and passed the Smoot-Hawley Tariff Act. As the economic downturn turned into a worldwide depression, the effect of the act backfired as other nations responded by raising tariffs on imports from the United States, worsening the situation for Americans. Hoover appointed former secretary of state Hughes to succeed former president Taft as chief justice of the Supreme Court. To address pressure from southwestern interests, Hoover allowed the controversial and racially charged forced deportation of Mexicans from the United States—eerily previewing twenty-first-century deportation debates. He was reluctant to sponsor public works projects or programs for fear of budget deficits. As matters deteriorated, Hoover did opt for direct federal intervention.

However, by 1932, nearly 25 percent of Americans were unemployed, five thousand banks had failed, and the homeless called shantytowns "Hoovervilles." The low point for Hoover was during the summer of 1932. Thousands of World War I veterans camped out in Washington, calling for the immediate payment of a bonus legislated by the World War Adjusted Compensation Act of 1924 for payment in 1945. Against Hoover's orders army chief of staff Douglas MacArthur sent troops to break up the encampments. The Democrats brutally attacked Hoover as the cause of the Great Depression and for being blind to the suffering of millions. Governor Franklin Delano Roosevelt of New York won the 1932 election with 57.4 percent of the popular vote and a landslide 472 Electoral College votes.

The new president had overcome a staggering blow when he fell ill vacationing at Campobello Island, Maine, in August 1921. Permanently paralyzed from the waist down, FDR's physicians diagnosed him with poliomyelitis. Experts have come to believe that the symptoms are more consistent with the autoimmune neuropathy Guillain-Barré syndrome.[11] Being tied to a wheelchair and "carrying around ten pounds of steel attached to my legs" profoundly changed how the energetic and ambitious politician worked, and it profoundly altered his conception of the human condition.[12] In 1926 FDR discovered a hydrotherapeutic rehabilitant center in Warm Springs, Georgia, where he would make repeated visits during the rest of his life to rest and experience curative solace. Though his disability was known, FDR avoided appearing in public in his wheelchair, preferring to stand with assistance. In 1938 he founded the National Foundation for Infantile Paralysis, leading to the development of polio vaccines.

In his inaugural address FDR famously said, "we have nothing to fear but fear itself." But it would take more than words to lead the nation out of the Great Depression. His administration focused on relief for the unemployed, recovery of the economy, and reform of the financial system. FDR decided to communicate to the people using radio, and he launched a continuing series of regular "fireside chats," in which he projected optimism and activism. FDR's first term was an unprecedented series of legislative initiatives and the creation of a range of government programs and agencies under the aegis of a "New Deal." One of the first popular decisions he made was to repeal Prohibition, which had led to a rise of organized crime.

An alphabet soup of agencies sprang up to tackle national challenges, including the popular Civilian Conservation Corps (ccc), which hired 250,000 unemployed young men; the Tennessee Valley Authority (tva) to modernize the poverty-stricken Tennessee Valley; the Securities and Exchange Commission (sec), and the Public Works Administration (pwa) to oversee large-scale projects such as dams, bridges, and schools. The Supreme Court declared unconstitutional another initiative, the National Industrial Recovery Act. FDR later launched the Works Progress Administration (wpa), which employed three million people for various construction projects and funded youth and arts programs. Although both criticized or lionized as establishing socialism, FDR's decisions appear to have been pragmatic rather than ideological. His objectives always remained American economic liberty, national security, and social progress. Prussian-born Sen. Robert Ferdinand Wagner (D-NY) spearheaded FDR's New Deal legislation, including the Social Security Act and the Wagner Labor Act. The quintessential New Dealer Wagner arguably put more laws on the books than anyone since America's founders.[13]

Nowhere did the Great Depression cause more dramatic change than in Germany, which took a quite different course than the United States to cure economic collapse. On January 30, 1933, President Paul von Hindenburg of the Weimar Republic appointed the leader of the new and provocative National Socialist Party, Adolf Hitler, as chancellor of a coalition government. Within months Hitler seized absolute power by decree without legislative participation, and Germany quickly became a single-party fascist dictatorship. Hitler and the Nazis centralized power and took advantage of the deep resentment, humiliation, and deprivation felt by the German people to rebuild the economy though ambitious public works and a military buildup. The German nation was thus set upon a pagan totalitarian trajectory that would enslave millions and inevitably collide with the liberal democratic values of the United States in a cataclysmic struggle for the planet.

From 1933 through 1939, war-weary European leaders and diplomats consistently underestimated Hitler's agenda and appeased a series of Nazi threats and territorial seizures, including the Rhineland, the Austrian Anschluss, and Czechoslovakia. The Reich helped the Fascist Nationalists of Gen. Francisco Franco during the Spanish Civil War to test men, equipment, and tactics. By 1939 Nazi Germany commanded the best-trained and -equipped military on the planet, constituting a real threat to civilization, including the Western Hemisphere. But many in Britain and France were fully prepared to accommodate Hitler, who arranged a Grand Alliance with fascist Italy and Imperial Japan. Then, in 1939, Hitler and Stalin signed the Nazi-Soviet Non-Aggression Pact, which CBS commentator Elmer Davis characterized as "the death warrant for the rest of the world."[14]

In 1931, faced with labor unrest and the need to develop sources of goods, resources, manpower, and manufacturing infrastructure, Japan invaded China and seized Manchuria.[15] By 1938 the Japanese forces occupied China's strategic and industrial centers, including Shanghai, and the Nationalist Chinese government retreated to Chongqing (Chunking). Imperial Army troops committed genocide, murdering millions in incidents such as the Nanjing (Nanking) Massacre. The Chrysanthemum Empire also fortified the Micronesian and Melanesian territories it held, in violation of its mandate from the League of Nations.

FDR was reelected in a 1936 landslide, carrying every state except Maine and Vermont. Eight million workers remained unemployed, but the economy had stabilized. However, FDR overreached in his second term by trying to "pack" the Supreme Court, when he wanted to replace "the nine old men" led by chief justice Hughes. Met with bipartisan disapproval led by Sen. Burton Wheeler (D-MT) and Sen. Arthur Vandenberg (R-MI), FDR abandoned the plan in July 1937. Conservative southern Democrats did not always follow FDR's wishes, and he campaigned in 1938 to replace some of them with friendlier or more liberal Democrats. The move backfired as Democrats lost six Senate seats and seventy-one House seats. In 1939 Republicans and Southern Democrats aligned to effectively end FDR's creative domestic agenda. However, most of these coalition members came to support FDR's foreign and national defense policy.

Relations with Nazi Germany were peaceful as isolationists held FDR's foreign policy hostage. Many Americans admired German culture, and some even respected Hitler. It was therefore shocking when, on May 6, 1937, the magnificent but hydrogen-laden Deutsche Zeppelin Reederei airship *Hindenburg*, D-LZ129, ominously exploded while trying to moor at NAS Lakehurst, New Jersey, for connections to westbound American Airlines flights, with a live radio broadcast by Herb Morrison of WLS, Chicago, over the NBC Blue Network that dramatically described the terrible event.[16]

After the Munich accord and surrender of Czechoslovakia to Hitler, American public opinion slowly began to shift, and FDR quietly but steadily crafted a coalition of internationalist Hamiltonian Republicans and Jeffersonian Democrats to support national defense spending for airplane and weapons manufacturing and shipbuilding programs.

During the 1930s jazz became intermingled with popular music and even classics during a unique period, which came to be known as the swing or big band era. An explosion of mass media undeterred by the Depression helped bandleaders, musicians, and singers become social icons. In 1937, on the heels of the Warner Brothers musical *Hollywood Hotel*, the media anointed bandleader Benjamin David "Benny" Goodman as the "king of swing" as his sensational organization appeared on late night network broadcasts from around the nation and the weekly *Camel Caravan* commercial series for Camel Cigarettes on CBS. Future successful bandleaders Harry James, Gene Krupa, Lionel Hampton, and Teddy Wilson were among Goodman's talented and racially integrated group. The notion of jazz on par with serious music took a giant leap forward on January 16, 1938, when Goodman and his men appeared for a concert at New York's fabled Carnegie Hall, the cathedral of serious music.

Following the traumatic circumstances of their son's kidnapping and death, Charles and Anne Morrow Lindberg hoped to escape by moving their family to England. Maj. Truman Smith, the American military attaché in Berlin, learned that Lindbergh was touring aviation concerns in Britain and France and thought a visit to Germany was an excellent idea. Smith believed that Nazi authorities might invite Lindbergh to see German aviation assets, and he might be able give the Army Air Corps valuable insight. The Germans eagerly took the bait and happily invited Lindbergh as a guest of Deutsche Lufthansa.

On July 22, 1936, Charles and Anne flew to Germany, where Nazi royalty embraced them. Lindbergh toured military bases and civilian aviation facilities and was impressed with German production capability and their "superb technical designs." On July 28 Hermann Göring hosted Charles and Anne for a lavish luncheon at his opulent residence. The boastful but indiscreet Göring shared many secrets with Lindbergh because he admired the Lone Eagle as a fellow Aryan aviator. Smith reported to Washington that Lindbergh had gained valuable intelligence. But the American public and FDR saw newsreels showing a beaming Göring welcoming the cheery Lindberghs and the couple attending the 1936 Berlin Olympics, where exceptional American athletes, such as the legendary University of Washington rowing team, Louis Zamperini of the University of Southern California, and African American Jesse Owens of Ohio State University were defeating competitors from the "master race." On October 11, 1937, Charles and Anne returned to Germany, and Lindbergh visited the Focke-Wolfe factory. Luftwaffe director-general of equipment Ernst Udet showed Lindbergh the Rechlin air training center in Pomerania. Lindbergh met manufacturer Willy Messerschmidt and was the first American to see the Messerschmidt ME-109 fighter. Udet also briefed him on the new ME-110 twin engine fighter. Lindbergh reported his findings to Smith, who prepared report no. 15440, "General Estimate of Germany's Air Power," on November 1. In Washington, Gen. H. H. Arnold of the Army Air Corps was reading Lindbergh's reports with great interest. With encouragement from Arnold, Lindbergh returned to Germany during October 1938. He saw the Junkers factory and had a private conversation with Göring about the JU-88 bomber. Then Göring surprised Lindbergh with the cameras rolling and awarded him the Service Cross of the German Eagle. The award was a disaster for Lindbergh.

On November 9, 1938, Kristallnacht occurred, with synagogues burned, Jewish businesses destroyed, and thousands of German Jews arrested and sent to concentration camps. The American media eviscerated Lindbergh. His hero status, already tarnished, now vanished. Even TWA removed the slogan "The Lindbergh Line" from its airliners. It was time for Lindbergh to return home, where he would argue for an American policy of strength and neutrality. He shared the opinion of the American ambassador to the United Kingdom, Joseph P. Kennedy, that the United States should not actively support a doomed Britain under any circumstances. This set both Kennedy and Lindbergh on a collision course with FDR.[17]

Arriving in the United States, Lindbergh met privately with General Arnold, who asked him to return to active duty as an Air Corps colonel. Lindbergh threw himself into working on helping to develop the Air Corps, and the media let up on him. Lindbergh then went to the White House on April 20, 1939, for a fifteen-minute appointment with the commander-in-chief. It was the first time the men had met. Lindbergh wrote in his journal: "He is an accomplished, suave, interesting conversationalist. I liked him and feel that I could get along with him well. Acquaintanceship would be pleasant and interesting. But there is something about him I did not trust, something a little too suave, too pleasant, too easy. Still, he is our president and there is no reason for any antagonism between us in the work that I am now doing . . . it is better to work together as long as we can . . . yet somehow I have a feeling that it may not be for long." Later FDR told Secretary of the Treasury Henry Morgenthau, "If I should die tomorrow, I want you to know this. I am absolutely convinced that Lindbergh is a Nazi."[18]

Easter Sunday, April 9, internationally acclaimed contralto Marian Anderson appeared at a concert arranged by Secretary of the Interior Harold Ickes and broadcast by NBC Blue Network from the Lincoln Memorial in Washington DC. The Daughters of the American Revolution had denied the African American singer the use of Constitution Hall, which they owned. In protest, First Lady Eleanor Roosevelt led thousands in resigning their DAR memberships.[19]

Over the weekend of June 7–11, their majesties HRH George VI and Queen Elizabeth traveled to Washington, New York, and the Roosevelt home in Hyde Park, New York. The dignified and pleasant royal couple captivated their hosts and, by glowing press reports, newsreels, and radio, the nation. The highlight of the visit was an all-American picnic FDR hosted at his Hilltop Cottage on June 11. The menu included hot dogs, potato salad, baked beans, and strawberry shortcake.[20]

Four Freedoms

Nazi Germany and the Soviet Union signed their cynical ten-year non-aggression or neutrality treaty on August 23, 1939.[21] Then, on September 1, 1939, the calm midwestern voice of Elmer Davis on CBS announced to the American people that Germany had ruthlessly invaded Poland without a declaration of war. Shortly afterward Davis shared that Great Britain and France declared war on

Germany. On September 17 Americans learned that Russia was also invading Poland.[22] As the fascist and communist forces closed in from west and east, CBS carried moving shortwave broadcasts from besieged Warsaw of Chopin's haunting "Polonaise, Op. 53." Listeners around the world were gripped by the last broadcasts, including September 23 with pianist Wladyslaw Szpilman playing Chopin's "Nocturne in C Sharp Minor," which was interrupted by bombing, and the final heartbreaking broadcast of September 28, with the announcer proclaiming "Jesczcze Polska nie zginęla" (Poland has not perished yet) and "Niech zyle Polska" (Long live Poland) before a recording of "Mazurek Dąbrowskiego," the Polish national anthem.[23] Then came word via the BBC and the American networks that Japan and the Soviet Union had also signed a non-aggression treaty.

During 1939 FDR started moving slowly but inexorably toward a coalition government. He and his advisers developed many informal working relationships with the second- and third-generation members of dynastic industrial families to move American industry toward a war footing, create better working relationships between the political parties, and improve ties with foreign governments, particularly in the Western Hemisphere. These were considerable challenges with no guarantee of success. FDR understood the need for a national mobilization on an unprecedented scale. Among the minds he enlisted were Republican dynastic heirs Edsel Ford and Nelson Rockefeller. FDR and his advisers also reached out to media and entertainment leaders.

On October 11 Alexander Sachs of Lehman Brothers personally delivered a letter to the president at the White House. On August 2 the internationally eminent physicist Albert Einstein, a German refugee and pacifist humanitarian, wrote or at least signed the letter after meeting with a group of physicists, some of whom had also fled the Nazis. The men feared that Nazi Germany was developing a uranium-based weapon and that President Roosevelt must learn of their concerns right away.[24] Einstein said it was his duty to inform FDR about "recent work" by Enrico Fermi and Leonard Szilard to develop uranium into a "new and important source of energy," which could be weaponized, and that Nazi Germany was working on it as well. Roosevelt read the letter and told his military adviser Gen. Edwin "Pa" Watson "this requires action." The action that FDR suggested would, combined with British research that would soon be available, evolve into the Manhattan Project.[25]

For his first radio address after war broke out in Europe, Lindbergh quoted Washington's Farewell Address about "entanglements in European alliances." He showed the address to a disappointed Arnold, who suggested that Lindbergh was free to do what he wished but that, under the circumstances, his current Air Corps relationship would end if Lindbergh wished to be involved in politics. Major Smith, back in Washington, told Lindbergh that the Roosevelt administration would prefer he not give any political addresses. Lindbergh ignored Arnold and Smith and gave his speech over NBC, CBS, and Mutual at 9:30 p.m. on Friday, September 15.

On November 4, 1939, FDR signed the Neutrality Act, allowing the sale of arms to belligerents so long as they paid cash and did not transport them aboard American-flagged ships. Lindbergh saw this as an American attempt to aid Britain and France.

In April 1940 Lindbergh took to the air several times as Germany invaded Denmark, Norway, Belgium, and Holland. The Wehrmacht blitzkrieg bypassed the vaunted and impregnable Maginot Line and made fools out of the French army. German forces rapidly surrounded the British Expeditionary Force as their perimeter tightened around the coastal town of Dunkirk as proud France collapsed. Lindbergh broadcast that the danger was not because "European people (Germany) have attempted to interfere in the internal affairs of America . . . but because American people have attempted to interfere with the internal affairs of Europe."

British prime minister Neville Chamberlain spoke of "peace in our time" when he returned from the Munich Conference with Adolf Hitler in 1938. Now Chamberlain's ephemeral effort to buy time was in tatters. He resigned in May, and the controversial and combative Winston Churchill replaced him. Handed a hopeless situation, a defiant Churchill offered "blood, toil, tears and sweat." Rallying the English language to steady Britain, Churchill also spoke to another important audience, FDR and the American people. It was imperative to convince the United States that Britain could hold out. At the close of a speech on June 4 before the House of Commons, as Operation Dynamo miraculously rescued British troops from certain entrapment in France, the prime minister avowed, "we shall fight on the beaches, we shall fight on the landing grounds, we shall fight in the fields and in the streets, we shall fight in the hills; we shall never surrender, and even if, which I do not for a moment believe, this island or a large part of it were subjugated and starving, then our Empire beyond the seas, armed and guarded by the British fleet, would carry on the struggle, until, in God's good time, the New World, with all its power and might, steps forth to the rescue and the liberation of the old."[26]

By this time coded messages and a secure transatlantic telephone circuit connected the "former Naval Person" and the president of the United States, bypassing the problematic and untrustworthy Ambassador Kennedy. The Grand Alliance formed, although for the moment it was informal and secret. Nazi Germany was under no illusions about which side the United States was on. The colonies would come to the rescue of the British Empire.[27]

Throughout the 1930s, Hollywood continued to improve film and audio technology, including the introduction of technicolor. The number and quality of motion pictures exploded, from features to serials and short subjects. Depression-era Americans flocked to theaters for affordable entertainment and escape. Thousands of talented producers, directors, screenwriters, musicians, actors, and technicians staffed the major studios of Metro-Goldwyn Mayer, Paramount, RKO, Twentieth Century-Fox, Universal, Warner Brothers–First National, and more. The studio moguls supported the Roosevelt administration and went far during the early 1930s to help the government convey significant social messages in gripping commentaries as well as to offer escape into handsome productions. A large expatriate British colony thrived in Southern California. By the mid-1930s many historical costume dramas highlighted all eras of British history and Empire. It was a cast of hundreds, including actors Leslie Howard, Charles Laughton, Claude Rains,

Laurence Oliver, Vivien Leigh, David Niven, and Olivia De Havilland and director Alfred Hitchcock. There was also a brilliant Germanic expatriate colony. The difference was they had fled the Nazis. Among the many German and Austrian directors, actors, and musicians who made Hollywood their home were prolific composers Eric Wolfgang Korngold and Maximillian "Max" Steiner.

The big band era was at its zenith by 1939. Among the most popular on radio and records were the "swing" bands of Benny Goodman, Tommy Dorsey, and Artie Shaw and the "sweet" bands of Guy Lombardo, Kay Kyser, and Horace Heidt. Radio was colorblind, so white listeners also became "hep to the jive" of African Americans William "Count" Basie, Cabell "Cab" Calloway III, and Edward Kennedy "Duke" Ellington. During the summer of 1939 a new band led by Glenn Miller, broadcasting nationally over the NBC Red and NBC Blue networks from the Glen Island Casino in New Rochelle, New York, leapt to the number one spot in popularity polls and record sales and would stay in that position until Miller disbanded to join the army in September 1942.

FDR made the unprecedented decision to run for a third term. He removed a thorn in his political side by recalling the ambassador and critic Joseph P. Kennedy from London, a decision applauded by Churchill and the British intelligence services, who had run out of patience. The cable from FDR to Kennedy said:

THE LIQUOR TRADE IN BOSTON IS NOW CHALLENGING AND THE GIRLS OF HOLLYWOOD MORE FASCINATING. STOP. I EXPECT YOU BACK HERE BY SATURDAY.[28]

Upon his abrupt departure, chaperoned by British authorities to a waiting Pan Am Boeing 314 Clipper at Southampton, Kennedy endured an uncomfortable flight home at eight thousand feet directly to Baltimore rather than New York, where the Secret Service unceremoniously escorted the ambassador and his wife, Rose, to a private White House dinner with FDR and the First Lady. The America-first isolationist and Lindbergh ally then made an extraordinary public about-face in a national radio address and supported FDR for reelection. Kennedy offered his resignation as ambassador to the Court of St. James, which FDR accepted after his reelection.[29]

On August 4, 1940, Lindbergh spoke in Chicago at the invitation of ally Robert McCormick, publisher of the *Chicago Tribune* and a fierce FDR foe. Lindbergh insisted that no matter who won the war, Western civilization depended upon a strong America and that cooperation with a victorious Germany need not be impossible. To keep America out of the war, Lindbergh urged an "impregnable system of defense." Lindbergh had a staunch supporter in Father Charles Coughlin, the anti-Semitic Catholic priest who broadcast the radio series *Social Justice* and published a tabloid of the same name from the Shrine of the Little Flower in Royal Oak, Michigan. At the insistence of the government, Detroit affiliate wjr and the cbs network pulled Coughlin off the air when his commentaries became too inciteful. He continued broadcasting on a syndicated basis, labeling FDR a liar, a communist, and anti-god, and he implied it was fine for someone to shoot the president in a speech in Cincinnati. At that point the Catholic Church cut Coughlin off.

During August Americans began hearing live reports from London by broadcasters Edward R. Murrow of cbs and Robert St. John of nbc, describing Luftwaffe air attacks. The "This . . . is London" voice of Murrow, broadcasting from London rooftops and streets, gripped audiences as they could hear the air raid sirens and bombs falling while Londoners ran for the air raid shelters in the tube. Meanwhile Murrow's colleague, William L. Shirer, sent Americans a distinct perspective, broadcasting from the cbs Berlin Bureau a portrait of a calm capital bursting with Nazi pride rather than the London perspective of a besieged capital showing British resolve.

On November 5 FDR won his third term, defeating the dark-horse Republican candidate, Wall Street executive and Indiana native Wendell Willkie. On December 29 FDR made his Fireside Chat and proposed to make America "the great arsenal of democracy." He noted the threat of the September 27, 1940, Tripartite Treaty between Germany, Italy, and Japan by stating that these nations' policies were incompatible with the values of the United States and that they planned to enslave and dominate the

Fig. 9. Edward R. Murrow and William L. Shirer, Columbia Broadcasting System correspondents, at CBS studios in New York before their return to Europe, April 1, 1942. Columbia Broadcasting System publicity photo, University of Maryland Library of Broadcasting History.

world. FDR asked for "all out aid" for the democracies. Isolationist Sen. Burton K. Wheeler gave a scorching radio rebuttal. In his State of the Union speech on January 6, FDR asked Congress for a Lend-Lease bill, empowering him to transfer war material to any country considered vital to American national interest, deferring payment for ships and arms.[30] In the State of the Union address, the president detailed a set of principles that became known as the Four Freedoms: "In the future days, which we seek to make secure, we look forward to a world founded on four essential freedoms: The first is freedom of speech and expression—everywhere in the world. The second is freedom of every person to worship God in his own way—everywhere in the world. The third is freedom from want—which, translated into world terms, means economic understandings which will secure to every nation a healthy peacetime life for its inhabitants—everywhere in the world. The fourth is freedom from fear—which translated into world terms, means a worldwide reduction of armaments to such a point and in such a thorough fashion that no nation will be in a position to commit an act of physical aggression against any neighbor—anywhere in the world . . . that is no vision of a distant millennium. It is a definite basis for a kind of world attainable in our own time and generation."[31]

The Four Freedoms are the foundational principles that evolved into the Atlantic Charter of August 18, 1941, and the United Nations Declaration of January 1, 1942, and they crystallized FDR's vision of intervention as a moral imperative, thus linking America's two historic competing ideals of expansionism, now interventionism, and moral purpose.

Lindbergh testified before the House Committee on Foreign Affairs and a thousand spectators on Thursday, January 23, 1941. A congressman asked, "Do you think that either Germany or England is the more to blame for the present conflict?" He replied, "Over a period of time, neither." Then he testified before the Senate Committee on Foreign Relations. Sen. Claude Pepper (D-FL) asked, "When did you first go to Europe?" And there was major laugher when Lindbergh replied, "1927, sir." But Pepper was interested in showing that Lindbergh was pro-Nazi. Lindbergh did not take the bait, but he came off cold and indifferent to Nazi aggression.[32]

Within a week House Speaker John McCormick (D-MA) and Senate Majority Leader Alben Barkley (D-KY) introduced the Lend-Lease bill in each chamber. Under Lend-Lease the British received World War I–era destroyers in exchange for airbases at British possessions. The deal freed British air assets and expanded American air coverage of the Atlantic and Caribbean for antisubmarine and air transport operations. The United States built or expanded airfields for land-based and amphibious planes at many locations including Bermuda, Nassau, Newfoundland, St. Lucia, and Trinidad.

On January 19, the day before FDR began his third term, Wendell Willkie paid a highly publicized visit to the White House. They met following the 1940 election, at which time FDR told his advisers that he ought to have Willkie work with him on a bipartisan basis. Willkie was on his way to Britain, where FDR suggested that he ought to get together with Harry Hopkins, his adviser and special envoy.[33] Willkie's visit to Britain was the result of a suggestion that the chief British intelligence officer in the United States, William Stephenson, made to FDR in December 1940.[34] The president asked Willkie to hand-deliver a note to Winston Churchill that he wrote out in longhand. The message, dated January 20, 1941, said, "Dear Churchill, Wendell Willkie will give you this—he is truly helping to keep politics out over here." Then FDR cited a quotation from Longfellow's "Building of the Ship," although he did not specify the author or work: "Sail on, O ship of State. Sail On, Union Strong and great. Humanity, with all its fears, with all the hope of future years, hangs breathless on thy fate."[35]

The Lend-Lease bill cleared the House 260–165 on February 8. The next day Wendell Willkie returned from Britain and dramatically testified on Capitol Hill. Breaking with many in his party, Willkie firmly endorsed Lend-Lease. Pointedly harassed by Sen. Gerald P. Nye (R-ND) about comments he (Willkie) had made during the election campaign about FDR leading the nation into war, Willkie replied that he saw no constructive purpose in discussing the campaign, saying, "I struggled as hard as I could to beat Franklin D. Roosevelt and I tried to keep from pulling my punches. He was elected president and he is my president now."[36] The bill got through the committee on a 15–8 vote. On March 8 the Senate approved Lend-Lease by a 60–31 vote, and three days later the House approved the Senate bill by a 317–71 vote.

Atlantic Charter

In April 1941 Lindbergh joined the America First Committee, a non-interventionist group formed on September 4, 1940, at Yale Law School by a student committee that included future president Gerald R. Ford, Supreme Court justice Potter Stewart, and Peace Corps director Sargent Shriver. The non-interventionist movement was originally popular on college campuses but rapidly grew to eight hundred thousand members from all strata of society. Isolationist politicians, industrialists, and media moguls joined the cause and centered the activities of the group in Chicago. The committee chairman was Gen. Robert E. Wood, chairman of Sears, Roebuck and Co. In addition to Lindbergh, the key notables were architect Frank Lloyd Wright, publishers Joseph Patterson of the *New York Daily News* and Robert McCormick of the *Chicago Tribune*, and isolationist senators Wheeler, Nye, and David Ignatius Walsh (D-MA).[37] The radio networks were bound by equal time regulations so that if FDR gave an interventionist speech, Wheeler, Nye, or Walsh could get equal time.

By May 1941 Nazi Germany was at the apex of its conquests and poised to seize Egypt, the Suez Canal, and all the vast Middle East oil fields. Muslims were favorable or at worst indifferent about the Nazis, and they disliked the British. And these developments imperiled the Empire beyond. On May 6 General Sir John Dill wrote Churchill a stark assessment that effectively wrote off Egypt and the Suez Canal in favor on concentrating on homeland defense because once the Middle East was secure, the Nazis would free up troops and equipment to at last invade the British Isles. Losing Egypt was a calamity, but an invasion risked absolute defeat.[38]

In December 1938 the conservative Catholic lay activist and chief censor Joseph Breen of the motion picture industry's Production Code had serious difficulty with Warner Brothers' *Confessions of a Nazi Spy*, which the studio asked him to keep confidential so the German American Bund or German counsel in Los Angeles would not see it in advance. The film met the PCA Hays Code, but it was provocative. A nervous Breen sidestepped a decision by asking Warner Brothers about reconsidering because many foreign governments would ban the film, but the studio decided to release it.[39] Edward G. Robinson, playing an FBI agent, declares that Germany is already at war with the United States; and in a closing courtroom scene, a prosecutor reminds the jury about the dangers of isolationism and that America must learn from the European experience and be prepared to defend the Constitution and Bill of Rights.[40] Breen was correct about foreign censorship: Germany, Italy, and Spain predictably banned the film.

Neutrals Ireland and Switzerland and Latin American nations banned it at German insistence, along with MGM's *The Mortal Storm* and Charlie Chaplin's *The Great Dictator*.[41] On August 17, 1940, Nazi Germany banned all American films from the Reich and occupied territories, and Italy followed suit. From that point forward, Hollywood had every incentive to go all in and support FDR, as their one legitimate concern, continental European market pressure, was gone. Breen, the PCA, and most of the industry had been at best ambivalent about fascism, staunchly opposed to communism and protective of European markets. But now Hollywood and Berlin were at war and competing for the hearts and minds of peoples around the world.

In a letter to the Academy Awards banquet in February 1941, FDR remarked, "we have seen the American motion picture become the foremost in the world. We have seen it reflect our civilization throughout the rest of the world—the aims, aspirations and ideals of a free people and freedom." He went on to thank the motion picture industry for its "splendid cooperation with all who are directing the expansion of our armed forces" and asked for continued support. FDR's aide and media liaison Lowell Mellett reported, "practically everything being shown on the screen from newsreel to fiction that touches on our national purpose is of the right sort."[42]

Fritz Hippler of the Reich Ministry of Propaganda sarcastically blasted FDR's remarks by saying, "if it is true that the Americans movie has carried out the ideals of a free nation throughout the world, then America's ideal must be light amusement, song hits and tap dancing. In no country in the world are so few films of real value or actual artistry produced in relation to total production as in America. Whenever an American movie turns to serious subjects, it does so in a critical manner and presents social disproportions, democratic disorders, capitalistic injustices, corrupt' courts or the untenable, gangster system in such a manner that a spectator can scarcely desire to see such conditions in his own country."[43]

On April 23, 1941, a reporter asked FDR whether Lindbergh had rejoined the Army Air Corps as a colonel. The president avoided a direct answer but wryly compared Lindbergh to a Civil War "copperhead" sympathetic to the Confederacy. An incensed Lindbergh felt his "loyalty, character and motives" questioned and his honor impugned; he impulsively sent FDR an imprudent letter resigning his Air Corps commission, which the adroit president readily accepted.

On June 25 FDR signed Executive Order 8802, prohibiting ethnic or racial discrimination in the defense industry. The order also set up the Fair Employment Practice Committee. Civil rights organizations and leaders had demanded the decision, which affected all defense contracts. This made possible the widespread employment of minorities in shipyards and factories during World War II.[44]

The United States was the only major power without a national information, or propaganda, agency. There was no American government international shortwave radio service, only CBS, NBC, and several independent commercial operations. The Axis Powers ran hundreds of transmitters broadcasting on dozens of frequencies to every nation on the planet, far surpassing the reach of the respected BBC. In Latin America Nazi Germany had made inroads in terms of public opinion. FDR was anxious to do something before Pearl Harbor, but politically he could not get too far ahead of public opinion. The president took his first step toward forming an information agency with the Office of Government Reports. He named adviser Lowell Mellett, the former editor of the *Washington Daily News* and Scripps-Howard executive, to run it.[45]

During 1941, FDR's information policy was a combination of caution, ambiguity, half-measures, and duplication of effort.[46] Outspoken liberal members of Roosevelt's cabinet such as Secretary of the Interior Ickes urged emphasis on the type of overt and heavy-handed propaganda that Creel employed in World War I and used by Dr. Joseph Goebbels in Nazi Germany. Mellett cautioned against this approach. He recommended that the administration should limit messaging to the international sphere "until there is an accepted national policy," and that heavy-handed messaging in domestic media would be counterproductive.[47]

In a monumental decision with grave implications, Hitler unleashed the Wehrmacht against the Soviet Union on June 22.

Asked about the policy of His Majesty's Government, Churchill said, "If Hitler marched into hell, I would at least consider an alliance with the devil."[48] There was never any doubt in FDR's mind that the United States would send the Soviets whatever aid they would need. The president was no friend of communism but, like Churchill, intuitively understood that the enemy of his enemy was his friend. Meanwhile, the Deutsches Afrika Korps of Gen. Erwin Rommel was threatening to sever the British Empire at the Suez Canal.[49] In Congress Sen. Robert Taft (R-OH) said, "the victory of Communism would be far more dangerous to the United States than a victory of Fascism." Sen. Bennet Champ Clark (D-MO) added, "It's a case of dog eat dog and I don't think we should help either one." Colonel McCormick's *Chicago Tribune* and other conservative media opposed aid to the Soviets. Clark's Missouri colleague, Sen. Harry Truman, concurred. Colonel McCormick's *Chicago Tribune* and other conservative media opposed aid to the Soviets. More serious was the potential opposition of the Catholic Church. In his encyclical *Divini Redemptoris*, Pius XI said, "Communism is intrinsically wrong and no one who would save Christian civilization may give it any assistance in any undertaking whatsoever."[50] However, His Holiness also issued the encyclical *Mit Brennender Sorge*, written in German, in which he proclaimed that Nazi philosophy was pagan and evil.[51] The encyclical asserted the inviolability of human rights and abuse of Christian values. Amazingly, the media in the United States ignored the strong encyclical, which the pontiff called "a conspiracy of silence."[52] The Vatican secretary of state, Cardinal Eugenio Pacelli, succeeded Pius XI on March 2, 1939. Taking the name Pius XII, his first encyclical, *Summi Pontificatus*, spoke about the unity of human society against racism, with specific reference to Jews, as had his predecessor, saying "there is neither Gentile nor Jew, circumcision nor uncircumcision."[53]

From 1941 to 1945 the United States would deliver an unprecedented volume of supplies and equipment to the USSR, including Studebaker trucks, Willeys and Ford jeeps, and Bell P-39 Airacobra fighter planes via treacherous North Atlantic convoys to Murmansk, extended routes through Iran, and from Alaska to Siberia. American support was vital to keeping the Soviets in the war.

In the epitome of the pre–Pearl Harbor interventionist films, Warner Brothers cast Gary Cooper as World War I hero Sgt. Alvin York in *Sergeant York*. Howard Hawks directed the story of the Tennessee mountaineer pacifist who won the Medal of Honor. The film's premiere on July 2 in New York drew, among others, Eleanor Roosevelt, Gen. John J. Pershing, and Wendell Willkie. *Sergeant York* was the highest grossing box office attraction of 1941, and it drew great criticism from isolationists.

On August 9 the battleship H M S *Prince of Wales* slipped quietly through heavy mist into Placentia Bay, Newfoundland, with Prime Minister Churchill and his staff aboard. The cruisers U S S *Augusta* and U S S *Tuscaloosa* and several American destroyers rode at anchor in the harbor. President Roosevelt and his staff awaited their British counterparts on *Augusta*. With newsreel cameras abuzz, Churchill came aboard *Augusta* and met Roosevelt for their first wartime summit conference. The next morning, a Sunday, FDR and his staff went over to *Prince of Wales* for meetings. American and British officials and American and British sailors attended a religious service on deck that the newsreel cameras filmed. For anyone with a sense of history it was an extraordinary moment as the leaders, their chiefs of staff, and the ships' companies sang "Onward Christian Soldiers." There could no longer be any doubt about which side the United States was on, as if there had really been any.[54]

FDR and Churchill released a joint declaration on August 14 that came to be known as the Atlantic Charter, which made it clear that the United States supported Great Britain in the war. The joint declaration gave a broad statement of eight "common principles" that the United States and Great Britain would be committed to supporting in the postwar world. They agreed not to seek territorial expansion; to seek the liberalization of international trade; to establish freedom of the seas and international labor, economic, and welfare standards. Most importantly, both the United States and Great Britain were committed to supporting the restoration of self-governments for all countries occupied during the war and, furthermore, allowing all peoples to choose their own form of government. In other words, Britain would free its empire, including India, and end the British Raj, which was a major diplomatic objective for FDR.[55]

Churchill's abandonment of Imperial Preference (colonial empire) was a great domestic political risk.[56] FDR did not specifically commit to enter the war, nor did the Atlantic Charter motivate the American people to intervene. However, the declaration affirmed the solidarity of the United States with Britain, boosted British morale, and defined FDR's vision for a postwar world including freer exchanges of trade, self-determination, disarmament, and collective security. The Atlantic Charter inspired colonial subjects in the Third World, such as Ho Chi Minh in French Indochina, to fight for independence, and it led to the formation of the United Nations and NATO.[57]

The Atlantic Charter was, however, a dramatic change in the traditional American debate between expansionism and morality. By renouncing territorial expansion and motivating Churchill to consider self-determination of colonies in exchange for a "Grand Alliance," FDR replaced expansionism with intervention as an American precedence. Intervention was therefore a moral prerogative, given the debased character of Nazi and fascist tyranny and because intervention had no territorial motivation as defined by the Atlantic Charter. Therefore FDR brilliantly closed the traditional American cultural debate by making expansionism into intervention, which was moral.

In taking the high ground, FDR created unity of purpose for the first time in American history. He now had an empty canvas to paint with expressive and vivid colors of exceptionalism. FDR would soon gather an extraordinary coalition of government and media talent that would complete the picture that he was painting. United, they would set America on a course toward a cultural renaissance, total victory, and enlightened world leadership.

At the same time Roosevelt and Churchill were conferring at Placentia Bay, Charles Lindbergh spoke before an audience of twenty-five thousand at Madison Square Garden. On September 11 he made an ill-considered address in Des Moines, Iowa, remembered as one of the most counterproductive talks in the history of American political discourse.

The networks delayed Lindbergh's scheduled speech to cover a statement by FDR about a September 4 Nazi attack on the destroyer uss *Greer* near Iceland. FDR did not speak to the nation about the incident until, coincidentally, the very moment Lindbergh was about to speak. The audience of eight thousand in the Des Moines Coliseum heard FDRs speech. When FDR finished, Lindbergh awkwardly opened as the loudspeakers were acting up. For most of his speech the Iowa audience applauded supportively. Lindbergh repeated his assertions that "powerful elements" were pushing the United States into war, although this time he did not refrain from saying who he believed those elements were. He titled his speech "Who Are the Agitators?" and this time he named them: Britain, the Roosevelt administration, and the Jews, saying in part,

> It is not difficult to understand why Jewish people desire the overthrow of Nazi Germany. . . . No person with a sense of the dignity of mankind can condone the persecution of the Jewish race in Germany. But no person of honesty and vision can look on their prowar policy here today without seeing the dangers involved in such a policy both for us and for them. . . . Their greatest danger to this country lies in their large ownership and influence in our motion pictures, our press, our radio and our government.[58]

Lindbergh set off a nationwide bipartisan firestorm of protest. Newspapers normally sympathetic to the non-interventionist cause trashed the speech as un-American. Republican leaders Wendell Willkie and Thomas E. Dewey condemned Lindbergh. The American First Committee considered censuring Lindbergh but realized (from their perspective) that his speech was correct. But Lindbergh's reputation was compromised and the America First Committee was now on the defensive trying to explain his remarks.

Lindbergh's activities contrasted sharply with the actions of many young Americans who were volunteering for Air Corps and

Navy flight training. A sizable group of Americans went north to join the Royal Canadian Air Force for training and service with the Royal Air Force in Britain. Between September 1940 and July 1941, three RAF fighter squadrons, collectively known as the Eagle Squadrons, organized with American pilots.

The bipartisan Selective Training and Service Act of 1940 was the first peacetime conscription in American history. The White House did not introduce the bill, and because it was an election year, FDR treaded lightly on announcing his support. Both FDR and his opponent, Wendell Willkie, supported the bill. Willkie said, "I would rather not win the election than [oppose the draft]." On September 14 the Senate passed the bill by a 47–25 vote, and the House passed it 232–124.[59] FDR signed it, and on October 16 more than sixteen million men between ages twenty-one and thirty-five registered for the draft. On August 12, 1941, a bill to extend the draft passed the House by only one vote, 203–202.[60]

On September 9, 1941, Willkie testified before a specially empaneled Senate subcommittee on interstate commerce on behalf of the motion picture industry and was present because Wheeler, Nye, and others wished to investigate "war propaganda disseminated by the major motion picture industry and of any monopoly in the production, distribution or exhibition of motion pictures."[61] Chairman Wheeler stacked the subcommittee with bipartisan isolationists. Nye was the first witness. He read an elaborate forty-one-page statement that, like Lindbergh's Des Moines radio address, led to his own downfall. Nye emphasized Jewish control of motion pictures; and therefore Hollywood was inclined to help take America into war. He felt that it was time to get this "out into the open."[62] Willkie was an excellent bipartisan choice to represent interventionism and the motion picture industry. The former utility industry attorney had a flair for the dramatic and a disarmingly direct manner."[63] Wheeler reminded Willkie that he could not cross-examine witnesses. However, Willkie released a 2,600-word press release denouncing Nye's thinking as un-American. Willkie pointedly noted that "if the Committee feels that the racial and geographic background of American citizens is a condition to be investigated,

Fig. 10. Wendell Willkie gives "Report to the American People" national radio address upon his return from his global fact-finding trip as a representative of Pres. Franklin Roosevelt, his opponent in the 1940 election, on October 26, 1942. Associated Press wire photo, collection of the author.

there is no need for the investigation. We frankly state that on the motion picture industry, there are in positions both prominent and inconspicuous, both Nordics and non-Nordics, Jews and Gentiles, Protestants and Catholics, native and foreign-born."

On the third day of the hearings, after sitting in silence, Willkie interrupted endless sermonizing to note that the committee had so far not offered any legislation, the supposed purpose of the hearing, and was repeatedly arguing for fair and balanced treatment of subjects and topics. Willkie snapped, "This, I presume, means that since Chaplin made a laughable caricature of Hitler, then the industry should be obliged to employ Charles Laughton to do the same with Churchill."[64]

Willkie continued with his serious point, adding, "The motion picture industry and its executives are opposed to the Hitler regime. We make no pretense of friendliness to Nazi Germany." He noted that anti-Nazi films were not propaganda because they told the truth, and he "emphatically and indignantly" denied that the industry made any such films at the command of the Roosevelt administration. "Frankly," he concluded, "the motion picture industry would be ashamed if it were not doing voluntarily what it is now doing in this patriotic cause."[65] Studio executives followed Willkie, including Harry Warner, who summarized his remarks by noting about the acclaimed *Sergeant York*, "if that is propaganda, we plead guilty!"[66]

First-term interventionist Sen. Ernest McFarland (D-AZ) turned out to be a feisty match for Nye, exposing his colleague's weak command of the facts and confusion about the details of specific films, which caused Nye to blurt out incoherent replies. It was a disaster for the America First movement. Nye came across as anti-Semitic and ill-informed. Other isolationists retreated from their militancy and praised films like *Sergeant York*.[67]

Willkie had changed the issue from propaganda to a question of fact, exposing the moral weakness of the isolationist position. He instinctively knew that although Americans dreaded war, they hated Hitler and Nazism. His strategy was brilliant. Stressing that Hollywood portrayed the world "as it is," Willkie proved that Hollywood was patriotic. The hearings adjourned on September 26, and the subcommittee never issued a report.

In 1933 Pan Am purchased the China National Aviation Corporation (CNAC), the pioneer airline in China, with major operations at Hong Kong and Shanghai. As the Japanese advanced during the late 1930s, CNAC withdrew from Shanghai to Chongqing. Aviation entrepreneur and CNAC adviser William Douglas Pawley organized the Central Aircraft Manufacturing Company for the Kuomintang government and set up a manufacturing operation in Rangoon, Burma, to assemble Curtiss P-40 Warhawk fighter planes. With the tacit support of FDR and the logistical assistance of Treasury Secretary Morgenthau, retired Air Corps officer Claire Chennault, air adviser to Chiang Kai Shek, Mme. Chiang, Soong

May-ling, and China's ambassador to Washington, her brother T. V. Soong, recruited American military pilots and Chinese American mechanics whom Pawley's firm trained and equipped in Burma. The First American Volunteer Group went into action against the Japanese in December 1941. They became media sensations as the legendary "Flying Tigers" because of shark's face painted on the P-40 engines and their combat success using Chennault's tactics against faster and nimble Mitsubishi A6M Zero fighters.[68]

Relations between Washington and Tokyo deteriorated during 1941 as Japan's aggressive war with China triggered an American oil embargo, forcing Japan to find other sources of raw materials. Veteran Japanese naval officer and diplomat Adm. Kichisaburō Nomura was the highly respected ambassador to the United States, and he tried to prevent war. Tokyo ignored Nomura's repeated pleas for concessions. In November the government of Hideki Tojo sent special envoy Saburō Kurusu to Washington. Kurusu served in the United States for six years, and his wife, Alice Little Kurusu, was American. The diplomats met FDR and conferred with Secretary of State Cordell Hull. Japan wanted America to stop supporting China and resume normal trade. The United States wanted Japan to withdraw from China and end the 1940 Tripartite (Axis) Pact with Germany and Italy. The nations were at an impasse.

In the weeks leading up to Saturday, December 6, the Army Signals Intelligence Unit and Navy Communications Special Unit noticed increased Japanese diplomatic cable traffic. The Americans had deciphered the Japanese diplomatic code, labeled Purple. However, Japanese military and naval codes such as JN-25 used a different crypto-system, so Purple gave cryptographers no clue about military movements. The British had cracked the German Enigma military code, captured several code machines, and helped the Americans crack Purple. The Allies code-named deciphered Axis military communications Ultra, called deciphered Japanese diplomatic communications Magic, and shared the top-secret information.[69]

On Sunday morning, December 7, at 7:40 a.m. in the Hawaiian Islands and 12:40 p.m. in Washington DC, Cmdr. Mitsu Fuchida of the Imperial Japanese Navy arrived over the island of Oahu in command of 183 bomber and fighter aircraft that took off from a fleet of aircraft carriers that had come within 250 miles north of the island and the city of Honolulu. The U.S. Army SCR-270 radar site at Opana detected the IJN planes, but authorities mistook them for an incoming ferry flight of B-17 bombers from the mainland. Upon seeing no activity as American naval and military personnel were enjoying a quiet weekend, Fuchida opened the canopy of his Nakajima B5N2 torpedo bomber and fired a signal flare directing the aerial armada to attack. At 7:53 a.m. Fuchida's radio operator sent the coded message "Tora, Tora, Tora" (or Tiger, Tiger, Tiger). The Japanese flyers had caught the Americans completely by surprise. The United States changed forever when a Japanese horizontal bomber scored a precise hit on a battleship powder magazine with one bomb that obliterated the beloved USS *Arizona*, instantly killing 1,177 officers, sailors, and marines.

When the news bulletins broke, CBS, NBC, and Mutual scrambled to get announcers, commentators, and reporters on the air to describe the attack, its meaning, and its ramifications. Sober if surprised voices spoke from New York, Washington, and London and in chilling on-the-scene reports from Hawaii. Within hours, news came that Japan was also attacking the Dutch East Indies, Guam, Hong Kong, Malaya, Midway Atoll, the Philippines, Singapore, and Wake Island. Most of the experts knew little more than the public about what was really happening. The calm voice of Elmer Davis came over CBS, and among other observations he quipped, "Well, it looks like the debate in Washington about continued American aid to Britain and what to do about Japan has just been made . . . in Tokyo."[70]

That evening FDR confirmed the Japanese attack to Churchill by telephone, saying, "It's true; looks like we're all in it together now." The prime minister recalled "sleeping the sleep of the delivered."[71]

On the morning of December 7 in Washington, Nomura and Kuruso received a lengthy fourteen-point cable from Tokyo that they had to decode. Their staff had to come in since it was a Sunday morning. The process delayed their scheduled meeting with

Hull, so they did not hand him the message breaking off diplomatic relations at 1:00 p.m. Washington time, or 8:00 a.m. Hawaiian time. At 2:20 p.m., and 9:20 a.m. in Hawaii, Nomura and Kurusu sorrowfully presented the message to an infuriated Hull, who was aware of the attack and knew exactly what the fourteen points were because he had already read the deciphered Magic copy.

On December 10 Japanese planes bombed and sank the HMS *Prince of Wales* and the HMS *Repulse* in waters northeast of Singapore, killing Adm. Sir Tom Phillips. The *Prince of Wales* and Admiral Philips had brought Churchill to the Placentia Conference and hosted the Atlantic Charter conference. The prime minister was thunderstruck and grief stricken.[72]

Charles Lindbergh realized that his two-year struggle was over. On December 8, when the president addressed a shaken Congress and asked for a Declaration of War, Lindbergh released a statement of support. On December 11, when Germany and Italy imprudently declared war on the United States, and Congress returned the favor, the America First Committee voted to disband. Led by President and former sergeant Fulgencio Batista y Zaldívar (elected in 1940), Cuba declared war on Japan December 9 and on Germany and Italy December 11.

PART II

The Great Crusade

With Thy blessing, we shall prevail over the unholy forces of our enemy. Help us to conquer the apostles of greed and racial arrogance. Lead us to the saving of our country, and with our sister Nations into a world unity that will spell a sure peace a peace invulnerable to the scheming of unworthy men. And a peace that will let all of men live in freedom, reaping the just rewards of their honest toil. Thy will be done, Almighty God. Amen.

Pres. FRANKLIN DELANO ROOSEVELT, June 6, 1944

Fig. 11. Pres. Franklin Delano Roosevelt, from an official campaign portrait session by Leon A. Perskie at Hyde Park, New York, August 21, 1944. Franklin D. Roosevelt Presidential Library, 09–109.

FOUR

Why We Fight

State of Emergency

American exceptionalism found an unlikely champion in Franklin Delano Roosevelt, the privileged son of a comfortable Dutch New York legacy. He was a man of contradictions; charming if cunning; principled if political, and pragmatic if progressive. He could inspire but disappoint. As congenial and remote as Ronald Reagan forty years later, FDR counted millions of admirers and few intimates. He never abandoned his Southern Democratic Party base and did not pass any significant civil rights legislation, but people of color worshipped him. FDR would fight a global war of survival with no quarter asked and none offered. He endured a physical disability, however, that gave him an exceptional empathy for Americans that they could hear, see, and feel. This combined with his native intelligence, intuition, and insight gave the United States the right man, at the right time, to do what was right.

On December 8, 1941, Franklin Delano Roosevelt rose to address a Joint Session of Congress, the nation, and the world, leaning on the podium to support himself. In eight minutes he succinctly defined a state of emergency and soberly called the American people to war. At the same time, he was gathering an extraordinary group of government and private sector leaders to direct America through the gravest crisis in its history, including a government and media alliance that explained to the American people and the world "why we fight." During the next four years he and his lieutenants would define and embody American exceptionalism.

Adm. Chester William Nimitz stepped off a PBY Catalina flying boat at Pearl Harbor on Christmas morning, December 25, 1941, and inhaled the stench of fuel oil, burnt wood, and rotting human remains. He faced a daunting assignment as the new commander in chief of the Pacific Fleet. Among the carnage and debris he found reasons for optimism: his aircraft carriers had escaped the attack, and the Japanese had not touched either the fuel tank farm containing 4.5 million barrels of fuel oil or the Pearl Harbor repair facilities. Ninety percent of the men in the fleet were onshore during the attack and survived.[1] Adm. Isoroku Yamamoto's audacious attack had destroyed older and slow battleships. What the IJN had accomplished, and as Yamamoto had warned, was to awaken and galvanize America.

A frail and unassuming Iowan loyally served FDR as his "behind the scenes" troubleshooter. Harry Hopkins functioned as an assistant president. At dinner with Churchill in 1940, Hopkins said, "I suppose you wish to know what I am going to say to President Roosevelt on my return. Well, I am going to quote you one verse from the Book of Books in the truth of which Mr. Johnston's mother and my own Scottish mother were brought up, "wither thou goest, I will go; and where thou lodgest, I will lodge; thy people shall be my people, and thy God my God." Hopkins paused, took a deep breath, and quietly added, "even to the end." Moved to tears, Churchill knew exactly what Hopkins's comment meant.

Churchill arrived in Washington to confer with FDR on December 22, 1941, just in time for Christmas. The leaders lit the National Christmas Tree together on Christmas Eve. The prime minister made a stirring address to a Joint Session of Congress on December 26, in which he noted that "we're now in it together" and paused to make the memorable quip that brought down the house, "after all, I cannot help but reflect that had my father been American and my mother British, instead of the other way around, I . . . I . . . might have got here on my own."[2]

FDR and Churchill had serious business to conduct at a conference with their military chiefs of staff that was code-named Arcadia. After a triumphant four-day trip to Ottawa to address the Canadian Parliament, Churchill returned to Washington, where, in the

Oval Office of the White House, he and FDR signed a joint declaration by twenty-six nations that were at war with the Axis powers. By 1945 forty-seven nations became signatories.[3] The United Nations Declaration was a formal follow-up to the Atlantic Charter. The signers agreed that being "convinced that complete victory over [our] enemies is essential to defend life, liberty, independence and religious freedom, and to preserve human rights and justice in their own lands as well as in other lands [we] are now engaged in a common struggle against savage and brutal forces seeking to subjugate the world." Each government pledged to employ their full resources to winning the war against the Tripartite Pact and its adherents and would not make a separate peace.[4]

The Third Meeting of Consultation of Latin American Ministers of Foreign Affairs, or the Rio Conference of 1942, met between January 15 and 28. The United States wanted to know the posture of the hemispheric nations that had not yet signed the United Nations Declaration. Brazil, Colombia, Ecuador, Mexico, Paraguay, Peru, Uruguay, and Venezuela severed diplomatic relations with the Axis nations. Mexico declared war on May 22, and Brazil declared war on August 22. Argentina and Chile held out. Argentina severed diplomatic relations with the Axis countries on January 26, 1944, but did not declare war until March 27, 1945. Chile severed diplomatic relations with the Axis nations on January 20, 1943, but did not declare war until April 11, 1945, and then only against Japan.[5]

There were many scares and outright hysteria along the Pacific Coast and western states in the immediate aftermath of Pearl Harbor. For days, many military authorities, personnel, and civilian populace suspected or imagined enemy activity at sea or in the air directed at population centers and even remote towns. There were several Japanese submarines probing American coastal waters, although nowhere near as many or as much of a concrete threat as the many Nazi U-boats brazenly patrolling the East Coast of North America, Gulf of Mexico, and Caribbean under the orders of Grand Admiral Karl Dönitz in his audacious and successful Operation Drumbeat. The precise opposite of frightened westerners was the attitude of Miami Beach hoteliers who initially balked

at brownouts and pleas to turn down their bright lights. The glow
of the resort silhouetted freighters and tankers for U-boat skip-
pers to attack close to the coast in the Gulf Stream with deadly
and accurate torpedoes. Miamians saw big freighters and tankers
explode, burn, and sink right off Government Cut and Haulover
Beach Park. If merchant crews did not burn to death, they had to
go into the water and deal with voracious sharks.

The same was true north to Cape Hatteras, North Carolina,
Cape May, New Jersey, and Cape Cod, Massachusetts; west into
the Gulf of Mexico, the mouth of the Mississippi, and Galveston,
Texas; and even inside New York harbor. The United States had
no effective antisubmarine warfare capability, so the Kriegsmarine
enjoyed what became known as the "happy time" of many kills.
Nazi wolfpacks interdicting essential supply convoys crossing the
North Atlantic was one thing. Suddenly the shooting war invaded
American territorial waters—everywhere—and in a deadly professional manner.[6]

By the end of January 1942 the U-boats sank thirty-one ships
weighing two hundred thousand tons in American coastal waters.
Churchill recalled, "For six or seven months, the U-boats ravaged
American waters almost uncontrolled, and in fact almost brought us
to the disaster of an indefinite prolongation of the war."[7] Although
the Roosevelt administration and the Navy Department did not
tell the American public, Operation Drumbeat was far more dangerous to the United States and caused significantly more damage
than the Japanese attack on Pearl Harbor. Having Atlantic convoys and shipping traffic in American waters vulnerable to U-boat
attacks compromised the entire war effort.[8]

Fearing Japanese attacks, paranoid military authorities ordered
West Coast broadcasters off the air following the attack on Pearl
Harbor. The fifty-thousand-watt signals of KOA in Denver and
KSL in Salt Lake City came through loud and clear at night on
the West Coast, and military authorities almost ordered them off
the air, too, out of fear that Japanese airmen could tune to them
for directional aid, just like they might use the signals of KFI and
KNX in Los Angeles or KGO and KPO in San Francisco. Although

the radio stations were quickly back on the air when federal and state officials realized Japanese attacks were not imminent, questions remained about whether to censor hourly weather reports and morning agricultural programs, including frost warnings, as if such reports gave imaginary Japanese invaders vital information.[9]

For the better part of a year before Pearl Harbor, the War Department Bureau of Public Relations (BPR), under the command of Gen. Alexander Day Surles, had given advice and information to broadcasters through its Radio Branch. In December 1940 Surles brought in Edward Kirby, director of public relations for the National Association of Broadcasters (NAB) and former promotion manager of WSM, Nashville, Tennessee, to run the BPR Radio Branch. After assuming his responsibilities, Kirby brought in seven experienced broadcasters to work with him, including his protégé, WSM news manager Jack W. Harris. Kirby and Harris suddenly found themselves deluged with requests for guidance and information from nervous broadcasters.[10]

Many were afraid the federal government would nationalize radio and suspend free speech because of the war emergency. Neville Miller, president of the NAB, felt the future of American radio as a free enterprise was at stake. However, there was never any such plan by the federal government. What appeared was a general national policy, working with the idea "what does not concern the war does not concern censorship." As would occur decades later in the "war on terror," government and media had to strike a careful balance between civil liberty and a free press versus national security. Within weeks, sober changes in news content and delivery came about as the shock of Pearl Harbor gave way to the grim news of setbacks across Asia and the Pacific, and the forces of the Empire of Japan inexorably advanced to build a "Greater East Asia Co-Prosperity Sphere."

The Japanese advance triggered United States War Plan Rainbow 5, which presumed a long, drawn-out conflict in Asia and the Pacific. Rainbow 5 calculated that the indefensible Commonwealth of the Philippines and the United States Army Forces in the Far East (USAFFE) commanded by the celebrated Gen. Douglas MacArthur could survive, at best, six months in the event of a Japanese invasion.[11]

Japan had long coveted and sought to subvert and seize the Philippines. Although American authorities had a nine-hour advance warning following the attack on Hawaii, they misread weather reports and delayed launching an attack on Japanese airfields in Formosa and moving airplanes out of range from a Japanese strike. The Japanese beat them to the punch and caught most of the Far East Air Force and many irreplaceable B-17 bombers on the ground. The same type of radar that detected Japanese planes approaching the north shore of Oahu also detected the planes approaching Luzon to strike Clark, Del Carmen, Iba, Nichols, and Neilson airfields, but as in Hawaii, the alert failed to reach the bases.[12]

When the Japanese bombed Manila, Bert Silen and Don Bell of KZRH transmitted vivid eyewitness accounts via the NBC White Network and shortwave station KGEI in San Francisco. NBC broadcast the reports over its Red and Blue mainland networks. For the first time, Americans could hear reporters describing events in real time from across the Pacific.[13]

A stunned Philippine president Manuel Quezon suggested that Gen. Douglas MacArthur declare the Philippines neutral in a doomed attempt to forestall the Japanese. MacArthur refused and executed War Plan Orange 3, withdrawing the USAFFE American and Philippine army forces on Luzon to the Bataan Peninsula and declaring Manila an open city.[14] On March 12, 1942, MacArthur obeyed a presidential order and escaped Corregidor by PT boat to Mindanao and then aboard a B-17 bomber from Del Monte airfield to Australia.

As the Japanese landed on Luzon and advanced toward Manila, the KZRH staff moved to Corregidor to operate the Voice of Freedom, broadcasting from the Malinta Tunnel. Their first broadcast opened dramatically with "The Star-Spangled Banner" followed by "Lupang Hinirang" and the famous voice of Maj. Carlos P. Romulo defiantly broadcasting in English and Tagalog.[15]

On December 23, 1941, a Japanese Naval Landing Force subdued the feisty 449-man U.S. Marine Corps Defense Battalion and

68 U.S. Navy personnel on Wake Island, capturing the survivors along with 45 Chamorro Pan Am employees of and 1,221 civilian construction employees of the Morrison-Knudson Company, Boise, Idaho. The marine detachment and F4F Grumman Wildcat Fighter Squadron VMF-211 had stubbornly held out since the first Japanese attack on December 8. Americans could not imagine the horrific treatment of the marines and civilians, whose Japanese captors had tied their hands behind their backs with wire, stripped them of their clothing, and repeatedly beat them with rifle butts while forcing the captives to kneel along the Wake Island airfield runway indefinitely in blazing and burning sunshine, awaiting an uncertain fate. The garrison surrendered after a fight that captured the imagination of Americans who mistakenly believed from media reports that all the Americans and Chamorros had sacrificed their lives in a battle reminiscent of the 1836 massacre at the Alamo. Paramount rushed into production the rousing film *Wake Island*, one of the first of many action films with wartime themes. It received four Academy Award nominations and starred Brian Donlevy as the marine garrison commander Maj. James Deveraux. The film ends with the marines fighting on, giving viewers the opportunity to imagine if the men all perished or not. What happened was that the Japanese sent the real-life marines and most of the civilians to prisoner-of-war camps. They kept 98 of the civilians on the island as slave labor to continue building an air base. On October 7, 1943, when he feared an imminent American landing after heavy air attacks on the atoll, Rear Adm. Shigematsu Sakaibara summarily executed the 98 civilians by machine-gunning them.[16]

On January 1, 1942, by order of the Federal Communications Commission, RCA (Radio Corporation of America) divested the NBC Blue Network to settle a long-running antitrust action. NBC kept the NBC Red Network and put Blue into an RCA operating trust pending purchase by a new owner. All Blue technical operations and facilities continued running with the former NBC managers and supervisors, and the network was identified on the air as the Blue Network.[17]

Since the mid-1930s, CBS and NBC had broadcast international programming services from CBS stations WBOS, WCBA, and WCBX, NBC stations WRCA and WNBI, and General Electric (GE) stations broadcasting the nbc signal, WGEA and WGEO, beamed toward Europe from directional transmitters in the afternoon hours on the East Coast of the United States. Engineers adjusted the transmitter signals for service to Latin America during evening hours in the Western Hemisphere. On the West Coast KCBA and KCBF broadcast CBS programs, and GE's KGEI broadcast the NBC international service, or White Network, to Asia and the Pacific. CBS and the NBC White Network also supported affiliated stations in several Latin American nations, such as Cuba and Mexico. Spanish-speaking NBC announcers including Alfredo Barratt hosted musical and information programs specially produced for Latinos and featuring popular bands such as Tommy Dorsey. Appearing at New York's Hotel Astor, Dorsey's band appeared on a 1940 series called *Carnivale de Broadway.* NBC transmitted Xavier Cugat's *Camel Rumba Review*, hosted by young announcer Bert Parks, to Europe, the Pacific, and Latin America. The CBS and NBC services had been more about prestige and a long-term investment than profits, as neither were making money running their small overseas operations.[18]

During a flurry of 1941 executive orders, FDR set up the Office of Coordinator of Inter-American Affairs (OCIAA) to focus on Latin America, and he chose fellow New Yorker Nelson Rockefeller of the Rockefeller Foundation to run it. The president selected another New Yorker from Buffalo, World War I Medal of Honor winner Gen. William J. Donovan, to run the Office of Coordinator of Information (OCOI). Donovan was a prominent United States attorney and celebrity. The 1940 Warner Brothers' James Cagney feature, *The Fighting 69th,* depicted Donovan's wartime command with George Brent playing Donovan and Pat O'Brien playing famous chaplain Fr. Francis Patrick Duffy (Lt. Col., U.S. Army).

Donovan convinced FDR that the United States needed a foreign intelligence service, and that part of that mission was information gathering and dissemination. Donovan proposed to use disinformation, or psychological warfare, as a weapon. For the moment the OCOI would get involved in overseas print and broadcast media activities to communicate America's message to the world. FDR asked his friend Robert Emmett Sherwood, the prominent playwright, to form a Foreign Information Service within the OCOI to counter anti-American Axis propaganda. Setting up offices in New York and San Francisco, Sherwood advocated a strategy of inspirational propaganda that promoted democracy and American values.[19]

During 1941 the OCOI and the OCIAA entered into voluntary agreements with CBS and NBC for time on their commercial shortwave transmitters and space on their international program schedules to broadcast war news and commentary. Germany and Japan used over one hundred government-operated shortwave transmitters in 194l, and the American commercial shortwave broadcasters ran thirteen, giving the Axis a considerable advantage in winning hearts and minds.

Following Pearl Harbor, the OCOI and OCIAA each took steps to begin direct programming, including consolidation of the NBC and CBS international operations into a jointly operated government service for the duration of the war. Sherwood assembled a high-level group including Joseph Barnes, *New York Herald Tribune* news editor, journalist Edd Johnson from CBS, and James Warburg, a banker and German expert, to lead the new team of OCOI FIS journalists, broadcast technicians, and foreign language experts. Sunday, February 1, 1942, the OCOI transmitted the first government broadcast, *Stimmen aus Amerika* (Voices from America), to the people of the German Reich. "The Battle Hymn of the Republic" preceded the welcoming words of journalist and author William Harlan Hale. The new radio service became the Voice of America.

The Crosley Broadcasting Company of Cincinnati, Ohio, owner of NBC affiliate WLW, ran the most powerful of the thirteen commercial shortwave transmitters in the United States. Crosley had a 75kw shortwave transmitter transmitting the signal of international station WLWO to Europe and Latin America using two

antennas. In January 1942 the OCIAA asked WLWO to install a
new 50kw transmitter to offer four signals instead of two. Crosley also pledged to install an astonishing array of 200kw transmitters that were capable of broadcasting six signals at once and
that would be operational by 1943. The powerful U.S. transmitters in Ohio caught the attention of Hitler, who called them "the
Cincinnati liars."[20]

By February1942 there were twenty-six defense information
offices spending $26 million and employing three thousand peo-
ple across the Departments of War, Navy, State, and Treasury and
the OCOI and OCIAA. War Department Chief of Staff Gen. George
C. Marshall urged FDR to get control of information quickly.[21]

FDR pulled public communications and morale from several
of his executive order agencies, such as the Office of Civil Defense
(OCD), chaired by the Republican New York mayor Fiorello La
Guardia, and formed a new Office of Facts and Figures (OFF).
The poet and Librarian of Congress Archibald MacLeish agreed
to run the OFF on a part-time basis, aided by full-time deputy
Ulrich Bell. The OFF was a domestic equivalent to Sherwood's
Foreign Information Service. It met with skepticism from both
interventionist and isolationist newspaper editorial boards upon
its creation. The media giants were worried that OFF would be a
domestic propaganda agency akin to Goebbels. Sarcastic remarks
included doubt that any Roosevelt administration agency could
ever tell the truth.[22]

FDR appointed Lowell Mellett as coordinator of government
films within the existing Office of Government Reports (OGR).
He directed Mellett to set up liaison with Hollywood studios and
ensure that they were helping the war effort. Mellett had no censorship power, but the media certainly thought that the OGR might
act as a censor.[23] Mellett was unknown in Hollywood, and industry insiders suggested that Hollywood financier John H. Whitney,
who was working with the OCIAA, or director John Ford, who had
recently joined the OCOI, might be better suited for the job. In
January 1942 Mellett made his first trip Los Angeles. He lavishly
praised the film industry and appeared to make progress in set-

ting up the wartime role of government with motion pictures. In April he set up a Bureau of Motion Pictures office in Hollywood and named Nelson Poynter, publisher of the *St. Petersburg Times*, as director. Poynter was another official unknown to motion picture industry insiders.[24]

After Pearl Harbor the government compelled automobile, steel, and other major manufacturing industries to divert their entire production of machines and materials from civilian to military use. The nature of the enemy and the mortal threat they posed to the existence of the United States made a state of emergency necessary. As British intelligence master William Stephenson confided in FDR, "The Füehrer is not just a lunatic. He is an evil genius. The weapons in his armory are like nothing in history. His propaganda is sophisticated. His control of the people is technologically clever. He has torn up the military textbooks and written his own."[25]

Although not conscripted in a physical sense, media including motion pictures and broadcasting were, nonetheless, vital to winning the war. Lowell Mellett offered Hollywood a proposal where Nelson Poynter and the Bureau of Motion Pictures would be the clearinghouse between the government and the motion picture industry. In return, Mellett promised that the government would not interfere with the business of motion pictures, film distributors, and theater owners. The government was not asking Hollywood to turn over film production to wartime use, as the manufacturing industries had to do. Mellett correctly understood that Hollywood would agree to a voluntary system of "guidance" in exchange for non-interference with the bottom line. Mellett needed Hollywood to sell the war aims of the nation and boost morale, but overt propaganda would negatively affect the entertainment value of motion pictures. The studio heads wanted to win the war but not at the loss of their profits. The government and Hollywood tacitly agreed on a mutually beneficial, if undefined, arrangement.[26]

One World

During a March 1942 CBS broadcast, Elmer Davis commented, "The whole government publicity situation has everybody in the

Fig. 12. Elmer Davis testifies before the Senate Judiciary Committee to the effectiveness of American propaganda in North Africa by pointing out the large number of surrendering Italian soldiers, saying that Mussolini's men were carrying OWI leaflets promising food when they surrendered, April 22, 1943. Office of War Information Photo, collection of the author.

news business in despair, with half a dozen different agencies following different lines . . . under one head, with real power, thy might get somewhere . . . objection has been made that it might be hard to pick the man to head them. But almost nobody would be better than half a dozen heads."[27]

Davis would be surprised with what was to come next. FDR finally set up a central authority to channel the flow of public information by reorganizing the Office of Coordinator of Information into the Office of War Information (OWI) with Executive Order 9182 effective June 12, 1942. The OWI would have responsibility for the dissemination of wartime information to the people of the United States and the nations of the world. It had two distinct missions, domestic and international. The OWI inherited the Office of Facts and Figures and Archibald MacLeish, the Foreign Information Service and Robert Sherwood, and the Office of Government Reports Bureau of Motion Pictures with coordinator Lowell Mellett. Overseas broadcasting in the form of the new Voice of America came under the authority of the new Foreign Branch of the OWI. The coordinator of inter-American affairs and responsibility for Latin America remained separate.[28]

Gen. William Donovan became head of the newly organized Office of Strategic Services (OSS). The OSS would gather and analyze information, becoming a wartime national intelligence agency.[29] The OSS became actively involved in special operations, asymmetrical warfare, paramilitary activities, support of partisans and guerillas behind enemy lines, sabotage, espionage, and the penetration of Nazi Germany. The agency included military personnel and recruited and trained indigenous groups around the world, including both Mao Zedong's revolutionary Chinese Communist Army and the official Kuomintang (Nationalist) forces of Chiang Kai-shek in China, the Viêt Minh of Ho Chi Minh in Indochina, and the communist partisans of Josip Broz Tito in Yugoslavia. The OSS was a particularly attractive agency for highly educated and motivated individuals, including foreign-born American citizens with language skills. The Overseas Branch of the OWI would attract similar individuals, although the agency had a different and distinct mission.

FDR did not select a corporate executive or government official to run the new OWI. He selected a broadcast journalist with impeccable credentials and public trust: Elmer Davis became director of the OWI. Davis did not seek the position. He was not a Roosevelt confidante, nor did he have an undiluted admiration for FDR. He had never hesitated to praise or criticize the president or point out FDRs strengths and weaknesses in print or in on-the-air commentaries. Davis had no administrative experience, so FDR appointed the experienced manager Milton Eisenhower, the brother of Maj. Gen. Dwight D. Eisenhower of the Pentagon War Plans Office, as deputy OWI director.[30]

Davis told reporters that the strategy of the OWI was "to tell the truth." MacLeish, Sherwood, and Mellett agreed. On the other hand, truth and accuracy were subjective guidelines under conditions of wartime military security. The owi would not always have the luxury of being exact in real time, and the agency was as interested in showing context and interpretation as it was in issuing information.[31]

Domestic responsibility was the most contentious aspect of the owi. To broadcasters and publishers the owi meant censorship. To housewives and businessmen it meant rationing. To everyone it meant propaganda. However, Japan's surprise attack came across to Americans as "a stab in the back." FDR's Declaration of War on December 8, 1941, emphasized Japanese treachery. Nazi Germany swept itself up into the storm of public outrage by supporting its ally and declaring war on the United States. Doubts about a government information agency at home and abroad were now secondary to national survival. As with many aspects of the war, an air of necessity and inevitability took hold. It helped to have enemies who were ready-made villains right out of central casting. Because the existence of the nation was on the line, public and private sector leaders were willing to suspend their concerns for the duration or at least try to go along with as much of the new owi agenda as they could.

Davis appointed Archibald MacLeish director of the owi Domestic Branch and Robert Sherwood director of the owi Overseas Branch. Publisher and broadcaster Gardner "Mike" Cowles became director of the owi Domestic Branch when MacLeish resigned in December 1942.

It was inevitable that Davis would come to blows with other agencies and agendas, but he enjoyed FDRs absolute trust and confidence. FDR's executive order had said, "the Director of the new owi will have authority, subject to powers held directly by the President, to issue directions to all departments and agencies of the government with respect to their information services. He will have full authority to eliminate all overlapping and duplication and to discontinue in any department any information activity which is not necessary or useful to the war effort."[32]

Davis and Eisenhower got to work restructuring the agencies the OWI inherited into a new organization. They had 2,348 employees and between $15 and $20 million in the annual budget. In a statement to the House Appropriations Committee in August 1942, Davis remarked, "The war is going to be won primarily by fighting, but history, both recent and remote, proves that victory of the fighting forces can be made easier by what is called psychological or political warfare, the prosecution of which has been entrusted primarily to this office [the OWI]. We are in a sense an auxiliary to the armed forces—an organization whose operations can pave the way for their operations and make their success easier."[33]

On April 9, 1942, the American and Philippine forces besieged on the Bataan Peninsula surrendered. The sick and starving "Battling Bastards" had delayed Japan for three critical months. The Japanese forces commanded by Gen. Masaharu Homma were unprepared logistically or culturally to cope with the 78,000 haggard American and Philippine prisoners they captured and considered contemptible. The result was the infamous Bataan Death March, where Japanese personnel brutally murdered thousands. Survivors fared no better as emaciated guests of the Empire in squalid camps as slave laborers. British Commonwealth and Dutch prisoners captured elsewhere suffered the same fate.[34]

At this grim juncture Davis felt the American people "had the right to be truthfully informed" and for defeats to be reported as honestly as victories. His policy was consistent with the BBC, which valued reliability and objectivity as the most effective form of propaganda. Davis allowed photos of battlefield casualties to appear in print and on newsreels. His sense of fair play and candor led him to recommend that Japanese Americans serve in the armed forces. When FDR looked to deprive Japanese Americans of their citizenship and intern them for the duration of the war, Davis correctly predicted the policy would aid Japanese propaganda in proclaiming that America was fighting a racial war. Davis constantly instructed OWI officials to judge their efforts from the point of view of enemies, allies, and the public. He argued with the navy, and won, over when and how candidly to report ship losses. In the eyes of the OWI, the navy had withheld or delayed disclosure of unwelcome news to a degree that invited legitimate suspicion. The navy hid losses, including the USS *Lexington* at the Battle of the Coral Sea, but Japanese broadcasts from NHK and Radio Tokyo had told the truth.

On April 18, 1942, sixteen Army Air Forces B-25 "Mitchell" bombers under the command of Lt. Col. James H. Doolittle took off from the carrier USS *Hornet* to bomb targets in Tokyo, Yokohama, Osaka, Kobe, and Nagoya. The results were negligible, but it was a big morale booster for Americans and a psychological blow to the Japanese military. All the planes but one crashed in China, but the crews survived. One plane diverted to Vladivostok, and the neutral Soviets interred the crew. The embarrassed Japanese captured two of the crews, who they put on trial as "war criminals." Tokyo executed some of the flyers in contravention of international law. Radio Tokyo announced the criminal reprisal, which only further infuriated Americans. The IJN sank the *Hornet* on October 27, 1942, at the Battle of Santa Cruz Islands.

Davis broadcast a fifteen-minute weekly summary of the American war progress and requirements every Friday evening at 10:45 p.m. Eastern War Time over all four national radio networks. He trusted the American people with the facts, commenting, "We could lose this war. We have never lost a war; but it has been remarked that this means only that our ancestors never lost a war . . . but our ancestors were never up against a war like this. To win a total war we must fight it totally, and we are not yet fighting it that hard. Many individual Americans have made great sacrifices but as a nation we are not yet more than ankle deep in the water. We might win this war, but we are not winning it yet."[35]

The media was not always on the same page with the OWI and military. Following the June 1942 Battle of Midway, Stanley Johnson and the *Chicago Tribune* indiscreetly published an amazingly accurate and detailed story that would lead any knowledgeable reader to deduce that the Americans had broken the Japanese naval code. Johnson's source was an inside leak, but there was no trial to avoid further exposure. The Japanese missed the tipoff and continued to use their JN-25 code.[36]

One of the first challenges the OWI had to tackle was the portrayal of the Japanese in motion pictures, in magazines, and on radio. During the first half of 1942, Hollywood rushed out seventy-two features that the OWI classified as "war features," which the OWI found to be sensationalistic, inarticulate, in poor taste, and racist. Early wartime features made Japanese treachery the only pretense for the war. Without proper context the American public developed a vividly false understanding of why they were at war and who their enemy really was. The OWI noticed that the "unconvincing" war films stereotyped the Japanese as brutal and treacherous fascists but did not examine the motives and ideology of the Japanese government.[37] Dorothy Jones, the agency chief film analyst, determined that serious treatment of war issues was completely absent from motion pictures.[38]

Poynter told the studios that the OWI wanted them to incorporate serious government-directed themes into feature films. He suggested that the OWI would be most helpful if the studios would send scripts to the Bureau of Motion Pictures in advance so that the government could review them. Poynter emphasized that he had no right to demand the scripts and such a program was voluntary.[39] Although the studios wanted to help, the industry remained uneasy about the possibility of censorship. An unidentified studio executive said, "We don't want people whom we would not employ, because they are not qualified through experience and training, telling us what to do."[40]

During the summer of 1942 Poynter's staff assembled the *Government Information Manual for the Motion Picture Industry*. It was a comprehensive statement of the OWI's vision for America and the liberal worldview of the OWI staff.[41] In the section "The Issues: Why We Fight," the OWI summarized the war as a struggle for democracy. It was the people's war and a war for the Four Freedoms of speech, religion, want, and fear; which, unlike World War I, would end with a just and lasting peace. As Wendell Willkie characterized in his milestone 1943 book, total victory over the Axis would bring a united "One World."[42] The manual defined World War II as a continuum of a revolutionary struggle that started in

1776. According to the OWI, every class, race, creed, and nationality fought the "People's War."

The guidelines recommended the studios avoid stereotypes, such as blacks in comedic or menial roles. "The Enemy" emphasized that the enemy was not the German, Japanese, or Italian people, but, rather, poisonous ideology. The manual described thirty countries as the "United Nations," including the Soviet Union. It said that "yes, we Americans reject communism, but we do not reject our Russian allies." The OWI downplayed British imperialism and underscored the British struggle against fascism. The manual neither whitewashed or criticized Latin American caudillo dictatorships that had declared war on the Axis and joined the United Nations. The OWI told the studios to avoid demeaning stereotypes of all Allied peoples, especially of different races. They stressed unity as the theme of the "Home Front." American democracy was not perfect. The underprivileged and minorities had a stake in the outcome of the war. This section implied that through the New Deal, the government had improved the living standards of all Americans, and this trajectory toward justice and equality would continue, while all progress would disappear if the fascists conquered the world and American became a vassal state.

"Unity" became the theme of all civilian participation and cooperation with the war effort. The studios thus had to portray labor and management harmony. Americans should embrace volunteerism and personal sacrifice for the common good, including food rationing and buying war bonds. Women in films must assertively take their rightful role as equals in the war effort, including in the armed forces and manufacturing. Hollywood should depict women as strongly coping with wartime challenges such as separation from spouses and child care.

Hollywood had started releasing formulaic plots as combat films. The OWI asked the studios to consider something less melodramatic with the "Fighting Forces." The government wanted to deemphasize the glorification of war with realistic and thoughtful presentations. They wanted Hollywood to prepare the American people for casualties and, while respecting combat victories and military valor, to also respect the tragedy of war and why the sacrifices of the fallen were worthwhile.[43]

The OWI guidelines became a parallel Motion Picture Code for the duration of the war, even as their liberal guidelines contrasted with the conservative Hollywood Production Code. The OWI sent updates and additions to the original loose-leaf binder manual that expanded the guidelines and confused the motion picture studios. All the movies reviewed by the OWI Motion Picture Bureau received a classification theme. The reviewer of *Casablanca* slotted it into the major theme "pigeonhole" of III B (United Nations—Conquered Nations). The minor theme classification was II C 3 (Enemy—Military). Four members of the Bureau saw *Casablanca* on October 26, 1942, before American forces landed in North Africa, and gave it a glowing review: "Judged from the standpoint of the war information program . . . [*Casablanca* shows that] personal desires must be subordinated to the task of defeating fascism" and "graphically illustrates the chaos and misery which fascism and the war has brought." America was "the haven of the oppressed and homeless." By including the background of lead character Rick Blaine [Humphrey Bogart] fighting fascism in Ethiopia and Spain, the film reminded audiences that "our war did not commence with Pearl Harbor, but that the roots of aggression reach far back."[44]

The OWI did not have to force its will on Hollywood. The conservative studio owners, directors, and managers all wanted to win the war and agreed with the OWI that motion pictures were strong moral-building and messaging assets. The most liberal people in the business were the writers, some of whom were even self-avowed communists, who all backed the war effort 100 percent. This was a unique convergence of ideals because of a clear and present danger. Writers such as Dalton Trumbo, later blacklisted as part of the "Hollywood Ten" in the Cold War, were supportive of the liberal OWI directives.

Meanwhile radio and the print media were dealing directly with censorship. On December 17, 1941, FDR appointed Byron Price of the Associated Press as director of the Office of Censorship. Price had been with AP for thirty years and was executive news editor when FDR called on him to find a way to balance wartime security with the constitutional freedom of the press. Price prepared and administered a voluntary regulatory code that the collaborative media would come to praise. Yet, with it, Mr. Price's office would keep secret such critical Allied plans as the 1942 invasion of North Africa, the precise time and place of the 1944 invasion of Normandy, and the successful effort to develop the first atomic bomb.[45] At the 1942 convention of the National Association of Broadcasters in Washington, Price described censorship as a military weapon that is "a necessary evil" in time of total war. His office, he said, tried to avoid restrictions so strict that they would keep Americans ignorant of the progress of the war. Price named J. Harold Ryan of WSPD in Toledo and vice president of Fort Industries, which later became Storer Broadcasting Company, as his deputy.[46]

Edward Kirby became a lieutenant colonel in the army on May 1, 1942, and assumed military control of the BPR Radio Branch. He recommended to Surles that the military to take full advantage of radio. The BPR thus went directly to the people with a radio series accurately informing the public about the progress of the war. *The Army Hour* debuted on Sunday, April 5, 1942, Army Day, at 3:30 p.m., as a one-hour feature on NBC. General Marshall ordered Kirby to present the story of the army in an honest manner and not "exaggerated to hide our losses because our people will see right through it."[47] There were no retakes, digital recordings to edit and assemble, and no satellites to reliably feed signals from around the world. Engineering problems fouled up the broadcasts, including enemy jamming and fickle atmospheric conditions. Reports from the field cut out during the live actualities. The staff could lose entire scripted sections of a broadcast and had to scramble to improvise. They also had to precisely synchronize and cue remotes. One of the first broadcasts included dramatic segments coming in via shortwave from Corregidor before Gen. Jonathan Wainwright surrendered to the Japanese.[48] NBC invested a considerable budget to *The Army Hour* to reach millions of listeners and present the most descriptive battlefield reporting of the war. The army wrote and produced the program, and NBC shared the costs. By 1943 the program would have three million listeners, and it won Kirby a coveted Peabody Award. According to the Hooper ratings service, *The Army Hour* was the highest-rated Sunday daytime radio program.[49]

National Interest

On December 7, 1941, Radio Corporation of America president David Sarnoff sent FDR a telegram saying, "All our facilities are ready and at your instant service. We await your commands."[50] Sarnoff had come a long way since working as a radio operator during the 1912 RMS *Titanic* disaster for the American Marconi Company. The Italian engineer and entrepreneur Guglielmo Marconi developed long-range radio transmission and founded the pioneering firm. Sarnoff went on to become president of RCA after the General Electric subsidiary bought the assets of the American Marconi Company. Sarnoff ran RCA's NBC broadcasting networks, built radio receivers and transmission equipment, and made a considerable investment in innovative technologies, including Dr. Vladimir Zworykin's electric eye, which became television. On April 20, 1939, Sarnoff joined President Roosevelt and New York mayor Fiorello La Guardia to open the New York World's Fair. Engineers set up an RCA television camera, connected by coaxial cable to a transmission van fifty feet from the podium. Two thousand viewers could see Trylon and Perisphere, the fair symbols, along with the speakers. But with war clouds gathering, Sarnoff became immersed in shuttling to Washington since RCA's facilities, research, engineers, and radio broadcasting assets were all vital national assets. In 1941, expecting American entry into the war, he centralized RCA research in a new facility in Princeton, New Jersey, where he brought together RCA's 1,300 scientists and engineers "in the national interest."[51] RCA was essential in the development of radar and electronic navigation systems, an underwater detection device known as sonar, powerful magnetron tubes, two thousand types of vacuum tubes needed for military communications, twenty million miniaturized tubes, and small communications devices known as walkie-talkies.

In 1924 Sarnoff received a reserve commission as a lieutenant colonel in the Army Signal Corps, a responsibility that the Russian immigrant took very seriously. On June 25, 1942, Sarnoff reported for his two weeks' service as vice chairman and then chairman of the Signal Corps Advisory Council and returned on August 27 for a two-month tour of duty and travel, handling troubleshooting assignments. On October 19 Sarnoff reported on the "Secrecy of Communications." He called attention to the danger of the enemy tapping into underwater cables to monitor communications. He determined that the geographical pattern of U-boat attacks was close to the transatlantic cables. The Germans had cut the cables in World War I but had not done so this time around. Sarnoff logically deduced that they were tapping and decoding cables to determine convoy routes. The navy ran a test that confirmed Sarnoff's fears and revised the codes. After the two-month stint, Sarnoff returned to his office at Rockefeller Center and did not put his uniform back on until 1944.[52]

With the coming of war, several fundamental changes faced popular bandleaders and their booking agencies, including fuel rationing and transportation priorities. Bus and rail travel became costlier and less available. The flexibility of bands to support schedules of one-night appearances crisscrossing the country was seriously impaired. The military draft expanded and depleted bands of talented musicians. And there was another and potentially more serious challenge:

ALL RECORDING STOPS TODAY

Disc Firms Sit Back; Public's Next Move

Government May Step In; Several Months' Record Supply On Hand

New York—From today on there will be no recording of music, classical or jazz, in this country by union musicians. Prexy Petrillo [American Federation of Musicians President James Caesar Petrillo] has not backed down by his claim recording was running the jobs of 60 percent of the AFM membership and he meant to do something about it. As a result, only Soundies and Hollywood are exempted from the "no mechanical reproduction of any kind" order. Petrillo has shifted his position as to the sale of records. He had previously told the companies they could record for home and Army use but when it was pointed out to him the companies would be violating the law if they tried to regulate who bought their records, Petrillo made the edict a complete stoppage. The recording firms, transcription firms, radio networks and even small stations are sizzling. Executives all pointed out at no time had the AFM indicated what terms it wanted, merely had casually sent out carbon copies of a rubber-stamped order putting them out of business. The howls of the small stations emphasized by James Lawrence Fly, Chairman of the FCC, who pointed out 60 percent of all the country's radio stations depended on records to exist and without them they would go under and 'this is a matter of public interest demanding thorough investigation. Not only do the wax firms have a large backlog but in the past month they have been recording at a frantic rate. Most of the firms are ready to wait for the effects of public opinion and possible government action, which is already being demanded by Arthur Vandenburg (R-MI).[53]

The target audience for the BPR's *The Army Hour* was the American public. The American soldiers stationed in all corners of the globe also needed information and entertainment. Kirby, consultant Lou Cowan, and Hollywood scriptwriter Glenn Wheaton developed a concept around the idea of the soldiers commanding entertainment of their choice, which became the most successful variety program in radio history. Wheaton gathered commitments from the networks, advertising agencies, music licensing firms, and the musicians' union. Vic Knight, the producer of *The Fred Allen Show,* agreed to handle the same chore for the new program pro bono. Sunday, March 1, 1942, to the sound of a bugle call and the opening bars of George M. Cohan's "Over There," the BPR recorded the first *Command Performance* program, in New York.[54] To take advantage of motion picture industry talent, the War Department moved *Command Performance* to Hollywood.

Glenn Wheaton and Vic Knight transferred to the West Coast and produced the series at CBS. The support of the newly organized Hollywood Victory Committee expanded the pool of entertainers available for the program.[55]

In 1939 Secretary of War Henry Stimson asked Frederick Osborn, chairman of the Rockefeller Foundation, to chair a committee to set goals for military morale and avoid a repetition of morale problems experienced in World War I. These efforts coalesced into the BPR and OCOI. Archibald MacLeish and Robert Sherwood were members of the Osborn committee.

During 1941 Osborn's Army Welfare and Recreation Committee recommended the merger of various local troop welfare agencies into United Service Organizations (USO). Following Pearl Harbor, the Morale Branch became the Special Services Division, which the Pentagon put into the Army Services of Supply commanded by Gen. Brehon B. Somervell. The Services of Supply later became the Army Service Forces, one of the three autonomous components of the army in World War II, the others being the Army Ground Forces and Army Air Forces.

Osborn became a brigadier general in September 1941 and took over Special Services information and education activities.[56] At the direction of General Marshall, Osborn arranged the transfer of the Hollywood film director Maj. Frank Capra from the Signal Corps to Special Services. Capra's job would be to use the medium of film to explain to American troops why they had to fight. Capra, who was not pleased with the transfer, reported to Col. E. L. Munson of Osborn's staff. Like others in similar positions, Capra had entered the service to get close to the fight and loathed a cozy rear-echelon assignment.

Italian immigrant Capra proved his keen patriotism in *Mr. Smith Goes to Washington,* one of the many classic films made in 1939. At the time, the film was controversial because it dealt with political corruption in the United States just as Germany was igniting war. Government officials worried about a potential negative political impact in Europe, and Hollywood moguls feared negative repercussions from Washington. Columbia Pictures president Harry Cohn went ahead and released the film, starring James Stewart, which received eleven Academy Award nominations and was a smash hit.

When the forty-four-year-old Capra enlisted on December 11, 1941, giving up his successful career and presidency of the Screen Directors' Guild, his posting put him into the War Department HQ at the Pentagon and into direct contact with General Marshall, who had selected Capra for a vital assignment for which Capra was the best qualified officer in the army to handle, hence his transfer from the Signal Corps to Special Services. Having discussed the idea with an eager FDR, Marshall wanted Capra "to make a series of well-documented, factual-information films, that will explain to our men why we are fighting and the principles for which we are fighting . . . you have an opportunity to contribute enormously to your country and the cause of freedom."[57]

Capra coordinated the production of a brilliant seven-episode war information documentary series titled *Why We Fight*, consisting of *Prelude to War* (1942), *The Nazis Strike* (1942), *Divide and Conquer* (1943), *The Battle of Britain* (1943), *The Battle of Russia* (1943), *The Battle of China* (1944), and *War Comes to America* (1945).

The *Why We Fight* production quality and style evolved through the episodes as film footage from Allied sources replaced enemy sources, but all the episodes received high praise. A group of studios and contributors including the Walt Disney Studios worked with Capra's military team to assemble the series. *Why We Fight* appeared at military installations and in theaters across the United States. The well-produced and powerful documentaries made a strong impression on military and civilian audiences. They were a cornerstone in the FDR-inspired creation of Americans' sense of their own exceptionalism. The War Department translated *Why We Fight* into French, Spanish, Portuguese, and Chinese, and the series appeared throughout Britain and the Commonwealth nations.

Capra's army production unit also made many short subjects and features for military and civilian circulation, including *Tunisian Victory*, *Two Down and One to Go*, *Know Your Enemy: Japan*, and *Here Is Germany*. Capra became a colonel and won the Legion of Merit and the Distinguished Service Medal. Among his Army Signal Corps colleagues was director John Huston from Warner Brothers and *Maltese Falcon* fame. Captain Huston produced and directed films including the critically acclaimed *Report from the Aleutians*, *The Battle of San Pietro*, and *Let There Be Light*. Huston's works were so honest and realistic that military officers thought the films were detrimental to morale and quarantined them. Huston filmed *The Battle of San Pietro* in combat in Italy; the film shows the loss of American lives due to poor intelligence. Huston became a major and won the Legion of Merit. He went on to create classic films such as *Treasure of the Sierra Madre* and *The African Queen*.

When the skeptical Capra arrived in Washington and learned of his challenging assignment, among other things Munson asked if he was acquainted with an advertising executive named Thomas H. A. Lewis and if he felt Lewis was the right man to manage a potential military radio network. Capra knew Lewis as the husband of actress Loretta Young and the vice president for radio at Young & Rubicam and Audience Research, Inc. When Munson explained what he envisioned for Capra and for Lewis, and the vital importance of the assignments, Capra came on board and recommended Lewis, but not without trepidation. He knew the job of setting up a worldwide radio service potentially larger than all the commercial networks combined was a daunting task. Lewis was Munson's choice because he had a reputation for simplifying problems and getting things done. Fellow Catholic Capra remembered telling Munson, "The Army and the country will be lucky to get Tom Lewis . . . a man who asks God for help and gets it."[58] Munson asked Lewis to resign from Young & Rubicam, become an army major, and tackle the job. Lewis accepted on the spot without realizing what he was getting himself into. Lewis was commissioned May 26, 1942, and came to Washington with plans the army quickly approved. He selected Los Angeles for his base of operations and after a brief sojourn at the Taft Building in Hollywood moved his staff to 20th Century Fox, where Capra's film team worked. Lewis did not yet have formal approval to do so, but Capra advised him to "Just do it. Don't ask questions. We

Fig. 13. Col. Thomas H. A. Lewis, commander of the Armed Forces Radio Service, gives "Victory Through Air Power" speech commemorating the twenty-fifth anniversary of radio and radio's contribution to the war effort, at the Advertising Club of Los Angeles, February 6, 1945. Library of American Broadcasting, University of Maryland.

were both crazy to do this in the first place. What will they do? Fire You? Just get the job done!"[59]

For a variety of reasons ranging from patriotism to draft evasion, Lewis was quickly able to recruit an administrative, production, and engineering staff of experienced broadcasters. However, with Lewis in command, broadcasters could not expect a cushy Hollywood assignment. They had to set up a global network from scratch.

Beginning in February 1942, a policy of forced relocation moved between 110,000 and 120,000 people, including Americans of Japanese ancestry, from their homes and into internment camps akin to how the government treated enemy aliens. Some 62 percent of the detainees were American citizens. This was one of the most unnecessary and cruel decisions in American history. Faced with an emergency, FDR prioritized national security above constitutional liberties. The part of Executive Order 9066 detaining Japanese citizen aliens was a justified wartime measure. But the inclusion of American citizens of Japanese ancestry was an overreaction to Japanese aggression that had nothing to do with loyal American farmers in Modesto or storekeepers in Pasadena.[60] Secretary of War Stimson initially opposed relocation. Hawaiian military authorities reported that no organized fifth-column activities or sabotage occurred when Japan attacked on December 7, 1941. The FBI announced that no danger realistically existed on the mainland either. But on March 18, 1942, in Executive Order 9102, FDR created the War Relocation Authority to detain and intern American citizens of Japanese ancestry. Racist agricultural and real estate interests openly and proudly confirmed to the media that relocation was a way of seizing the homes, businesses, and farms of Japanese Americans for no compensation. The *Los Angeles Times* demanded relocation and justified theft in a series of editorials.[61]

If he ever saw them, a series of Magic intelligence decrypts may have given FDR a rationale for relocation and explain the context in which he saw the emergency. Declassified Japanese communications provide evidence that Tokyo operated espionage and potential sabotage networks in the United States and Latin America.[62] But agents had misgivings about recruiting Japanese Americans. Takeo Yoshikawa, the chief Japanese spy in Hawaii, said, "I couldn't trust them to help me. They were loyal to the United States." On the other hand, the Imperial Army expected locals to actively welcome them if they ever invaded Hawaii.[63]

On December 18, 1944, the Supreme Court handed down two decisions: a 6–3 decision upholding a Nisei conviction for violating the exclusion order, meaning that removal was constitutional; but a 9–0 unanimous decision that the government could not detain without cause loyal American citizens regardless of ancestry. This closed the detention camps, but citizens had already lost their property.[64]

Young patriotic Japanese Americans felt they had something to prove, and with their parents' support, they did so in blood. The 442nd Regimental Combat Team of Japanese Americans was one the most decorated units for its size and length of service in the history of the U.S. Army. Fourteen thousand men eventually served in the four-thousand-man unit due to casualties, and they earned 9,486 Purple Hearts. There were 21 Medal of Honor winners, and the unit won 8 Presidential Unit Citations. The motto of the 442nd was *Go for Broke*, and MGM made a film about them by the same name in 1951. These exceptional Americans proved their loyalty to the United States with their sacrifice, courage, and lives on the battlefields of Italy and France.

Like Frank Capra, motion picture director John Ford (John Martin Feeney) painted a rich canvas of Americana with prewar films such as *Stagecoach, Young Mr. Lincoln,* and *Drums along the Mohawk* and films on the human condition including *The Grapes of Wrath* and *How Green Was My Valley*. Best known for his postwar western classics, Ford was an avid sailor, fond of all things nautical and the U.S. Navy. He was more at home on his 110-foot, two-masted yacht *Araner* than on land.

When Ford won his second Academy Award for *The Grapes of Wrath*, he commented, "Awards for pictures are a trivial thing to be concerned with in times like these."[65] As early as 1939 Ford had the idea that he and other mostly overage Hollywood technicians could be of value to the navy as a field photographic unit to chronicle the war and help in intelligence work. The prolific Ford had already made over a hundred films, and there was no doubt about his genius, but most in Hollywood thought his military ideas were eccentric. Ford was serious and hoped the navy would see the value in his filmmaking auxiliary, but for some months the navy did not take Ford seriously. But he was persistent.[66] In 1941, 20th Century Fox studio chief Darryl Zanuck gave Ford his first wartime project for the War Department, the training film *Sex Hygiene*. Based on experience, the military considered venereal and communicable diseases as important a foe as actual combat. The odd film was effective and widely distributed, and it met a vital army need.[67]

In September 1941 the chief of naval operations Adm. Harold R. Stark summoned Ford. At the recommendation of his colleague, film producer, soldier of fortune, aviator, Pan Am board member, and Army Air Forces reservist Merian C. Cooper, Gen. William Donovan wanted the ad hoc Ford Field Photographic Unit, including all its members, for the Office of the Coordinator of Information's new intelligence service that became the oss in June 1942.

Ford became chief of the Field Photographic Branch of the ocoi and later the oss and was promoted to the rank of commander in the U.S. Navy Reserve (usnr). His Field Photographic unit included some of the best talent in Hollywood, including writers Garson Kanin and Budd Schulberg, cinematographer Gregg Toland, editor Robert Parrish, and special effects expert Ray Kellogg. Their first assignment from Donovan was the production of a report about the U.S. Atlantic Fleet escorting British convoys; the second was a report about Panama Canal defense.[68]

The Japanese attacked Pearl Harbor between the North Atlantic and Panama Canal assignments. Pleased with the results, Donovan ordered Field Photographic to the Pacific, beginning with a secret report on the damage in Hawaii. After Ford flew to Honolulu, he learned of the pending Doolittle Raid using aaf b-25 bombers from the uss *Hornet*, which sailed from nas Alameda, California, right under the Golden Gate Bridge during morning rush hour with the bombers fully visible, lashed on the flight deck of the ship. Leaving Toland in charge at Honolulu, Ford and several cameramen boarded the uss *Salt Lake City*, part of Admiral Halsey's Task Force 16 that was forming the escort for the mission. Upon returning to Hawaii, Toland informed Ford the navy had confiscated their Pearl Harbor footage as being too controversial.[69]

Meanwhile, Cmdr. John Rochefort and the Navy's op-20-02 Combat Intelligence Office (code-named Hypo) at Pearl Harbor broke the Japanese jn-25 naval code. The decrypts, classified as Ultra (military signals intelligence) revealed that the self-confident ijn was seeking to lure the inferior Americans into a decisive confrontation with their powerful Kidō Butai (combined carrier battle groups) near Midway Atoll, 1,304 miles northwest of Hawaii. Armed with the jn-25 intercepts, Nimitz was preparing to ambush the Japanese, and Donovan ordered Ford to film the battle.[70]

The filmmaker returned to Pearl Harbor and with photographer's mate Jack MacKenzie went to Midway. From the moment a pby Catalina spotted the Japanese fleet on June 3, 1942, Ford had a vast blue Kodachrome landscape to film an actual battle. Ford and MacKenzie, and by extension, the American public, became eyewitnesses to real war in real time. On June 4, 1942, Japanese planes attacked the Midway garrison while offshore America and Japan fought the most decisive naval battle since the 1805 Battle of Trafalgar. Ford and MacKenzie calmly captured the entire chaotic scene when Japanese bombers and fighters attacked Midway at dawn. Filming from the airfield control tower, Ford was both terrified and exhilarated when Japanese fighters zoomed in and riddled the structure. Ford aimed his camera at a group of marines hoisting the Stars and Stripes while smoke and flames swirled in the background. The dramatic shot eventually became one of the best-known images of World War II. When shrapnel from a bomb blast struck him, Ford sought medical attention and kept on filming.[71] At sea young American naval aviators from the uss *Enterprise*, *Hornet*, and *Yorktown* attacked and sank the *Akagi*, *Hiryu*, *Kaga*, and *Soryu*, four of the carriers that struck Pearl Harbor. In a decisive victory the Americans only lost the *Yorktown*. From that point forward, Japan was on the defensive, having lost irreplaceable ships, planes, and highly skilled samurai airmen. Outrageously claiming victory, Japanese media hid the truth, and the IJN quarantined survivors of the battle to conceal the fateful loss. By contrast, the unpretentious battle communiqué from Nimitz noted that the USN had "ended the nonsense" of retreat since "a Sunday morning six months ago." He went on to humbly acknowledge that "we have made substantial progress in that direction."[72]

Ford returned to the West Coast and made a rush print of an eighteen-minute documentary, titled *The Battle of Midway*, which he saw as a morale booster. "It's for the mothers of America . . . to let them know that we're in a war and that we've been getting the s— kicked out of us for five months, and now we're starting to hit back."[73]

Donovan and Ford rushed the film to the White House, where FDR, Eleanor Roosevelt, Harry Hopkins, and Adm. William D. Leahy viewed it. The footage included a shot of Marine Corps Maj. James Roosevelt attending a memorial service for the Midway dead. When FDR, who had been chatting during the film, recognized his son, he froze into silence. The film also included a moving segment about Torpedo Squadron 8 from the USS *Hornet,* commanded by Cmdr. John C. Waldron, of Oglala Lakota descent, that courageously lost every plane and crew in the battle except one pilot, Ens. George Gay. All the VT-8 personnel heartbreakingly appear in the film, smiling and confident, before they took off. After the viewing the film, the first lady wept, and FDR was ashen. Turning to Leahy, the president said, "I want every mother in America to see this picture."[74] 20th Century Fox distributed five hundred prints to theaters across the country, and the first public screening was at New York's Radio City Music Hall on September 14, 1942. Parrish reported, "It was a stunning, amazing thing to see. . . . women screamed, people cried, and the ushers had to take them out. . . . The people, they just went crazy." Ahead of its time, the film was propagandist yet realistic and inspirational and showed that victory in the Pacific was possible. *The Battle of Midway* won the Academy Award for best documentary short subject of 1942. Ford never made a more cinematically challenging and perfect film.[75]

Fig. 14. Cmdr. John Ford, USNR. Photo by Film Photographic Unit, Office of Strategic Services, June 1944. Courtesy Records of the Office of Strategic Services, RG 226, NARA.

FIVE

Good Neighbor

Saludos Amigos

By 1940 the United States decided that the time had come to exert political pressure and stop the ominous spread of Nazi influence. This meant ending German airline activity in Latin America. The father of aviation in Columbia was the Austrian Dr. Peter Paul von Bauer, who developed the airline SCATDA, which had originally flown Junkers planes and received technical support, pilots, and mechanics from Syndikat Condor Colombia. SCATDA was Sociedad Colombio-Alemana de Transportes Aéreos, or the Colombian-German Air Transport Company. The German personnel of SCATDA were excellent workers. During the 1930s, Pan American Airways became the majority owner of SCATDA, and over time SCATDA bought and flew American airplanes. Alarmed by Nazi aggression, the Austrian Anschluss, and the outbreak of war in Europe, von Bauer had returned to Colombia following a brief retirement. Working with his colleague Juan Trippe of Pan Am, von Bauer tried to phase out the German footprint at SCATDA. This did not satisfy the State Department, which reminded the Colombian government and Pan Am that SCATDA remained a risk and that Colombia should nationalize the airline and employ a majority Colombian staff. On June 8, 1940, SCATDA dismissed all German employees, Nazi or not. Pan Am personnel replaced them for the time being, and on June 14 the name of the airline became Aerovías Nacionales de Columbia (AVIANCA), which remains the name of the airline into the twenty-first century.[1]

The airline industry of Brazil was heavily German influenced.

France and Germany each pioneered air services to South America during the 1920s and 1930s. Italy also made attempts to serve South America: Aéropostale from Marseille and Toulouse via Dakar to Natal, Rio de Janeiro, Montevideo, and Santiago, Chile. Aéropostale eventually served nine Latin American nations until Air France bought it. Italian service by Linee Aeree Transcontinentali (LATI) did not begin until December 1939 and could not overfly or stop at British or French possessions, so the Italian route to Brazil was via Spain, Villa Cisneros, Spanish Sahara (Dakhla) and Cape Verde to Natal, Recife, and Rio de Janeiro.

Deutsche Lufthansa flew scheduled flights from Stuttgart via Bathurst to Recife, Rio de Janeiro, Buenos Aires, and Santiago, Chile. Syndicato Condor won rights to serve domestic Brazilian, Argentine, and Chilean cities. Luftschiffbau Zeppelin GmbH and the Hamburg Sudamerikanische famously flew the airship *Graf Zeppelin* from Friedrichshafen to Brazil from 1931 until the 1937 loss of her sister ship *Hindenburg* permanently grounded the stately hydrogen airship. As Brazil began to favor the allied cause, the German airline presence became problematic. On August 19, 1941, a government decree changed Syndicato Condor's name to Serviços Aéreos Condor, Ltda., and by April 1942 control transferred to Brazilian interests, although the airline had to train a Brazilian staff. Condor owed Deutsche Lufthansa $2.7 million, or 55 million cruzeiros, a great deal of money in 1942. Brazilian president Getúlio Vargas gave ample government support to the group of businessmen who bought the airline. However, essential German personnel remained, and this was of great concern to the United States.[2]

The problem was that Germany had used Condor for political and military purposes, and it had become entrenched in Argentina, Brazil, and Chile. Condor serviced airplanes for Brazilian carriers VARIG and VASP and gave technical support for airlines in Bolivia and Peru. Pan Am owned the largest Brazilian carrier, Panair do Brasil, so it was not an issue. One worry was that the continued German presence in neutral nations gave them a potential network of airfields north along the Pacific Coast, enabling long-range Luftwaffe bombers to reach and disable the Panama Canal. In fact, the four-engine Deutsche Lufthansa Focke-Wulf Fw-200 airliner was also a long-range bomber. However, there was never any evidence that the German expatriates working for Condor were Nazi agents. Brazil solved any Condor problem when it declared war on August 22, 1942. Serviços Aéreos Condor fired all the German nationals, and Brazil interred them for the duration.[3]

Pan Am profited from the purge of German airline influence in Latin America, as the American carrier stepped in to give financial support and operational expertise. "America's Merchant Marine of the Air" and its affiliated Panagra (Pan American–Grace Airways) personnel were also experts at dealing with the political challenges of the Axis collaborators and sympathizers throughout Argentina, Brazil, and Chile. FDR entrusted fellow New Yorker and Republican Juan Trippe, the Pan Am chief executive, to build vital strategic airfields in Latin America and across to Africa. America's international airline or "chosen instrument" went on to perform yeoman service as an integral element of the wartime Air Transport Command and Naval Air Transport Service.

The corporation and family most associated with American capitalism is that of John D. Rockefeller, who founded the Standard Oil Company in 1870. The administration of Theodore Roosevelt invoked the Sherman Anti-Trust Act in 1906 to break up the company, which by then controlled about 90 percent of oil production and sales. Following the breakup of Standard Oil in 1911,[4] the intuitive Rockefeller heirs thereafter gravitated toward socially responsible philanthropy. However, the Standard Oil legacy remained conflicted, seen as a symbol of both American progress and capitalist excess. John D. Rockefeller's grandson, Nelson Aldrich Rockefeller, developed a keen interest in Latin America. His focus included development of the Lake Maracaibo oil fields in Venezuela and the fact that Bolivia had nationalized Standard Oil property. Of more importance to Nelson, his personal interest was art and cultural history, and he became enamored with the southern continent. Rockefeller also developed a genuine concern about the economic and political disparity between the nations of the Americas and the peoples within the nations. He realized that memories of gunboat diplomacy and Marine Corps interventions made Latin America a ripe target for German and Italian business and political interests. Mexico, which had also nationalized all American petroleum property, was developing closer ties with Berlin. A quarter of Chile's foreign trade was with the Third Reich, and the German-controlled airline subsidiaries had gained strong footholds across Latin America. It was clear to FDR and Rockefeller that the Nazis challenged the security of the Western Hemisphere. On March 16, 1939, Republican Rockefeller met with FDR before making another trip south. There he took concrete steps to change attitudes and promote FDR's Good Neighbor policy with action rather than just words, putting family assets into liberal education and health care improvements in Venezuela.[5]

During 1939 presidential adviser Harry Hopkins came to see that Rockefeller could be a valuable member of Roosevelt's developing wartime team. Nelson was fully prepared to jump in and assist, although he was busy with efforts to open and fund the Museum of Modern Art (MoMa) in New York. On May 10, 1939, MoMa opened its new building as Lowell Thomas introduced Edsel Ford, Thomas Hutchins, and Walt Disney, and then the broadcast cut away to the White House, where a national radio audience heard FDR praise the new art museum. Rockefeller was thrilled. He continued his freelance diplomacy in Mexico, where negotiations stalled between American oil companies and the Mexican government. He initially hit a brick wall with President Lázaro Cárdenas, who reminded him that the Roosevelt administration had criticized his regime and, in his view, pushed him toward Nazi Germany. Cárdenas also set Rockefeller straight about Mexican-American history, which to him was the humiliation of losing Texas, California, Arizona, and New Mexico and the recent mistreatment and deportation of Mexicans in the United States.

Cárdenas believed that it was a matter of national spiritual and economic liberation for him to nationalize the oil fields and infrastructure, but Mexico did not have the technicians to extract or process the oil. Cárdenas and Rockefeller were able to narrow a historic and psychological gulf and begin the process of working out an agreement.[6] Meanwhile, in addition to commercial aviation, Germany continued to make hemispheric inroads in motion pictures and radio. German radio broadcasts outnumbered American broadcasts, and German investment subsidized pro-German newspapers. The United States not only was faced with a hostile Nazi-controlled Europe but a Nazified Latin America, where Germany was actively promoting fascist regime change.

Sizable German expatriate communities and a multitude of German commercial interests penetrated Latin America, where Latino nations and peoples held a traditional aversion for the Anglo United States. From the American point of view, liberal democracy was not present in most of the Latin American republics, and policy makers worried that well-established Latin American authoritarianism might be compatible with European fascism. Indeed, there were pro-Nazi groups publicly marching around and holding rallies in many cities across the Americas, where the martial spirit of the Nazis held some fascination. The war interrupted international trade and the flow of capital. Chile, for instance, lost the ability to trade with major shipping partners Germany and Japan. The Latin American economies were heading into a downturn that could result in political destabilization, so the Americas were fertile ground for Axis mischief. Regime changes manipulated by the fascists were a major fear, and one contributing factor was officially neutral Spain. Other than in Portuguese Brazil, there were Spanish Nationalists everywhere. Until the tide of war turned, the pragmatic Gen. Francisco Franco and his government were officially neutral but emotionally pro-Nazi.[7]

Americans for and against intervention in Europe, including Charles Lindbergh, favored a strong hemispheric posture. Most Americans embraced FDR's notion of a Good Neighbor policy. FDR had to create trust with Latin America, much as he had to made peace with American industry. His government had competing aims: the State Department and Sec. Cordell Hull, free trade; the Agriculture Department and Sec. Henry Wallace, leftist agrarian reform; the Treasury Department and the Commerce Department, and Secretary Jesse H. Jones, American economic interests.

On June 14, 1940, Rockefeller gave Hopkins a thousand-word memo of recommendations to reconcile these competing interests and better focus the activities of the United States in Latin America. FDR circulated Rockefeller's memo to his cabinet. Aides James Forrestal and Paul Nitze devised plans for a new agency, the Office of the Coordination of Commercial and Cultural Relations between the Americas. Nelson, the logical choice to lead the agency, asked presidential candidate and friend Wendell Willkie for advice. Willkie said, "If I were president in a period of crisis such as we face now, and I asked somebody to undertake what I considered was an important assignment in the national interest and that person turned it down for political considerations, I would lose my respect for him totally."[8]

Forrestal and Nitze made added modifications to their proposal. By July 26 the proposed name of the agency was the Commission for Pan American Affairs, and that afternoon FDR asked Rockefeller to run it. The president was not concerned with Nelson's connection with Standard Oil; as far as he was concerned, Rockefeller stood for the philanthropic Rockefeller Foundation. On August 16 FDR announced the Office for Commercial and Cultural Relations between the American Republics, which Rockefeller shortened to the Office of the Coordinator of Inter-American Affairs (ociaa). The new wartime agency existed until April 1946.[9]

From August 1940 until December 1941 the ociaa focused on countering Axis influence in Latin America, where German and Italian expatriate communities were long established. After Pearl Harbor, the ociaa adopted a policy of economic development to earn the wartime allegiance of Latin American nations, with the longer-term goal of promoting constructive social change beyond the war. Rockefeller expected a battle for the minds and hearts of Latinos with communism once the allies defeated fascism. In September 1940 Rockefeller enlisted J. Edgar Hoover and the fbi to probe the Nazi connections of American commercial interests in eighteen Latin American nations. The ociaa also had the secret

Fig. 15. Nelson A. Rockefeller, coordinator of Inter-American Affairs, 1941.
Courtesy Rockefeller Archives Center.

cooperation of the British MI6 Intelligence Service, via the covert British Security Coordination (BSC) office run by William Stephenson, coincidentally from Room 3603 at Rockefeller Center in New York. The British were extensively involved in Latin America and eager to help the officially neutral Americans.[10]

The FBI and OCIAA became aware of large-scale purchases of strategic commodities by Japanese agents, shipped through the Soviet Union to Germany. Rockefeller successfully argued for the United States to buy up industrial diamonds, rubber, lead, and other commodities to keep them away from the Nazis. In January 1941 the OCIAA went public with news that several major American industrialists with Latin American interests were colluding with the Nazis. Leading the list was Alfred B. Sloan Jr. and General Motors. At a private meeting Under Secretary of State Sumner Welles and Rockefeller met with Sloan's deputy. General Motors agreed to replace all offending employees and agents, and by May 1941, when FDR announced a state of emergency, many corporations had voluntarily severed ties with thousands of individuals shown by the OCIAA to be Nazi collaborators or sympathizers.

Rockefeller genuinely loved and respected Latin culture, which gave him the temperament to communicate American aims and candor to Latinos but also the viewpoint and needs of Latin America to Americans. It was important to him to build bridges in both directions. The OCIAA therefore encouraged and sponsored abundant cultural exchange, particularly in the arts. Famed architect and Rockefeller friend Walter Harrison directed the OCIAA cultural programs. Harrison's many major projects included Rockefeller Center, the Trylon and Perisphere structures for the 1939 New York World's Fair, and the United Nations Headquarters complex in 1952.

During 1941, frustrated by a lack of cooperation between the FBI and the American Army and Navy military intelligence agencies, British spymaster William Stephenson recommended that the United States should set up an American counterpart to his British Security Coordination office. Moreover, he had a candidate in mind, his friend Colonel William J. Donovan. When FDR appointed Donovan the coordinator of information (COI), he gave Donovan authority to collect data on national security. Rockefeller was quick to work out what he thought was an arrangement with Donovan to reserve the Western Hemisphere to OCIAA.

Rockefeller's radio information efforts got off to a slow start. The OCIAA convinced NBC and CBS to expand their outreach, and CBS president William Paley contracted to broadcast fifteen-minute newscasts. The OCIAA took over independent WRUL in Boston for $200,000. Rockefeller was trying to cobble together a radio service in the face of overwhelming German shortwave dominance. Then Donovan demanded that all radio content had to pass his (Donovan's) approval. This was a major power grab for all of radio. But Donovan had angered other agencies such as the FBI, and Hoover was not prepared to put his agents under Donovan's control. Rockefeller kept control of Latin America radio.

Then on October 11, 1941, Donovan presented Rockefeller with an ultimatum, saying, "only one agency can deal with the broadcasting companies . . . in the transmission of news, and in the matter of program schedules, direction of beams (transmitter signals) and all the mechanical matters pertaining to transmission and retransmission . . . this is no mere jurisdictional question. It is a matter of policy."[11]

Donovan's ultimatum appalled Rockefeller. He felt strongly that allowing Donovan to conduct independent psychological warfare while the State Department and OCIAA were trying to develop positive hemispheric relations as directed by FDR was dangerous.[12]

Disputes over radio frequencies and news editorial control masked the real issue, which was the autonomy of the OCIAA and, with it, an approach to Latin America that recognized what was unique about the region and its historically troubled relationship with the United States. With the support of Sumner Welles and the State Department, Harry Hopkins, and Henry Wallace, Rockefeller prepared a document that FDR signed, which kept control of Latin American communications and information dissemination with the OCIAA.[13]

By December 1941 Rockefeller's vision had extended to a "New Deal" for the Americas. The OCIAA was already sponsoring health and sanitation efforts in Brazil in anticipation of major American wartime air bases that Pan Am was presently building and a buildup of Brazilian naval bases. Depending on Nazi movements, Rockefeller took into consideration the stationing of American ground troops in Brazil.

He saw an opportunity for increased aid to Latin America but, sensitive to Latino pride, did not favor unilateral aid but partnerships, under which America would offer technological and managerial aid through local government agencies. He also proposed to devise multiyear contracts on sliding scales with America paying 80 percent of costs up front and then declining over time, with the decision to continue resting with local authorities.

Rockefeller unveiled a Basic Economy Program in March 1942. Gen. George Marshall transferred Gen. George Dunham to the program; he was a public health expert with an intimate knowledge of tropical medicine. Within months Rockefeller was introducing crop diversification, staging livestock demonstrations, and distributing thousands of baby chicks and pigs throughout Latin America. A massive public health effort rolled out into the rubber-rich Amazon Basin, which was suddenly more critical than ever to the war effort with the loss of Malaysia, Singapore, and Indonesia (the Dutch East Indies). American-built filtered water plants cut bacterial pollution, the cause of widespread dysentery. Hundreds of American nurses helped local nurses care for the people. Major efforts addressed a multitude of diseases across the hemisphere. Years after the wartime information campaigns ended, the impact of the 1941–1945 involvement of the OCIAA in Latin American economics, agriculture, and health care continued to have a positive impact. Receiving a grudging compliment years later from a State Department official about the success of the OCIAA, Rockefeller assertively noted, "and we haven't had decent relations with Latin America since!"[14]

When he launched the OCIAA, Rockefeller tapped his friend and fellow millionaire John Hay "Jock" Whitney to run the OCIAA

Motion Picture Division with the assignment of getting American films rather than Axis films shown on Latin American theater screens. Whitney, an important financier of *Gone with the Wind*, asked attorney Gunther R. Lessing to serve on his Short Subject Committee. Lessing happened to be the head of the legal department of Walt Disney Studios. By 1941 Lessing was at the epicenter of a bitter labor dispute and infamous strike that tore apart the Disney workforce. He opposed an effort to unionize the Disney studio and managed to alienate people on all sides of the issue.

Long perceived as a tranquil oasis with benevolent management, the Disney lot had grown tense by 1941, to some degree because of a volatile relationship between Walt Disney and animator Art Babbitt. Much of tension was due to politics. Babbitt was a leftist intellectual who hardened during the 1930s, never compromising and always appearing to preach to his fellow animators and other Disney employees. Babbitt confronted Disney during the production of *Fantasia* to demand a raise for his assistant animator, and Disney, angered, declined, saying "Why don't you mind you own goddamn business; if he was worth it, he'd be getting it." Disney continued, "The trouble with you is that you and your Communist friends live in a world so small you don't know what's going on around you." Disney was not the only one concerned with possible communist infiltration into Hollywood. Union leader Herb Sorrell, Babbitt, and others were under FBI surveillance.[15]

Lessing enlisted Babbitt to lead an in-house Federation of Screen Cartoonists, which Babbitt came to realize was simply an effort to block accredited unions from the studio. In the fall of 1940 the Screen Cartoonists Guild contacted Babbitt about formally unionizing Disney, and he became a key organizer of the American Federation of Labor (AFL) initiative. Babbitt recruited Disney employees off campus and on the Disney lot. Warned to stop doing so on company property, Babbitt refused. Hollywood union leader Herb Sorrell presented Disney with four hundred signatures from employees asking to join the AFL-affiliated Screen Cartoonists Guild. During the spring of 1941 the Screen Cartoonists Guild appealed to the National Labor Relations Board (NLRB), which declared the Federation of Screen Cartoonists illegal. By coincidence, the Burbank Police Department arrested Babbitt for carrying a concealed weapon, which appeared staged. On May 17, 1941, employees learned that only qualified "artists" would be eligible for union representation and continued job security. On May 26, 1941, two studio policemen came to Babbitt's office with a letter of termination from Lessing and escorted Babbitt off the property. Disney fired twenty animators. That evening the Screen Artists Guild voted to strike Disney. Babbitt became the strident public face and voice of the strike, although only one other senior animator walked out in support.[16]

Babbitt intensified his attacks. He labeled Walt an "America Firster" who "saw Communists behind every tree and bush." Babbitt circulated rumors that Disney attended German-American Bund (or Nazi Party) meetings with Lessing and prominent actors and musicians.[17]

Enabling Babbitt was the fact that in 1938 Disney had hosted German filmmaker Leni Riefenstahl during a Hollywood visit by Hitler's famed filmmaker. At best, Disney's timing and optics were poor; at worst, this confirmed the suspicion of leftists that the capitalist and conservative Disney was their enemy if not an actual Nazi, and that negative impression continues into the twenty-first century.

The strike had come at a critical juncture for Walt Disney. Although *Snow White* and *Pinocchio* were big hits, *Dumbo* (October 1941) and *Bambi* (August 1942) were still in preproduction, and the absorbing *Fantasia* was not doing as well as expected at the box office. The war in Europe cut off markets and capital.

The problem was that unions ran against Disney's work ethic and self-made individualism. The paternalistic Disney could not bring himself to believe that his studio family would strike him. In early 1941 he went before his employees in a studio theater to explain his thinking in a carefully worded speech, which he explained was necessary for legal reasons. Disney gave a candid if defensive speech that explained his worldview and core values.[18] Disney believed in majority rule and wanted an open studio and a vote by secret ballot among his employees to choose their bargaining agent. Herb Sorrell demanded that the Screen Cartoonists Guild was the sole collective bargaining agent and that there would be no vote.

Disney was ill-served by Lessing, who always bragged about the fact that he had once represented Pancho Villa. Lessing urged Disney to stand tough, which only further alienated the strikers. The normally congenial Disney came across as inflexible.[19]

On July 2 Walt Disney ran a full-page ad in *Variety* and other trade publications. The ad was a letter to "my employees on strike" and offered reinstatement, union recognition, a closed shop, retroactive pay, increased wages, and paid vacations.[20] Disney stated: "I believe that you have been misled and misinformed about the real issues underlying the strike . . . I am positively convinced that Communist agitation, leadership and activities have brought about this strike and have persuaded you to reject this fair and equitable settlement. I address you in this manner because I have no other means of reaching you."[21]

This ad appeared the morning after the Screen Cartoonist Guild membership approved a proposed contract submitted by AFL negotiators.[22] The day after Disney's ad, the strikers replied with an ad that said: "Dear Walt, Willie Bioff is not our leader. Present your terms to OUR elected leaders, so that they may be submitted to us and there should be no difficulty in quickly settling our differences."[23] William Morris Bioff led the International Alliance of Theatrical Stage Employees. On June 30 Bioff met with the strikers and told them that if they joined the IATSE there would be a favorable settlement. The same day a federal grand jury indicted Bioff on the charge of trying to extort $500,000 from several studios. The strikers declined Bioff's offer and ended further negotiations.[24]

On July 8, on orders from FDR, the Department of Labor contacted the parties to affect a settlement.[25] Gunther Lessing refused the president's offer to arbitrate. This came as a surprise to Whitney, who was a major Disney shareholder. Union representatives naturally pounced on Lessing's refusal as being unpatriotic.[26] By July 23 the media reported that Sorrell was holding out for 100 percent of pay retroactive to the start of the strike. They also noted that Bioff had withdrawn from trying to muscle in on an AFL deal.[27] Picket lines greeted the RKO release of Disney's *The Reluctant Dragon* at theaters around the country, as well as *Fantasia*, which was in its thirty-seventh week of exhibition. Disney had just wrapped *Dumbo*, which was set for release in October. Finally, on July 30, the trades announced that government arbitration was underway. The company agreed to retroactive pay from May 15 forward and permanent reinstatement of the employees let go before the strike, including Babbitt. The AFL instructed workers at Technicolor Processing, who had refused to process Disney films, to end their boycott.[28] On August 11 Roy Disney, Walt's brother and the studio financial chief, proposed to lay off 207 strikers and 49 nonstrikers, saying that the studio would have to cut costs to accommodate a new union agreement. Disney was under intense pressure from lead lender Bank of America to straighten out its finances, rationalize its workforce, and settle the strike.[29] On August 15 Roy Disney closed the studio until September 15, except for a skeleton crew finishing *Dumbo* and several other features. Roy traveled to Washington to resolve the strike. On September 9 he agreed to settle via binding arbitration, and on September 12 the federal conciliators issued a ruling settling the ratio of layoffs of strikers to nonstrikers. The strike officially ended on September 14, and work resumed on September 16 with 694 employees on the payroll, down from 1,200. Roy and Walt felt sandbagged by the government, who favored the union.[30]

In May 1941 Walt Disney met with Whitney and his assistant Frances Alstock at the studio. By June, Roy Disney and Lessing met with Whitney in New York to arrange a $150,000 OCIAA contract for short subjects with Latin American themes. Rockefeller and Whitney wanted more. They asked Walt to make a goodwill tour to South America, where he was well known and liked. By the time Disney agreed, the tour became a filmmaking venture as well as a "movie ambassador" assignment. The OCIAA offered to underwrite the entire tour and guarantee Disney that he would recoup the costs of any motion pictures made from the trip.[31] Disney considered the tour a combination business and pleasure tour, and he needed a change of scenery.[32]

"El Grupo," as they called themselves, left Burbank's Lockheed Air Terminal on an American Airlines DC-3 on August 11, 1941. Aboard were Walt, his wife, Lillian, and seventeen associates. They had to fly east via Fort Worth and Nashville before changing planes to Eastern Airlines for Jacksonville and Miami. After a layover they embarked on Pan Am from Miami to Rio de Janeiro via San Juan, Belem, and Barreiras aboard a Boeing 307 Stratoliner. The Boeing 307 was a four-engine landplane and the first pressurized airliner. It allowed Pan Am to compete in terms of range and speed with the four-engine Focke-Wulf Fw-200 Condor airliners that Deutsche Lufthansa had assigned to Syndicato Condor.

For years Pan Am flew seaplanes from Miami to Brazil that had to land on water and therefore fly east and south around Brazil rather than a direct line over the interior. With the approval of the Brazilian government, Pan Am and Panair do Brasil constructed an airport at Barreiras, the westernmost point of the state of Bahia. They also put in paved runways at Belo Horizonte and Belém. It took Pan Am seven years to complete engineering surveys. In 1939 the Pan Am. technical committee and President Getúlio Vargas approved the plan. Construction started in 1940, with supplies, building materials, and aviation fuel sent in by ship and rail. The Barreiras "cutoff" opened on September 1, 1940, when the B-307 *Clipper Comet* landed on the ceremonial first southbound trip.[33]

At Barreiras, El Grupo experienced their first taste of what was a celebrated and rejuvenating tour. Hundreds of schoolchildren had unexpectedly gathered at the airport to greet Walt Disney when the Stratoliner landed.[34] Word of his arrival spread. Arriving at Rio de Janeiro, local officials and the general population welcomed Disney as a sort of a folk hero. El Groupo set up a studio and began to shoot 16mm color film of their activities for the animated feature *Saludos Amigos* and the OCIAA feature *South of the Border with Disney*. The studio later assembled another feature film, *The Three Caballeros*, using ideas and film footage gathered during the tour.[35]

The OCIAA subsidized *Saludos Amigos*, but Disney ended up making money on it anyway. Disney released *Saludos Amigos* in English, Spanish, and Portuguese. The animated film has vignettes focused on Argentina, Brazil, Chile, and the Andes. Disney enlisted Brazilian composer Ary de Resende Barroso and introduced his hit composition *Aquarela do Brazil* in the film, along with a new animated character, the smooth parrot "el papagayo" Jose Carioca, to terrorize silly gringo Donald Duck.[36]

During their August 16 to September 8 sojourn in Rio de Janeiro, El Grupo made a side trip to Sao Paulo, and then they settled in Buenos Aires from September 8 through September 28. During a trip to Montevideo and Uruguay, schools closed for the day in Colonia del Sacramento when "the father of Mickey and Donald" arrived. Although Disney had wanted a working trip, it was also the successful goodwill tour that the OCIAA had envisioned.

"Walt Disney is far more successful as an enterprise and a person than we could have dreamed," Whitney reported to Rockefeller from Rio on August 29. "His public demeanor is flawless. He is unruffled by adulation and pressure. He just signs every autograph and keeps smiling."

Film footage shot by El Grupo and media photographs show a relaxed Disney enjoying Copacabana Beach in Rio or putting on a gaucho outfit on the Pampas, looking much like his animated character Goofy would look like in *Saludos Amigos* as a funny gringo Texas cowboy visiting the Argentine. An unending series of receptions, parties, screenings, interviews, and public appearances interrupted the trip's working itinerary. The Argentine part of the trip coincided with the premier of *Fantasia* in Buenos Aires. Disney had agreed to make a series of short subjects with Latin American themes and OCIAA underwriting and returned with enough ideas and material for the OCIAA shorts, his two theatrical features, and the OCIAA featurette. Disney did more than just shake hands, and the dizzy pace of the tour helped restore his confidence and "joie de vivre."

Leaving Buenos Aires, El Grupo split up to cover more territory. Walt and Lillian, accompanied by Bill and Hazel Cottrell,

Fig. 16. Walt Disney (*third from right*) with El Grupo in Brazil on a goodwill and working tour of Latin America for the Office of the Coordinator of Inter-American Affairs, August 1941. The tour led to the production of *South of the Border with Disney, Saludos Amigos, The Three Caballeros*, and four short-subject films. From the records of the Office of the Coordinator of Inter-American Affairs, RG 229, NARA.

went to Mendoza, Argentina. Others scattered to La Paz, Bolivia, and Lake Titicaca as well as locations in Argentina and Chile. Disney flew over the Andes to Santiago, Chile, and Cottrell filmed the flight, where some of the artists thought up a new character, a little airplane named Pedro. El Grupo members also toured Peru, Ecuador, Colombia, Venezuela, Panama, Costa Rica, Nicaragua, El Salvador, Honduras, Guatemala, and Mexico.[37] Walt and Lillian boarded the Grace liner *Santa Clara*, transited the Panama Canal, and reached New York on October 20, 1941, in time to attend the premiere of *Dumbo*.

Caught in the Draft

Disney returned to Burbank to learn that the settlement gave the union everything they had wanted. Also, his father Elias had passed away while Walt was in South America. Shortly thereafter, the United States was at war. Disney made the OCIAA-oriented shorts and expanded its government contracts for military training and information shorts for the OWI Domestic and Overseas branches. Animators designed popular logos for military units and answered thousands of requests. One of the first non-OCIAA shorts was *Donald Duck in Nutzi Land*, wherein Donald Duck has a nightmare that he is working in a Nazi ammunition factory. Disney renamed the short because Spike Jones and his City Slickers had a runaway hit with the song featured in the cartoon, *Der Fuhrer's Face*.[38]

Disney found his old enthusiasm with *Victory through Air Power*, based on a book by Russian émigré Alexander P. de Seversky that aviation buff Disney had read and felt was vitally important. Walt made the feature with his own money, and he convinced de Seversky to appear in it. Disney wanted the government and public to hear and see de Seversky's compelling and, as it turned out, generally correct theories, although cynical *New York Times* film critic James Agee thought the message was "high pressure" and "open to question." FDR and Churchill saw it and disagreed with Agree. They felt it was a valuable educational and motivational tool. *Victory through Air Power* proved Disney as a legitimate producer of quality documentary and educational films. Some of de Seversky's recommendations were impractical, such as basing long-range bombers in the Aleutians to attack Japan. But the film had a significant impact and cemented Disney's value to a unified nation in wartime and beyond.[39]

At 7:07 p.m. on January 16, 1942, veteran Transcontinental & Western Airlines Capt. Wayne C. Williams taxied TWA Flight 3 into position for takeoff at Las Vegas, Nevada, for the final leg of a cross-country flight. from New York's La Guardia Field to the Burbank Air Terminal serving Los Angeles. There were nineteen passengers aboard the daily DC-3 "Sky Apache." In addition to fifteen Army Air Forces personnel assigned to the Ferrying Command at Long Beach, there were four civilians, Lois Hamilton of Lincoln Park, Michigan, traveling to join her husband in the service stationed in California, Otto Winkler, MGM publicity representative, actress Carole Lombard, and her mother, Elizabeth K. Peters.

Registered as NC 1946, the plane was running late. The Army Air Forces personnel with travel priority bumped civilians, including violinist Joseph Szigeti, off the plane at Albuquerque. Lombard refused to give up her seat. When Flight 3 left Las Vegas, the dry desert sky was clear, dark, and full of stars. About twenty minutes later the men at the Blue Diamond Mine heard a loud explosion and saw a bright flash of light. A ball of fire rose from near the summit of Potosi Mountain, thirty miles southwest of Las Vegas. A search team from the Clark County sheriff's office and the army were not able to reach the crash site until 9:00 a.m. the next morning due to the remote location and rugged terrain. When the men arrived at the wreckage at 7,700 feet, it was tragically clear that NC 1946 had slammed directly into the wall of the mountain just below the peak, broke apart, and slid into a ravine. Pine trees had burned, and snow had melted away. There were no survivors. Clark County sheriff Gene Ward placed the site under armed guard.

Escorted by several MGM executives, Lombard's husband, actor Clark Gable, flew to Las Vegas. Eddie Mannix and Ralph Wheelright persuaded the distraught Gable not to climb all the way up to the crash site. Mannix identified what was left of Carole Lombard's dismembered body in the crushed forward section of the DC-3.

On July 20, 1942, the Civil Aeronautics Board (CAB) found that the captain did not follow the proper course after takeoff. When the pilots filed their flight plan at Albuquerque, they planned to stop at Boulder City and not Las Vegas. The compass heading from Boulder City for the airway to Silver City, California, was 218 degrees. TWA Flight 3 flew a 218-degree heading out of Las Vegas and directly into the mountain range instead of over the desert. Flying a 218-degree heading at 8,000 feet from Boulder City was perfectly safe. The compass heading for the airway from Las Vegas was 205 degrees. Due to wartime security, beacons along the routes were off at night, and the pilots simply flew NC 1946 directly into Mt. Potosi.[40]

After Lombard's funeral a devastated and remorseful Gable told former Hollywood screenwriter Capt. Sy Bartlett of the AAF public relations office in Washington that he wanted to enlist in the AAF.[41] General Arnold sent a message addressed to Gable: "Capt. Sy Bartlett, whom you know informs me you wish to join the Air Forces. If we do not, repeat do not, conflict with your studio's plans for you, I believe in my capacity as chief of the Army Air Forces, we have a specific and highly important assignment for you. Capt. Bartlett will be in California within a fortnight and will discuss my plans with you."[42]

At the direction of MGM chief Louis B. Mayer, publicity manager Howard Strickling did not give the message to Gable because Mayer did not believe Gable was emotionally ready to join the military. After finishing the film *Somewhere I'll Find You* with seductive Lana Turner, an unsuspecting Gable walked into a Los Angeles recruiting office to enlist. MGM quickly got back to Bartlett and asked what the studio could do to help.

MGM pulled strings for cinematographer Andrew McIntyre to enlist and go with Gable through training. The forty-one-year-old Gable and McIntyre enlisted in Los Angeles August 12 with the press, public, and AAF public relations officers present. The men went to the Officer Candidate School at Miami Beach, and on August 17 they entered Class 42-E. Gable and McIntyre completed training on October 28 and became second lieutenants.[43] Gable's assignment was to produce a film about aerial gunners in combat with the Eighth Air Force in England. He attended Flexible Gunnery School at Tyndall Field, Panama City, Florida. An avid hunter, Gable had no difficulty at gunnery school and graduated January 6, 1943. When he and McIntyre joined the 351st BG at Pueblo Army Air Field, Colorado, their six-man motion picture unit included screenwriter John Lee Mahin, camera operators Sgt. Mario Toti and Sgt. Robert Boles, and sound man Lt. Howard Voss. The 351st BG arrived at Polebrook, Northamptonshire, on May 1. Gable flew on five combat missions. On August 12, during an attack on Bochum, Germany, a 20 mm shell came up through the B-17 flight deck, cut off the heel from Gable's boot, and exited one foot from his head without exploding. On September 23, Gable took part in a strike to the port area of Nantes, France. He left his film crew in the waist of the bomber and manned a gun in the nose.[44]

Gable was embarrassed to win the Air Medal on October 4 and later the Distinguished Flying Cross.[45] He left the 351st BG November 5, returning to the United States with over fifty thousand feet of 16 mm color film. He joined the AAF First Motion Picture Unit in Hollywood to edit and complete his film, and in May 1944 he became a major. The AAF and the OWI released *Combat America* in September 1944 for nationwide theater exhibition.[46]

A remarkable transformation was creating the most powerful air force in the world. To market the Army Air Forces, General Arnold made the most assertive use of radio and motion pictures by any of the uniformed services and enlisted top-level media talent to do so. The American public of 1942 did not really know what an air force was. Heavily invested in innovative science and engineering, the AAF amounted to a "high tech" branch of the armed forces.[47] Arnold gathered around him a brilliant group of officers who intuitively knew how to secure the support of industry and government to build modern planes and air bases. They developed the largest educational system in the world to train flying and ground personnel. Colleagues including aviator Lt. Col. Jimmy Doolittle went on active duty before Pearl Harbor to convince industrialists such as Edsel Ford to convert from automobile manufacturing to building massive airplane manufacturing plants at locations such as Willow Run, Michigan. Arnold recruited the airline industry to create a global air transportation network. And the AAF reached out to the entertainment industry for talent to staff radio and motion picture production units.

The AAF envisioned radio production units in Hollywood and New York, The First AAF Radio Production Unit formed in 1942 at Santa Ana Army Air base near Hollywood. Maj. Eddie Dunstedter was commanding officer, and Sgt. Felix Slatkin initially shared musical directing duties with Sgt. Harry Bluestone. Slatkin and Bluestone had worked as musical directors for Hollywood motion picture studio orchestras and were highly respected and classically trained musicians. In 1943 Capt. Glenn Miller formed what became the Second A A F Radio Production Unit at the A A F Technical School, Yale University, New Haven, Connecticut, near the New York network radio and recording studios.[48]

The A A F formed its First Motion Picture Unit (F M P U) on July 1, 1942. The F M P U consisted of officers and enlisted personnel who had been employed as civilians by the motion picture industry. It produced over four hundred A A F training films and publicly exhibited documentaries, including *Memphis Belle: The Story of a Flying Fortress* and *Thunderbolt!* produced by Maj. William Wyler, as well as *Combat America*, produced by Maj. Clark Gable. Wyler filmed *The Memphis Belle* at great personal risk, flying on highly dangerous bombing missions over enemy territory. During one attack Wyler lost consciousness from lack of oxygen. Wyler's cinematographer, Lt. Harold J. Tannenbaum, lost his life while filming aboard a B-17 that went down when hit by enemy fire.[49]

After Pearl Harbor Arnold commissioned Jack L. Warner as a lieutenant colonel assigned to the A A F Public Relations office and working from Hollywood. Producer Hal Wallis and screenwriter Owen E. Crump went with Warner to meet with Arnold in Washington, and Arnold also commissioned Crump as a captain. Warner's chief pilot, Paul Mantz, a reserve officer, returned to active duty after completing *Captains of the Clouds* on location in Canada. Wallis was in production of the film *Casablanca* and could not accept a commission.[50] Col. Roy M. Jones became commander of the entire F M P U studio and aviation operation with Maj. Crump running the motion picture studio and Lt. Col. Mantz doing the flying. Crump discovered the Hal Roach Studio in Culver City was available and well suited to the A A F's needs. He set up the F M P U at the Hal Roach lot, which quickly gained the nickname "Fort Roach."

The A A F needed one hundred thousand pilots. The first project, started before the F M P U was anything more than a concept, was the recruiting film *Winning Your Wings*, filmed under contract by Warner Brothers and starring Lt. James Stewart, the former M G M actor and active duty pilot. Stewart was loath to do film work, having just escaped the industry. However, when Crump explained the importance of the project, Stewart relented. Director John Huston was able to wrap *Winning Your Wings* in only two weeks.

Capt. Ronald Reagan served as Crump's administrative officer. When Reagan resumed his civilian career and became head of the Screen Actors Guild, governor of California, and president of the United States, observers were surprised the actor was capable of administering organizations. Reagan's experience as the FMPU officer responsible for managing several hundred temperamental film industry professionals in uniform gave him early experience in handling egos, coordinating projects, and meeting deadlines. Media and political critics would later dismiss Reagan's FMPU experience as that of someone who had avoided combat or was merely a propagandist. The reality was that all the "Culver City Commandos" were of high value to Arnold and the AAF because of their résumés. The same was true of the men who served in the AAF Radio Production Units. There were many thousands of young men who could learn to fly or fix planes but fewer than a thousand who knew how to make movies, produce radio broadcasts, or professionally make music. Crump remembered, "Reagan was too identifiable to be used as an actor, so we used him as a narrator. I made him personnel officer. He was wonderful at it. Warm."[51]

B. Reaves Eason directed *Men of the Sky*, the second of four films produced by Warner Brothers for the AAF. Crump wrote the script and narrated the film. General Arnold appears in the opening scene and speaks on location at Santa Ana. *Men of the Sky* was shot in Technicolor and, like *Winning Your Wings*, addressed concerns of potential airmen and their families about AAF service. Warner Brothers made two more films before Fort Roach went into operation, *Beyond the Line of Duty*, directed by Louis Seiler, and *The Rear Gunner*, directed by Ray Enright and starring Lt. Burgess Meredith.

In May 1941 Irving Berlin approached the army about staging his World War I play *Yip! Yip! Yaphank*, updated to 1941 for the benefit of the troops stationed at Camp Upton, New York, who were mostly fresh draftees. Gen. Alexander Surles was interested and recommended a full-scale Broadway production. General Marshall approved a plan allowing Berlin to personally conduct arrangements and rehearsals at Camp Upton.

Berlin insisted upon an integrated all-solider cast including African American troops, a major concession the army accepted. The men involved had to continue military drill and training duties while taking part in the production. *This Is the Army* ran at the Broadway Theatre from July 4 to September 26, 1942. The successful production then went on the road with a national tour concluding in San Francisco on February 13, 1943. The production earned over $2 million for the Army Emergency Relief Fund. Despite the recording ban, Decca Records issued an original cast album with the approval of the AFM. There were ironic moments during the planning and rehearsals of *This Is the Army*. The producer Sgt. Ezra Stone was trying to explain his concept of using the melody of Berlin's "Puttin' on the Ritz" for "That's What the Well-Dressed Man in Harlem Will Wear," a rousing routine that the African American soldiers would perform. To his astonishment Stone discovered Berlin did not read or write music.

Jack L. Warner offered $250,000 for the motion picture rights to the play and at Berlin's direction donated the funds to the Army Emergency Relief Fund. Warner also pledged to donate all profits from the film to the fund. The 359 members of the army production troupe went to Hollywood to make the film version of *This Is the Army*. The AAF loaned Lt. Ronald Reagan to the production, and heavyweight boxing champion Sgt. Joe Louis appeared in the film. Kate Smith performed her signature Berlin classic, "God Bless America." Berlin cast himself, re-creating "Oh! How I Hate to Get Up in the Morning" from *Yip! Yip! Yaphank*. Warner Brothers released the motion picture with great fanfare in August 1943. The Army Emergency Relief received the film's profits of $9 million. In October 1943 a slimmed-down 150-man *This Is the Army* troupe sailed for Great Britain to start an overseas tour. Berlin flew ahead to London to lead them.[52]

Upstaged by the army, the AAF wanted its own piece of Broadway. In May 1943 General Arnold approached prominent playwright

Moss Hart to write a play based on the AAF Training Command. At Arnold's suggestion Hart "drafted" himself as a buck private. With a bomber and crew assigned to him, he covered some twenty-eight thousand miles getting acquainted with the programs offered at twenty different basic training units, technical schools, and flying schools.[53] Hart wrote a patriotic and uplifting stage play he titled *Winged Victory*. He did his homework and squeezed in as much of a feel for the AAF as he could onto a Broadway stage. Lt. Irving "Swifty" Lazar and Lt. Benjamin Landis joined Hart to produce the play and assemble a cast. The players had to be AAF personnel, and Arnold ordered that the theater company had to be racially integrated. Arnold also recommended that the story be about men training to fly the Consolidated/Ford B-24 Liberator bomber, which Americans were assembling in enormous plants at Fort Worth and Willow Run in greater numbers than the Boeing B-17.[54]

The *Winged Victory* cast included Lt. Leonard de Paur's forty-two-member choral group from among the company, which carried most of the musical weight of the play about a group of recruits struggling through pilot training. Capt. Glenn Miller helped organize the Winged Victory Orchestra. One of his suggestions was to bring in M/Sgt. Norman Leyden from the Twenty-Eighth AAF Band to conduct. Composer T/Sgt. David Rose conducted the premiere of the production and received extensive publicity. He left the nightly performances of the production for other duties soon after it debuted. Leyden conducted for the rest of the New York theater run.[55] After a trial run in Boston, *Winged Victory* opened to a packed house at the 42nd Street Theatre on Broadway the evening of Saturday, November 20. As with *This Is the Army*, the Army Emergency Relief Fund received the proceeds from the production. *Winged Victory* was a major success, playing to over 350,000 people in 226 performances. Darryl F. Zanuck of 20th Century Fox secured the rights for the play after seeing it on Broadway. When the theater company moved west in May 1944, Leyden joined Miller's Second AAF Radio Production Unit staff. Production started June 15, 1944, and George Cukor directed the film.[56] 20th Century Fox released *Winged Victory* December 22, 1944. When the film wrapped, the theater company went on a national tour that included 445 performances for over 800,000 people.[57]

The Army Specialist Corps (ASC) was a military expediency to fast-track musicians, producers, actors, theater managers, dramatics professors, and recreational and hospitality professionals into the army with the aim of ramping up Special Services to serve the vast influx of Americans streaming into the armed forces. From the start the controversial program drew the resentment of the military bureaucracy and scrutiny from members of Congress concerned about "special treatment" for celebrities to avoid the draft.[58] Political pressure forced the army to fold the ASC in November 1942, but not before 918 officers completed the ASC orientation course at Fort Meade, Maryland. The most notable among them was Capt. Glenn Miller, who enlisted after disbanding his popular dance band on September 27, 1942. On November 25, two days after completing the course, Miller received orders to report to Maxwell Field, Alabama, and the Army Air Forces.[59]

Sec. of War Henry Stimson held a press conference on September 17, 1942, to address congressional concern about special service commissions. The War Manpower Commission (WMC) sought the cooperation of the armed services to regulate the enlisting and commissioning of civilians employed in any of thirty-four "essential industries" or government agencies.[60] The WMC was concerned about potential manpower shortages in key industries and making nonessential personnel available for Selective Service. The WMC did not consider the entertainment industry essential, but the WMC was among the government agencies that expected the entertainment industry to support the war effort.

On December 7, 1941, isolationist Sen. Gerald P. Nye was giving an America First address and did not stop when handed a message about the attack on Pearl Harbor. He came under withering press criticism for only announcing the attack after he finished. However, Nye did vote the next day to declare war.[61] Nye remained a wartime thorn in FDR's side as a leading critic of the OWI. He alleged that broadcasting and entertainment industry professionals received favoritism for military commissions, the draft, and the war effort. By November 1942 Nye was on the warpath.[62] He opposed everything that the Roosevelt administration proposed, which is why it was ironic that the unrehabilitated isolationist would find an ally in liberal activist First Lady Eleanor Roosevelt, who was usually a staunch supporter of the OWI. Nye's issue with the existence of the Army Specialist Corps was one reason the Pentagon had phased it out. Nye had allies not only in the Senate but also on House budget committees. The unsuspecting, unassuming, and sincere bandleader Jerome Kern "Kay" Kyser, who was not in uniform, became Nye's number one high-profile target. Only Glenn Miller matched Kyser's record sales and financial earnings. His homespun NBC *Kollege of Musical Knowledge* series may have come across to sophisticated listeners as corny, but it was one of the highest-rated programs on network radio. Kyser registered for the draft and received a call-up notice in November 1942 that the OWI asked to be set aside. Nye promptly accused the OWI of helping Kyser avoid the draft, painting Kyser as a draft dodger trying to buy a cushy commission. An unlikely villain, Kyser spent the next six months repeating only that he wanted to serve his country in the best way he could.

The AFM was seeking an executive order from FDR to declare music an "essential wartime industry" and protect musicians from the draft. Broadcasters were seeking similar draft protection for radio station employees. Elmer Davis supported the musicians and the broadcasters, telling the press "entertainment and morale in wartime is an urgent national necessity." To Davis, this included Kyser, who by this time was commuting to Washington as chairman of the OWI music industry advisory group. Davis believed that this vital work was in the best interest of the nation and properly exempted Kyser from the draft.

Nye challenged Davis, who confirmed that the OWI contacted draft boards on behalf of Kyser and fifteen other "persons vital to the OWI mission" to recommend exemptions. Davis said, "Mr. Kyser can do much more to help us win the war by continuing in his present role and with his productive public activities than by handing him a rifle." Nye and Paul V. McNutt, chief of the wmc, disagreed. McNutt did not act favorably on the petitions of the musicians' union and broadcasting industry in their rare show of solidarity in seeking draft deferments for performers and radio station staffers.[63]

As the whirlpool of controversy swirled around him, Kyser continued to keep a low profile, maintaining his radio, motion picture, and personal appearance commitments and working with the owi to coordinate radio series such as *Uncle Sam Presents* and *Music from America*. He worked with the Treasury Department to develop the *Treasury Star Parade* series. Kyser was also helping uso Camp Shows, Inc. to coordinate bands and form entertainment troupes.

Then Eleanor Roosevelt joined the public debate. When asked about celebrities and the draft, the First Lady declared everyone of any status ought to submit to the draft and not be given special privilege to become officers or receive deferments for morale purposes. She mentioned Kay Kyser by name in her *My Day* syndicated newspaper column, although she mistakenly thought that the bandleader could become an enlisted man and then go back to the type of work he was already performing. As if on Eleanor's cue, Selective Service announced that they would call up for service individuals classified 3-a, and they were penciling-out a 4-h classification for entertainers. In response to the First Lady, Davis said the band business was as essential for civilian morale as military morale. The private proprietors such as hotels, theaters, and ballrooms where many essential civilians and war workers sought their recreation could not employ an army band. As a civilian, Kyser could divide his time between the civilian venues and the army camps, with each benefitting without a loss to the other.[64] The owi also pointed out that Kyser had spent $104,000 out of his own pocket to cover the added expenses of broadcasting *Kollege of Musical Knowledge* from army camps; the bandleader had sold vast numbers of War Bonds, and he had made transcontinental plane trips weekly at his own expense to consult the owi.

It was Kay Kyser, or more precisely, his physical condition, that ended the controversy. His draft board rejected his appeal for deferment. The North Carolina Selective Service Board took an appeal of Kyser's 1-A classification filed by the OWI all the way to the White House, and FDR personally upheld the rejection. Kyser appeared for his induction physical at Rocky Mount, North Carolina, with the attendant press fanfare. Then he promptly flunked due to severe chronic arthritis.[65]

Overseas Circuit

Immediately after showing *The Battle of Midway* to FDR in August 1942, Cmdr. John Ford flew to Britain aboard a Pan American Boeing 314 serving with the Naval Air Transport Service, accompanied by Chief Petty Officer (CPO) Jack Pennick. They settled into the luxurious Claridge's and started preparing Field Photo units for Operation Torch, the pending invasion of French North Africa at Oran, Algiers, and Casablanca. His men went to British Commando School at Achnacarry in Scotland for special training and physical conditioning. American forces went ashore on November 8. Ford, with Pennick and photographer's mate Robert Johannes, arrived at Algiers from Gibraltar on November 14. In Bone, Algeria, Ford caught up with Col. Darryl F. Zanuck, who had put on an Army Signal Corps uniform and was full of bravado. Zanuck's commission was controversial, as no one really knew what he was supposed to be doing, and he soon returned to the inactive list. Taking leave of Zanuck, Ford and his crew of thirty-two cameramen saw considerable action in Algeria and Tunisia.[66] By late January 1943 Ford was back at OSS headquarters in Washington and learned of his promotion to captain. Ford and Gregg Toland resurrected their embargoed Pearl Harbor footage and trimmed it to an eighty-five-minute feature titled *December 7th,* which explores the period leading up to Pearl Harbor and then the attack itself. Ford made a shorter thirty-four-minute version that cut negative if honest recrimination about who was to blame into a positive story of how America took the blow and bounced back.[67] The government did not put either film into general release, but the military and the OWI exhibited the shorter version at military bases and industrial plants as a morale tool. On the heels of 1942's *The Battle of Midway*, the shorter version of *December 7th* received an Academy Award for Best Documentary of 1943, Ford's second award in a row while in uniform.

Notable social welfare associations had set up canteens, reading rooms, and meeting places on and off bases to serve the needs of America's growing military population during 1941, among them the American Red Cross, Salvation Army, Young Men's Christian Association (YMCA), the Young Women's Christian Association (YWCA), National Catholic Community Services, National Jewish Welfare Board, and National Traveler's Aid Association. President Roosevelt and the government wished to create a unified effort aimed at military welfare and joined with the social welfare organizations to form the United Service Organizations (USO). To provide entertainment for the military, the Hollywood Victory Committee and other entertainment groups formed USO Camp Shows, Inc., a corporation affiliated with the USO, on October 30, 1941. The War and Navy Departments designated USO Camp Shows, Inc. as the official entertainer of the armed forces, and General Marshall gave USO Camp Shows, Inc. exclusivity for overseas entertainment tours under control of theater commanders. No commercially sponsored productions could travel overseas for the duration of the war.[68]

USO Camp Shows organized activities around four basic "circuits" or types of tours:

The Victory Circuit, full-sized revues and concerts

The Blue Circuit, smaller touring companies

The Hospital Circuit, to visit wards and auditoriums at military hospitals

The Overseas Circuit, known also as the Foxhole Circuit, for foreign trips

In 1942 the first small overseas entertainment troupes followed the American forces across the Atlantic to Great Britain and North Africa. Subsequent groups ventured into the South Pacific. Prominent stars Jack Benny, Joe E. Brown, Bob Hope, and Al Jolson led the pioneering USO troupes into England and North Africa. Radio celebrities traveled between network seasons, or between July and October. Female stars Kay Francis, Carole Landis, Mitzi Mayfair, and Martha Raye had their exploits memorialized by 20th Century Fox in the 1944 film *Four Jills and a Jeep*. Originally titled *Command Performance*, the film resembled the radio series.

On Tuesday, May 6, 1941, Leslie Towns "Bob" Hope broadcast *The Pepsodent Show* episode no. 111 on the NBC Red Network live from March Field, the major Army Air Forces base at Riverside in San Bernardino County, with his entourage including Jerry Colonna, Frances Langford, Vera Vague, announcer Bill Goodwin, and Skinnay Ennis with his band. It was Hope's first personal appearance and broadcast from a military base. The warm reception the military audience gave to Hope convinced the comedian to do more. The routines he and his famously large retinue of writers crafted for military audiences became a model for all wartime service entertainment.[69] Following his 1942–1943 radio season finale, Hope, Langford, guitarist Tony Romano, and vaudevillian Jack Pepper left La Guardia Field for Britain aboard a Pan Am Boeing 314 Clipper serving with the Naval Air Transport Service. The troupe went on to North Africa, Sicily, and Italy. They returned to Britain before heading home, and Hope appeared on the cover of *Time* on September 20, 1943. The caption under his picture read, "First in the Hearts of the Servicemen." Hope and company, with Jerry Colonna, traveled to the South Pacific during the summer of 1944 and returned to Europe during the summer of 1945.[70]

In 1935 Congress awarded George M. Cohan a Congressional Gold Medal, the civilian equivalent of the Medal of Honor, in recognition of his many patriotic tunes. Cohan was embarrassed and would not accept the award from President Roosevelt until 1940. Around the same time, with Cohan's blessing, students at Georgetown University in Washington staged a college production called *Yankee Doodle Boy*, the story of his life told through his music, and Jack L. Warner bought the rights to the play. Retitled *Yankee Doodle Dandy* and starring James Cagney, Warner Brothers released the film version of the musical on May 29, 1942. Cohan's patriotism was back in vogue, and the film was a major success, earning Cagney the Academy Award for Best Actor. Cohan was thrilled with Cagney's performance but developed cancer and died November 5, 1942.

By 1942 Irving Berlin was clearly at the top of his profession. "White Christmas" was the quintessential wartime ballad of home-sick troops. It became his most successful composition thanks to the best-selling record of all time, recorded by Bing Crosby (with John Scott Trotter's Orchestra backing him), although the Columbia record by Charlie Spivak and His Orchestra, with Garry Stevens handling the vocal chores, was the first record released. Crosby debuted "White Christmas" on his NBC Red *Kraft Music Hall* program on Thursday, December 25, 1941. The tune was one of twelve songs that Berlin wrote for the Paramount film *Holiday Inn* starring Crosby and Fred Astaire. The film premiered August 4, 1942. "White Christmas" became a perennial holiday classic and assumed extra emotional meaning because of its sentimental significance in wartime.

After launching the SSD Radio Section, Maj. Thomas Lewis discovered shortwave transmissions alone could not give reliable coverage for the troops overseas. He formulated a new model for his Special Services Division Radio Section, deciding to use transcription discs and medium wave local stations as his primary program distribution channel rather than shortwave radio, citing the unreliability of shortwave and the prohibitive cost of building new long-distance transmitter sites. He did not propose to abandon shortwave altogether but to use it to augment the transcription discs and local stations. Elmer Davis ordered the OWI to cease production and transmission of its own programs for the military on September 1, 1943, and to make OWI shortwave equipment available to the SSD Radio Section.[71] Lewis supported this decision as "common sense" because he was able to field a twenty-four-hour, seven-days-per-week global system of shortwave operations free of propaganda.[72] Lewis proposed a mix of commercial network broadcasts and original programming, recorded with studio audiences and recorded in studios. The SSD Radio Section used network facilities and leased offices and production studios.[73]

During August 1942 the SSD Radio Section inaugurated a variety program produced at NBC Hollywood called *Mail Call*, which was like *Command Performance*. This was the first of three big SSD Hollywood productions. The others were *G. I. Journal* and *Jubilee*, which featured African American entertainers. The BPR turned over control of *Command Performance* to the SSD on December 15, 1942, and the SSD produced their first *Command Performance* from Hollywood on Wednesday, January 6, 1943, at CBS.[74]

Lewis decided to use a Union Carbide resin called vinylite for the transcription discs. Developed by Hollywood recording engineer Irving Fogel, the vinylite records were flexible and almost unbreakable. Electrical insulation, life rafts, and other vital products used vinylite, so the army also used Formvar, a similar Canadian polyvinyl acetal resin developed by a subsidiary of Monsanto Chemical Company for transcription discs. Lewis recruited Fogel to help the SSD Radio Section adapt vinylite and Formvar for the production and shipment of transcription discs. Lewis had no budget for the procurement of these discs, so he approached the advertising agencies and advertisers for support, reminding them that millions of service personnel would continue to hear their programs if the SSD Radio Section could dub and ship the discs in large quantity. The broadcasting industry donated one million discs. Manufactured in Southern California, the discs saved shipping costs but more importantly allowed the SSD Radio Section to edit programs and remove commercials.

Army Special Services had earlier received a $100,000 grant from the Carnegie Foundation for Fogel to aid in the development of vinylite records for the V-Disc program. Receiving an added $400,000 from the Carnegie Foundation, Fogel developed vinylite discs that packed grooves closer together and allowed for fifteen minutes of time per side on a twelve-inch disc. Lewis recruited Fogel's assistant, Victor Quan, who became a captain and head of SSD Radio Section production. T/Sgt. Edward de la Penna came from the Signal Corps to be recording director.[75]

Warner Brothers was preparing the new war movie *Air Force* with the blessing of General Arnold. Director Howard Hawks took liberties with the otherwise solid script that had added typecast Japanese "fifth columnist" activity in Hawaii. When a B-17D bomber approaching Hickam Field on Oahu diverts during the attack on Pearl Harbor, the crew meets Japanese American snipers at an emergency field on Maui (Warner Brothers filmed the scene in Florida). The same difficulties surrounding the treachery of Japanese Americans living in the Philippine Commonwealth repeats when the bomber reaches Clark Field.[76] The scenes were complete nonsense. Although the OWI complained, *Air Force* went out with full Army Air Forces approval, complete with unnecessary blatant racial stereotyping, fiction purporting to be fact, and offensive racist language.[77] Other than that, it was a well-made and stirring wartime story.

On the heels of *Air Force*, Lowell Mellett moved to bolster the clout of the OWI. He posted Ulric Bell to Hollywood on the pretense that the OWI Overseas Branch would be better able to obtain scripts in advance. Mellett calculated that denying foreign distribution could influence the studios to make changes recommended by the OWI, and thus the agency would be able to affect domestic audiences as well. The strategy of focusing on the foreign market worked.[78] By 1943 Mellett and Nelson Poynter knew that left alone, Hollywood would keep putting out films that undermined the war effort. However, intervention in the script submission phase of a film, and not the production phase, bore fruit. In a November 12, 1942, speech to the National Board of Review, Mellett praised Hollywood, but he was critical of war movies and stereotyping. Industry insiders were privately worried that Mellett was preparing to move toward outright censorship.[79]

Mellett sent a letter on December 9, 1942, to all the studio heads. He told them that "it would be advisable" to routinely give finished scripts to his Hollywood office for review, suggestions, and changes. He wanted the studios to make all contact with the armed forces and foreign governments through the OWI.[80] The next day newspapers and the trade press reported that Mellett and the OWI were moving to impose direct censorship on the motion picture industry.[81] The odd thing was that Mellett was not asking for anything that the film studios did not already give to the Hays Office and the Production Code. Davis defended Mellett in a December 23 press conference and repeated that the OWI had no power of censorship.[82] Jean C. Herrick of *Look* told Mike Cowles, head of the OWI Domestic Branch, "there is an almost unanimous opinion among important producers" that they were "incompetent to advise on changing scripts" and that "they will never be able to obtain a healthy cooperation from the motion picture industry . . . you need to clean house."[83]

SIX

Command Performance

Casablanca

During the humid early morning hours of Monday, January 11, 1943, a military train with the presidential railway coach *Ferdinand Magellan* slipped quietly into the Florida East Coast Railway passenger terminus in downtown Miami. As military police and the Secret Service stood guard before dawn at 5:00 a.m., railway red caps removed the luggage from the train as Army Air Forces officer candidates across Biscayne Bay on Miami Beach awakened at reveille for mess and exercise. Elsewhere in southern Florida thousands of young men and women were preparing for their daily duty at stations including Naval Air Station (NAS) Miami, NAS Fort Lauderdale, NAS Richmond Field, Homestead Army Air Field, Boca Raton Army Air Field, Morrison Army Air Field in West Palm Beach, and many auxiliary air fields. Along with hundreds of military bases across the nation, these modern facilities were part of the vast military buildup by the Roosevelt Administration since 1939. The commander-in-chief and his presidential party remained on the train and disembarked further south at S. W. 27th Avenue and South Dixie Highway. FDR rode the short distance to the Pan American Airways International Airport at Dinner Key in a convertible, where he boarded the big Pan Am Boeing B-314 named the *Dixie Clipper* (NC18602) for the first presidential trip outside of the United States during wartime and the first overseas airplane flight by any president.[1]

An upbeat FDR was airborne in the large flying boat off the waters of Biscayne Bay by 6:00 a.m. The commander-in-chief and his party were heading 1,162 miles southeast across the Caribbean and West Indies to Trinidad, British West Indies, aboard two Pan American B-314 planes for an overnight stay at the Macqueripe Beach Hotel. The next day FDR continued to Belem, Brazil, where Vice Adm. Jonas Ingram, commander of the joint U.S. and Brazilian South Atlantic Force, welcomed him. The president visited with officers and personnel stationed at the AAF Air Transport Command base and Naval Air Station at Belem while the Pan American flying boats refueled.

Shortly after 6:30 p. m. on Tuesday, January 12, the Clippers took off for a 2,100-mile flight across the Atlantic Ocean to Bathurst, Gambia. After another overnight layover, the president transferred to a new AAF Douglas C-54 passenger plane outfitted to accommodate his wheelchair. Two C-54 planes flown by former TWA pilots transported FDR's presidential party, which included Harry Hopkins, General Marshall, Admiral King, and General Arnold. From Bathurst, the deputy commander of the Air Transport Command, Brig. Gen. Cyrus Rowlett Smith, the peacetime president of American Airlines, escorted the presidential party. They arrived without incident at Casablanca, French Morocco, on January 14 at 6:20 p. m. For security reasons the planes did not fly a direct route from Bathurst to Casablanca over land but a dogleg route over Dakar, Senegal, which they would repeat on their return trip from Marrakech, French Morocco, on January 25. Bathurst was among a network of airfields that Pan Am's Africa Division built from scratch across Africa and the Middle East to India. Pan Africa transported critical equipment and supplies from Miami to the British in Egypt and, eventually, over "the hump" (the Himalayas) to China.

The two Boeing 314 Clippers carried the presidential party westward on January 27 via Natal, Brazil, where FDR met with President Vargas. After returning to Miami via Trinidad, FDR relaxed in South Florida before boarding the *Ferdinand Magellan* for Washington on January 31. Between Trinidad and Miami, the president celebrated his sixty-first birthday by enjoying a birthday cake in flight.[2]

At Casablanca, FDR reviewed American troops commanded

by Gen. George S. Patton, and Moroccan officials graciously welcomed him. His journey was vital and consequential. The Casablanca Conference met on January 14, 1943, at the Anfa Hotel in Casablanca, French Morocco, and ran to January 24. FDR and Churchill attended with their combined chiefs of staff. Premier Joseph Stalin declined to attend, as Soviet forces were fiercely battling the German Sixth Army at the decisive battle of Stalingrad. Between October 23 and November 11, the British Commonwealth Eighth Army commanded by Lt. Gen. Sir Bernard Law Montgomery defeated Field Marshal Rommel's Afrika Korps near the Egyptian railway halt at El Alamein. On June 4–6, 1942, the United States Navy had defeated the Imperial Japanese Navy at the Battle of Midway, and on August 7 American Marines landed on Guadalcanal in the Solomon Islands. The Axis Powers' remarkable streak of victories and steady territorial advance had ended. Churchill commented, "This is not the end; it is not even the beginning of the end, but it is perhaps the end of the beginning."[3]

The Allies invited rival Free French generals Charles de Gaulle and Henri Giraud to the meeting in French Morocco, which American forces had invaded on November 8, 1942, in Operation Torch, a series of simultaneous landings at Casablanca and Oran and Algiers in French Algeria, all occupied by the Nazi-subjugated Vichy French regime. The plan was to launch an American advance across North Africa from the west, coordinated with a British advance from the east, and to trap the Afrika Korps in Tunisia.

Though the Casablanca Conference addressed pressing strategic and tactical issues, the headline from the summit was "unconditional surrender." This was a statement of purpose favored by FDR, which he said that he borrowed from Civil War Gen. Ulysses S. Grant. FDR's controversial insistence that the Allies fight the war to an ultimate end was an instinctive and sincere moral stance, although calculated to bolster domestic morale and to prevent Stalin from negotiating a separate peace with Hitler. American diplomats frowned because the policy would tie their hands in the event German resistance groups managed to depose Hitler. Churchill officially supported FDR's ultimatum, but the British privately agreed with the American diplomats. General Donovan's OSS intelligence chief in Berne, Allen Dulles, said that the ultimatum was "a piece of paper to be scrapped without further ado if Germany sued for peace. Hitler had to go." The OSS and MI6 were diligently trying to remove Hitler with the support of German officers including Abwehr chief Adm. Wilhelm Canaris, chief of all German military intelligence, through covert operations behind enemy lines. This made no difference to FDR, who felt that the Allies had to obliterate fascism and hold the fascist rulers accountable for their crimes against humanity.[4]

On June 4, 1942, Metro-Goldwyn-Mayer released *Mrs. Miniver*, directed by William Wyler and starring Greer Garson and Walter Pidgeon as an unassuming British couple trying to cope with wartime circumstances such as Dunkirk and the Blitz. Receiving twelve nominations, *Mrs. Miniver* won six Academy Awards, including Best Picture, Best Director, Best Actress, and Best Supporting Actress (Theresa Wright). The film went into production long before Pearl Harbor. Wyler reshot certain scenes in early 1942 to strengthen the wartime message.

The film ends in the badly damaged local church with a rousing sermon by the local vicar, played by Henry Wilcoxon. Wyler and Wilcoxson tweaked the dialogue right up to the moment of shooting. In its final form the vicar says,

> This is not only a war of soldiers in uniform. It is the war of the people, of all the people. And it must be fought not only on the battlefield, but in the cities and in the villages, in the factories and on the farms, in the home and in the heart of every man, woman, and child who loves freedom. . . . This is the People's War. It is *our* war. *We* are the fighters. Fight it, then! Fight it with all that is in us! And may God defend the right.

The congregation sings "Onward Christian Soldiers," the same hymn sung by FDR and Churchill at Placentia Bay, and Wyler pans the camera up to the bombed-out ceiling open to the sky, where a squadron of RAF Spitfires fly overhead in a "V for Victory" formation as the hymn dissolves into "Pomp and Circumstance."[5]

With *Mrs. Miniver* Hollywood had finally gone all out with the war effort. Distributors no longer had European markets to protect, and producers did not have to cater to isolationist American audiences. Born in Alsace-Lorraine of Jewish religious heritage, William Wyler well understood the threat of Nazism and realized that *Mrs. Miniver* was a pro-British propaganda piece when he took the assignment in 1941. But he did so eagerly. Indeed, after making *Mrs. Miniver*, Wyler joined the army. He later remarked that, upon reflection, *Mrs. Miniver* was too soft on the enemy. Nelson Poynter and the Bureau of Motion Pictures praised the film.[6]

Mrs. Miniver had a strong impact on audiences and national leaders. Moved to tears, Churchill offered effusive praise. FDR insisted that MGM rush the film to theater screens across the United States. *Time* and *Look* published Wilcoxon's closing speech verbatim, and the OWI broadcast the Wilcoxson speech over the Voice of America. *Mrs. Miniver* even received grudging praise from an unlikely source. Nazi propaganda minister Dr. Goebbels said that the film "shows the destiny of a family during the current war, and its refined powerful propagandistic tendency has up to now only been dreamed of. There is not a single angry word spoken against Germany; nevertheless, the anti-German tendency is perfectly accomplished."[7]

Warner Brothers, who had been more daring than its competitors with anti-Nazi material before Pearl Harbor, produced their own acclaimed wartime classic that premiered Thanksgiving Day, November 26, 1942 in New York. The studio rushed the premiere to take advantage of Operation Torch and the American occupation of Casablanca and Algiers. Then, when Warner Brothers released it nationally on January 23, 1943, the film coincided with the Casablanca Conference.[8] The feature was the aptly named *Casablanca*, well cast with Humphrey Bogart, Ingrid Bergman, Paul Henreid, Claude Rains, consummate screen Nazi Conrad Veidt, Sydney Greenstreet, Peter Lorre, S. Z. Sakall, and dozens of character actors who were exiles from occupied European nations.[9] Producer Hal B. Wallis did not expect much of the film, although it was an "A" picture with a large cast.

Following the invasion of North Africa, American commander Gen. Dwight D. Eisenhower made the decision to keep the former Vichy government and military leaders in Morocco and Algeria in place. FDR and the State Department supported this course of action, which infuriated Gen. Charles de Gaulle, the Free French leader. Before American troops landed, Robert Murphy, the American counsel in Algiers, contacted Admiral François Darlan, commander of Vichy forces, to determine if he would resist or cooperate. When American troops landed, the Vichy forces at first put up an unexpected fight. Eisenhower recognized Darlan as high commissioner of French North Africa, and in return Darlan ordered all French forces to cease resistance and cooperate. Learning this, Hitler ordered German forces to occupy all of France. The Free French and the American public were angry because they considered all Vichy officers to be Nazi collaborators. Eisenhower, however, was concerned about driving his troops east to fight the Afrika Korps and not fighting a rear-guard action. A disgruntled officer assassinated Darlan on December 24. Gen. Henri Giraud replaced him, and the stage was set for the de Gaulle and Giraud meeting at the Casablanca Conference.[10]

Nazi Germany coveted control of the intact and formidable French fleet. Churchill had to consider that the French fleet would fall into Nazi hands. The combination of the French, German, and Italian fleets could control the Mediterranean. On July 3, 1940, the Royal Navy at Gibraltar cornered a major part of the French fleet in the Algerian harbor of Mers-El-Kebir. Ordered to surrender, the Vichy officers replied that their orders from Darlan were to sail to the United States if Germany violated the armistice. Meanwhile the British intercepted a message from Vichy ordering Oran reinforced and not to surrender or scuttle the fleet. That was enough for Churchill, and ninety minutes later the Royal Navy opened fire. Within ten minutes, 1,297 French sailors were dead, and three big warships including the battleship *Richelieu* were out of commission. Vichy repaired the ships and moved them to Toulon. When the Germans occupied Vichy following Operation Torch, Darlan scuttled the fleet, and no French ships fell into German hands.

The Royal Navy peacefully interred French ships at Alexandria, Plymouth, and Portsmouth.[11]

French sensitivities were therefore quite pronounced when the motion picture *Casablanca* appeared, complete with the worldly Vichy officer Capt. Louis Renault, played by Claude Rains, who says, "I blow with the wind and the prevailing wind comes from Vichy."[12] Against this backdrop, on January 8, 1943, the OWI Overseas Branch Motion Picture Division director Robert Riskin blocked *Casablanca* from exhibition to anyone in North Africa, including American troops.[13]

American forces made a dash for Tunisia that became a crawl due to inexperience, inadequate training and equipment, and weather. The hesitant French Tunisian governor, Adm. Jean-Pierre Esteva, could not decide which side he supported. As Montgomery's seasoned Eighth Army closed in from the east, Esteva's dithering allowed the Germans to create a strong defensive perimeter. The American II Corps commanded by Gen. Lloyd Fredendall could not advance in force until February 1943 when airfields became available in eastern Algeria and western Tunisia. Between February 14 and 24, elements of the Afrika Korps and Fifth Panzer Army decimated the inexperienced Americans before II Corps stopped them at Kasserine Pass. At Faïd Pass and Sidi bou Zid, Gen. Hans-Jürgen von Arnim's elite units overran the 168th Infantry Regiment of the 34th "Red Bull" Infantry Division. The Afrika Korps killed or captured an entire National Guard unit from the southwestern Iowa towns of Red Oak, Villisca, Clarinda, Shenandoah, Glenwood, and Council Bluffs.[14] Patton replaced the humiliated Fredendall, and after three months of bitter fighting, Tunis and Bizerte fell on May 7. The next day, ending a stunning collapse, von Arnim surrendered the remaining 230,000 German and Italian troops of Army Group Africa.

By the end of 1942 the United States reversed the success of the U-boat attacks on the Atlantic and Gulf coasts with a combination of innovative radar and sonar technology, better procedures, more submarine-hunting ships, long-range airplanes, blimps, and skilled personnel. Enigma code machines fell into Allied hands

without the Germans knowing it when the Royal Navy captured
U-171 and later U-570 intact. Breaking the Kriegsmarine Naval
code, the Allies could listen in to U-boat orders and movements,
as they had deciphered Wehrmacht communications following
the snatch of ground forces Enigma machines in Poland.[15] The
"happy time" was over. The shallow and clear waters of the Caribbean were never good U-boat operating areas. The Kriegsmarine
started losing valuable U-boats and veteran crews. Dönitz and his
boat commanders now had to deal with prowling U.S. Navy PB4Y
Liberators, PBM Mariners, and PBY Catalinas, many flying from
the airbases picked up in the Lend-Lease agreement.[16]

On July 14, 1943, Bastille Day, the pro-Vichy French governor
Adm. Georges Robert surrendered control of the French Antil-
les, including Martinique and Guadeloupe, to Ambassador Henri
Hoppenot of the Free French Committee of National Liberation.
Earlier, on July 2, following a rebellion of his pro–Free French
republican troops, he surrendered his command to American
vice admiral John H. Hoover, USN, commanding officer of the
Caribbean Sea Frontier, San Juan de Puerto Rico. Since the fall of
France, the U.S. Navy quarantined the elements of the French fleet
at Fort de France, including the aircraft carrier *Béarn*. Vichy also
had 106 new American-built planes stuck on Martinique, although
most were still in shipping crates. The cruiser *Jeanne d'Arc* was at
Guadeloupe. Robert allowed Kriegsmarine U-boats to refuel and
provision at Fort de France, although once the United States was
at war, they were vulnerable to air attack from the Naval Air Station at nearby St. Lucia.

The June 1940 Conference of American States in Havana had
given the United States authority to run neutrality patrols, which
later became wartime missions. The American nations had a sense
of urgency concerning vital oil refineries in Dutch Aruba and
Curaçao that processed Venezuelan crude, and, of course, the
security of the Panama Canal was paramount. If Robert had not
capitulated the United States was prepared to seize Martinique
and Guadaloupe.[17]

Following the Lend-Lease agreement, the United States developed airbases in Antigua, the Bahamas, British Guiana, Jamaica, St. Lucia, and Trinidad, which combined with American facilities in Puerto Rico, Cuba, the Virgin Islands, and Panama offered almost complete coverage by patrol planes. Undeterred, Dönitz decided to heavy up Caribbean attacks in mid-1943. Fortunately the Americans sank most of the U-boats. In addition the navy trained Allied airmen and sailors in antisubmarine warfare. In a coordinated attack an American Vought-Sikorsky OS2U Kingfisher of VS-62 operating from Cayo Francés spotted the type IXC U-176 off Cayo Blanquizal, Cuba, on May 15, 1943, and dropped a smoke float to mark its position. The Cuban sub-chaser CS-13 found the U-176 with sonar, attacked with depth charges, and sank the crash-diving submarine commanded by Kapitänleutnant Reiner Dierksen with the loss of all hands. CS-13, commanded by Lieutenant Alférez de Fragata Mario Ramirez Delgado, made good contact through the sonar and launched two perfect attacks with depth charges. This was the only successful attack against a submarine carried out by a surface unit smaller than a Patrol Craft Escort (PCE) of 173 feet. The small but efficient Cuban Navy properly regarded this kill by an 83-foot sub-chaser with pride.[18] The action was, in a way, a fulfillment of the Monroe Doctrine and an example of hemispheric defense coordinated by the United States and a Latin American ally.

The Brazilian Navy sank nine U-boats in Brazilian waters and conducted 574 convoy operations across the Atlantic. They protected the South and Central Atlantic in concert with Admiral Ingram and the U.S. Navy's South Atlantic Force. The Brazilian Expeditionary Force fought alongside the American Fifth Army and British Commonwealth Eighth Army in Italy, and the Mexican Air Force flew Republic P-47 Thunderbolt fighters in the southwest Pacific, showing hemispheric solidarity.

On April 18, 1943, while the noble samurai Adm. Isoroku Yamamoto was flying on an inspection and morale-boosting trip from Rabaul to Balalae near Bougainville in the Solomon Islands, sixteen AAF Lockheed P-38 Lightning fighters intercepted his flight of two Mitsubishi G4M Betty bombers and Mitsubishi A6M Zero fighter escort. Yamamoto died when a P-38 shot down the bomber that he was aboard. The Americans knew about Yamamoto's whereabouts from Ultra JN-25 intercepts. FDR himself ordered the ambush to "get Yamamoto."[19]

During May 1943 Churchill and the British military chiefs of staff returned to Washington for their third conference with FDR and the American military chiefs of staff. During the conference, code-named Trident, Churchill argued for a "soft underbelly" approach of advancing toward Germany from the Mediterranean through mountainous Italy and the Balkans. Gen. George C. Marshall favored an invasion of northwest Europe and a more direct route to Berlin. Churchill argued that an Italian campaign would divert Nazi resources from the Eastern Front against the Soviet Union, knock Mussolini out of the war, and give the Allies time until they assembled resources for a decisive northwest Europe campaign. The combined chiefs agreed to push a cross-Channel invasion back to May 1944.

The leaders kept their focus on defeating Germany by the end of 1944 and then shifting resources to knock out Japan in 1945. There were no good alternatives concerning China except continued material support by air. In the end, despite American concerns and although the United States was becoming the stronger member of the alliance, the conference approved the Italian strategy.[20]

Voice of America

The OWI made a serious attempt to get Hollywood to address real wartime issues, to curb its output of spy and action hero films, and, importantly, to tone down the racist depiction of the Japanese. Although Hollywood appropriately portrayed all Nazis as evil, cunning, and brutal, depictions of good Germans resisting the Nazis populated many war films, such as Carl, the anti-Nazi German refugee and maître d'hôtel of Rick's Cafe Americain, played by S. Z. Sakall in *Casablanca*. And Italy got a pass. The studios depicted Italians as victims. They limited anti-fascist Italian messaging to Il Duce himself, and mostly dismissed Mussolini with sarcasm.

Disagreements between Mellett, Poynter, and Bell were among

internal feuds that were exposing the OWI Domestic Branch to criticism in Washington and Hollywood. Officials favoring thoughtful analysis such as Mellett and Poynter were finding themselves on the defensive versus others with advertising backgrounds, such as publisher and broadcaster Mike Cowles, who succeeded Archibald MacLeish in December 1942 as director of the Domestic Branch. The shift of focus to advertising caused several key resignations.

In April 1943 Henry Pringle, Francis Brennan, Arthur Schlesinger Jr., Della Tuhn, Milton MacKaye, W. McNeil Lowry, Katherine Douglas, Louis Baker, and several others resigned and published a statement criticizing the "promoters" at the OWI who "prefer slick salesmanship to honest information."[21] Pringle, a Pulitzer Prize–winning biographer, did not want to "sell the war to the American people by methods used to sell Coca Cola."[22] The Domestic Branch was floundering and trying to move into the center of political and social discourse, and its enemies pounced. Many in the House and Senate, suspicious of artists and intellectuals, believed the OWI was too liberal.[23]

Many talented men and women of the branch were too individualistic and ideological to accept the management style and directives of director Cowles and his colleagues who had come into the agency from advertising rather than academia. In their view it was inevitable that advertising people, whose impulse was persuasion, would sugar-coat the facts. To stress their point, the dissatisfied writers and artists drew up a poster of the Statue of Liberty holding up four Coca-Cola bottles and circulated it around the OWI offices before they resigned en masse.[24]

An awkward problem was that some of the intellectuals in the Domestic Branch openly admired the Soviet Union. Davis would let go about three dozen employees for suspected past communist associations, although the FBI did not find evidence of party membership.[25] The FBI and a Soviet operative later identified OWI Overseas Branch Pacific operations director Owen Lattimore to have been a Soviet agent.[26] When Davis received the resignations of the group, they said they wanted to stay if they could all report directly to him and not Cowles. But Davis could not tolerate insubordination, even if he privately agreed with some of the complaints. Otherwise all loyalty in the organization would be undermined. He also disagreed with their premises. He held a press conference to say that he respected the sincerity of the group, but he was convinced they were wrong. Davis told the media that the OWI never swerved from the truth, and no such change was in prospect. And that is where he left the matter. In normal situations that would be the end of it, but the OWI was an extraordinary agency affecting all levels of society.

Congress and the media ignored Davis's arguments and heavily criticized the former journalist.[27] A House committee recommended cutting the funding of the Domestic Branch. The full House voted to cut the Domestic Branch budget entirely. The Senate whittled the Domestic Branch budget from $7.6 million down to $2.135 million. The Domestic Branch narrowly survived, but its workforce dropped from 1,300 to 495 people. Davis said that it gave just enough money to avoid "the odium of having put us out of business and carefully not enough to allow us to accomplish much."[28] Mellett and Poynter did not survive the cut. The Bureau of Motion Pictures and its mostly female reviewing staff transferred to the Overseas Branch and continued working for Ulric Bell.

The OWI Overseas Branch did not elicit the debate the Domestic Branch met, likely because of its focus outward from the United States. Although the Overseas Branch was subject to the same congressional scrutiny, undermining enemy morale was not a controversial war aim. Elmer Davis had kept Robert Sherwood on board as chief of the Overseas Branch when FDR created the OWI. Sherwood hired John Houseman (Jacques Haussmann) as the first director of the Overseas Branch Radio Bureau and the Voice of America.[29] The six-foot-eight-inch-tall Sherwood was a pacifist who became so appalled with German and Italian fascism that he came to embrace intervention. He later confessed he and other pacifists had helped create Hitler and cause World War II.[30] Houseman was known for his stage, screen, and broadcasting achievements and collaboration with Orson Welles, including the provocative 1941 film *Citizen Kane* and the notable 1938 CBS *Mercury Theater on the Air* radio broadcast, *War of the Worlds*.

Sherwood and Houseman rapidly expanded and upgraded VOA transmission facilities, production capability, and program content. They centralized VOA announcers and technicians at the New York studios of the now-nationalized CBS and NBC international divisions, where they had ready-made and world-class talent and technology. They quickly negotiated an agreement for cooperation with the BBC and aided the Army Special Service Radio Section with studios, transmitters, and broadcast time. The VOA leased the network and GE shortwave transmitters and built new towers in Ohio to augment the Crosley site that the government eventually acquired.

The OWI added Arabic and African services to the former CBS and NBC European and Latin American services. They opened a European office in London and expanded Pacific services, adding Chinese and Japanese language programs broadcast from the NBC studios in San Francisco. By 1945 the OWI operated thirty-nine transmitters broadcasting over a thousand programs per week from New York, San Francisco, and London.[31]

The OWI Psychological Warfare Branch was part of the Overseas Branch. In Europe the PWB coordinated radio psychological warfare with the Supreme Headquarters, Allied Expeditionary Force Military Psychological Warfare Division, using the OWI's American Broadcasting Station in Europe, the SHAEF radio broadcasting service, known as Allied Expeditionary Force Programme, the BBC European Service, and, later, the facilities of Radio Luxembourg. Enemy military and civilian audiences received an avalanche of broadcast and published messages the OWI PWB also coordinated with the OSS. The psychological warfare operations have historically blurred institutional memory and often confuse OWI and OSS. The OWI PWB also handled dissemination of magazines, leaflets, and specialty items flown and dropped by AAF and navy airplanes.

When American forces invaded North Africa, Lt. Andre Baruch, a peacetime network radio announcer, and a team of army personnel liberated the French radio transmitter in Casablanca. Baruch, a bilingual French speaker, was soon on the air with news and entertainment in English and French to the delight of General Patton. When Tom Lewis learned what was happening, he claimed Baruch, who became the ssd radio chief for a Mediterranean Network that would eventually include stations in Morocco, Algeria, Tunisia, Egypt, and Italy.[32]

Gen. Dwight D. Eisenhower well understood the importance of morale, remembering, "Morale is the greatest single factor in a successful war . . . morale will always suffer unless all ranks thoroughly believe their commanders are concerned first and always with the welfare of the troops who do the fighting."[33]

In 1942 Sherwood sent Brewster Morgan, a former cbs executive, to London. His responsibility was to create an owi European Service. Morgan and his new London staff were able to quickly forge a good working relationship with the bbc.[34] The owi handled discussions with the bbc about the possibility of an American military radio service in addition to an owi radio service. The owi had the funding to help launch a military radio service. Morgan listened to all concerned and gathered information; on November 1, 1942, Eisenhower approved his recommendation.[35] On June 21, 1943, the owi and the bbc signed a formal operating agreement. They named the new service the American Forces Network (afn), and it went on the air July 4, 1943.[36] Capt. John S. Hayes, from wor radio, New York, soon became afn director. He insisted the afn military staff control all commentary, news, and news analysis so the afn would not be confused with the owi, which was the voice of the government and was in the business of broadcasting the policies of the U.S. government to foreign audiences rather than apolitical information and entertainment to the American armed forces.[37]

The first afn studio was 11 Carlos Place, just off Grosvenor Square and near the U.S. Embassy. In May 1944, afn moved to larger quarters provided by the bbc at 80 Portland Place. Within a year, afn would have fifty-five transmitters broadcasting in the United Kingdom.[38]

Following intense aerial and sea bombardment, Operation Husky started with American and British paratroopers dropping into

Sicily just after midnight on July 10, 1943. Amphibious landings followed. By the evening of July 10, seven Allied divisions were ashore, and they captured the port of Syracuse.[39] Montgomery advanced from Syracuse to Catania on the east coast while Patton raced west to capture Palermo. The German and Italian forces fought a tough withdrawal to the Etna line underneath Mount Etna. Field Marshal Albert Kesselring and Gen. Alfredo Guzzoni successfully evacuated most of their troops from Messina across the heavily fortified and very narrow Strait of Messina. American troops entered Messina on the morning of August 17, and the Allies secured Sicily.[40]

On the cloudy and moonless night of August 2, 1943, the Japanese destroyer *Amagiri* ran over and sliced in half an American PT boat in the Blackett Straight of the Solomon Islands. The boat was among several of Motor Torpedo Squadron 2 from Tulagi Island patrolling the Solomon Island waters to interdict Japanese troop and supply movements. The skipper of PT-109 gathered the survivors of the collision and swam them to several nearby islands where native scouts found them, and Australian Coastwatcher Arthur Reginald Evans arranged their rescue. The American skipper was Lt. (jg) John Fitzgerald Kennedy, the son of Ambassador Joseph Kennedy, and he would suffer lifelong back trouble because of the collision and ordeal.[41]

A series of deadly naval battles raged in "the slot" between Guadalcanal and Bougainville with the loss of proud ships named *Astoria, Atlanta, Quincy, Vincennes,* and *Juneau,* the latter including the five Sullivan brothers of Waterloo, Iowa. Many native scouts bonded with the Americans, including Sir Jacob Vouza, KBE GM, a sergeant major in the Solomon Islands Constabulary and chief U.S. Marine Corps scout. Japanese troops captured and tortured Sir Jacob on Guadalcanal. Left for dead by his captors, he somehow staggered back to American lines to gasp warning of an impending enemy attack. The United States awarded Vouza the Legion of Merit and the Silver Star, and Queen Elizabeth II knighted a most exceptional honorary American.[42]

Lt. Robert Vincent was a technical officer in the SSD Radio Section offices in New York. He was involved with the shipment of transcriptions overseas of the Radio Section's radio programs and commercial programs. Until the July 31, 1942 recording ban, the ssd Recreation and Welfare Section distributed popular records to military bases in the form of "Buddy" Kits that included a battery-operated radio receiver, hand-wound phonograph with 78 rpm and 33 1/3 rpm speeds and two speakers, so recreation officers could play the records in mess halls and recreation rooms. But with the strike, they were stuck. Vincent had an idea. In July 1943 he went to Washington to propose a special recording project as a means of offering currently popular and other music on records for overseas packages. The War Department approved and funded the project. Promoted to captain, Vincent left the ssd Radio Section to devote his full attention to the new recording program. He set up offices at 205 East 42nd Street in New York and reached agreements with the afm (American Federation of Musicians) and afra (American Federation of Radio Artists) about the waiver of all fees, royalties, and copyright payments.[43]

The army agreed V-Discs would be for the use of military personnel only, and there would be no commercial exploitation of the recordings. The agreements made it possible for the army to afford the V-Disc program by focusing funds for processing and pressing records. The Armed Forces Radio Service (afrs) reached similar agreements with the afm and afra.

Working for Vincent on his immediate staff were Tony Janak and Morty Palitz, formerly of Columbia records; Steve Sholes and Wally Heebner, formerly of rca Victor, and, later, Cpl. George T. Simon, formerly editor of Metronome Magazine and unit historian of the Capt. Glenn Miller Radio Production Unit (replacing Palitz). Songwriter Pvt. Frank Loesser joined the Music Branch and worked with the V-Disc staff on various projects. In March 1944 the team moved to 25 West 45th Street, New York. The navy joined the project and assigned Lt. Edmond "Digi" DiGiannantonio as their representative. In July 1944 a V-Disc radio program produced by Cpl. Simon, *For the Record* appeared over the nbc flagship station weaf. By October 1944, the Marine Corps also joined the V-Disc program and assigned Capt. Lee Kamern as their representative.[44]

The producers scheduled special V-Disc recording sessions in New York at Columbia Records, RCA Victor Records, CBS studios, NBC studios, and the World Broadcasting System studios (Decca records owned World). They also used Hollywood's CBS and NBC studios for V-Disc sessions. Radio programs came by direct line from CBS and NBC in New York for recording. The producers also had access to radio transcription libraries. Commercial 78 rpm records were very fragile shellac discs, and records shipped overseas broke. The main sources of shellac were the Japanese-occupied Malay Peninsula and French Indochina. Like the SSD Radio Section and later AFRS, Vincent decided to use vinylite and Formvar for the V-Disc records.

As devised by Lt. Col. Irving Fogel of the SSD Radio Section, the V-Discs were 12-inch 78 rpm vinylite and Formvar records, recorded with a fixed number of lines or grooves per inch. For recording times of up to 4 minutes and 30 seconds, the technicians used 96 lines per inch. For up to 6 minutes and 30 seconds, they squeezed 136 lines per inch onto the record. By comparison, standard commercial 78 rpm records used 85 to 97 lines per inch. The V-Disc playing time of 6 minutes and 30 seconds compares to the maximum playing time of standard 10-inch 78 rpm records of 3 minutes and 25 seconds and 12-inch 78 rpm records of 4 minutes and 20 seconds.

The V-Disc program pressed the records at the RCA Victor Camden, New Jersey, plant. They shipped and collated all the records from different plants at Camden, assembling records into complete releases and packing the releases in boxes. The factory coated the boxes with wax and waterproof glues that were shockproof and impervious to varying climatic conditions. The boxes included one hundred Duotone or Microphonic steel needles and a letter from Captain Vincent inviting requests and comments. Camden shipped the first V-Discs on October 1, 1943. The "A" release consisted of 1,780 boxes with 30 records each (V-Discs 1–30) for a total of 53,400 records. The boxes went to eight ports of embarkation ran by the army for shipment overseas. The boxes went to theater headquarters in Alaska, Iceland, England, Italy, Sicily, North Africa, the Persian Gulf, India, China, Guadalcanal, and Australia. The theater headquarters distributed the boxes to individual military units. The military reduced shipments to 20 records per box beginning with the "E" release in February 1944 (V-Discs 121–140). Unlike AFRS transcriptions, the V-Discs traveled by ship and not by air. By the end of the program, the V-Disc program distributed more than eight million V-Discs.[45]

Listeners to *The Army Hour* broadcast of Sunday, August 1, 1943, heard the first announcement of the American air raid on the Ploesti oil fields and refineries in Romania. Among the surprised listeners was Gen. H. H. Arnold, commanding general of the Army Air Forces. During the program commemorating the thirty-sixth anniversary of the air force, General Arnold called in commanders from the various theaters of action for combat reports. When Maj. Gen. Lewis H. Brereton, commanding the Ninth Air Force, Middle East, reported from Cairo, he said, "I have big news for you and America, General Arnold. Your Ninth Air Force has just delivered a blow against the Nazis which may conceivably change the course of the war." Gen. Brereton then told of the bombing of the Ploesti fields, the source of more than a third of Germany's oil ("Operation Tidal Wave"). General Arnold's face lit up when he heard the news, related Maj. Jack Harris, acting chief, Radio Branch, War Department Bureau of Public Relations, who was with General Arnold during the broadcast. "Here was a report from a general to his commanding general," Harris pointed out, "that was the first inkling of the news to the world. Gen. Brereton made his report at 3:43 p.m. while the bombers were still returning from the mission. He discarded a prepared script in favor of the late action. The anniversary broadcast represented one of the most complicated operations ever undertaken in radio, according to Maj. Harris. Pickups aggregated 142,014 miles, or more than half the distance to the moon. Col. Edward M. Kirby, chief of the Radio Branch of the War Dept. Bureau of Public Relations had returned to Washington after spending several weeks in England

and Africa in connection with plans for use of magnetic wire-sound recorders and Army radio matters."[46]

The first mention of changing the SSD Radio Section name appeared in October 1943 program scripts. Lewis changed the name to the Armed Forces Radio Service effective November 12. The name better described the organization, which served all the armed forces. The rebranded AFRS had grown the number of overseas stations from 21 to 306. The number of transcriptions pressed monthly increased from 7,891 in January 1943 to 117,695 by October 1945. AFRS replaced 12-inch transcription discs with 16-inch discs by the end of 1943.[47]

Fogel had stated the larger discs were practical and held more content. As of January 1, 1944, AFRS offered the widest variety of programs ever tried by a single network. There was jazz, popular, classical, Latin American, easy listening, western swing and hillbilly (country western), and ethnic music and programs for African American or Latino service personnel. Musical director Maj. Meredith Willson suggested that the SSD Radio Section should ship sets of prerecorded records to radio stations as music libraries. The first set of five *Basic Music Library* transcriptions shipped in September 1943. Of all its major off-network and original programming, the most popular program among the servicemen based upon their mail was the fifteen-minute disc jockey offering *G. I. Jive*, featuring Martha Wilkerson as "G. I. Jill" with the AFRS "jukebox of the air." Wilkerson was astonishingly popular, a lot less expensive than elaborate productions and nicknamed "America's answer to Tokyo Rose" by the media. Her trademark sign-off—"This is Jill saying good morning to some of you, good afternoon to some more of you and to the rest of you, good night"—effectively summed up the global reach of AFRS.

Wilkerson exuded a wholesome "girl next door" quality but also the elements of an attractive woman who cared for the servicemen overseas. Her sign-off was unabashedly suggestive. In addition to *G. I. Jive*, produced six days per week and featuring currently popular records, Wilkerson also hosted the once-per-week feature *Jill's All Time Juke Box*, which featured older records.[48]

"Tokyo Rose" was the nickname of several women who worked for the Japanese network NHK and broadcast from the studios of JOAK and Radio Tokyo. During 1942, as the OWI and the SSD Radio Section struggled to broadcast by shortwave to the Pacific, the female Japanese announcers filled the gap by playing American popular music. Although the records were all made before December 1941, allied military personnel and civilians across the Southwest Pacific, Australia, and New Zealand could clearly hear the broadcasts. As AFRS expanded its reach with stations across the Pacific, the NHK *Zero Hour* and several other well-produced Japanese English-language features became irrelevant as no one other than intelligence personnel were listening to them. Most of Japan's extensive and sophisticated wartime radio activity, including transmitters across Southeast Asia, was to firm up the Greater East Asia Co-Prosperity Sphere with anti-Allied, reverse racist propaganda and to subvert British rule of India with an extensive multilanguage India service. Radio Tokyo also sent a clear signal to North America. NHK's tradition mirrored the BBC editorial integrity, and early in the war Radio Tokyo was often more exact than American sources. But as the war turned against Japan, increasingly false and shrill military announcements forced upon NHK by the Tojo regime ruined Radio Tokyo's credibility.[49]

On September 3, 1943, Sir Harold Alexander's Fifteenth Army Group, consisting of Gen. Mark Clark's American Fifth Army and Montgomery's British Eighth Army, invaded the Italian mainland. The Allies announced the surrender of Italy and the arrest of Mussolini on September 8, and the Wehrmacht promptly seized control of Italy. On September 9 Alexander launched Operation Avalanche. The British Eighth Army landed unopposed at Taranto, and the Americans faced strong resistance landing near Salerno. Gen. Albert Kesselring brilliantly pivoted away from the encircled Salerno sector to form the first of what would be several strong defensive lines across the rugged Italian peninsula. There would be another costlier invasion and bloody siege of the American beachhead at Anzio to come before the Allies liberated Rome. And then there was a prolonged slog up to Florence, Milan, and the Po Valley.[50]

Modus Vivendi

There was fertile ground in Italy for the seeds of owi propaganda, and Sherwood's Foreign Branch made the most of it. Whether Italian morale would have collapsed without Allied radio broadcasts is unknown, but the bbc and the voa, in conjunction with leaflets and other printed materials, gave Italians every opportunity to learn what was really happening and make up their minds about what to do. Nazi Germany had as much to do with Italian morale or lack of it as did Allied propaganda. The Germans occupied much of Italy and had no respect for the Italians, who likewise hated the Germans. The voa Italian desk staff in New York tended to argue among themselves about scripts and themes. Many conservatives in the group chafed at what they labeled the communistic tendencies of other owi staff. Davis had to reprimand Luigi Antonini of the Italian desk to "cool it." Differences of opinion boiled over, however, as the State Department and the military were handling sensitive negotiations with the Italian military and politicians to affect the surrender of Italy and removal of Mussolini. This would cause ruptures between owi Washington and owi New York, and between Davis and Sherwood.[51]

As of July 1943 American policy toward Italy held that owi broadcasts should not personally attack King Victor Emmanuel because the Allies might need him as a peace solution, and that Italy's commanding general, Marshal Pietro Badoglio, had broken with fascism and likewise ought not to be criticized as the State Department, oss, and military tried to effect a bloodless transition from Mussolini and the fascists. But when Italy fell apart, the owi Overseas Branch New York office formed a different policy. The troublesome Italian desk thought that the way to keep Hitler, the ss, and Wehrmacht from seizing control was to denounce all Italian leadership and that events in Rome had no significance.

When the king received Mussolini's resignation and installed Badoglio, the voa told Italians nothing has changed because the king and Badoglio were still fascists. At the same time, Italian radio was proclaiming, "with the fall of Mussolini and his band,

Italy has taken the first step toward peace. Finished is the shame of Fascism. Long live peace. Long live the King!" At Studio 8-H in Rockefeller Center, Arturo Toscanini and the NBC Symphony Orchestra were broadcasting the stirring "Garibaldi War Hymn" in celebration. The OWI statement was completely out of line with American policy. Although James Warburg and Joseph Barnes took responsibility, Davis concluded that the New York office was out of control. FDR rebuked the OWI for its indiscretion. Arthur Krock of the *New York Times* accused the agency of seeking to "discredit the authorized foreign policy of the United States or to reshape it according to the personal and ideological preferences of communists and their fellow travelers in this country . . . the OWI has always been closer to Moscow than the Washington-London line."[52] The conservative *Chicago Tribune* editorialized that members of the OWI were trying "to foment a communist revolution in Italy."[53] FDR and the State Department walked a fine line with a Badoglio modus vivendi. The problem for Davis was that the VOA had broadcast, in twenty-four languages, Samuel Grafton's commentary that "this moronic little King, who has stood behind Mussolini's shoulder for twenty-one years, has moved forward one pace. This is a political minuet, and not the revolution we have been waiting for. It changes nothing, for nothing can change in Italy until democracy is restored."[54]

It was this sort of indiscretion that grabbed headlines, and not the consistent day-to-day work of the OWI personnel scattered by July 1943 at twenty-six overseas outposts, or local/regional radio stations and information offices. The OWI sent the 16-inch transcription discs of *Music from America* and *Uncle Sam Presents* out to the outposts along with an *Outpost Series* of record library discs like the SSD/AFRS *Basic Music Library*. The outposts in mid-1943 included Reykjavik, London, Dublin, Berne, Madrid, Stockholm, Algiers, Oran, Casablanca, Accra, Lagos, Brazzaville, Johannesburg, Cairo, Asmara, Beirut, Ankara, Teheran, Karachi, Bombay, Calcutta, Delhi, Chunking, Canberra, Honolulu, and Anchorage. The OWI added more as Allied forces advanced. The erection of 50,000 kw transmitters in the Mediterranean and Middle East meant that enemy and neutral audiences now heard the owi loud and clear throughout Italy, Southern France, Austria and the Balkans. The owi also now had a clear signal in Lebanon, Syria, Palestine, Egypt, the Arabian Peninsula, Iraq, and Iran. When American forces went ashore at Salerno and Anzio, the owi broadcasts went with them. Davis noted that "propaganda is only an auxiliary weapon, but properly used, it can powerfully reinforce the effect of military operations . . . owi served this purpose in Sicily and Italy. . . . [This] was acknowledged by the enemy; after the Italian government's surrender in September 1943, Japanese government spokesmen warned their people that this could partly be ascribed to 'British and American propaganda aimed at the disintegration of the home front.' They added that intensified propaganda might be expected 'against the solidarity of the Japanese nation,' which was a prediction that owi soon fulfilled."[55]

Robert Sherwood was one of the most talented writers of his time. If it was difficult for journalist Davis to run an organization, it was impossible for Sherwood, who had no talent for delegation of authority or reporting to management. Without strong management from Sherwood, Warburg, Barnes, and Edd Johnson, chief of the Overseas Editorial Board, had made themselves effectively independent. They were all powerful professionals before joining the owi and quite self-assured. But complaints were coming back from outposts, particularly London, and within Washington that the triumvirate was getting out of control. Davis ordered an investigation, which his new associate director, Edward Klauber, conducted. Klauber took over from Milton Eisenhower, who had become president of Kansas State University. The investigation produced disturbing findings, and Davis held Sherwood responsible. He ordered Sherwood to fire Warburg, Barnes, and Johnson, but Sherwood refused. According to Executive Order 9182, Davis had the right to fire anyone, including Sherwood. Bending over backward to be fair, Davis allowed Sherwood to take the matter to FDR, who ordered Davis to refrain from firing anyone until he (FDR) saw evidence of why Davis was proposing to do so. In other words, FDR supported Sherwood. The president had not read a detailed letter that Davis sent him four days earlier, outlining the facts of the matter. It noted that Sherwood was threatening to split the Overseas Branch apart from Davis and the Domestic Branch, which was outright insubordination. Davis told FDR that the New York clique had caused resignations in London. He also noted that Sherwood would accept any redefinition of duties. Davis waited ten days for a reply and sent another letter, which prompted a fully informed FDR to act.

FDR met with Davis and Sherwood at the White House on February 2, 1944.Davis kept a detailed summary of the meeting. FDR scolded them but reiterated that Davis was the boss. The president was fond of both and could not afford to lose either, but he did not want Sherwood "shipped to Guam."[56] Davis and Sherwood signed an agreement that acknowledged Davis's control. Sherwood kept the title of Overseas Branch director but moved to London to run owi psychological warfare operations. Davis called Edward W. Barrett back from North Africa to become executive director of the Overseas Branch, and he accepted the resignations of Warburg, Barnes, and Johnson.[57]

When FDR saw the original long version of Capt. John Ford's documentary *December 7th*, he found it injurious to morale and ordered Donovan that all oss Field Photo unit work was subject to censorship. Angry cinematographer Gregg Toland went to Brazil to film a report on South Atlantic Naval and Air Operations, and Ford joined him during May 1943. Donovan then sent Ford and a Field Photo team to the China-Burma-India Theatre of Operations (cbi). The cbi was dangerous: during August 1943 cbs correspondent Eric Sevareid narrowly survived a Curtiss c-46 Commando crash, with twenty-one other survivors, by walking through 138 miles of Japanese-controlled Burmese jungle to Jorhat, Assam, with the help of Naga tribal headhunters.[58]

Ford arrived in Calcutta on November 25. After spending time in New Delhi, Ford and his team flew to Rangoon, Burma, to film *Victory in Burma* for Admiral Lord Louis Mountbatten, the Allied theater commander. Ford met Donovan and went with the oss chief to Nazira, Assam, where they made a practice parachute jump at the clandestine OSS Detachment 101 training base.[59] Donovan wanted to prove the value of OSS operations behind enemy lines, so Ford and his team parachuted into the jungle to film *Galahad Forces* scenes with Kachin tribal guerillas preparing the advance of Gen. Frank Merrill's 5307 Composite Regiment, nicknamed "Merrill's Marauders."

Ford met a real-life version of one of his film characters, Fr. James Stuart, a militant and bearded Dominican priest who led Kachin guerillas and claimed to have once been a member of the Irish Republican Army. A member of Ford's team, Arthur "Butch" Meehan, lost his life when Japanese fighters shot down the airplane that he was aboard on January 18, 1944.

Ford incorporated some of the Kachin film into the Mountbatten documentary and flew on with Donovan over the Hump to Chongqing and Kunming to set up Chinese OSS operations under the auspices of the Fourteenth Air Force and Gen. Claire Chennault. The AAF had absorbed the original American Volunteer Group or "Flying Tigers" on July 4, 1942, although the new Twenty-Third Fighter Group retained the tiger shark airplane nose art.

Field Photo had become involved in aerial mapping, and Ford spent a month in China getting that program up and running. He even managed to visit Tibet. Ford's team also made the films *OSS Camera Report: China-Burma-India, Burmese Troops, Chinese Commandos and Preview of Assam* in the CBI.[60]

Ford flew back to Miami via the long Air Transport Command Route from India to Florida and reached Washington on January 23, 1944. He had set foot in every theater of war. After a brief rest Ford learned that he was to oversee Allied photography and film operations during the coming invasion of Northwest Europe. In April he returned to London for his important OSS assignment with Supreme Headquarters, Allied Expeditionary Force.[61]

During 1941 famed photographer Edward Steichen came to share the pessimism of his brother-in-law Carl Sandburg, who had become poet laureate of the United States, that a "hurricane of fate" lay ahead and that he wanted to serve his country. The army refused the sixty-one-year old photographer for active duty. Steichen went about creating art and photography shows at the Museum of Modern Art in New York to dramatize the need for national defense. Steichen renamed *Panorama of National Defense*, which became *Road to Victory*, which was an immediate and rousing success. Steichen had also applied to the navy. Impressed with his professional credentials and World War I decorations as an army colonel, the navy quickly commissioned Steichen as a lieutenant commander. Admiral Arthur Radford wanted to build up Naval Aviation with photographs and film, and Steichen was his man. Steichen would soon have a team of navy photographers deployed with him on ships at sea and at naval bases, and his team expanded. Major magazines carried photos made by the unit that became embedded in national consciousness as the graphic history of the Pacific War and wartime sacrifice of sailors and pilots. Color film shot by Steichen's unit aboard the USS *Yorktown* and other aircraft carriers during 1944 became the basis for the Louis de Rochemont and 20th Century Fox documentary *The Fighting Lady*, including gripping real scenes of aerial combat, narrated by the former MGM actor Lt. Robert Taylor, USNR. Steichen personally made several trips to the Pacific and shot many memorable photographs about the USS *Lexington* in late 1943. The United States was assembling an incredible fleet of twenty-four *Essex* class aircraft carriers. Aboard those carriers and across the Pacific, Steichen's exceptional unit created the stunning photographic history of the United States Navy in the Pacific during World War II and formed Americans' impression of that conflict for decades to come.[62]

On November 20, 1943, the Marines Corps attacked the Japanese fortress at Tarawa Atoll in the Gilbert Islands with the main fighting on the island of Betio. Nimitz would bypass the Japanese fortresses at Chuuk (Truk) and Rabaul as he advanced across the Central Pacific, and MacArthur leapfrogged key Japanese installations in New Guinea and the southwest Pacific. But the Japanese airfield at Tarawa blocked any advance to the Marianas Islands, and the Americans had to seize it.

Tarawa was the first battle in a Micronesian offensive that would lead to the landings at the Marianas Islands, Iwo Jima, and Oki-

Fig. 17. Cmdr. Edward Steichen aboard the USS *Lexington*, photographed by Lt. Victor Jorgensen, November or December 1943. Courtesy U.S. Naval History and Heritage Command, Washington DC.

nawa. The amphibious landing at Tarawa was a frontal assault on a heavily fortified island with 3,636 Japanese defenders. The landing was complicated by a neap tide that kept ocean water from rising over the coral reef offshore Betio, which caused LCVP landing craft or "Higgins boats" to run aground five hundred yards offshore. Only LVT Amtraks or "Alligators" with tracks could get across the reef, and heavy enemy fire knocked out half of them during the first day of the operation. After several days of intense fighting, the marines subdued the Japanese garrison. Only one Japanese officer and 16 enlisted men survived. About 1,200 Korean construction workers had built the Japanese fortifications, and only 129 survived. Nearly 27 percent of the 12,000-man marine landing force were casualties, and the American public was outraged at the cost of seizing a remote atoll. The shocked public was still digesting photographer George Strock's timeless image a month earlier in *Life* of the bodies of three GIs half-buried in the sand on Buna Beach in New Guinea.[63]

At significant risk, Capt. Louis Hayward led a Marine Corps team of skilled film and still photographers who recorded graphic images and shot a 35 mm Technicolor film of the battle for potential public distribution. The military knew the final cut of the twenty-minute short feature was too graphic to meet the Production Code, and only the president could approve it. FDR trusted *Time* and *Life* correspondent Robert Sherrod, who covered the assault, and asked for Sherrod's advice. Sherrod pulled no punches, telling the president that the marines wanted the true story told so that the American people knew how horrible war was and that the marines did not always win gloriously. Sherrod recommended showing the film without restriction. FDR ordered the film released uncensored, and critics unabashedly praised it. The astonishing film includes some of the most stunning images ever taken of war, including the gallant assault on a Japanese bunker by Lt. Alexander Bonnyman Jr. that cost him his life and for which he won the Medal of Honor. It brought viewers into the experience, from the somber mood during preparation through the chaos of battle, the overwhelming sadness of counting and caring for the dead, and the sense of accomplishment as the marines raised the American flag over the island. The sobering footage also focuses on how competent medical personnel saved many lives with timely blood transfusions, a fact that gave hope to those with loved ones on the front lines. However, public opinion gravitated back toward the necessity of the operation and the heroism of the marines. *With the Marines at Tarawa* won the 1945 Academy Award for Best Short Documentary Subject. The film was an important milestone in coverage of the war because of its honesty.[64]

On a positive note, the landing difficulties at Tarawa led to improvements in assault tactics and equipment and the formation of Navy Underwater Demolition Teams, known as "frogmen," the forerunners of twenty-first-century Navy Sea, Air and Land Teams, or SEALS.

The Tarawa footage also appeared in the *Army-Navy Screen Magazine* feature *I Was There—Tarawa*, produced by Col. Frank Capra, which was for military audiences. In *I Was There—Tarawa*, combat cameraman marine S/Sgt. Norman T. Hatch recounts the story of the battle as he shows the footage to other cameramen.

The marine film and photo team went on to record the assault at heavily defended Saipan in June 1944. At fortified Peleliu, reminiscent of Tarawa, they chronicled an expected two-week campaign in September 1944 that took a ghastly two months and caused many additional marine casualties. The team was not present for the 1945 Academy Award ceremony because they were busy filming the assault on Iwo Jima, and that Technicolor footage became part of another documentary, *To the Shores of Iwo Jima*. Hatch's colleague Sgt. William Genaust filmed the marines' legendary flag raising atop Mount Suribachi. They installed a small flag, but a larger one replaced it on the island's highest point. Genaust's footage confirms that the marines and press did not stage the historic photograph of the flag raising by Joe Rosenthal of the Associated Press. Sergeant Genaust lost his life one week later.[65]

The 1942 Japanese advance directly threatened Australia and the supply line between Australia, New Zealand, and the United States in Polynesia. The Allied defense held at the Battle of Coral

Sea in May 1942. During the Solomon Islands and New Guinea campaigns the Allies systematically cleared Melanesia of Japanese garrisons. Gaining strength and momentum, large new naval fleets swept through Micronesia from the Gilberts to the Marianas. The 1944 capture of Saipan and the occupied American territory of Guam made it possible for the new Twentieth Air Force to station ultramodern Boeing B-29 Superfortress bomb groups within striking distance of Japan.

The pressurized and automated B-29 was the epitome of sweeping wartime industrial and scientific progress. Boeing augmented B-29 production in Seattle with a new and lager plant in Wichita, Bell Aircraft in Marietta, Georgia, and the Glenn L. Martin Co. in Bellevue, Nebraska. Airframe and engine production for diverse types of airplanes became an efficient network of decentralized sites that employed millions of workers. Henry Kaiser in the west and Bethlehem Steel in the east expanded and constructed dozens of enormous shipyards. In Detroit the automobile industry was on full wartime production status building planes, tanks, armored vehicles, trucks, jeeps, and utility vehicles. The Merchant Marine shipped thousands of planes and vehicles overseas to outfit American forces and Allies. Running at maximum employment, the booming wartime economy introduced significant social change as large numbers of citizens migrated to work in defense plants, including blacks moving north and west. The sixteen million men and women in uniform left their homes, communities, and regions to mix together with other Americans and to train and work all over the country, particularly the former Confederacy. America thus forever transformed itself geographically, culturally, technologically, and politically. Wartime unity itself was exceptional. It was a shared transformative experience that in some way touched every person in the nation. The OWI, at home and abroad, gave voice and context to the exceptionalism defined by FDR, as individual Americans met the challenge and became part of the momentous national transformation.

As emphasized by OWI Domestic Branch media guidelines, women famously played a critical role in World War II, replac-

ing men in every line of work, most notably as workers in manufacturing plants, airplane factories, and shipyards. Women also
played a vital role in the military. After decades of media in advertising and entertainment emphasizing the dependence of women
on men, the OWI directed advertisers, the motion picture industry and broadcasters to encourage female independence.

Women and minorities experienced opportunities previously
unknown and proved themselves, whether as workers or in uniform, with dynamic new organizations such as Col. Oveta Culp
Hobby's Women's Army Corps, Jacqueline Cochran's Women Air
Service Pilots, or Col. Benjamin O. Davis Jr.'s 332nd Fighter and
442nd Bombardment Groups, the Tuskegee Airmen.

During a meeting on May 19, 1943, about Latin America, FDR
shared thoughts about the Soviet Union with Nelson Rockefeller. The president said that so long as Stalin ruled, he would mute
the aggressiveness of international communism. FDR repeated
an oft-used rule of thumb to say, "Communism has gone 20% of
the way to capitalism and would go a total of 40% and the United
States has gone 20% of the way toward communism and would
go a total of 40%, [which] would bring us close enough so that we
could have a working understanding between the two nations."[66]
But as FDR was looking forward to a convergence of interests, his
OCIAA director believed that the "liberal leadership" of the United
States was paramount in Latin America. Sensitized to communism,
Rockefeller saw a real threat as proximate as the Rio Grande. By
this time Rockefeller had twenty-two major projects putting Mexico at the forefront of postwar development. He hoped to do the
same across the Americas. Secretary of State Cordell Hull had an
issue with Argentina, as the government of Ramon Castillo shel-
tered Nazi spies and continued to welcome German investment.
Eight months after a June 1943 coup toppled Castillo, a second
coup installed a figurehead, with the real power concentrated in
the hands of fiery nationalist Col. Juan Domingo Perón, the Argentine minister of war and vice president. This caused an enraged
Cordell Hull to dig in his heels and set up a collision course with
OCIAA and Rockefeller's vision of hemispheric unity.[67]

It was no secret that some openly socialist staff of the OWI and the OCIAA sympathized with the Soviet Union and advocated greater emphasis toward the wartime communist ally, including favorable treatment of the notorious premier Joseph Stalin. Elmer Davis and Nelson Rockefeller unconditionally rejected this approach, leading to more resignations. After the fall of the Soviet Union, historians discovered in Soviet-era files that a few OWI and OCIAA people served as paid Soviet agents, much like the Soviets infiltrated the left-leaning scientific community.

After absorbing the gravity of the October 1939 Einstein-Szilárd letter, FDR formed an Advisory Committee on Uranium, which became the National Defense Research Committee on June 27, 1940, and which included chemist James Bryant Conant of Harvard University. Lyman Briggs of the National Bureau of Standards proposed spending $167,000 to fund uranium-235 isotope and plutonium research. On June 28, 1941, FDR signed Executive Order 8807 to create the Office of Scientific Research and Development directed by Vannevar Bush, whom the president empowered to engage in large-scale engineering projects as well as research. Meanwhile British scientists determined the critical mass of uranium-235 and its potability via airplanes. In July 1940 Britain decided to share its atomic secrets with the United States and by August 1941 convinced the Americans an atomic weapon was workable. FDR approved an atomic weapons program on October 9, 1941. He suggested to Churchill that they stay in regular touch about atomic research. The army set up a massive project so secret that the government deliberately compartmentalized it to disguise its true nature.

The project budget included $54 million for construction by the Army Corps of Engineers and $31 million for research and development by the Office of Scientific Research and Development. Research led by theoretical physicist J. Robert Oppenheimer of the University of California, Berkeley, Enrico Fermi of the University of Chicago, and other prominent scientists tentatively confirmed that a fission bomb was theoretically possible.[68]

The army code-named the project Manhattan as recommended

by engineering officer Col. Leslie Groves, because Col. James C. Marshall of the Corps of Engineers was coordinating the secret effort from New York. The original name was "Development of Substitute Materials." Groves became a brigadier general, moved to the Pentagon, and took command of the project on September 23, 1942, reporting directly to General Somervell of the Army Service Forces.

Groves had to pull together many facilities scattered around the nation and build secret construction and research sites on a massive scale. He compartmentalized projects that would not appear to relate to one another. The army and the FBI were concerned about Oppenheimer and other scientists who had friends and relatives who were card-carrying communists. Their fear of Soviet espionage, infiltration, and theft turned out to be quite real. Nevertheless, Groves believed that Oppenheimer was the right man to lead the scientific team.[69]

The project headquarters moved to Oak Ridge, Tennessee, where a huge facility named the Clinton Engineering Works produced enriched uranium. Up to 82,000 people eventually worked at Oak Ridge. Weapons design and construction, or "Project Y," occurred at the Los Alamos Laboratory in New Mexico, deliberately placed at a location remote from Oak Ridge. The Metallurgical Laboratory, or Met Lab, at the University of Chicago studied plutonium and used the world's first nuclear reactors to produce it. Hanford, Washington, was the site of the world's first full-scale nuclear reactor.

After dinner on November 11, 1943, FDR motored to the Marine Base at Quantico, Virginia, where he boarded the presidential yacht USS *Potomac*. Early the next morning the *Potomac* anchored off Cherry Point, Virginia. As the president slept, the crew of the *Potomac* could see the dark silhouette of the battleship USS *Iowa* on the predawn horizon. At 8:50 a.m. the little *Potomac* came alongside the mighty *Iowa* to transfer the president and his traveling party. That evening *Iowa* set sail for Oran, Algeria, with FDR, Harry Hopkins, Gen. George C. Marshall, Gen. H. H. Arnold, Gen. Brehon Somervell, Adm. William D. Leahy, and Adm. Ernest J. King aboard. At 11:55 p.m. on November 16 Task Group 27.5 crossed the thirty-fifth meridian, west longitude, and entered the European-African-Middle Eastern Theatre of Operations; at 9:11 p.m. on November 19 *Iowa* passed through the Straits of Gibraltar, arriving on the Barbary Coast of North Africa 141 years after Commodore Stephen Decatur and anchored at Mers el Kebir at 8:09 a.m.

Waiting for FDR at Mers el Kebir were his sons, Elliott and Franklin D. Jr., along with Gen. Dwight D. Eisenhower. The president motored to La Senia airfield where his specially equipped c-54 airplane and Air Transport Command pilot Capt. Otis Bryan of TWA flew him to El Aouina airfield near Tunis. FDR spent the night at a guest house near the ruins of ancient Carthage, and escorted by Eisenhower, he toured the Medjez el Bab and Tebourba battlefields the following morning.[70]

That night the presidential c-54, now nicknamed the "Sacred Cow," left El Aouina and arrived at Cairo West aerodrome at 9:35 a.m. on November 22. Gen. Ralph Royce, commanding general of the Middle East Army Air Forces, met the president upon landing. FDR went to the villa of Ambassador Alexander C. Kirk in the Mena district of Cairo. During the afternoon he met with Prime Minister Winston Churchill and Generalissimo Chiang Kai-Shek of China, who both had arrived the previous day. Joining the president at dinner were Churchill, Hopkins, Adm. Leahy, and the commander in chief of the China-Burma-India Theatre of Operations, Adm. Lord Louis Mountbatten.[71] FDR and Churchill were on their way to a summit with Premier Joseph Stalin of the Soviet Union. Since the USSR was not at war with Japan, the Western Allies had to meet separately with Chiang Kai-Shek, who rounded out the wartime "Big Four": a democrat, imperialist, communist, and fascist.[72]

The meetings with Chiang and Allied military officers involved Japanese war strategy. After dinner on November 22 Roosevelt and Churchill met with Mountbatten, Hopkins, Marshall, King, Arnold, and Somervell, along with Lt. Gen. Joseph Stilwell, Maj. Gen. George Stratemeyer, Maj. Gen Raymond Wheeler, Adm. John Cunningham, Field Marshal Sir John Dill, and Lt. Gen. Hastings Lionel Ishmay. The following day the leaders met with Generalissimo and Mme. Chiang Kai-Shek (Soong May-ling). May-ling was present at all meetings to translate for her husband but also to protect him. Allied officers could not tell who they were dealing with. The generalissimo was unimpressive, and Soong did her best to impress them and speak for her husband. American and British officials quickly learned why the China-Burma-India theater commanders Adm. Mountbatten and Gen. Stilwell were frustrated dealing with the couple.[73]

In September 1942 Wendell Willkie made a "fact-finding" trip as FDR's representative. One of his stops was Chongqing, the wartime capital of the Kuomintang. Impressing Willkie was important, so Chiang and Soong spared no expense to stage Willkie's visit for maximum advantage. Accompanying Willkie was publisher and broadcaster Mike Cowles, soon to become director of the Domestic Branch of the OWI. Willkie's itinerary was carefully managed; he saw only what the couple wanted him to see, and he was impressed. One exception was that Willkie wanted to see communist official Zhou Enlai, whom he had met twice before and liked. But it was Soong who impressed Willkie the most—literally.

On several occasions Willkie and Soong disappeared together for copious lengths of time. Cowles and American diplomats had the distinct impression that she had physically seduced the ambassador, who was known to have a roving eye. Willkie certainly led his colleagues to believe he had become intimate with Soong. When Willkie and Cowles returned to the United States, Soong followed. She sought a medical diagnosis and had a standing invitation from Eleanor Roosevelt to stay at the White House. On November 27, 1942, Soong arrived in Miami aboard an Air Transport Command Pan Am Boeing 307 Stratoliner especially assigned to her for the trip from China to Florida. Soong had severe abdominal pains and thought she had stomach cancer, but the cause turned out to be an intestinal parasite.[74]

At Cairo, the Kuomintang sought increased material aid, and the Western allies wanted a more focused and effective effort to push the Japanese out of Burma. Regarding Europe and the war against Germany, the American and British chiefs of staff hammered out plans for the Italian campaign and, importantly, progress concerning the command and timetable of the forthcoming invasion of Northwest Europe, code-named Overlord. FDR and Churchill also conferred with their diplomats, W. Averell Harriman and Anthony Eden, to prepare for their meeting with Stalin.[75]

FDR and his party left Cairo West aerodrome aboard the Sacred Cow at 7:07 a.m. on November 27. En route to Teheran the c-54 flew over the Suez Canal and Jerusalem. American minister Louis Dreyfus Jr. and Brig. Gen. Patrick Hurley met the plane when it arrived at Teheran's Gale Morghe airport at 3:00 p.m.[76]

Before the Teheran summit, code-named Eureka, there was no unified military strategy between the Western Allies and the Soviet Union. Stalin was insistent upon the opening of a second or Western Front, and he sought assurances about American material support. There was tension seeping into the American and British alliance over the future of the British Empire, but neither government was prepared to surrender Eastern Europe.[77] Stalin was determined to separate the Western Allies, and Roosevelt was equally interested in engaging him one-on-one. Roosevelt met Stalin for the first time, alone, on November 28. FDR the capitalist and Stalin the communist both desired a positive working relationship and formed a wary if outwardly friendly rapport, FDR introduced Stalin to one of his beloved dry gin martinis. Stalin's reaction when asked by FDR if he liked the drink was a polite "all right, but it is cold on the stomach."[78]

The Soviet Union and Britain occupied Iran. In 1941 they deposed Reza Shah for pro-Nazi leanings and replaced him with his son. Before meeting FDR, Stalin paid a visit on the young Shah Mohammed Pahlavi, who later remembered Stalin as charming but dangerous.[79] FDR and Churchill also individually met with Pahlavi. Over the next three days, the leaders and their teams hammered out a communiqué they called the "Three Power Agreement." Stalin was pleased to learn about the planned invasion of northwest Europe and promised to launch an offensive in the east to coordinate with Operation Overlord. He agreed to enter the war against Japan after the Allies defeated Germany.[80]

FDR left Teheran for Cairo on December 2 aboard the Sacred Cow and circled for a view over Baghdad, Iraq, along the way. In Cairo he met again with Churchill to discuss the meetings with Stalin. On December 4–5 FDR met privately with Pres. Gen. Ismet Inonu of Turkey and together with Churchill, and he dined privately with Field Marshal Jan C. Smuts of South Africa. On December 7 FDR returned to Tunis and the villa at Carthage. The following day the president toured Malta and Sicily, meeting Lord Gort on Malta and General Patton at his Castelvetrano headquarters. He returned that evening to the villa and left the next morning for a long flight to Dakar, French West Africa. FDR transferred to the uss *Iowa*, and Task Group 27.5 headed west. At 8:27 a.m. on December 16, *Iowa* arrived at the entrance of Chesapeake Bay. The next morning, aboard the uss *Potomac*, FDR arrived at the Washington Navy Yard, and the First Lady welcomed him home.[81]

PART III

Pax Americana

Let every nation know, whether it wishes us well or ill, that we shall pay any price, bear any burden, meet any hardship, support any friend, oppose any foe to assure the survival and the success of liberty.

Pres. JOHN FITZGERALD KENNEDY, January 20, 1961

Fig. 18. Pres. John F. Kennedy. Photograph by David Iwerks, 1960. National Portrait Gallery, Smithsonian Institution, Washington DC (NPG.77.344).

SEVEN

Road to Victory

D-Day

The American people had innocent nineteenth-century notions of China as a mysterious Confucian and Mandarin realm, and Hollywood reinforced these illusions. This was not acceptable to the OWI. Chiang's China had to modernize and democratize. Col. Frank Capra's *Battle of China* and the OWI both noted that although Americans had warm feelings for the Chinese, they did not understand that China was "an important world power and ally" that had been already fighting the Japanese for ten years.[1]

Early war films like *Flying Tigers* with John Wayne only used China as a backdrop for American action against Japan with the Chinese as spectators. Up through 1944 the OWI was particularly irritated with a continuing stream of *Charlie Chan* "B" features with wartime themes that the agency was certain would insult Chinese audiences. The OWI banned the *Charlie Chan* films for export to Asia.[2]

Two serious films about China, *Dragon Seed* and *Keys to the Kingdom*, had considerable OWI input. The OWI reviewed and returned the *Dragon Seed* script to MGM because the agency felt that the Pearl Buck story should strengthen the portrayal of the Chinese characters. MGM returned the script with the OWI recommendations added.[3] Critics, however, eviscerated the film. They criticized Caucasians including tall Katherine Hepburn playing Chinese characters and Chinese actors playing Japanese characters. Critics could also not accept the glamorization and democratization of China. James Agee called it an "unimaginably bad movie."[4]

Fox produced *The Keys of the Kingdom,* a turn-of-the-century historic drama from an A. J. Cronin novel about a Catholic missionary priest, Fr. Francis Chisholm from Scotland, played by young Gregory Peck. Posted to China, Fr. Chisholm discovers poverty, famine, war, corruption, banditry, and resistance to Christianity. Production Code Administrator Joseph Breen warned Fox in 1941 that the script would provoke vigorous protest from Chiang's diplomats in the United States. Fox sat on the script until January 1943 and sent it to the OWI. The screenplay by Nunnally Johnson and Joseph Mankiewicz stunned the OWI. Their treatment presented China as a nation beset by civil war, racial conflicts, and superstitions; populated by ignorant, backward, and cowardly people. Although the story was set circa 1900, Ulric Bell refused to approve it and gave Fox specific ideas for changing the script.[5] With the input of the Chinese counsel in Los Angeles, T. K. Chang, Fox hired Wei Fan Hsueh, Fr. Albert O'Hara, S. J., and Fr. Wilfrid Parsons, S. J. as technical advisers. Fox altered the story to be set over a thirty-year time to show material progress in China. They revised the script, as Fr. O'Hara put it, to show China in a more "favorable light than the actual conditions at the time would have required." The OWI was satisfied with these changes that fit FDR's China policy and passed the film.

During 1943 Hollywood's treatment of Japan was improving but still riddled with stereotypes. *Guadalcanal Diary* from Fox in 1943 was technically an improvement. Based on a bestselling book by author Richard Tregaskis, the film shows the efforts of the first Marine Corps units to land on the island in August 1942 and the fierce fighting that enveloped the Solomon Islands into 1943. The OWI found the film and script by Lamar Trotti "the most realistic and outstanding picture" about the Pacific war to date.[6] Critical reviews varied, although most praised the use of real combat footage to bring realism to the story. None of the critics commented on the continued racism that Elmer Davis found abhorrent and counterproductive.

The Doolittle Raid on Japan in April 1942 was ready-made for Hollywood once the military declassified enough of the details.

One of the pilots, Capt. Ted Lawson, authored a book with popular writer Bob Considine titled *Thirty Seconds over Tokyo* about his experience, and MGM bought the film rights. Mervyn Leroy directed the film, and Dalton Trumbo wrote the screenplay. The studio put Van Johnson into the starring role with Phyllis Thaxter as his wife and Spencer Tracy playing Doolittle. The OWI was pleased with the script. The film closely followed the real-life story with few dramatics and excellent aerial scenes shot on location in California and Florida. MGM artfully used actual film shot by Cmdr. John Ford to portray the dramatic takeoff of B-25 Mitchell bombers from the USS *Hornet*. The Chinese come across in this film in an intelligent and positive manner, and the film is remarkably free of anti-Japanese slurs. This was a credit to Dalton Trumbo's ability and sensitivity.[7]

The Purple Heart, released by Fox in 1944, also dealt with the Doolittle Raid but focused on an American aircrew that the Japanese captured, and Darryl F. Zanuck took personal charge of the production. This was the first film to deal directly with the treatment of American POWs by the Japanese. The subject was controversial because the War Department had not previously approved any POW film for fear of reprisals. They lifted that ban in 1943 after revealing Japanese atrocities in the Philippines. Zanuck took control of the script and realized that dramatics were unnecessary. The plot centers around a trial of the captured Americans in Tokyo. The Imperial Army prosecutor, played by Chinese American actor Richard Loo, wants the men to admit that they came from an aircraft carrier, so as to embarrass the rival Imperial Navy. He tortures the men who do not break. Their refusal induces the prosecutor's suicide before the Americans' probable execution, which we do not see. The OWI praised the script and Zanuck's alterations.[8]

Directed by William Wellman, *The Story of G. I. Joe* was the ultimate World War II combat feature. Made in 1945 and set in Italy, the film has a realism and maturity far removed from earlier and less intelligent war films. It was based upon the Pulitzer Prize–winning reporting of Scripps-Howard war correspondent

Ernie Pyle, played by Burgess Meredith. Pyle became a beloved journalist who honestly reported on the sacrifices of the ordinary infantrymen of the war. A Japanese sniper killed Pyle on Ie Shima near Okinawa in 1945. The film is a tribute to both the soldiers he represented well and Pyle himself. Wellman achieved realism by mixing scenes from John Huston's *Battle of San Pietro* combat footage into the production.

Robert Mitchum gave an excellent performance as the infantry company commander, and the cast included 150 combat veterans. The film includes a segment about the controversial bombing of Monte Cassino, which the foot soldiers beneath the Benedictine Abbey applaud. At the end of the sensitive story, the enemy kills the captain. In a fitting epitaph to four years of war films, Pyle says in a voice-over, "This is our war . . . We will carry it with us from one battleground to another. In the end, we will win. I hope we can rejoice in our victory, but humbly . . . as for those beneath the wooden crosses we can only murmur, thanks, pal, thanks."[9]

In January 1944, with Secretary Hull in declining health, General Marshall recommended that FDR appoint Rockefeller as undersecretary of state for Latin American affairs and thus incorporate the OCIAA into the State Department. The conciliatory, charming, and well-intentioned forty-four-year old former head of U.S. Steel, Edward J. Stettinius Jr., had just replaced Welles as undersecretary of state. Hull was racing to form a postwar peace organization, and Rockefeller was struggling to keep postwar Latin American relations a priority and wanted the OCIAA made permanent. Anything less would confirm Nazi claims that the Good Neighbor Policy was a mere wartime expedient.[10]

On March 31, 1944, two Japanese Kawanishi H8K2 Emily flying boats departed from Palau in the Caroline Islands for Davao, Mindanao. The first carried Adm. Mineichi Koga, commander in chief of the Japanese Combined Fleet. For security reasons Koga's chief of staff, Rear Adm. Shigeru Fukudome, boarded the second plane. The flying boats flew into a typhoon, and both crashed. All aboard the lead plane perished. Fukudome survived and became the first flag-rank Japanese Naval officer ever captured. Filipinos fished

Fukudome's red leather portfolio out of the water. It contained a set of top-secret documents, Operation Z, the Japanese defensive plan for the entire Central and Southwest Pacific. The American guerilla leader on Cebu, Lt. Col. James M. Cushing, found himself besieged by Japanese forces intent on rescuing Fukudome. Worried about reprisals against civilians, he released the admiral but kept the portfolio. Cushing packed and sent the documents to Lt. Col. Edwin Andrews on Negros, where submarines regularly made runs to Australia. Meanwhile, Ultra intercepts indicated that the Japanese were hunting for the portfolio. From Negros the submarine USS *Crevalle* survived depth-charge attacks to deliver the documents to Darwin, where MacArthur's intelligence staff expedited them by air to the Allied Translator and Interpreter Section (ATIS) in Brisbane. There the exceptional Nisei and Caucasian military intelligence team from the University of Colorado Boulder Defense Language School and under the command of Col. Sidney Forrester Mashbir deciphered Operation Z. Because the Japanese did not recover Fukudome's portfolio, Adm. Soemu Toyoda, Koga's successor, adjusted his strategy. But it was too late. Ultra intercepted Japanese messages containing the adjustments. Nimitz used the captured documents to decisive advantage in the battles of Leyte Gulf and the Philippine Sea.[11]

At the Casablanca Conference, the Allies created the Chief of Staff to the Supreme Allied Commander, a group responsible for the organization and planning of forthcoming Allied operations for Western Europe, including the cross-Channel invasion. British Lt. Gen. F. E. Morgan ran COSSAC, and American Brig. Gen. Ray Barker was his deputy commander.[12]

On January 17, 1944, Gen. Dwight D. Eisenhower became supreme commander of Supreme Headquarters, Allied Expeditionary Force (SHAEF) and commanding general of the European Theatre of Operations, United States Army. SHAEF absorbed COSSAC on February 13, 1944, and activated a Public Relations and Psychological Warfare Division (G-6) under Brig. Gen. Robert A. McClure on February 14, 1944, to coordinate all Allied information and psychological warfare activities.[13] G-6 became two divisions on April 13, 1944, with McClure in charge of the Psychological Warfare Division (PWD) and Brig. Gen. Thomas J. Davis running the Public Relations Division (PRD).[14]

McClure believed that SHAEF had to have consistent messages German troops depend on as being truthful. The information had to be reliable, stress Allied unity, and stress the certainty of German defeat.

Eisenhower believed that an effective psy-ops campaign could save many lives on both sides by shortening the war. SHAEF PWD realized that the German military and public would expect punishment in some form for Nazi policies and would not react favorably to messages either pledging mercy or making accusations. Instead, messages focused on Allied superiority in manpower and equipment, the impossible nature of a two-front war, the weakness of the Luftwaffe, the ineffectiveness of Hitler, the unlikelihood of German victory, and the idea that German soldiers had done their duty and could surrender with honor. These themes would permeate Allied propaganda and radio broadcasts.[15]

The SHAEF Public Relations Division (PRD) controlled press, radio, and photographic censorship, press communication, communiqués, and policy for news correspondents in the European Theatre of Operations (ETO).[16] The role of SHAEF PRD was to communicate accurate and candid war information within the limits of operational security. Any information released to correspondents could be potentially helpful to the enemy. Innocuous movements of correspondents reported in their dispatches could draw attention to invasion preparations. Correspondents could accurately guess Allied plans from the bits and pieces they heard over cocktails after hours. The sizable number of Allied and neutral news representatives who had swarmed into Britain made the situation worse.[17] The authorities could not control correspondents and photographers around London as they could on military bases or in the field. SHAEF PRD therefore selected a limited number of accredited correspondents to cover D-Day with dispatches subject to military censorship.

Eisenhower gave a personal "off the record" briefing for the press on May 16. He told correspondents accredited to SHAEF he considered them as quasi-staff officers and responsible for the safety of Allied troops and the success of forthcoming operations. The supreme commander said he would allow the accredited correspondents to speak freely with officers and mix with enlisted men to "see the machinery of war in operation in order to visualize and transmit to the public the conditions under which the men from their countries are waging war against the enemy." He read this order to the correspondents at the beginning of his personal briefing, reiterating his belief "public opinion wins wars."

Eisenhower went on to say, "without public opinion behind us, we would be nothing but mercenaries." Like Elmer Davis at the OWI, Eisenhower believed that SHAEF ought to inform the people of success and failure alike, and he reminded the correspondents that the fault for any errors rested with his leadership, not the men in the forces. He promised he would not condone censorship of any criticism correspondents might make of him or his decisions, because "a military man in high places should not use his extraordinary power to protect himself." Eisenhower's candor and self-depreciation impressed the correspondents. As of June 5, 1944, there were 530 accredited members of the press at SHAEF.[18]

The SHAEF press contingent included the cbs team that Ed Murrow built up in London, including Charles Collingwood, Bill Downs, Richard C. Hottelet, Howard K. Smith, and Larry LeSueur. Eric Sevareid and William L. Shirer also reported from Europe. Among the legion of American correspondents soon to invade France were Walter Cronkite, *United Press*, Ernest Hemingway, Marguerite Higgins, *New York Herald Tribune*, Edward M. Kennedy and Margaret Bourke White, *Associated Press*, Ernie Pyle, *Scripps-Howard*, and Quentin Reynolds, *Collier's*.

When BPR radio chief Col. Ed Kirby visited Britain and the Mediterranean during 1943, he met with Eisenhower's HQ staff. There he renewed an acquaintance with Cmdr. Harry Butcher, Eisenhower's aide-de-camp. They discussed an idea to set up a SHAEF broadcasting service, and Butcher passed along Kirby's recommendation to Eisenhower, who liked the idea. This set up a debate within SHAEF and with the BBC that led to the launch

Fig. 19. Gen. Dwight D. Eisenhower, supreme commander, Allied Expeditionary Force. Portrait by Thomas Edgar Stephens, 1947. National Portrait Gallery, Smithsonian Institution, Washington DC (NPG.65.63).

of an American, British, and Canadian radio service. On March 20, 1944, Eisenhower added Col. David Sarnoff as his communications adviser, and on May 1, 1944, he asked Surles for permission to bring in Kirby from Washington to direct the new SHAEF Broadcasting Service.[19]

The BBC initially opposed the idea, so Eisenhower appealed to Churchill, who convinced Brenden Bracken and the Ministry of Information (MOI) to go along with Eisenhower's plan. Maurice Gorham, the BBC Foreign Service North American director, became the director of the newly christened Allied Expeditionary Forces Programme (AEFP), an Kirby became troop broadcasting director for SHAEF. Gorham and Kirby had twelve days between approval on May 23 and D-Day, set for June 5, to put the new service on the air.[20] Sir Noel Ashbridge and the BBC engineering staff had already prepared a transmitter with a strong medium wave (AM) signal to give the new service excellent coverage in Normandy. Gorham and Kirby got to work rounding up personnel, and Eisenhower sent a cable to Marshall and Arnold in Washington requesting the services of Capt. Glenn Miller and his Army Air Forces Radio Production Unit and Orchestra, which they approved.[21]

Preparing for Operation Overlord, Eisenhower believed that media coverage of D-Day and the succeeding campaign was second in importance only to military victories.[22] He needed an officer who was a senior-level communications leader and who was an experienced negotiator, understood the issues, and had the credibility to carry out the mission. Col. David Sarnoff fit the specifications better than any officer in the armed forces.[23] On the blustery day of March 20, 1944, he arrived at Hendon Aerodrome and checked into Claridge's Hotel. There an annoyed if amused Sarnoff discovered that the hotel mixed up his room with competitor William Paley of CBS, also in London on wartime duty, and Sarnoff had mistakenly received Paley's laundry and meal tab. On his second day in London Eisenhower gave Sarnoff three urgent tasks: create a SHAEF broadcasting service to inform and entertain all Allied forces in Europe, evaluate current and planned military communications systems for D-Day and the campaign in Northwestern Europe, and arrange for news coverage from the scenes of action. Eisenhower wanted the American people to get the straight news in a prompt manner.[24] Later that day Sarnoff met with Sir Noel Ashbridge, who proposed the BBC transmitter antenna farm at Start Point and a powerful 100 kw medium wave (AM) transmitter that he and BBC engineering wanted to make available for the Allied Expeditionary Forces Programme (AEFP). Gorham and Kirby had to quickly work out the setup for the new AEFP service, and Sarnoff had just made their lives much easier. Ashbridge also assigned a Start Point transmitter to SHAEF for psychological warfare broadcasts.[25]

Sarnoff then focused on preparing for new media coverage of D-Day. His obligation was to cut through red tape and maneuvers for competitive advantage and assure the fourth estate equality of opportunity to cover the impending drama. He could only do this if transmission facilities could handle the expected traffic. He set up a single and unified Signal Center at the MOI.[26] He directed the Army Signal Corps to erect a new transmitter so that the American networks could broadcast simultaneously from England and by London relay from Normandy. He held a Signal Center dress rehearsal on May 25, and everything seemed to work. On May 29 he went to the south coast to inspect facilities, including the USS *Ancon*, AGC-4, a cruise ship that the Army Signal Corps and the navy remade into a floating communications center. There were a thousand radio and electronics specialists aboard *Ancon*, and the ship housed several large radio broadcasting studios. Sarnoff and the SHAEF Signals Division were satisfied that all preparations for D-Day were in order.[27]

At 9:30 a.m. DBST (Double British Summer Time) on June 6, 1944, Col. R. Ernest DuPuy, deputy commander, Public Relations Division, Supreme Headquarters, Allied Expeditionary Force, read SHAEF Communiqué #1 from the London University radio room, "Under the command of General Eisenhower, allied naval forces supported by strong air forces began landing allied armies this morning on the northern coast of France."[28] The next morning at 5:30 a.m. DBST, the AEFP signed on with an opening statement by Capt. Franklin Englemann.[29]

Within twenty-four hours of D-Day, SHAEF was able to cable the War Department that all communications and signals had worked properly. It was clear to everyone that Sarnoff had succeeded.[30]

In 1942 Capt. John Ford left a Field Photo unit team led by Mark Armistead in London to photograph in detail French coastal waters, beaches, and terrain from dangerously low-flying photo-reconnaissance planes. Eisenhower told Donovan that Armistead's D-Day preparation work alone justified the entire OSS. Armistead worked closely with PT-boat squadron commander Lt. John D. Bulkeley, who had won the Medal of Honor in 1942 for evacuating Gen. Douglas MacArthur from Corregidor. When Ford arrived in London during April 1944, Armistead introduced him to Bulke- ley. Author William L. White had memorialized Bulkeley's exploits in the best-selling book *They Were Expendable*. Ford's associates Frank "Spig" Wead, a Navy veteran, and Jim McGuinness, among others, wanted Ford to direct a film version of the book for MGM. Ford told them that it would have to wait.[31]

On the evening of June 5, having dispersed his camera crews among Allied assault troops, Ford went aboard the USS *Augusta*, flagship of Rear Adm. Alan G. Kirk's Western Task Force. During the early hours of June 6, he watched the perilous Omaha Beach assault by American troops. Wanting to get closer to the action, he joined Armistead and Bulkeley aboard one of Bulkeley's PT boats, where Ford stayed aboard for five days, getting a taste of combat as Bulkeley's squadron fought enemy E-boats off Cher- bourg. Later, Ford accompanied Bulkeley to film a PT boat mis- sion to support Tito's Yugoslav partisans. Bulkeley told Ford that White's book exaggerated his exploits and that he did not deserve the Medal of Honor, but their days together convinced Ford that Bulkeley's story was important, and Ford felt he was the one to do it.[32] Ford handed off color film work to fellow Hollywood director Col. George Stevens, whose Army Photo Unit went ahead with American combat ground forces all the way to Berlin.[33]

Restoration of French radio and telegraph services was vital for both military and psychological reasons. Sarnoff prioritized the restoration of direct radiotelegraphy from Paris to London and

New York, suspended ever since the Nazis had occupied La Ville-Lumière in 1940. There were technical and political challenges, including regulations and management of facilities destroyed or abandoned by the retreating Wehrmacht. At times Sarnoff ran head on into Gen. de Gaulle's concept of national prestige, but he was careful to negotiate an agreement with the French PTT (Postes, Télégraphes et Téléphones) that specified SHAEF would handle any disputes about priorities or maintenance.[34]

As early as July 15 Sarnoff also began to concern himself with telecommunications in Germany. The invasion of Germany was still very much in the future, but Sarnoff believed that SHAEF had to start planning for the special problems they would meet in the enemy homeland. He outlined a series of Signal Corps guidelines for Germany that became the foundation of a working plan that he would later develop.

Sarnoff traveled to North Africa to set up another communications center for Operation Dragoon, the August 15 invasion of Provence and the Rhône Valley. The Allies liberated Rome on June 4, and Sarnoff went on to the Eternal City to confer with Gen. Mark Clark, commander of the U.S. Fifth Army, before returning to SHAEF. In North Africa Sarnoff found an unused 50 kw OWI transmitter, which he diverted to AEFP to enhance the SHAEF broadcasting signal coverage on the continent.[35]

Cultural Renaissance

La Résistance, the French Forces of the Interior, or the FFI, was nominally under the wing of SHAEF and commanded by Gen. Pierre Koenig. American forces were in the Paris suburbs and approaching the Seine on August 24 when rioting led by La Résistance broke out in and around the city. Eisenhower preferred to bypass Paris, but events forced him to divert resources to occupy the city. As the Wehrmacht hurriedly withdrew, the FFI was able to make it impossible for Gen. Dietrich von Choltitz to carry out Hitler's order to destroy Paris landmarks and infrastructure. The FFI included communist elements that presented a threat to de Gaulle consolidating control over Paris. On his own authority de Gaulle

Fig. 20. Col. David Sarnoff (*left*), U.S. Army Signal Corps, special communications consultant of Supreme Headquarters of Allied Expeditionary Force and president of Radio Corporation of America, in London with Col. Edward Kirby, director of troop broadcasting of Supreme Headquarters of Allied Expeditionary Force, August 1944. Courtesy Library of American Broadcasting, University of Maryland.

ordered Gen. Phillippe Leclerc and the French Second Armored Division to advance into the city. Eisenhower had no choice but to support the unauthorized diversion. In Paris von Choltitz had twenty thousand men to control a city of three million.

Although von Choltitz had no intention of destroying Paris, he also did not want to surrender to the FFI and get lynched. He needed safe passage from the Americans. As Leclerc's Sherman tanks with white American stars entered the city at dusk on August 24, thrilled Parisians at first thought that the Americans had arrived. At 10:00 the next morning, welcomed by ecstatic crowds, the U.S. Fourth Division's tanks and troops reached Île de la Cité and Nôtre Dame.[36]

When von Choltitz surrendered, Hitler ordered V-2 guided

missiles turned upon Paris, but Gen. Hans Speidel ignored der Führer. Speidel survived the war and served alongside Allied officers in NATO as a founder of the Bundeswehr. A fellow Swabian, Speidel served as Field Marshal Erwin Rommel's chief of staff and was answering the phone for Field Marshal Walter Model when Gen. Alfred Jodl called with Hitler's insane order.[37]

American officials and journalists within striking distance of Paris converged on the city, among them Ernest Hemingway and Ernie Pyle. Those who were there that day remembered it as the most exciting day of their lives. Ernie Pyle reported, "the war should have ended at that moment."[38]

A triumphant de Gaulle welcomed Eisenhower to Paris on a picture-perfect Sunday, August 27, for a victory celebration as Parisians chanted "Eisenhower, Eisenhower!" The supreme commander recognized de Gaulle's status even though FDR and the State Department did not.[39]

On August 25 Sarnoff had set off by jeep for Paris from SHAEF Forward HQ at Granville, a two-hundred-mile trip. The next morning he headed for Boulevard Haussmann and the studios of Radio France. There he reunited with Radio France director Emile Girardeau, who gave an emotional account of what had been happening under Nazi rule since 1940. Sarnoff ordered Girardeau to reassemble the personnel of Radio France and restore contact with London and New York. He requisitioned supplies to feed the employees and sent armed American Military Police to guard the facilities. He inspected the wreckage at Émetteur de Sainte-Assise and was delighted to find that the Wehrmacht had botched the demolition job. The Germans were in a hurry and had blown the big medium-wave towers and antennae but left inside equipment intact as well as smaller towers and antennae, or the heart of the shortwave system. Sarnoff restored communication with London and New York within several days.[40]

Correspondents did not always adhere to SHAEF PRD rules. Some of the transgressions were due to communications difficulties between the front lines, rear-echelon stations, and London. Larry LeSueur of CBS entered Paris on August 25 with Free

French forces. When he could not find a military censor to provide a clearance stamp for his reports at the Scribe Hotel, headquarters for the Allied press corps, he went to a French underground radio station on the Rue de Grenelle and broadcast on its transmitter without a censor's clearance. LeSueur provided Americans with the first radio account of the liberation, but SHAEF PRD suspended his credentials for thirty days.[41]

By mid-September American forces penetrated the German Reich at two points as units of Patton's quick-moving Third Army ran out of gas. The Twenty-First Army Group liberated the vital port of Antwerp, although Field Marshal Montgomery did not capture the vital crossings over the Albert Canal that controlled sea access to the port. The Wehrmacht realized the importance of Antwerp and reinforced the strategic sixty-mile Scheldt Estuary, Walcheren, North Beverland Islands, and South Beverland peninsula to deny the use of the port to the Allies. The Allied supply lines ran hundreds of miles from Normandy ports and Marseilles to the front lines, so it was important to make use of closer Antwerp as the staging area for the invasion of Germany. The Canadian First Army drew the nasty assignment of clearing the Scheldt Estuary. As the operation stalled, Montgomery proposed a different plan, an airborne assault code-named Operation Market Garden, to dislodge the German defenses and open Antwerp.[42]

During August 1943 Brewster Morgan appointed broadcaster Oliver Nicoll from the OWI in New York as his deputy. Morgan visualized an independent American radio station serving Europe, and Nicoll envisioned an affiliate of the Voice of America. Their ideas came together as the American Broadcasting Station in Europe (ABSIE), which would originate 50 percent of its own programs but serve as an outlet of the VOA with the other 50 percent of its programs coming from New York. The OWI shipped transmitters and equipment to Britain in September of 1943. Morgan requisitioned studio space and installed switching equipment lines and cables to link the studios with the BBC. The ABSIE offices were at 2 Sharaton Street, and studios were around the corner at Film House, 142 Wardour Street.

The ABSIE English, Danish, Dutch, French, German, and Norwegian sections started rehearsals and dry runs on April 10, 1944. The sections also handled broadcasts in Flemish and to Czechoslovakia. OWI shipped several more 50 kw transmitters for installation on the Continent after Allied forces had liberated potential sites. One of these transmitters was the one Sarnoff diverted to the AEFP.[43]

Robert Sherwood arrived in March 1944 to direct OWI psy-ops in coordination with SHAEF PWD. There were 1,200 OWI staff in London, and 279 of them worked with Sherwood to engage in propaganda to confuse and discourage the enemy, hearten occupied peoples, and prepare guerilla forces for liberation. Sherwood's group prepared newspapers, leaflets dropped from American planes, and messages contained on ABSIE and SHAEF PWD broadcasts.[44]

William S. Paley had taken a leave of absence as president of CBS. He received an informal army commission and became deputy commander of the SHAEF PWD, reporting to General McClure. He coordinated the activities of SHAEF PWD with the OWI and ABSIE, the BBC, the British government, and representatives of occupied nations in London. One of Paley's assignments was arranging with the Dutch government to record their Radio Orange program for broadcast by ABSIE. Paley also arranged with the BBC for ABSIE to broadcast their *Les Française Parlent Aux Française* program. The Radio Orange and BBC programs helped fill out the ABSIE broadcast schedule.[45]

ABSIE went on the air April 30, 1944, at 5:30 p.m. DBST. Brewster Morgan spoke the first words and introduced Robert Sherwood, who addressed the purpose of the new service. BBC director general William Haley spoke following Sherwood. ABSIE broadcast translations of their announcements all evening in French, Danish, Dutch, German, and Norwegian. The BBC Home Service and the VOA rebroadcast both speeches worldwide. Mutual and the Blue Network carried Sherwood's address in the United States. Radio Algiers transmitted a three-minute message from Henri Laugier, rector of the University of Algiers, to open the ABSIE French service. The opening French program also included a message of greeting from Gen. Pierre Koenig, the French representative on Eisenhower's staff. ABSIE transmitted in Danish, Dutch (with fifteen minutes produced by Radio Orange), English, Flemish, French, German, Norwegian, and, later, Czech. By direct relay from New York ABSIE carried the daily "ACES" programs, *America Calling Europe*, *Amerika Aufruf Europa*, and *Appel Amérique l'Europe*.

In June 1944 Philip Cohen, chief of the OWI Domestic Radio Bureau, replaced Morgan as OWI London director of broadcasting, and Morgan became the OWI representative with the U.S. Army in Europe (ETOUSA). Cohen brought in Robert Saudek, on leave from the Blue Network, as station manager. Cohen and Saudek arranged for an underground office and studio in case a V-1 flying bomb hit the Wardour Street studios. The "crash" quarters were set up in the basement at 49 Carlos Place, near the American Embassy on Grosvenor Square.[46]

As instruments of psychological warfare, ABSIE and the BBC European Service adhered to the directives of SHAEF PWD. ABSIE and BBC producers and editors worked with SHAEF PWD "guidance notes" for scripts. On all matters of handling military news in the ETO, ABSIE followed SHAEF directives. ABSIE and the BBC European Service broadcast coded messages from SHAEF under a schedule drawn up by SHAEF PWD. ABSIE also broadcast coded messages to the European underground from the OSS. Such messages consisted of meaningless-sounding phrases like "it is time for Charles to lock the ceiling window."

The policy of the OWI was never to directly answer Nazi propaganda. Sherwood did not want to engage in polemics with the enemy. The OWI wanted American propaganda to be positive and designed to counteract and remove the basis for the enemy's propaganda offensives.[47]

Robert Bauer, who had worked in the German Section of the OWI New York office, organized the ABSIE German Section on March 29, 1944. When ABSIE went on the air, the section included William H. Hale, former chief of the German desk in New York, and Alfred Puhan, who identified himself on the air as Alfred Zimmerman. Bauer stayed as chief until August 1944 and then went to the Continent. Puhan succeeded him and stayed until December 1944, when he, too, went to the Continent. George Hanfmann replaced Puhan and remained chief of the section for the rest of ABSIE's existence.

From April to August 1944 ABSIE's German broadcasts supported Allied military operations and focused on Wehrmacht troops. From September 1944, as the Allied armies advanced to Germany and SHAEF took over radio stations such as Radio Luxembourg, ABSIE's role shifted to a campaign of surrender and the occupation. ABSIE served as the voice of SHAEF to prepare the German people for defeat and Allied occupation.

Hanfmann reported in February 1945, "while it is impossible to say how many of the 870,000 Germans captured on the western front to-date have been influenced by ABSIE German broadcasts, our interrogators do encounter prisoners who make definite statements to this effect." In June 1944 ABSIE began reading the names of German prisoners of war. Henry Hatfield of the German section took charge of the prisoner broadcasts to obtain prisoners' reactions to ABSIE broadcasts and to record talks from the prisoners themselves. Hatfield designed these recordings to attract family members listening in Germany for news about their loved ones as well as to support the surrender campaign among the German soldiers.[48]

Radio Luxembourg became the center for tactical military psyops while ABSIE continued to have a strategic focus. ABSIE concentrated on the audience within the shrinking Reich. The German section began to broadcast an informational series to prepare the German people for what the principles and details of Allied occupation would be. A strong propaganda theme was the contrast between the rule of law and order in the Allied-occupied part of western Germany as opposed to the increasingly chaotic conditions in the rest of Germany under the disintegrating Nazi regime.

Directed by Paley, SHAEF PWD and the OSS used Radio Luxembourg to broadcast "Operation Annie" at night, consisting of broadcasts in German on another frequency, which they announced as originating in Germany. This was the type of psy-ops known as a "black" operation. The Germans were doing the same thing with Radio Arnhem and similar operations based in Cologne, where they broadcast a signal with recordings of actual AEFP broadcasts mixed with fake news presentations.[49]

George Herald screened intelligence material to inform German listeners of bad news they could not receive from Nazi media. He used these demoralizing stories in news broadcasts and interspersed them with music in a musical program for German soldiers called *Musik für die Wehrmacht*. Herald gave Germans the confidence that ABSIE would honestly answer their questions and that what they heard was worth the risk of listening.

Gottfried "Golo" Mann, deputy chief of the German Section and the son of German literary legend Thomas Mann, produced a weekly summary of events in Germany and a daily word on the situation in Germany. Mann also prepared a daily feature called *The Lie of the Day* (*Die Lüge des Tages*) where he singled out a current German propaganda theme and exposed it.

In addition to *Musik für die Wehrmacht,* the principal ABSIE German-language programs included the aforementioned *Amerika Aufruf Europa* (*America Calling Europe*), *Für Ihre Freunde* (*News for Your Friends*), with women's and labor features produced by announcer Gloria Wagner; *Programm für die Bundeswehr* (*Program for the German Forces*) (also relayed by Radio Luxembourg), *Nachricten aus dem Pazifik* (*Pacific War News*), and a weekend feature, *Nachrichten für die Luftwaffe* (*News for the Luftwaffe*).

ABSIE tried to improve the projection of America using interviews with German-speaking members of the United States armed forces. *Die Amerikaner "Yanks" Kommen Nach* (*The Yanks Are Coming*) served this purpose A German sergeant captured in Holland said on a prisoner broadcast, "It is not quite six weeks ago that I was still with a parachute regiment . . . we had the opportunity to listen to the radio . . . then we heard 'This is the Voice of America, one of the United Nations.' At first there were many things that we did not believe and appeared impossible to us. But after some days, sometimes after only a few weeks, we realized that it was the truth they told us, the truth that our radio concealed from us."[50]

William Klein supervised the production and writing of the music programs including *Musik für die Wehrmacht*. Bing Crosby and Dinah Shore recorded programs during their tours of England and the Continent. German listeners nicknamed Crosby "Der Bingle." German native Marlene Dietrich was a regular ABSIE and SHAEF PWD contributor. A series of weekly broadcasts by Maj. Glenn Miller and the American Band of the Allied Expeditionary Forces (ABAEF) with German continuity instantly became a highlight of the ABSIE schedule and received favorable comment.[51]

ABSIE irritated the Nazis. The enemy was never able to jam or block every frequency at the same time, so ABSIE broadcasts got through on multiple frequencies. In addition to reliable news and provocative commentary, ABSIE offered listeners authoritative interpretation of the news by persons of international reputation, including exiled European monarchs and political leaders, and American correspondents and commentators. The Nazis called ABSIE *Der Amerikanische Agitation-Station in Europa* (The American Agitation Station in Europe).[52]

For much of December 1944 bad weather caused the cancellation of passenger flights between London and Paris. Maj. Glenn Miller was supposed to be aboard one of those flights on December 14, 1944. Miller, Lt. Col. David Niven, and SHAEF were ready to complete arrangements for AEFP Paris broadcasting studios and to move Miller's ABAEF to France. Miller's Air Transport Command flight was canceled, and prospects looked bad for the next day or more. Frustrated, he accepted an invitation from an Eighth Air Force officer to hitch a ride on a Noorduyn C-64 "Norseman" courier plane on the afternoon of December 15. Not authorized for casual travel, an impatient Miller disobeyed orders, did not inform SHAEF of his intentions, and boarded the plane. The C-64 vanished over the English Channel, but authorities did not know that Miller was aboard until three days later.[53]

The poor weather also concealed a bold gamble by Hitler to seize the port of Antwerp and divide the Western Allied armies.

Before dawn on December 16 a ninety-minute artillery barrage lit up the sky along the front lines from Maastricht to Trier. The Fifth, Sixth, and Seventh Panzer Armies struck at the weakest point in the American lines to open Operation Wacht am Rhein (Operation Watch on the Rhine). Americans came to know this offensive as the Battle of the Bulge.

The Nazi armies neutralized several stunned American divisions that took heavy casualties and had no air support. German special forces dressed in American uniforms tried to sow confusion behind the American lines. The panzers soon encircled the strategic crossroads of Bastogne. At Versailles Eisenhower was celebrating the award of his fifth star, and the Allied command did not yet grasp the gravity of the situation.

The 101st Airborne Division commanding officer Maj. Gen. Maxwell Taylor was in the United States on December 16, 1944. Adverse weather delayed his deputy, Brig. Gen. Bernard Higgins in London. That left division artillery officer Brig. Gen. Anthony McAuliffe as acting commander when the "Screaming Eagles" rushed into the bulge and became surrounded at Bastogne. It was McAuliffe who famously answered a German surrender demand with one word, "Nuts." Following that dramatic moment, the skies cleared, exposing the advancing Panzers to attack from marauding Ninth Air Force Republic P-47 Thunderbolts and allowing the Troop Carrier Command Douglas C-47 transports to drop much needed food and ammunition.[54]

On Saturday, November 11, 1944, James Caesar Petrillo announced RCA Victor and Columbia records had come to an agreement with the AFM, settling the recording strike that had dragged on for twenty-eight months. But despite the strike, the draft, and wartime travel restrictions, top bandleaders continued to prosper due to wartime demand for entertainment, although former band singers had gained in popularity. RCA Victor and Columbia were catching up to Decca, Capitol, and transcription companies that had settled in September and October 1943.[55]

World War II was not only the apex of the big band era of popular music and jazz but was also a wide-reaching American cultural renaissance. Government, media, and private industry encouraged and supported the arts as never before. The nation, propelled by the extraordinary public and private sector push to win the war, was experiencing a dynamic explosion for arts and entertainment within a media, political, social, military, and industrial transformation.

Broadway flourished. In addition to the patriotic *This Is the Army* and *Winged Victory*, the first among successful wartime productions was undoubtedly Richard Rodgers and Oscar Hammerstein II's *Oklahoma*, directed by Rouben Mamoulian and choreographed by Agnes de Mille. The production opened at the St. James Theatre in New York on March 31, 1943, and was an immediate sensation. It ran for 2,212 performances, closing on May 29, 1948. The musical and dance motifs integrate into a story line that includes drama, comedy, and a wide range of emotions and messages that did not normally appear in musical productions until Hammerstein and Jerome Kern's *Show Boat* in 1927. In addition to Broadway, a national company started touring the country beginning in late 1943, and the USO assembled a military base tour. Decca released an album of original cast music in 1943, the first of its kind. *Oklahoma* received immediate and widespread critical praise. Before *Oklahoma*, the major Broadway productions of the early war years included *Louisiana Purchase* and *Panama Hattie* (1940), *Best Foot Forward* and *Let's Face It* (1941), *Priorities of 1942* and *Stars on Ice* (1942), and *Something for the Boys* (1943).

Many productions hit Broadway in 1944 and 1945 with the memorable standout being *On the Town*. The story of *On the Town* concerns three American sailors on shore leave in New York during 1944 and, as such, is a definitive wartime musical masterpiece. The production launched the distinguished musical career of Leonard Bernstein, who composed the music. Adolph Green and Betty Comden wrote the lyrics, based on Jerome Robbins's 1944 ballet *Fancy Free*. *On the Town* opened at the Adelphi Theater on December 28, 1944, directed by George Abbott and choreographed by Jerome Robbins. It closed on February 2, 1946, after 462 performances. The 1946 musical production *Call Me Mister* also captured the look and feel of wartime romance and fast-paced cultural change.

In January 1937 David Sarnoff approached Arturo Toscanini, who had retired to Italy after conducting the New York Philharmonic, about conducting a new world-class orchestra specifically for broadcasting and designed expressly for him. The world's most famous conductor conditionally accepted, provided he would be in complete control of the best orchestra in America, if not the world. Sarnoff went to all lengths to fund the prestigious project and build the enormous Studio 8-H at Radio City to house the new orchestra. After a momentary disagreement just as the first three broadcasts took place, Toscanini arrived in the United States to conduct his first NBC Symphony broadcast on Christmas night, December 25, 1937.

At the end of Toscanini's third season, 1939–1940, the NBC Symphony made a goodwill tour of South America. During Toscanini's fifth season he told Sarnoff that he reluctantly wished to again retire but left the door open for a return.

Sarnoff hired Leopold Stokowski to conduct, and other guest conductors appeared on broadcasts. Toscanini returned to conduct war-related performances for the Department of the Treasury and to record before the 1942 AFM strike. In the 1942–1943 season, Stokowski and Toscanini shared conducting duties. When Italy deposed Benito Mussolini in September 1943, the news bulletin came in during the NBC Symphony broadcast. After intermission, an emotional Toscanini and the orchestra finished their performance with "Garibaldi's War Hymn" and the "Star-Spangled Banner." The SSD Radio Section and AFRS made ample use of NBC broadcasts, and the V-Disc program issued many Toscanini NBC Symphony recordings. The collaboration of Sarnoff and Toscanini enriched the culture that America projected to the world during and after World War II.[56]

Conductor Andre Kostelanetz's *Pause That Refreshes on the Air* was one of three Coca-Cola vehicles produced before and during the war years in addition to *Victory Parade of Spotlight Bands* and *Songs by Morton Downey*. Kostelanetz and his wife, renown vocalist Lily Pons, traveled extensively during World War II on USO and military tours to the European, Pacific, and China-Burma-India Theatres of Operation.

During World War II serious music of the classical era received tremendous financial and ideological support from the U.S. government, particularly the OWI. Serge Koussevitzky said, "We, as musicians, are soldiers, too, fighting for the ever-growing spiritual need of the world. If music is our life, we give it joyfully to serve the cause of freedom."[57]

The OWI commissioned many composers including Aaron Copeland to write serious music. An OWI objective was to counter Nazi propaganda alleging the United States was a "jazz obsessed and mongrel nation of half-breeds" that had no cultural sophistication. Working with the OWI, Andre Kostelanetz commissioned composers to write musical portraits of famous Americans, including Copeland's *Lincoln Portrait* and Jerome Kern's *Mark Twain* (*A Portrait for Orchestra*). The VOA and ABSIE presented the United States as the last bastion of freedom, including freedom of the arts. This meant composers and musicians working in harmony and without fear of persecution or censorship.[58]

Although American troops naturally preferred big band swing as their favorite music, the classics were second. AFRS rebroadcast the CBS Kostelanetz commercial series *Pause That Refreshes on the Air* as *Music by Kostelanetz* and rebroadcast the NBC *Symphony Orchestra* with the same name. Harold Spivacke, director of the Library of Congress Music Division, was chairman of the Army and Navy Commission on Welfare and Recreation's Music Sub-Committee. Spivacke worked with the War Department BPR and Special Services to produce releases of serious music on V-Discs.

All through the war the OWI had difficulty dealing with the subject of the Soviet Union. Although Americans wanted the Soviets to defeat the Nazis, it was difficult for conservatives to embrace an atheist and communist ally. The American ambassador to Moscow, Joseph E. Davies, a World War I protégé of Woodrow Wilson, became the second American ambassador to the Soviet Union, following William Bullitt.

State Department professionals found Davies naive concerning Joseph Stalin. An admirer of Lenin, Davies found the State Department professionals to be conservative reactionaries. In 1941, when Hitler tore up the Nazi-Soviet Pact, FDR encouraged Davies to publish a book titled *Mission to Moscow*, which the president thought might encourage support for the Soviet common cause against Nazi Germany. Davies's book was a best seller, and Warner Brothers bought the film rights.[59] OWI reviewers liked Howard Koch's script, and the agency wanted to build American trust in the Soviets. The problem was that the script whitewashed Stalin's bloody 1930s purges, falsely making it appear that Stalin was stamping out a Nazi conspiracy.[60] The screenplay further depicted a benevolent Stalin focused on building Soviet society and not in exporting communism. Poynter was able to convince Warner Brothers to throw in criticism of prewar American conservative isolationists and to remove a scene that depicted Stalin's Bolshevik nemesis Leon Trotsky as a Nazi conspirator.[61]

The film builds up FDR as the successor of the visionary Woodrow Wilson, who is inaccurately portrayed as embracing the rise of Soviet communism. It opens with Davies speaking to the audience about the honesty and integrity of the Soviet leaders. Then Walter Huston, portraying Davies, says that no leader or nation has been "so misrepresented and misunderstood" as Stalin and the Soviet Union. The film becomes a preposterous fantasy to justify Stalin's record and to make his purges appear essential to the Allied war effort. A scene depicting a sage Stalin urging Davies to awaken America and Britain about the Nazi menace is nonsense.[62]

Critics disagreed about *Mission to Moscow*. James Agee was glad to see the Soviets praised for fighting fascism, but he said the rest of the film was "shameful rot." Agee criticized the OWI for going along with half-truths and falsifications in the name of national policy.[63]

Hollywood also presented positive Soviet portrayals, emphasizing resistance to the Nazis and solidarity with America, in films such as *North Star* (Goldwyn), *Song of Russia* (MGM), *Days of Glory* (RKO), and *Counter-Attack* (Columbia), which were not necessarily excellent films, but they were not as overtly political, misleading, or fabricated as *Mission to Moscow*.[64]

Four days after D-Day, on June 10, Col. Juan Perón publicly called for a mobilization of Argentine armed forces to combat what he called American imperialism. To Cordell Hull, this was tantamount to a declaration of war. He recalled Ambassador Norman Armour and froze Argentine gold reserves in the United States. Argentina retaliated by banning American ships from Argentine ports.

Wendell Willkie died on October 8, 1944, after suffering several heart attacks. Had he lived, he may have become the first secretary general of the United Nations. FDR was quick to praise his former opponent, who served his country by keeping aid to Britain out of the 1940 presidential campaign and who later traveled and campaigned to support FDR's foreign policy and their bipartisan "one word" global outlook.[65]

FDR and Democratic Party elders, with an eye toward succession, replaced liberal vice president Henry Agard Wallace with moderate Sen. Harry Truman of Missouri on the 1944 Democratic ticket. Many Democrats had strongly opposed Wallace, the brilliant Iowa State College agronomist and former secretary of agriculture, as being too liberal, naively pro-Soviet, eccentric, and ineffectual to become president at such an important moment in American history. FDR was visibly diminished and in declining health. On October 21 the president looked haggard riding in an open car with Truman during a driving rainstorm in New York.[66]

The Republican challenger, New York Gov. Thomas E. Dewey, had a stellar reputation as a "gangbuster" prosecutor and competent administrator. Dewey shared the worldview of Wendell Willkie and agreed with FDR's foreign policy and war aims. He and running mate Gov. John Bricker of Ohio managed to capture 46 percent of the popular vote despite a natural reluctance by voters to change leadership during wartime.

Truman earned the wartime media spotlight as a fierce war production Senate watchdog. The highly visible Truman Committee was not shy about going after waste, fraud, and inefficiency. Among Truman's targets were Edsel Ford's enormous B-24 Liberator bomber plant at Willow Run and a messy Curtiss-Wright defective aircraft engine scandal. The public knew Truman to be associated with the Kansas City political machine of Thomas Joseph Pendergast, which was an issue in Truman's 1940 Senate race.

Following FDR's reelection, Cordell Hull retired, and Edward Stettinius replaced him as secretary of state. Stettinius proposed six new undersecretaries including Rockefeller, Dean Acheson and Archibald MacLeash. Liberals were upset and nicknamed the group "Snow White and the Six Dwarfs" (Stettinius had prematurely white hair); Eleanor Roosevelt said that Thomas E. Dewey might as well be president.

Setting Sun

After D-Day the secretary of the navy detached Capt. John Ford from the oss to make the film *They Were Expendable* at MGM with members of his Field Photo group. The navy saw great public relations value in a realistic production. Associates Frank "Spig" Wead and Jim McGuiness wrote the screenplay. Actor Robert Montgomery, a navy PT-boat skipper and combat veteran, was the lead actor along with John Wayne. The shooting of the story of defeat in the Philippines began on Key Biscayne, in Miami, in February 1945, with Biscayne Bay substituting for Manila Bay and navy PT-boats and crews on loan for the production. The final film is a masterpiece that reflects a sobriety that wartime experience had given Ford. There is no false bravado in the grim story of American and Filipino defeat at the hands of the Japanese, who the audience never sees in the film except for planes dropping bombs or strafing. Critics praised *They Were Expendable* as moving and poetic. James Agee said it was "so beautiful and so real." The film premiered at Loew's Capitol Theater in Washington on December 19, 1945. Audiences had tired of war, and Ford's masterpiece had mixed success at the box office. By then Ford had returned to Europe and documentation of Nazi extermination camps and the Nuremburg War Crimes trials.[67] But with *They Were Expendable*, Ford fulfilled the OWI vision for a realistic, restrained, and rational war film that bore no resemblance at all to the 1942 war movies that the OWI worked so hard to curb. By 1945 intelligent films such as *They Were Expendable* delivered the quality messages that the OWI had wanted to send during the war.

The new, ultramodern Boeing B-29 Superfortress was the ultimate symbol of American power. But the game-changing airplane that Arnold had rushed into service was coming off assembly lines with numerous mechanical issues and defects.[68] A quantum technological leap, the B-29 had a wingspan wider than the length of the Wright Brothers first flight, a pressurized cabin, and electronic gun turrets. It had a range of 3,700 miles without refueling and a 350 mph airspeed. And it was complicated for crews to learn to operate. Boeing's ace test pilot Eddie Allen died in a B-29 crash. Arnold had already ordered 1,600 of the big bombers. They *had* to work, and engineers steadily made modifications.[69]

The B-29s were sent to India and China in Operation Matterhorn, commanded by Brig. Gen. Kenneth Wolfe. The surreal CBI, with the Himalayas and a myriad of climates and landscapes, was the worst place in the world to break in the buggy and complicated new planes. The first B-29 combat mission was an attack from Kharagpur, India, against targets at Bangkok, Siam, on June 5, 1944. The first mission to Japan was an attack from Chengdu, China, against the Imperial Iron Works at Yawata on June 15.[70]

On a July 29 mission against the Showa Steel Works in Manchuria, a B-29 made an emergency landing in Vladivostok. Stalin had no strategic bombers, so the Superfortress was a welcome gift that the Soviets soon "reverse engineered" into the Tupolev TU-4.

As Boeing engineers, AAF technicians, and aircrew sorted out the mechanical bugs and operational issues, CBI results were negligible, as Chinese bases proved difficult for workhorse Curtiss C-46 Commando cargo planes to supply. The United States had made a considerable investment in the B-29, and Arnold had to prove that it was worth it. On August 29 he sent the assertive Maj. Gen. Cutis LeMay to straighten things out. The cigar-chomping LeMay, a semblance of Ulysses S. Grant, changed tactics from nighttime to daylight raids and expanded targets to include Formosa. The staunch anti-communist LeMay met Mao Zedong and learned that he could rely upon the Chinese Communists to faithfully rescue downed American airmen. LeMay and Mao came to respect each other, exchanged gifts, and corresponded.[71]

Until now Japan's home islands had been safe. The complacency of Tokyo's citizens abruptly ended on October 13 as they looked up with fascination on a bright, clear day to see and hear the drone of one ultramodern Twentieth Air Force F-13A, a photo-reconnaissance B-29, boldly soaring unmolested, high above them and taking seven thousand high-quality still frames of the gleaming capital city. By November 1 Brig. Gen Haywood Hansell set up XXI Bomber Command in the Marianas Islands, and B-29 operations shifted to Guam, Saipan, and Tinian. On November 24, Brig. Gen. Emmett "Rosie" O'Donnell flew in the lead B-29, piloted by Maj. Robert K. Morgan, pilot of the B-17 *Memphis Belle,* immortalized by Maj. William Wyler's film. Their target was the Musashino-Nakajima aircraft engine factory near Tokyo, where the Japanese came to nickname the intimidating B-29s the B-san, or Bikko. Hundreds of new planes and fresh crews poured into the Marianas to rain devastation from the earth's troposphere down upon the home islands.

During 1944 and 1945 many international conferences determined the structure and practice of the postwar liberal democratic economic and political world order led by the United States. Among the initiatives was the Bretton Woods Conference held at the Mount Washington Hotel in Bretton Woods, New Hampshire, during July 1944. American and British economists agreed in principle in April 1944 to create an international monetary fund to stabilize markets, help trade, and enable postwar reconstruction. At the July 1944 conference formal agreements ratified the main aims of the economists, including an adjustably pegged foreign exchange market system, convertible currencies, and balance of payments ratios. The delegates created an International Bank for Reconstruction and Development (IBRD), chaired by British economist John Maynard Keynes, as well as an International Monetary Fund (IMF), chaired by American economist Harry Dexter White.[72] The concept behind all of this was to encourage open and free global markets. Secretary of the Treasury Morgenthau declared that the creation of the IMF and the IBRD marked "the end of economic nationalism." The United States was the world's largest economy, and it was growing. America was the main source of funds for the IMF and IBRD and therefore controlled the proceedings in a manner both magnanimous and in its own best interest. The IMF and IBRD needed ratification by countries with at least 80 percent of the capital subscriptions, and this threshold kicked in on December 27, 1945. An inaugural meeting formalized the IMF and IBRD on March 8–16, 1946, at Savannah, Georgia. The Soviet Union signed the July 1944 agreements but never ratified them. The communist state never joined the IMF or IBRD.[73]

The Washington Conversations on International Peace and Security Organization, otherwise known as the Dumbarton Oaks Conference, occurred in Washington from August 21 through October 7, 1944. The conference was the first meeting between the wartime Allies calling themselves the United Nations to enact the principles of the Atlantic Charter and create an international organization to succeed the League of Nations. Because the Soviet Union was not a belligerent in the war against Japan, it could not meet directly with China at the conference.

Dumbarton Oaks was a manor owned by Harvard University that the trustees and president of the university, Manhattan project member James B. Conant, placed at the disposal of the Department of State. The members of the conference came to agreement on the stated purposes for a United Nations organization, including collective security; peaceful means of adjustment or settlement of international disputes; international economic, social, and humanitarian cooperation; and a center to achieve these common goals. On October 7 they signed a tentative set of proposals to achieve these goals, including United Nations membership requirements and the makeup of a Security Council. The Soviets insisted that all sixteen Soviet republics become UN members; this was akin to the United States proposing individual memberships for each of its forty-eight states. The Big Three at the Yalta Conference and the UN San Francisco Conference settled the differences.[74]

Fig. 21. 1940 Republican hopefuls meet at the American Society of Newspaper Editors dinner at the Willard Hotel, Washington DC, April 21, 1940. (*Left to right*) William Allen White, president of the American Society of Newspaper Editors, Emporia, Kansas; Sen. Robert A. Taft of Ohio; Thomas E. Dewey of New York; and Sen. Arthur H. Vandenberg of Michigan. Harris & Ewing Photography Collection, LOC.

On January 10, 1945, Sen. Arthur Vandenberg, son of an old Dutch family from Grand Rapids, Michigan, shed what had been gentlemanly if isolationist views historically at odds with fellow Dutchman FDR. Since the beginning of the war, Vandenberg was a principled supporter of FDR's war policies although not a domestic policy advocate. By 1945 anti-communist Vandenberg, the uncle of Ninth Air Force commanding general Hoyt S. Vandenberg, was most concerned about the framework for a postwar world. Like Wendell Willkie, he had come to the realization that American isolationism was forever dead. Hosting a Republican gathering on Mackinac Island in 1943, Vandenberg earned the scorn of "Mr. Republican" Sen. Robert Taft of Ohio and Anglophobe Col. Robert McCormick of the *Chicago Tribune* when he supported New York Gov. Thomas E. Dewey in calling for a continuing postwar American and British global alliance and the establishment of a United Nations organization. Vandenberg and Dewey were launching the party that killed the League of Nations on a radically different course.[75] In what became known as "the speech heard 'round the world," Vandenberg famously defined a bipartisan viewpoint that "politics end at the water's edge" and that America needed a coalition foreign policy moving forward. Seeing an early draft of the speech, columnist James Reston urged Vandenberg to explicitly recommend a postwar security organization including the United States and Soviet Union that would remove any pretext that Stalin had for seizing and communizing Eastern Europe. Of all Republicans, Vandenberg was the one who had the gravitas to outline a major foreign policy initiative.[76]

Vandenberg summarized the course of the war to date and current events as Americans were holding out at Bastogne and bloody flighting evicted Japanese occupiers from island after island. "We not only have two wars to win," he said; "we also have yet to achieve such a peace as will justify this appalling cost." He tapped into a reservoir of feeling among Americans that international security was vital, and that something might happen with victory that would betray the Atlantic Charter for a repeat of Versailles. Americans expected their government to demand the end of colonial empires, but they did not necessarily support the spread of communism. The United States, he warned, faced a choice. This was also his personal choice to make: "unilateral spirit" or "joint action," whereby nations "undertake to look out for each other." America's relationship to the world had changed. Americans had not asked for the responsibilities of global leadership, but the task was upon them. Admitting his lifelong belief was in American self-reliance, Vandenberg concluded that the days had ceased when "our oceans were moats which automatically protect our ramparts." The solution was "maximum American cooperation, consistent with legitimate American self-interest." A vague endorsement of a postwar security organization was not enough. Vandenberg closed with Reston's conclusion that the Allies must form an actual United Nations organization and, specifically, a Security Council. The media proclaimed that isolationism was officially dead and put out of its misery by one of its former chief proponents. FDR was wary, but as members of his cabinet came around, especially Stettinius and the new hawkish secretary of the navy, James Forrestal, the president praised Vandenberg. A thrilled OWI broadcast his Senate speech overseas to foreign audiences, and AFRS broadcast it to the armed forces.[77]

Gen. William Donovan awarded Capt. John Ford the Legion of Merit for his wartime work. Ford returned to civilian life, and his first project was to make one final film before escaping Darryl F. Zanuck and Fox, *My Darling Clementine*. He went on to direct some of his most famous works, including, with his own production company Argosy, the cavalry trilogy *Fort Apache*, *She Wore a Yellow Ribbon*, and *Rio Grande*; then *The Searchers* and *The Man Who Shot Liberty Valance*. Ford examined his Catholic faith and the contradictions of Latin America with the compelling drama *The Fugitive* and his Irish roots with the colorful *Quiet Man*. He also harkened back to his wartime work with the navy-oriented films *Mister Roberts*, adapted from Joshua Logan's brilliant stage play, and *Wings of Eagles*, the story of Frank "Spig" Wead. The exceptional Ford had helped define a vigorous and just America with his wartime work, before later painting an epic and legendary America. At Ford's 1973 funeral his coffin was draped with the frayed American flag he filmed Marines hoisting at Midway in 1942.

Led by Irving Berlin, the *This Is the Army* troupe left England in March 1944 and traveled to North Africa and then Italy. When the Fifth Army liberated Rome in June 1944, Berlin and his men rode into the Eternal City six days behind the advance units. *This Is the Army* continued to Egypt, Iran, India, the Philippines, Guam, and Hawaii. During the final performance of *This Is the Army* on October 22, 1945, on the island of Maui, Berlin sang "Oh! How I Hate to Get Up in the Morning" one last time and concluded his appearance with a speech in which he said he hoped he would never again have to write another war song . . . and he never did.[78]

On January 3, 1945, FDR approved a plan by Rockefeller to secretly approach Col. Juan Perón via Rafeal Oreamuno of Costa

Rica, chairman of the Inter-American Development Commission, offering American recognition of his regime in exchange for transferring power to the chief justice of the Argentine Supreme Court, which would oversee fair and free elections, and for Argentina to declare war on the Axis and arrest Nazi sympathizers. The plan appeared reckless. Although Perón did not transfer power or declare war, he did commit to free elections. It was a start.

On February 20 Rockefeller held a hemispheric conference in Mexico City. Delegates from twenty nations assembled at Chapultepec Castle, the former home of Montezuma II and the site of Mexico's last stand against the 1847 assault by Gen. Winfield Scott. The symbolism was not lost on anyone. The conference pledged to enact a hemispheric security treaty consistent with any international peacekeeping organization emerging from the upcoming San Francisco Conference. The Mexico City Conference left the issue of Argentina unresolved. The Latin nations proposed the same offer as Rockefeller had secretly made to Perón, and he rejected them, too.[79]

The United States was busy training thousands of officers and personnel to occupy and administer Germany. The plan, code-named Operation Eclipse, envisioned the cooperation of the Soviet Union. Americans were carefully planning the details of civil administration, communications, food and medical services, civilian transportation, and other essentials. The task would be difficult and the cost enormous, but government leaders experienced with the aftermath of World War I were determined not to repeat the mistakes of Versailles.[80]

In his final assignment before returning home, Col. David Sarnoff chaired the Communications Division of the Control Council and drew up a detailed plan for German postal and radio services. His staff put together a complete blueprint including a table of organization and responsibilities for the Signals Division after the war. Sarnoff was back in the United States and at RCA in New York when he received a promotion to the rank of brigadier general on December 7, 1944, and returned to inactive status.[81]

Lt. Gen. Walter Bedell Smith, Eisenhower's chief of staff, and

SHAEF G-1 (Personnel) Maj. Gen. Ray Barker became embroiled in a debate with General Bradley and his field commanders of the Sixth Army Group and Gen. John C. H. Lee, ETOUSA chief. The argument was the controversial subject of whether or how to move African American troops into the front lines as stand-alone units or as man-for-man replacements in segregated white combat units during the Battle of the Bulge. There were over 150,000 noncombat African American troops in the theater in supply and construction units, and several black armored and infantry regiments already on the front line. Lee proposed mixing blacks into white units, much to the concern of Bradley.[82] Lee appears to have had Eisenhower's support. This was an explosive idea given the tenor of the times and the segregated United States. As an officer in the Army Corps of Engineers during the 1920s, Lee had been instrumental in addressing the serious floods that plagued the lower Mississippi River region. He had seen the poverty of both whites and blacks in the Deep South and grew to have an almost religious zealotry about racial discrimination and social welfare. His primary motivation in December 1944 was pragmatic. The army needed bodies in the front lines. Washington was concerned that African American organizations and prominent civil rights leaders would see the offer for noncombat black troops to integrate within white units as patronizing and beg the question why this was only happening in a time of emergency and not as ongoing policy. Barker worked out a compromise that put segregated units of noncombat black troops into front lines as replacements rather than using Lee's man-for-man proposal.[83]

On December 19, 1944, clever and well-produced German broadcasts went on the air, claiming to be a "recaptured" Radio Luxembourg. OWI director Davis contacted SHAEF and recommended that ABSIE and AEFP broadcast clear messages that the real Radio Luxembourg remained in Allied hands. False enemy broadcasts such as Radio Arnhem from Cologne had always mimicked AEFP, so this challenge was nothing new for Paley at SHAEF PWD and Niven at the AEFP to handle.[84] As the war situation became more desperate, Nazi messages warned Germans against listening to

Allied radio by publicizing prison or death sentences if caught. In turn, Paley accelerated efforts by Radio Orange and "Annie" to sow mayhem behind enemy lines. SHAEF PWD psy-ops increased pressure on the Wehrmacht high command to keep order as American units prepared to cross the Rhine and eviscerate the Reich.[85]

In July 1944 Elmer Davis went with FDR to Honolulu, where the president met with General MacArthur and Admiral Nimitz to coordinate strategy. The OWI chief convinced Nimitz to set up a psy-ops operation with the OWI in Hawaii that would later move west to the Marianas. When Davis returned, he gave a talk over CBS on August 15. In eloquent prose he paid tribute to the work of armed forces personnel and reminded the audience that although there was much good news, the Japanese government and military remained stubborn and desperate, even as Prime Minister Tojo's government fell when Tokyo lost Saipan and Guam.[86]

The navy softened up Iwo Jima and the surrounding Japanese Volcano Islands for months in anticipation of an assault. The American fleets had grown in numbers and quality of ships. The naval air arm now deployed smaller escort or "jeep" aircraft carriers to supplement the new and large *Essex*-class carriers. One of the smaller carriers was the USS *San Jacinto*. On September 2, 1944, during an attack on the Japanese garrison at Chichijima, anti-aircraft fire downed a Grumman TBF Avenger from VT-51 aboard the carrier. The pilot, Lt. (JG) George Herbert Walker Bush, survived, and the submarine USS *Finback* rescued him. Bush went on to become president of the United States.[87]

The Twentieth Air Force discovered the phenomenon of the previously unknown jet stream in the skies over Japan. Before the B-29, no airplane had ever flown so high. The constant 150–200 mph headwinds increased flight times, caused the airplanes to use extra fuel, and strained already trouble-prone engines. High-altitude bombing accuracy became problematic. Bombing with the jet stream, bombs fell long. Bombing against the jet stream, bombs fell short. Gen. Haywood Hansell believed in precision high-altitude bombing and sought to avoid civilian casualties. But it was taking too long to straighten things out. On January

20, 1945, LeMay arrived from India to relieve Hansell. B-29 operations in the CBI ended on March 31.[88]

On February 19, 1945, the marines assaulted Iwo Jima, and the Japanese garrison fought for the black volcanic rock to the last defender. But now the B-29s had a gas station, an emergency airfield, and runways within 760 miles of major Japanese cities. North American P-51 Mustang fighters could now escort the bombers. Everything moving in Japan was a target, despite the suicidal heroism of defending Japanese pilots, some of whom now became kamikaze.[89]

Urged by the navy to bypass the Philippines to concentrate forces on a direct strike at Japan, FDR paid close attention in July 1944, when MacArthur reminded him that America had a "sacred obligation" to save the Philippine people and liberate "occupied American soil consecrated with American and Filipino blood." On October 20, 1944, MacArthur waded ashore on Leyte and declared "I have returned." Then the battles of Leyte Gulf and the Philippine Sea finished off the Japanese Navy. Unlike von Choltitz in Paris, the fanatical Japanese naval commander in Manila decided to fight it out, massacre civilians, and destroy the "pearl of the orient" in an unnecessary and cruel last stand, but by March 1945 the United States had liberated the Philippines. In 1946 America made good its promise, and the Philippines became an independent nation.

Named after species of fish, American diesel fleet submarines, spawned mainly in New England, carried twenty-four torpedoes, were able to complete seventy-five-day patrols, and had a range of ten thousand miles without refueling.[90] In a deadly unrestricted submarine campaign Dönitz and the Kriegsmarine could only envy, Adm. Charles Lockwood's silent service overcame early problems with defective Mark 14 torpedoes to control the world's largest ocean.[91] Elite American submariners trained in New London, Connecticut, sank any enemy merchant vessel with the last name *Maru* that dared move between the East Indies and Asia to the vulnerable Japanese home islands. The Americans cut the long arteries that fed Japan's people and industries by sinking 1,314 ships weighing over five million tons.[92]

EIGHT

United Nations

Armageddon

FDR's internationalist America combining strength *and* a clear moral imperative had replaced the traditional and competing American imperatives of expansionism *versus* morality.[1] Darryl F. Zanuck and Fox had a project appearing ready-made for convincing war-weary Americans to stay engaged with the world. It was *Wilson*. An admirer of Fox board member Wendell Willkie, Zanuck was an internationalist, and by 1944 he reconsidered the subject of Wilson because the film "would match the new climate of the times."[2] Lamar Trotti, who wrote *Guadalcanal Diary*, wrote Wilson. His screenplay drew praise from OWI reviewers, who labeled it for rush distribution to liberated areas.

Fox portrayed Wilson as a champion of populism versus privilege from election to a fictional defeat at the hands of unscrupulous politicians led by villainous Henry Cabot Lodge.[3] Canadian Alexander Knox played Wilson, and Geraldine Fitzgerald played his second wife, Edith. Among a stellar supporting cast, Sir Cedric Hardwicke played Lodge superbly. Zanuck had taken on a weighty subject but did not honestly confront the aloof ideologue that Wilson really was and how he snatched defeat from the jaws of victory in 1919. In attempting to humanize Wilson, Zanuck made the scholar-president boring.[4] The real reason for the film, setting the stage for a new American-led world order, is incomprehensible in *Wilson*. The film premiered on August 1, 1944, with Wilson's widow, surviving Wilsonian officials, and Wendell Willkie in attendance at a gala New York benefit. Most reviews were favorable, and the box office was good, but not good enough for such a large budget feature.

During the late evening of January 22, 1945, the Secret Service escorted FDR to the *Ferdinand Magellan*, and the president departed for Newport News, Virginia. The next morning, FDR and his traveling party boarded the USS *Quincy*. On January 28 *Quincy* crossed the thirty-fifth meridian and into the European-African-Middle Eastern Theatre of Operation. Every evening on board, FDR and his party enjoyed first-run Hollywood films, including *To Have and Have Not*. At sunrise on January 31, *Quincy* passed through the Straits of Gibraltar. About 9:30 a.m. on February 2, with FDR out on the deck and thoroughly enjoying himself, *Quincy* steamed into Grand Harbor, Valetta, Malta, greeted by thousands of well-wishers on shore. Prime Minister Churchill met the president aboard *Quincy*.[5]

Following a busy day of meetings aboard *Quincy* in Malta, FDR boarded the *Sacred Cow* at Luqa aerodrome. At 12:10 p.m. the next day, the C-54 landed at Saki, Crimea. Churchill's plane landed fifteen minutes later. The leaders drove together in a jeep to the Livadia Palace, two miles south of Yalta, which was FDR's residence for the Yalta Conference. The prime minister went on to his residence at Vorontsov Villa, about twelve miles south of Livadia. Overnight a security-conscious Stalin arrived at Koreiz Villa, about six miles south of Livadia and not coincidentally directly in between the residences of the Western leaders. As at Teheran, Stalin was amazed at American naïveté regarding Soviet bugging of summit residences, telling his aides, "Do they not realize that we are listening to them?" FDR knew but thought it would build trust not to protest.[6] The Yalta Conference, code-named Argonaut, opened on February 5, 1945, at Livadia Palace.[7]

FDR and Stalin knew they were coming out of the war as the two world superpowers. Stalin agreed to enter the Pacific War after Germany's defeat with the condition that the Soviet Union receive a sphere of influence in Manchuria, upon which the three leaders agreed. They agreed not only that France would be included in the postwar governing of Germany, but also that Germany would pay reparations.

The Americans and the British conceded that future governments of the Eastern European nations bordering the Soviet Union should be friendly to Moscow while the Soviets pledged to allow free elections in all territories liberated from Nazi Germany, which never happened. These agreements may appear to be acquiescence to Stalin, but the Western Allies had no choice short of war. The Big Three also decided to create a United Nations Security Council of five permanent members, including France, that would each hold a veto.

Stalin dominated Yalta and achieved his aims. He had sacrificed twenty-five million Soviet lives with a scorched earth policy to save the motherland and his brutal form of communism. From his perspective it was now his right to build an unassailable empire and to subvert bourgeois capitalism everywhere. With substantial material support from the United States, the USSR was now a superpower, and the uneasy wartime marriage of convenience was about to end.

On February 11 FDR motored to Sevastopol, where he boarded the USS *Catoctin*. After spending the night aboard ship, the president went to Saki airfield and boarded the *Sacred Cow* for a flight to Deversoir, Egypt. The AAF airfield was near the Great Bitter Lake, seventeen miles south of Ismailia. From Deversoir FDR motored to the Suez Canal and the USS *Quincy*, which had sailed to Egypt from Malta. The next day, February 13, King Farouk of Egypt paid a courtesy call for a luncheon with FDR. Later that day the president received Emperor Haile Selassie of Ethiopia. Then a meeting of profound importance stretching into the twenty-first century occurred.[8]

The USS *Murphy* arrived from Jidda, Saudi Arabia, and the Red Sea on St. Valentine's Day, and aboard was King ibn Saud (Abdulaziz) of Saudi Arabia, who was afforded full honors by the president and the U.S. Navy. Accompanied by Princes Abdullah, Mohammed, and Mansour, the king met with FDR, Admiral Leahy, and their advisers for a luncheon aboard *Quincy*. The king traveled eight hundred miles to meet FDR, and it was his first trip out of his kingdom or aboard a ship, which FDR considered an unprecedented honor. Their discussions that day have led to the consequential diplomatic alliance between the United States and Saudi Arabia that has dramatically shaped the course of world events ever since.

The evening of February 14 *Quincy* transited the Suez Canal northbound for Alexandria, where Secretary of State Stettinius arrived from the Soviet Union to confer with FDR on the morning of February 15. Later Prime Minister Churchill joined the president at a luncheon. That evening *Quincy* and its escorts set sail, arriving at Algiers on February 18. Gen. Charles de Gaulle refused an invitation to meet with FDR, citing urgent military business. FDR concluded that de Gaulle was simply being stubborn. After refueling, *Quincy* left Algiers for Newport News, passing Gibraltar with air cover by U.S. Navy Lockheed PV-1 Ventura patrol planes. FDR's aide-de-camp and appointments secretary, Gen. Edwin "Pa" Watson, died of a cerebral hemorrhage onboard *Quincy* the next day. The frail president mourned the loss of his beloved confidante.

At about 5:20 p.m. on February 27, *Quincy* passed through a submarine net gate, entered Hampton Roads, and moored at Newport News. On his first day home the president joined mourners for Pa Watson's funeral at Arlington National Cemetery.[9]

FDR addressed a joint session of Congress on March 1 to report on the Yalta Conference. His appearance shocked members of Congress and the American people. He did not hide his failing health; indeed, he explicitly mentioned his disability and discomfort. His presentation about Yalta was as disconcerting as was concern for his health. The president's schedule thinned out, with some days devoted to motoring around the Virginia and Maryland countryside. Without her mother's knowledge, FDR's daughter Anna arranged for an old acquaintance, Lucy Rutherford, to go with FDR on such therapeutic adventures, which allowed the president an opportunity to relive younger and dreamier days.

On the Marianas Islands LeMay resolved to defeat Japan with the Twentieth Air Force. To LeMay, the logic of ending the war as quickly as possible was paramount. His Grant-like solution was a radical change to low-altitude, nighttime attacks using incendiaries to ignite vulnerable Japanese cities.[10] Just past midnight on March 10 high winds and cool dry air contributed to a disaster, as B-29s attacked highly flammable Tokyo, where there were a few air raid shelters and inadequate firefighting capability. Heat asphyxiated a hundred thousand people, mostly in the flat, working-class city municipalities, and a million more became homeless.[11] French catholic priest Fr. Joseph Flaujac ministered to the wounded and later bore witness to the conflagration, which mirrored the catastrophic Great Kantō earthquake of September 1, 1923, that shook Tokyo and Yokohama for five minutes.[12] Many in Washington were morally appalled, but FDR remained resolute that such were the terms of unconditional surrender and the price of eradicating fascism.[13]

Maj. Gen. Patrick Hurley was born in Choctaw Nation, Indian Territory, in 1883, which is within the present-day state of Oklahoma. During most of World War II the salty and erratic Hurley handled trouble-shooting assignments for FDR, including Iran. Hurley was sympathetic to Iran and instrumental in the insertion of an Iran Declaration into the Teheran communiqué that committed Britain and the Soviet Union to full Iranian sovereignty and territorial integrity following the war. He authored a report about Iran incorporating FDR's aims, envisioning a liberal democracy, aided and developed by an "unselfish" United States.

During the spring of 1944 Japan launched a major offensive in China, Operation Ichigo. This brought the contentious relationship of Gen. Joseph Stilwell and Chiang Kai-Shek to a head. "Vinegar Joe" and his chain of command in Washington were at wit's end with Chiang's military incompetence and endemic Kuomintang corruption. Marshall was ready to pull the plug on military support for China beyond a mere holding action. However, Gen. Claire Chennault of the Fourteenth Air Force was fully supportive of the Kuomintang. Chiang and Soong May-Ling used their close relationship with Chennault to undermine Stillwell.

Against this backdrop, FDR sent Hurley as a special envoy to China to straighten things out. Hurley did not speak Mandarin and knew nothing of China. He was accompanied by War Production Board chairman Donald Nelson, who acted as an economic adviser. Chiang and Soong May-ling welcomed Hurley and Nelson and appeared the modicum of civility and cooperation. At first Hurley believed that he convinced Chiang to turn over more military control to Stilwell, and Mao Zedong's communists pledged to accept Stilwell as their commander.

FDR still had the romanticized notion of China that the OWI communicated to the American people. Nevertheless, Marshall was able to convince the president to send a blunt message demanding that Stilwell be put in command of all Chinese forces with authority to enlist the Chinese Communists and putting strict conditions on continued American economic and military assistance. Written by Marshall's staff, FDR's terms amounted to an invasion of sovereignty and contradicted FDR's vision of Chiang's China as a viable world power on par with the Big Three. Aware of the message, Hurley recommended reconsideration.

But FDR's message was addressed to Stilwell for delivery, and Stillwell delivered the honest ultimatum in fluent Mandarin to a humiliated and enraged Generalissimo. From Chiang's point of view, he had to maintain control of American economic and military assistance and not open any door to the communists. As advised by T. V. Soong, Chiang believed that the United States would not abandon him. His reply, given to Hurley, was to demand Stilwell's immediate removal and control of all American material assistance. Hurley recommended that Gen. Albert C. Wedemeyer replace Stilwell or "we will lose China."

Marshall had pushed an ailing FDR to send an ultimatum that the sentimental president did not at heart really believe in. In the face of Chiang's intransigence and seeing no viable China alternative, FDR backed down and recalled Stilwell.[14]

The United States already had a small group of observers and OSS liaison stationed with the communists in Yan'an, commanded by Col. David D. Barrett and code-named Dixie. Barrett's job was to evaluate the communists as allies against Japan, and his recommendation was positive. On November 7 Hurley visited Mao and Zhou Enlai seeking cooperation between the communists and the Kuomintang but did not come across to his hosts in a cohesive or articulate manner. During their talks Mao recommended a coalition government and joint military council with an equal number of communist and Kuomintang generals, American military aid to the communist Chinese army, and the freeing of all political prisoners. The communists drafted a proposal that Hurley accepted, although he had no authority to do so.[15]

When Hurley returned to Chongqing, Soong said he had been "sold a bill of goods." Chiang would only accept the proposal if he had command over the communist army. When Hurley tried to persuade Mao to accept Chiang's proviso, Mao replied, "a foot in the door means nothing if the hands are tied behind the back." Hurley blamed Soong May-ling, the State Department, and the oss for his failure. Nevertheless, on November 17 FDR prevailed upon Hurley to accept the position of ambassador to China upon the resignation of a disgusted Clarence E. Gauss. The communists and the Kuomintang thereafter took turns manipulating Hurley, who was unable to understand facts or formulate solutions and who often was visibly intoxicated. In a December 2, 1944, cable to Washington, Hurley blamed China's problems on Britain and demanded that the British return Hong Kong to China after the war. In January 1945 Hurley exploded when he learned that oss Col. William Bird and Col. David Barrett of the Dixie operation planned to embed five thousand American paratroopers with Mao and that General Wedemeyer was considering assigning an American division to Shandong Province to fight alongside the communists. Hurley accused Bird and Barrett of recognizing Mao without permission and felt that General Wedemeyer was therefore plotting against him (Hurley). As it happened, Mao and Zhou did prefer to negotiate with Wedemeyer, which further inflamed Hurley.

Wedemeyer reported to Mountbatten and Marshall that Hurley was mentally unfit and out of his depth. When Hurley traveled to Washington, the entire Chongqing embassy senior staff sent a cable asking for Washington to relieve him on the grounds of incompetence and insanity. Hurley saw the cable and fired every person who signed it.

By now, Hurley had abandoned hopes of a compromise and

came to fully support the Kuomintang. He saw the military, OSS, and State Department favoring the communists and insubordinate to him. He believed that the decisions made at Yalta giving the Soviet Union favored status in Manchuria were a death warrant for the Kuomintang. Chiang asked Hurley, "Has China really been sold out at Yalta?"[16]

On March 14 Rockefeller got fourteen nations meeting in Washington to jointly offer Perón formal recognition in exchange for joining the war effort and adding Argentina's name to the forthcoming United Nations Charter. The Pan American Union and the State Department approved. As the war in Europe wound down, Rockefeller's persistence with Argentina paid off. The colonels in Buenos Aires entered the war and froze the assets of German and Japanese concerns. In turn the United States and the rest of the hemispheric republics, along with Britain and France, recognized the junta.[17]

FDR left Washington aboard the *Ferdinand Magellan* on the evening of March 29 for an overnight trip to his beloved therapeutic oasis of Warm Springs, Georgia. Secret Service agent Mike Reilly found it difficult to transfer the president to his car because "he was absolutely dead weight." FDR had lost considerable weight, appetite, and stamina. His secretary William Hassett told White House physician Cmdr. Howard G. Bruenn, USNR, that "he is slipping away from us and no earthly power can keep him here."[18]

After several days Bruenn observed improvement in the president's appearance, appetite, and attitude. FDR slept well, went on motor trips, and regained a jovial sprit. On April 9 Lucy Mercer Rutherford arrived from Aitken, South Carolina, with portrait artist Elizabeth Shoumatoff. Thursday, April 12, FDR sat in the living room at the Little White House as Shoumatoff painted. Shortly before 1:00 p.m. the butler came in to set the table for lunch. FDR glanced at his watch and said, "We have fifteen minutes more to work." Then he suddenly put his hand up to his head and said, "I have a terrific pain in the back of my head."[19] Dr. Bruenn recalled, "He was sitting in a chair while sketches were being made of him by an artist. He suddenly complained of a very severe occipital headache. Within a very few minutes he lost consciousness." Bruenn pronounced the president dead at 3:35 p.m.[20]

On Friday, April 13, the president's body boarded the *Ferdinand Magellan*. The next day, over five hundred thousand Americans lined the streets of the nation's capital to pay their respects to their fallen leader, as the horse-drawn carriage with the casket made its way in procession from Union Station to the White House. Americans from coast to coast were transfixed by the description poignantly narrated by CBS and WJSV morning host Arthur Godfrey. After a simple White House service, FDR's remains returned to Union Station for a final journey to Hyde Park, where the nation bid farewell to the only commander-in-chief that many in uniform had ever known. Meanwhile, America's new president had no idea that the Manhattan Project existed.

On a hill shown as #913 on army maps, southwest of Bologna and northwest of Florence in Italy near the otherwise picturesque town of Castel d'Aiano, soldiers of the Tenth Mountain Division's Eighty-Fifth Infantry Regiment were trying to dislodge Wehrmacht troops dug into the strategic high ground that characterized their Gothic Line of mountainous defenses. On the morning of April 14 Lt. Robert Dole of Russell, Kansas, and his platoon found themselves pinned down by machine-gun fire. A shell or bullet hit Dole in his right shoulder, fracturing the clavicle, scapula, and humerus, and penetrated the fourth cervical vertebra. His spinal cord was shocked, and all four extremities were paralyzed. Dole miraculously survived the ordeal and came home to face years of arduous convalescence. He would represent Kansas in Congress, serve as Senate Republican leader, and become a vice presidential and presidential candidate.[21]

After Pearl Harbor Hawaiian native and Japanese American Daniel Inouye could not enlist until the army lifted a ban on Japanese American enlistments in 1943. Inouye then found himself in the Japanese American 442nd Regimental Combat Team at Camp Shelby, Mississippi. He served as a platoon sergeant in Italy before his regiment moved to the Voges Mountains in Alsace, where Inouye won a battlefield commission to lieutenant. The regiment again redeployed to the Gothic Line in Italy. On April 21, 1945, Inouye was leading an attack on a heavily defended ridge near San Terenzo in Tuscany when first enemy fire hit him, and then a grenade almost blew off his right arm. Army physicians had to amputate Inouye's mutilated arm. Inouye won the Distinguished Service Cross and later the Medal of Honor for his bravery. While convalescing at Percy Jones Army Hospital in Battle Creek, Michigan, Inouye met another wounded officer, Lt. Robert Dole, and formed a lifelong camaraderie. Inouye also went on to represent Hawaii as a Democratic senator.[22]

The United Nations Conference on International organization, or the San Francisco Conference, opened on April 25 and ran through June 26. Delegates from fifty nations reviewed and rewrote the Dumbarton Oaks agreements and passed the UN Charter. Rockefeller escorted the Latin American bloc of delegates, who were determined to add the Act of Chapultepec regional security arrangements into the UN Charter. The Peronist regime in Argentina was hoping that its last-minute declaration of war could gain it a seat in the new world body and respectability on the cheap. Rockefeller shared Latin American concerns about permanent Security Council members and vetoes, reasoning that the Soviets could plant communist regimes in the Americas and veto collective UN action to stop them. That is not unlike what eventually really happened in Cuba, and later in Nicaragua.[23]

Among the American delegation to the conference was Vandenberg's adviser John Foster Dulles, grandson and nephew of Secretaries of State John W. Foster and Robert Lansing, who was legal counsel at the Versailles Conference. Dulles coauthored the preamble to UN Charter and became a delegate to the General Assembly.

President Truman attended the final session in San Francisco and addressed the delegates. All fifty nations ratified the UN charter by October 25, 1945, and the organization set up its permanent headquarters in New York on February 14, 1946.[24]

As daily life within Germany collapsed, anxious Germans needed guidance about what to expect when they awoke to see American soldiers on their streets. German soldiers learned that their gov-

Fig. 22. Pres. Harry S. Truman's official portrait, ca. 1945. Harry S. Truman Presidential Library, 530677, NARA.

ernment had ceased to exercise effective control over wide areas. ABSIE broadcast instructions from SHAEF PWD outlining surrender procedures. Wehrmacht officers became more receptive to the voice of authority from Eisenhower than their own disintegrating government. The biblical Armageddon had arrived, as Patton's Third Army tanks rolled down the autobahn into Munich and raced for Prague.[25]

On April 20, 1945, Hitler's birthday, the First Belorussian Front commanded by Marshal Georgy Zhukov started shelling the city center of Berlin. The First Ukrainian Front led by Marshal Ivan Konev smashed through Wehrmacht Army Group Centre and into the southern Berlin suburbs. Hitler committed suicide April 30 as the Soviets crushed the Berlin garrison and raised the red hammer and sickle flag over the Reichstag. Goebbels and ss leader Heinrich Himmler also killed themselves, and Göring surrendered to American troops. Before the final reckoning, the Nazis had executed Abwehr chief Adm. Wilhelm Canaris and other officers caught up in a failed July 20, 1944, assassination plot. Hitler compelled Rommel, who knew of the plot, to kill himself. Dönitz briefly succeeded Hitler as führer, but his only realistic task was to arrange for an orderly surrender. At 02:41 Monday, May 7, Gen. Alfred Jodl, representing the okw, signed the act of unconditional surrender at shaef Forward in Reims, France. Eisenhower's deputy Lt. Gen. Walter Bedell Smith signed for the Allies.[26]

Associated Press Paris Bureau chief Edward Kennedy broke the surrender story before shaef prd authorized clearance. shaef revoked his credentials and shipped him back to the United States for violating the embargo.[27] absie also inadvertently jumped the gun and broadcast news of the surrender prematurely, much to the irritation of the voa in New York.[28]

absie signed off just before midnight on Wednesday, July 4, 1945, when the voa took over with its postwar European Service. The bbc closed aefp on July 28. The wartime service became the bbc Light Programme and eventually bbc Radio 2. The American Forces Network moved to Germany and took over the Reichs-Rundfunk-Gesellschaft (rrg) domestic and Großdeutscher Rundfunk international broadcasting facilities according to Gen. David Sarnoff's Operation Eclipse blueprint.[29]

Charles Lindbergh distinguished himself during World War II. At first the Roosevelt administration blackballed Lindbergh and refused to reinstate his aaf commission. They prevailed upon his friends, including Juan Trippe of Pan Am, to decline his services. There were similar roadblocks at United and Consolidated Aircraft.

Harry Bennett of the Ford Motor Company contacted Lindbergh. Ford was interested in his help with the B-24 Liberator program at Willow Run. Within days Lindbergh was test-flying and recommending modifications to the B-24. He also flew P-51 Mustangs with Packard-built V-1650 Rolls Royce Merlin engines. Ford paid Lindbergh the salary of an AAF colonel, $666 per month.[30] Lindbergh volunteered as a high-altitude test chamber guinea pig for the Mayo Clinic's Aeromedical Unit for Research in Aviation. He taught pilots how to properly fly the Republic P-47 Thunderbolt outfitted with Ford-built Pratt & Whitney engines. Lindbergh test flew the B-29 Superfortress at Eglin Field, Florida. As a "technical representative" he went to the South Pacific for United Aircraft to resolve issues with the Vought F4U Corsair navy and marine fighter and flew with the marines on combat missions. To better judge the Corsair, Lindbergh then flew AAF Lockheed P-38 Lightnings with the 475th Fighter Group of the Fifth Air Force in New Guinea and unofficially shot down at least one Japanese fighter. After V-E Day he led a Naval Technical Mission to Europe to study jet airplanes, including the Messerschmidt ME-262 Schwalbe (Swallow). The Lone Eagle earned redemption.[31]

Trinity

Truman wanted his own man at the State Department. He pushed Edward Stettinius out and installed former senator James Byrnes (D-SC). Stettinius became ambassador to the UN and supported Rockefeller's recommendation to admit Argentina, which the USSR, Henry Wallace, and American UN delegate Adlai Stevenson opposed. Soviet foreign minister Vyacheslav Molotov quoted from Cordell Hull's earlier denunciations of the Peronistas, but Stettinius pointed out to the General Assembly the agreements reached at Mexico City, and Argentina was admitted by a 31–4 vote, but the delegates did not expressly add the Chapultepec accords to the UN Charter. Truman asked Rockefeller to find Tom Pendergast's nephew a job at the State Department, and Rockefeller replied that his staff would review the young man's qualifications. Byrnes got rid of Rockefeller and closed the OCIAA.[32]

On July 6, 1945, President Harry Truman left Washington by train at 11:00 p.m. for Newport News, where he and his traveling party boarded the USS *Augusta*. On Sunday, July 15, *Augusta* entered Pas Van Terneusen Channel and the Western Scheldt Estuary and continued into Antwerp harbor where a formation of AAF P-47 fighters flew air coverage. Supreme Commander Dwight D. Eisenhower greeted the president, who motored to Brussels. Men from Truman's World War I unit, the 137th Infantry Regiment of the Thirty-Fifth Division, helped guard the road. Three C-54s awaited the presidential party at Brussels Evre Aerodrome, and the president boarded the *Sacred Cow* piloted by Lt. Col. Henry T. Myers. The flight flew a ten-mile-wide air corridor over Soviet-occupied territory after passing over Frankfurt-Main, and the three C-54s landed at Berlin Gatow aerodrome between 3:58 and 4:28 p.m.

The president went to his residence for the Potsdam Conference (code-named Terminal) in the affluent Babelsberg district. The traveling party nicknamed his three-story stucco residence at No. 2 Kaiser Strasse as the "Little White House."[33] Flying over Germany, Truman saw the utterly hellish devastation of cities such as Kassel, contrasted with green rolling farmland that appeared unscathed. Touring Berlin his first day, he saw mountains of rubble and dazed survivors scrounging for food and shelter.[34]

Truman's objective for the conference was to get the Soviet Union to declare war on Japan. He also wanted to size up Churchill and Stalin. Before the conference the British people went to the polls in a parliamentary election Churchill could have postponed. Results were still pending while the military vote overseas came in. When they met for the first time, Churchill formed a very favorable impression of Truman, although the president thought the prime minister was trying too hard to be friendly.[35]

Joseph Stalin arrived in Germany aboard a special armored train, including four green carriages of the tsar pulled out of a museum. Thousands of security police and troops made up his security detail, to "guarantee proper order and purges of anti-Soviet elements." Stalin was a day late to arrive, but it did not

matter to him because the Soviets had already won the important decisions at Yalta. His first meeting with Truman was at the
Little White House on July 17.

Following the meeting, Stalin told Molotov, Andrei Gromyko,
and Sergo Beria that he found Truman unimpressive and "neither
educated or clever."[36] Truman told aides that he liked Stalin and
thought he could work with him, but that Uncle Joe reminded
him of Kansas City political boss Tom Pendergast.[37]

At 5:29 a.m. Mountain War Time on July 16, 1945, the United
States detonated the first nuclear weapon, code-named Trinity, in
the Jornada del Muerto desert about thirty-five miles southeast
of Socorro, New Mexico, on the Army Air Forces Alamogordo
Bombing and Gunnery Range. Manhattan Project scientists and
military personnel nicknamed the implosion-design plutonium
device "the gadget." Present at the birth of the "atomic age" were
Groves, Oppenheimer, James Conant, Enrico Fermi, and Vanne-
var Bush. Oppenheimer recalled that, seeing the explosion, he
thought of a verse from the Hindu holy book the Bhagavad Gita,
XI, 12: "If the radiance of a thousand suns were to burst at once
into the sky, that would be like the splendor of the mighty one."
People could see and feel the bright light and blast from Albuquerque to El Paso, and the military issued a decoy press release
that a large cache of high explosives and pyrotechnics accidentally
exploded. Truman had ordered Groves and Oppenheimer to test
Trinity before the Potsdam Conference opened.[38]

Stalin was aware of the Manhattan Project since his spies and
agents had infiltrated it in 1942. The USSR was trying to kick-start
its own nuclear weapons program, although Stalin did not trust
his scientists. Stalin's adviser Sergo Beria told him to feign igno-
rance and pretend that he did not understand when Truman inevitably divulged the existence of the new weapon.[39]

By the summer of 1945 Allied signals intelligence and Ultra
reached peak efficiency, intercepting thousands of Imperial Japanese Army and Navy messages. Magic revealed Japanese diplomats had approached the USSR about rapprochement and to seek
Soviet intercession toward a negotiated settlement of the war. The

Foreign Ministry, however, did not represent the military in Tokyo, and the militants were not aware of this initiative.

Gen. John Weckerling, Marshall's G-2 (Intelligence), forwarded a detailed analysis to Potsdam. Ambassador Naotake Satō, Japanese ambassador to the USSR, advised Tokyo that the USSR was coldly realistic and unlikely to cooperate. Satō recommended that Japan "should not harbor illusions" and had to face the reality of unconditional surrender as the only way to end the war. Satō was correct; the USSR rebuffed the Foreign Ministry initiative.[40]

At midmorning on July 18, Secretary of War Stimson read Truman an urgent message from George Harrison in the United States that the Trinity test was successful. On Saturday, July 21, Stimson received a top-secret report flown in from Groves with detailed Trinity test results. After reviewing the report with Marshall, Stimson briefed Truman, and from then on observers thought the president was more confident and certain in his dealings with Stalin. Admiral Leahy told FDR's Russian interpreter, Chip Bohlen, who had already formed a favorable opinion of Truman, "Watch the president. This is all new to him, but he can take it. He is a more typical American than Roosevelt, and he will do a good job, not only for the United States, but for the whole world.[41]

On July 23 Truman was considering the language of a Potsdam Declaration to Japan, and he favored the terms of unconditional surrender demanded of Nazi Germany. Stimson thought this unwise because the Japanese would interpret the terms as meaning they could not keep Emperor Hirohito. Truman could have cared less at that point about keeping the emperor, but Stimson had a wise point about governing postwar Japan. The next morning Harrison sent Stimson another coded message that the United States was ready to use the bomb against Japan. Stimson, Marshall, and deputy John McCloy recommended that the declaration include keeping the emperor and a veiled threat about the new bomb, so America would have the high moral ground if or when it was used. Truman and Byrnes said no.[42]

Later that day, as Stalin was leaving their meeting, Truman casually told him about Trinity. As rehearsed, Stalin was deadpan and simply said he was glad to hear of it. At that precise moment the wartime alliance between the two new superpowers ended. America had the bomb, and the Soviet Union had Eastern Europe.[43] On July 26 the United States, United Kingdom, and China jointly issued the Potsdam Declaration calling on Japan to unconditionally surrender or "suffer complete destruction." But Stimson and Marshall had won an important distinction: the declaration did not specify the status of the Japanese monarchy.[44]

Churchill returned to Britain to await the official election returns, and the Conservatives lost. On July 28 Clement Atlee of the Labour Party arrived to replace Churchill at the conference as prime minister. Meanwhile Truman received a message that the Senate had approved the United Nations charter by an almost unanimous vote.

Japan rejected the Potsdam Declaration on July 28, daring the United States to demonstrate what prompt and utter destruction meant. Military leaders in Tokyo imprudently saw the Allied demand as a sign of fatigue. The rational foreign minister Shigenori Tōgō argued on July 27 that it was "impolitic" to publicly reject the declaration and that Japan should seek clarification via the USSR. But by July 29 Tōgō correctly realized that Soviet silence meant concurrence. Satō observed that acceptance of the Potsdam terms meant Japan would enjoy the benefits of the Atlantic Charter, terms Nazi Germany never received, and left open the status of the monarchy. But Japan remained silent.[45]

It was objectively clear that Japan had lost the war, as Allied ships and planes had laid siege to the home islands. The only matter remaining was how the war would end. MacArthur was set to command Operation Downfall, the invasion of the home islands. Phase one was Operation Olympic, the invasion of Kyushu scheduled for November 1 by the Sixth Army. Phase two was Operation Coronet, the invasion of Honshū, scheduled for March 1, 1946, by the First, Eighth, and Tenth Armies and British Commonwealth forces. Both invasions would include Marine Corps divisions. Intelligence initially estimated Japanese troop strength on Kyushu at 300,000, but the Japanese defensive plan, Operation Ketsugō, called for 750,000. Five million troops would invade a Japanese nation defended by over four million military and up to thirty-one million civilian conscripts. Projections of Allied dead and wounded were horrific. Operation Downfall would cause such catastrophic Japanese casualties as to effectively render Japan extinct.[46]

By mid-July, armed with updated intelligence that the Japanese were fortifying Kyushu to a far greater degree than originally estimated, and that Japan had many thousands more airplanes than projected, Marshall and King in Washington and Nimitz on Guam had serious concerns about moving forward with Operation Olympic. MacArthur had no such doubts. He was prepared to invade but had a suspicion that Japan was already beaten, even if die-hard militarists in Tokyo wanted to needlessly kill millions in a desperate last act of national seppuku.[47]

President Truman left Berlin Gatow aboard the *Sacred Cow* on August 2, 1945. The three C-54s carrying the presidential party could not land at their intended destination of St. Magwan because of fog, so the planes diverted to Harrowbeer near Plymouth, where the *Augusta* awaited the president. HMS *Renown* was also at Plymouth Roads with HRH George VI aboard. The president visited the king aboard *Renown*, and his majesty visited Truman aboard *Augusta* before *Augusta* set sail for Newport News.[48]

The OWI and navy psy-ops set up by Nimitz and Davis played a crucial role in guiding Japan to the brink of capitulation. The OWI monitored and summarized Radio Tokyo broadcasts in San Francisco. OWI response and copy were composed and coded in Washington and relayed via Honolulu to Saipan. The OWI built KSAI, a 50 kw AM-frequency station, which relayed a 100 kw OWI signal from Honolulu. The OWI also broadcast to Japan from KGEI and the prewar CBS and NBC transmitters in California. Separately AFRS expanded its Pacific and Mosquito Networks from Noumea, New Caledonia, Guadalcanal, and the massive fleet anchorage at Espiritu Santo to Guam and restored service interrupted in 1942 with a Far East Network in the Philippines.

KSAI broadcast to the Japanese armed forces and people with war news, bombing warnings, messages from POW, and entertainment. It gave the Japanese civilian government and soldiers and sailors besieged across the Pacific objective news and information that the military dictatorship concealed. KSAI also served as a navigational beacon for Marianas-based B-29s.[49]

OWI guidance held that the emperor was a historic institution, that it was counterproductive to insult him, and that the military betrayed Hirohito, deceiving him into war. However, Davis agreed with Stimson, Marshall, and Forrestal not to broadcast any explicit promise of retaining the monarchy, which the military could see as weakness or reason to delay acceptance of the Potsdam Declaration.[50]

The Twentieth Air Force dropped tens of millions of leaflets over Japan to provide war news and air raid warnings. Leaflets dropped to Japanese forces abroad promised humane treatment to surrendering POWs. The message was that the Allies had already won the war, and the only question was ending the suffering without further bloodshed.[51]

On July 26 KSAI started broadcasting the Potsdam Declaration, calling for disarmament and abolition of the military, Allied occupation, respect for fundamental human rights, freedom of speech and religion, maintenance of Japanese industry, and prosecution for war criminals. Only the close of the message demanded unconditional surrender or "prompt and utter destruction." The Potsdam Declaration also reached the home islands by leaflets. When the government rejected the declaration, KSAI immediately warned civilians to evacuate thirty-five Japanese cities, and the AAF dropped millions of additional leaflets.[52]

After sunrise Monday morning, August 6, 1945, Col. Paul Warfield Tibbets of Miami, commanding the AAF 509th Composite Group and piloting a specially equipped Boeing B-29 Superfortress named for his mother, *Enola Gay*, crossed into Japanese airspace following a 2:45 a.m. departure from North Field, Tinian Island. Two B-29s with scientific measurement instruments and photography equipment accompanied *Enola Gay*. The formation flying at high altitude appeared to Japanese air defense controllers as a weather reconnaissance mission, so they did not waste aviation fuel and ammunition scrambling Nakajima Ki-87 fighters to intercept it. Carrying a device nicknamed "Little Boy," the *Enola Gay* was soon above Hiroshima, the capital of Hiroshima Prefecture, and the largest city in the Chūgoku region of western Honshū. Capt. William Sterling Parsons, USN, had armed the uranium-gun device over the Pacific Ocean. As Tibbets sharply turned his plane away, people below could see the sun reflect from the gleaming silver B-29. At 8:16 a.m. Little Boy completed a forty-three-second fall and detonated at 1,900 feet over the courtyard of Shima Hospital, releasing a blast equivalent to 12,500 tons of TNT and a bright flash of light for one-tenth of a second that measured 5,400 degrees Fahrenheit.

Following the attack on Hiroshima, KSAI and leaflets announced the existence of the atomic bomb, the true nature of the devastation it brought, and the immediate need to accept the Potsdam Declaration. KSAI repeated the message every fifteen minutes.[53]

Truman was lunching with the crew aboard *Augusta* on August 6 when news came of the successful Hiroshima mission. He commented, "This is the greatest thing in history." The next day *Augusta* arrived at Newport News, and the president boarded his train for Washington, arriving at 10:45 p.m.[54]

There was still no response to the Potsdam Declaration from Japan following the Hiroshima attack. It took several days for traumatized leaders to gather some idea of what had happened from confusing reports. Many military officials minimized the profound significance of the event and rationalized continued resistance. Tōgō presented the emperor a detailed report about Hiroshima on August 8 with a recommendation to immediately end the war by accepting the Potsdam Declaration.[55]

At 11:00 p.m. on August 8 in Moscow Molotov informed Sato that the Soviet Union was declaring war on Japan. At one-minute past midnight, Soviet troops invaded Manchuria from three directions and overwhelmed the million-man Japanese Kwantung Army.[56] Stalin communized Manchuria, and Korea split into separate states demarked by the thirty-eighth parallel.[57]

Most Americans were thankful that the atomic weapon would probably end the war without an invasion of Japan. Some military leaders, including Eisenhower and Nimitz, thought that either the invasion or atomic bomb was unnecessary and that a quarantined Japan would have eventually capitulated.[58] Others were morally outraged, including John Foster Dulles, who prophetically said, "If we, as a professedly Christian nation, feel morally free to use atomic energy in that way, men elsewhere will accept that verdict. Atomic weapons will be looked upon as a normal part of the arsenal of war and the stage will be set for the sudden and final destruction of mankind."[59] Describing the dawn of the atomic age, the September 1945 issue of *Scientific Monthly* noted, "Modern Prometheans have raided Mount Olympus again and have brought back for man the very thunderbolts of Zeus."

The Supreme Council for the Direction of the War remained deadlocked. Army Chief of Staff Gen. Yoshijirō Umezu, Navy Chief of Staff Adm. Soemu Toyoda, and War Minister Gen. Korechika Anami quixotically maintained that any surrender had to guarantee the emperor as a sovereign, prevent Allied occupation, and make Japan responsible for disarmament and war crimes prosecution. Prime Minister (and former admiral) Baron Kantarō Suzuki had opposed war with the United States from the outset. Suzuki, Foreign Minister Tōgō, and Navy Minister Adm. Mitsumasa Yonai accurately viewed the Potsdam Declaration as an ultimatum. As Ambassador Satō advised, the only negotiable ambiguity was status of the monarchy.[60]

At 10:00 a.m. on August 9, Hirohito granted Suzuki an audience. Marquis Koichi Kido, Lord Keeper of the Privy Seal, told Suzuki that Japan should terminate the war "by taking advantage of the Potsdam terms" and that the emperor wished to hear the views of his senior statesmen. Exactly forty-five minutes earlier, Tibbets's executive officer, Maj. Charles W. Sweeney of Quincy, Massachusetts, commanding the B-29 *Bockscar*, delivered a second atomic bomb, "Fat Man." The plutonium implosion device detonated over the city of Nagasaki, an alternate target due to overcast skies over the primary target of Kokura.[61]

The Supreme Council assembled as news of Nagasaki arrived. The three diehards insisted on their unrealistic conditions. The drama continued as the full Imperial Cabinet met and remained deadlocked. Hirohito then called an extraordinary meeting of the council at midnight. After listening to all opinions, the emperor intervened, telling his dejected cabinet that they had to "bear the unbearable" and accept the Potsdam Declaration. At 6:45 a.m. on August 10 the Foreign Ministry dispatched cables via Sweden and Switzerland accepting the declaration "with the understanding that the said declaration does not comprise any demand which prejudices the prerogatives of His Majesty as a Sovereign Ruler."[62]

The diplomatic cables caught Washington by surprise. Truman favored a nuanced reply, carefully stating that the authority of the emperor and Japanese government would be subject to the Supreme Commander Allied Powers. The president suspended the use of atomic weapons and conventional attacks by the Twentieth Air Force.[63]

Truman's reply arrived in Tokyo at 12:45 a.m. local time on August 12. Enraged, Anami and the army vowed to fight on. Suzuki called a cabinet meeting and said Japan should reject it. This emboldened Anami, and Tōgō rebuked Suzuki. Yonai feared a military coup d'état.[64]

As an atmosphere of great peril fell over Tokyo, the wavering Suzuki came to his senses, but deadlock persisted. Anami and Umezu controlled the resources to seize power. Junior officers were demanding a kamikaze fight to the death, no matter how many millions of Japanese perished. In Magic intercepts, Washington learned that Tōgō was warning embassies that the army and navy had not approved the surrender offer. Ultra intercepted a message from Imperial General Headquarters ordering all commands to prosecute the war to "preserve the Fatherland and annihilate the enemy."[65]

On August 14 B-29s resumed high-altitude daylight missions over Japan. KSAI broadcast continuous news of the Japanese surrender offer and American acceptance. The OWI-Navy team expeditiously produced millions of leaflets containing the new developments, which B-29s dropped all over Japan during the next several days.[66] Marquis Kido read leaflets that had drifted into the palace grounds and was alarmed that they could trigger a rebellion. At 10:20 a.m. senior military officers met with Hirohito. He told them to help him end the war. At 11:00 a.m. the emperor met the cabinet and ordered surrender. Suzuki resigned, and the Foreign Ministry transmitted the decision again through Sweden and Switzerland. The message reached Washington at 2:49 a.m. EWT on August 14 via a *Domei* report monitored by the FCC.[67]

In Tokyo a coup d'état broke out among junior officers, who briefly occupied the Imperial Palace. A mystery surrounds this episode, which is how they came so close without high-level support. After consuming a copious quantity of sake, Anami sliced his stomach open in the ritual of seppuku, or hari-kari, on the morning of August 15.

Hirohito recorded a radio address that NHK (Nippon Hōsō Kyōkai, or Japanese Broadcasting Company) personnel had to hide from the fanatical military officers. NHK broadcast the Imperial Rescript at noon Japan Standard Time on August 15, 1945. In the Gyokuon-hōsō (Jewel Voice Broadcast) His Divine Majesty announced that Japan had to "imagine the unimaginable" and accept the Potsdam Declaration. The emperor made the broadcast in his formal courtly Japanese, which most of his subjects did not understand, so there was confusion as to whether the emperor had surrendered. After the recording concluded, the NHK announcer explained in common language that Japan surrendered.[68]

Lt. Col. Jack Harris, now MacArthur's communications officer, had to find a way to contact Japan to make the arrangements for surrender and occupation. NHK had been broadcasting with the pseudonym Radio Tokyo after the Japanese military government under Prime Minister Hideki Tōjō nationalized it in 1941. The Army Signal Corps staff in Manila thought it would be logical to try contacting JUM, the Tokyo station that had handled the RCA commercial radio communications traffic between the United States and Japan before the outbreak of hostilities. The Signal Corps directed all transmitters including the powerful stations in the United States to broadcast messages to JUM and wait for a reply.

The first message from Harris in Manila went out: "JUM—from

WTA (Manila). We have an urgent message for you." A furious message came back from a confused Japanese operator, who had mistaken WTA for a Japanese station. Harris tried again. At first JUM did not reply. He repeated the message. There was a long pause, and then JUM dramatically transmitted the first message since December 1941 to RCA Overseas Communications in San Francisco: "KER from JUM. Receive okay. Go ahead. Send at 40 words per minute. How are receiving conditions? 9:05 p.m. Japan Time." KER then transmitted the statement prepared by Harris, in MacArthur's name, with specific instructions for setting up communications. It was 9:30 a.m. on August 15 in San Francisco. JUM acknowledged and started sending messages directly to WTA in Manila. Then something sensational happened. JUM started sending a lengthy series of messages to KER, with many hundreds of commercial cables that had accumulated since 1941. JUM was busy transmitting as if there had never been a war. JUM then advised WTA to send all official messages to JNP, the Japanese government station, so JUM could be free to restore commercial service to the United States. Harris sent a detailed message to JNP with instructions for the cessation of hostilities. He instructed a Japanese delegation to travel to Ie Shima on specifically marked G4M airplanes for transfer aboard an AAF C-54 to Manila for formal meetings to begin the transition to American occupation.[69] Harris then transmitted instructions for NHK and Radio Tokyo to prepare for unified Japanese-American broadcasting operations, as well as the time, place, and details of surrender to the Japanese government.[70] An advance team of 150 American communications personnel including Harris flew into Atsugi airbase, eighteen miles southwest of Tokyo, on August 28. Harris went directly to NHK, where he was warmly welcomed by courteous and cooperative civilian broadcasters, Within hours the U.S. Army was broadcasting from NHK and Radio Tokyo in Japanese and English.[71]

Donovan and the wartime OSS, including station chief Allen Dulles in Berne, took a pragmatic approach of ideological diversity in accepting a broad range of Allies, including Mao in China, Tito in Yugoslavia, and communist partisans in France and Italy.

Vietnamese communist insurgent Ho Chi Minh was in Kunming and with his colleague Pham Van Dong.[72] Lt. Charles Fenn, an OSS officer, asked Ho if he would be willing to return to Indochina with an OSS team, and Ho agreed. When Fenn asked what the OSS could do for him, Ho said, "American recognition for our league, medicine and arms."[73] The French knew Ho as the activist Nguyen Ai Quoc (Nguyen the patriot), a clandestine Comintern operative who trained in Moscow during the 1920s.[74]

Ho adopted the Ho Chi Minh (He Who Enlightens) identity for his cover as a Chinese journalist. He returned to Vietnam in 1941 and organized the first Vietnamese Communist Party. The Kuomintang arrested Ho on a journey to Chongqing in August 1942, but eventually released him.[75] Ho asked to meet with Gen. Claire Chennault, who realized Ho was a communist but wanted help from anyone who could rescue his downed pilots. Chennault autographed a photo for Ho, who used it and American sidearms to convince the Viet Minh he was their American-sanctioned leader.[76]

Capt. Archimedes Patti arrived to take over OSS Indochina operations. He knew who Ho was and approved of his recruitment. He was also under orders from General Donovan not to become involved in French Indochinese politics.[77] Patti realized Ho's purpose and that he was using the Chennault "endorsement" and OSS support to solidify his claim to be Viet-Minh leader.[78]

On July 16, 1945, an OSS team led by Maj. Allison Kent Thomas parachuted into Viet Minh headquarters at Kim Lung with small arms and explosives. More OSS personnel came in on July 29, at which point Ho had fallen ill and OSS medic Paul Hoagland treated him. Thomas selected about forty Viet Minh for the OSS operation, and a revived Ho nicknamed them "Bo Doi Viet-My," the Vietnamese-American Force. When Japan capitulated on August 15, the force was on its way to Hanoi. On August 16 Ho called on the people to revolt and signed the declaration Nguyễn Ái Quốc. The French thought that Nguyễn Ái Quốc was long dead. The Viet Minh entered Hanoi on August 19, and on September 2 Ho declared the independence of the new Democratic Republic of Vietnam. Hanoi newspapers reported the presence of the Americans and their support for Ho and called for massive anti-French demonstrations.[79] Patti had arrived in Hanoi on August 21with an oss and French team and tried to assuage the French and disassociate the oss from the Viet Minh, but it was too late. At Thai Nguyen, Viet Minh military leader Vo Nguyen Giap attacked a Japanese installation. French American Lt. Réne Defourneaux reported that Major Thomas took part in the attack. Defourneaux had not trusted the communists or Thomas since arriving in Vietnam.[80]

The oss did not put Ho in power but was an unwitting accomplice. They gave Ho and Giap the opportunity to claim the *appearance* of American support, which helped them legitimize the Viet Minh. Revisionist historians unconvincingly claim that Ho sought a long-term relationship with the United States. What Ho really did was manipulate the oss. By the first anniversary of Ho's return to Hanoi and the withdrawal of oss support, references to America's role in the victory over Japan had disappeared, and assistance to the Viet Minh had disappeared from Ho's pronouncements. Instead, the Viet Minh ludicrously credited the Soviet Union with "liberating the people subject to Japanese oppression."[81]

Finest Hour

Their divine leader's *kodo sempu* (dissemination of the royal way) broadcast bewildered Japanese soldiers and civilians.[82] Surrender and occupation were inconceivable. Many wanted to fight on. This was quite understandable given the years of conditioning. Militarily controlled Japanese media had insisted that Americans were barbarians and indiscriminate rapists. Corporations circulated cyanide pills, and local authorities in cities and prefectures instructed women to wear loose-fitting clothes to appear unattractive.

Gen. Douglas MacArthur had a remarkably different plan for Japanese women. He planned to give them the vote. He was about to begin a magnanimous and enlightened transformation of Japanese society. In addition to women's rights, his seven-point plan would include free elections, the formation of labor unions, opening schools with the elimination of military indoctrination and a course in civics, disarming Japanese soldiers, and dismantling

Fig. 23. Gen. Douglas MacArthur, supreme commander of Allied powers, deplanes from the Douglas C-54 *Bataan* at Atsugi Airbase, Japan, August 30, 1945. U.S. Army Air Forces photograph 210613-S, RG 18, NARA.

the war industry. MacArthur would also make a crucial decision about the emperor.

At Manila, when Japanese representatives arrived to discuss surrender details, the American draft of the surrender document opened, in Japanese, with "I Hirohito, Emperor of Japan," using the pronoun *watakushi* for "I." The Japanese officers were horrified because His Majesty always referred to himself using *Chin*, the royal "we." Col. Sidney Mashbir, MacArthur's interpreter, made the change. Afterward MacArthur put his arm around Mashbir's shoulder and said, "Mashbir, you handled that exactly right. I have no desire whatever to debase him in the eyes of his own people."[83]

Japan was the only major power that an enemy had never invaded. That ended on August 28, 1945, when the American advance team of 150 men peacefully landed at Atsugi. Theodore White of *Time* and *Life* was present and observed, "The [Japanese] attitude was curious. They acted as if we were partners in a common cause. *Domei* correspondents and photographers covered

Atsugi airbase. Japanese diplomats and newsmen shook hands with Americans and interpreters rushed back and forth beaming with goodwill."[84]

On August 30, an aide woke a napping MacArthur toward the end of a five-hour flight as his c-54 *Bataan* descended for approach. The aide pointed to a big snow-capped mountain that looked like an ice cream cone. MacArthur smiled and said, "Well, good old [Mount] Fuji! How beautiful! Did you ever have a dream come true?" Wearing his sunglasses and armed only with his corncob pipe, MacArthur dramatically stepped off *Bataan*, onto the tarmac at Atsugi. Nervous American troops escorted MacArthur to the Yokohama New Grand Hotel as thirty thousand Japanese troops with fixed bayonets lined the route facing away from the motorcade in a show of respect usually reserved for the emperor. Determined that the occupation be peaceful and constructive from the outset, MacArthur pointedly refused to have his food tasted, knowing that word would quickly spread. He ordered that American military personnel could only eat their own rations and forbid his forces to impose upon the Japanese people for sustenance. He also refused to impose martial law or curfews. This was the first step toward Japanese reformation, and MacArthur wanted to show generosity and compassion.[85]

During dinner on his second evening in Yokohama, the door opened to MacArthur's hotel suite. Liberated but ghostly Lt. Gen. Jonathan M. Wainwright stumbled in, leaning on a cane. MacArthur jumped up to emotionally embrace his friend. All Wainwright could utter was "General . . ." before they both broke down in tears. Two days later the dawned gray and overcast when Wainwright and Gen. Arthur Percival, who surrendered Singapore in 1942, stood with MacArthur on the deck of the battleship uss *Missouri*. An emotional Japanese delegation arrived after beholding hundreds of ships of war at anchor in Tokyo Bay. MacArthur spoke movingly to the packed gathering and radio listeners around the world. Lt. Gen. Yatsuji Nagai marveled at MacArthur's lack of vindictiveness. Toschikazu Kase, secretary to new Foreign Minister Mamoru Shigemitsu and a graduate of Amherst and Harvard, reported, "What a stirring eloquence and noble vision. Here is the victor announcing the verdict to the prostrate enemy. He can exact his pound of flesh if he so chooses. He can impose a humiliating penalty if he so desires. And yet he pleads for freedom, tolerance and justice . . . for the living heroes and dead martyrs of the war this speech was a wreath of undying flowers . . . MacArthur's words sailed on wings . . . this narrow quarterdeck was now transformed into an altar of peace."[86] Hundreds of American bombers and fighter planes flew overhead. Correspondents described MacArthur's demeanor and remarks as "Olympian."[87]

A total of 407, 316 Americas had paid the ultimate price to liberate the planet. Fulfilling FDR's vision of American exceptionalism, MacArthur was opening a chapter of history that would be the greatest evidence of the true American character. Healing the planet would be America's finest hour.

Unlike Halsey or others, Nimitz did not seek to humiliate his former adversaries. He went ashore to visit the enshrined battleship *Mikasa*, Admiral Heihachirō Tōgō's flagship when he annihilated the Russian fleet at the Battle of Tsushima in 1905. As a show of reconciliation, Nimitz, who had attended the beloved admiral's 1934 funeral, ordered a Marine Corps guard placed around the ship to protect it from souvenir hunters. In 1958 Nimitz helped finance a restoration of *Mikasa*. President Theodore Roosevelt, who respected Tōgō and Japan, would have approved.[88]

The next morning Shigemitsu appeared at the Imperial Court to read Kase's report about the events of September 2 aboard the *Missouri*. Kase reported that it was "rare good fortune" that a man "of such caliber and character should have been designated as Supreme Commander to shape the destiny of Japan . . . in [our] dark hour of distress, a bright light is ushered in, in the very person of Gen. MacArthur." Kase wondered "whether it would have been possible for us, had we been victorious, to embrace the vanquished with similar magnanimity. Clearly it would have been different . . . we were not beaten on the battlefield by dint of superior arms. We were defeated in the spiritual contest by virtue of a nobler idea. The real issue was moral—beyond all the powers of algebra to compute." Aboard *Missouri* Kase had noticed the many miniature rising sun flag decals on the steel bulkhead, symbolizing Japanese ships, submarines, and planes: "I could hardly bear the sight. . . . Heroes of unwritten stories, these were young boys who defied death gaily and gallantly . . . there were like cherry blossoms, emblems of our national character, swiftly blooming into riotous beauty and falling just as quickly." Hirohito lingered over this closing remark for a long time, sighed deeply, nodded, and murmured, "*Ah so, ah so deska.*"[89]

Many officials in the Truman administration were planning punitive postwar blueprints for Germany and Japan. MacArthur rejected this view. Japan was utterly devastated, with over two million citizens dead and 81 percent of its property destroyed.[90] MacArthur wanted Japan to save face, voluntarily disarm, and ultimately recover as a liberal democratic ally. He allowed Japanese fisherman to ply the waters of Tokyo Bay when Halsey forbade it in fear of terror reprisals. Nonsense, said MacArthur, they needed to catch fish for food. And so it was that everything MacArthur said or did endeared him to the shell-shocked people of Japan. He made it clear that he was not going to arrest or prosecute the emperor; quite the contrary, he wanted Hirohito to remain. Nor did he demand that Hirohito appear before him. Better the patience of the East than the haste of the West. MacArthur was introducing an innovative word to the Japanese language: *demokrashi.*

The headquarters of the Supreme Commander of Allied Powers (SCAP) had complete control over Japan and censorship authority over the Japanese media. SCAP could suspend Hirohito and the Japanese Diet (parliament). SCAP broke up a right-wing militarist party but legalized the communists just as Stalin clumsily broke a wartime agreement and kept 376,000 Japanese soldiers stationed in Manchuria as Siberian slave laborers. Japanese soldiers who did come home were peaceful; the Eighth Army occupied Japan with only 152,000 of its GIs. The entire Sixth and Tenth Armies went home, and seventy million Japanese people started rebuilding their nation with their own hands.

The citizens of the new Dai Nippon learned of wartime atrocities

Fig. 24. USS *Missouri*, September 2, 1945. Japan's Foreign Ministry representatives Katsuo Okazaki and Toshikazu Kase, and Lt. Gen. Richard K. Sutherland, deputy to Gen. Douglas MacArthur, correcting an error on Japan's copy of the Instrument of Surrender at the conclusion of ceremonies aboard the USS *Missouri* (BB-63), September 2, 1945. U.S. Army Signal Corps Photograph C-4626, RG-111-SC, NARA.

and the indictments of war criminals from their SCAP-approved newspapers. The compassionate behavior of the American GIs was a welcome surprise. Eager to learn anything and everything about the United States, the Japanese people closely listened to the AFRS Far East Network to learn the latest American news and music and to follow baseball from the States. Like war-weary survivors in Europe, they fell in love with jazz, and everything American was inspirational. Pleasant American Nisei announcers broadcast news and entertainment in fluent Japanese. Many listened to English-speaking broadcasts to learn the language, leading the Americans to add special English broadcasts, read at a slower pace with short sentences to help listeners with basic vocabulary.

In the weeks following the beginning of the honeymoon, die-hard samurai continued to harbor dreams of rising against the intruders. Then came another stunning imperial rescript that ended any delusions. Although the matter was going to be a nonnegotiable part of the new SCAP-designed Japanese Constitution, Hirohito freely decreed that he was not divine, and that Japan had therefore fought for a myth.

Everyone saw the photo on the front pages of Japanese newspapers on September 28. The mikado called on SCAP. Not knowing that MacArthur had stricken his name from the list of war criminals, Hirohito offered himself as the "one to bear sole responsibility for every political and military decision made and action taken by my people in the conduct of the war." This selfless and statesmanlike vow deeply impressed MacArthur. Thereafter Hirohito approved of every SCAP decision and met with MacArthur twice a year. Historians note that the respect SCAP gave to the mikado was a main reason why the occupation succeeded.[91]

Meanwhile most Americans were interested in the rapid return of men in uniform from overseas. Operation Magic Carpet was transporting millions of service personnel from Europe and the Pacific back to the continental United States by sea and air. On October 26 at Brooklyn Navy Yard, President Truman commissioned the new *Midway*-class aircraft carrier USS *Franklin D. Roosevelt*. Aboard *Missouri* the former army artillery officer reviewed a parade of fifty warships in the Hudson River, as thousands of aircraft flew overhead. It was an impressive display of a force that was about to disintegrate as the public demanded demobilization.

By mid-1944 Congress had already canceled defense contracts and cut manpower requirements in anticipation of victory. By June 1947 the armed forces contracted to just over one and a half million people. The navy mothballed most of its wartime ships. The AAF flew obsolete B-17 and B-24 bombers home and scrapped them. Futuristic jet aircraft now appeared along with guided missiles and the atomic bomb to both amaze and frighten Americans.[92]

Robert Sherwood wrote the screenplay for the successful Goldwyn Productions film *The Best Years of Our Lives*, based upon a story by war correspondent MacKinlay Kantor and directed by

William Wyler, about the adjustment of three war veterans to post-war life, where Americans wanted to take a break, earn money, raise families and enjoy their lives.

At this critical moment a world in ruins, beset by many long-simmering and newly released national, social, and cultural impulses, did not stand still while Americans relaxed.

Subversive forces moved into devastated Europe and the emerging third world to seduce anxious, starving, and displaced peoples. Legitimate and long-simmering independence movements sought support. Communist movements, inspired and often supported by the USSR, prepared to potentially seize and dominate much of the planet, beginning with China.

With Japanese hostilities at an end, Chiang Kai-Shek suggested a meeting with Mao Zedong. A suspicious Mao accepted the offer on the condition that Ambassador Patrick Hurley fly with him to Chongqing so that Chiang would not shoot his plane down. The summit predictably failed, and it appeared that all-out civil war would ensue. On November 26 Hurley met with Truman in the White House and told the president that everything was under control and that he would be returning to China. Two hours later Hurley made a speech at the National Press Club announcing his resignation because the State Department had "sided with the Chinese Communists." In a scathing letter of resignation he repeated that claim. A dumbfounded Truman said to his cabinet, "See what that son-of-a-bitch has done to me!"[93]

Truman made two popular announcements, naming victorious military leaders Eisenhower to succeed Marshall as army chief of staff and Nimitz to succeed King as chief of naval operations. Marshall had been retired for all of six days when Truman called and said, "General, I want you to go to China," and Marshall replied, "Yes, Mr. President" and hung up so he could tell his wife.[94]

A reluctant Marshall guardedly arrived in China on December 20, 1945, looking to unify the Kuomintang and communists, who were shooting at one another, into a coalition government that would not fall under Soviet domination. At war's end American forces had occupied key Chinese cities and ports and cooperated with the Kuomintang, leading Mao to correctly conclude that the United States in the person of Hurley was siding with Chiang. But Marshall was determined from the outset to be unemotional and rational. He suspended arms sales to the Kuomintang in July 1946 to force a cease-fire. The competitors agreed upon the precepts of a democratic constitution and a plan to merge their troops into one army. Mao proclaimed, "The entire people of our country should feel grateful and loudly shout, 'long live cooperation between China and the United States.'" He said that he wanted to visit America. Zhou Enlai was planning which agencies of the coalition government the communist officials would staff. But the euphoria was short-lived. The accord quickly broke down as the details were impossible to implement. Stalin undermined Marshall by urging Mao to accelerate guerilla warfare. At the end of 1946 Marshall said the obvious, "It is now going to be necessary for the Chinese, themselves, to do the things I endeavored to lead them into."[95]

Exasperated, Marshall left China in February 1947, and full-scale civil war ensued. He returned to the United States to succeed Byrnes as secretary of state and focus on the revitalization of Europe. Marshall was as careful as Hurley was eccentric, and as principled as Hurley was inconsistent. Yet China was beyond even Marshall's considerable skill and patience. His sense of duty compelled him to try, and for doing so he exposed himself to viscous criticism as the man "who lost China."

Dr. Franc L. McCluer, the president of Westminster College in Fulton, Missouri, invited former prime minister Winston Churchill to speak at the school. Truman traveled with Churchill from Washington to Missouri aboard the *Ferdinand Magellan*, where the men became better acquainted over poker and bourbon. Churchill passed around his speech on the train, and Truman commented that it might make quite a stir. On March 5, 1946, Churchill donned the scarlet robes and black cap of Oxford and rose to make his remarks. After thanking Stalin and the Soviet people for their heroic wartime sacrifices, and welcoming the Soviet Union as a world leader,

Churchill opined that it was his duty, however, to present "certain facts." And then he fired the opening salvo of the Cold War.

The British lion growled, "From Stettin in the Baltic to Trieste in the Adriatic, an iron curtain has descended across the continent. Behind that line lie all the capitals of the ancient states of Central and Eastern Europe, Warsaw, Berlin, Prague, Vienna, Budapest, Belgrade, Bucharest and Sofia, all these famous cities and populations around them lie in what I must call the Soviet sphere, and all are subject in one form or another, not only to Soviet influence but to a very high and, in many case, increasing measure of control from Moscow." Churchill went on to say that a strong postwar union between the United States, Britain, and Western liberal democracies needed to stand up to Stalin and protect the rest of Europe. This vision later became NATO, the North Atlantic Treaty Organization.[96]

Editorial reaction in the United States to Churchill's speech was negative. Columnist Walter Lippman called it a "catastrophic blunder," and Stalin responded by saying it was a "call to war." The criticism stunned Truman. He told reporters that he never knew what Churchill was going to say, which was a lie, because he had read the speech in advance. The president clumsily invited Stalin to speak at Westminster, and the dictator refused. Truman's advisers, particularly Undersecretary of State Dean Acheson, knew the truth, and they agreed with Churchill.

At this critical moment the chargé d'affaires at the American embassy in Moscow transmitted an eight-thousand-word "long telegram" to the State Department. George Frost Kennan urged the Truman administration to abandon plans for cooperation with the Soviets and adapt a sphere of influence policy to contain Soviet expansion. Kennan urged the formation of a western European confederation to counter Soviet influence and compete against the new Soviet power bloc of enslaved satellite nations. He wrote the message as a reply to Treasury Department concerns about why the Soviets were refusing to endorse the IMF and World Bank.

Kennan identified a toxic mix of a neurotic Soviet worldview, traditional Russian insecurity, and communist ideology. Stalin

Fig. 25. George F. Kennan. 1947. Harris & Ewing Photographic Collection, Library of Congress (LC-H261–112729).

needed a hostile world to justify his autocratic rule. Soviet leaders saw themselves living in a state of constant "capitalist encirclement" with which they could not peacefully coexist. This insecurity led to a belief that the Soviet Union must build ever-larger armed forces. Never losing their distrust of capitalism, the Soviets would cooperate in international organizations only to gain advantage or to inhibit the work of such groups. Using Marxist-Leninist dogma as a rationale, the Soviet Union would develop ties to countries opposed to the Western powers and discourage efforts at economic collaboration. Kennan recommended that Western institutions be strengthened to make them invulnerable to Soviet challenge until the Soviet regime changed.[97] Kennan later softened his pessimism by recommending economic and political containment of the Soviet Union and not necessarily military confrontation.[98]

In the confusion and uncertainty facing postwar Germany and Japan, AFN in Europe and FEN in Asia presented a positive view of America and desperately needed information and entertainment. By 1946 the American Forces Network operated major stations in Frankfurt, Munich, Berlin, and Bremen. The historic Hoechst Castle outside Frankfurt became headquarters for AFN and the Blue Danube Network in Austria. The former Großdeutscher Rundfunk AFN transmitters were so powerful that Munich reached listeners in South Asia and the Far East. Intended for the American forces, the stations became a magnet for Germans and Austrians eager for an escape from the grim daily reality of postwar survival and fear of the Soviets. The United States also set up Radio in the American Sector (RIAS) to serve Berliners. In Japan the Americans captured the cooperative NHK intact. NHK ran three networks prior to surrender and organized like the BBC. NHK-1 was the biggest network and had eighty local stations. It and NHK-3 remained on the air, subject to SCAP censorship. AFRS took over NHK-2, which joined the Far East Network. AFRS employed Japanese personnel, used NHK studios and transmitters, and renamed stations such as JOAK with the American call letters WVTR. FEN focused on returning American troops to civilian life and neighborly relations with their host nation, the same policy followed by

AFN in Europe. For curious Japanese listeners, FEN produced a series of programs portraying the virtues of American life, including *Ambassadors of Good Will*, and American troops received Japanese language lessons.[99]

Truman terminated the OWI with Executive Order 9608 on August 31, 1945. The controversial Domestic Branch disappeared, and the Department of State absorbed the efficient Overseas Branch, including the VOA. Rather than returning to CBS, Davis joined ABC (formerly the Blue Network). The president also closed the OSS with Executive Order 9621 on September 20, 1945, and Donovan headed to Germany to attend war crimes trials. The Department of State absorbed the Research and Analysis group of the OSS, which became the Bureau of Intelligence and Research. The War Department received the Secret Intelligence and Counterespionage branches of the OSS, which became a new Strategic Services Unit. Facing postwar reality, in January 1946 Truman created a Central Intelligence Group, into which the War Department placed the clandestine functions preserved by the SSU. The CIG formed the nucleus for what became the Central Intelligence Agency in 1948. The new CIA would also include the Bureau of Intelligence and Research and former OWI information gathering and analytical functions from the Department of State.[100]

In the immediate months following victory, Congress cut funding for the VOA. A Department of State committee chaired by Columbia University professor Arthur W. MacMahon advised that the United States could not be "indifferent to the ways in which our society is portrayed to other countries." The committee recommended that information services were necessary for foreign policy, and that government information activities should promote full and fair knowledge of the United States, international alliances, and free trade. Congress reluctantly approved continued funding for the VOA in 1946 and 1947. Their demeanor would change in 1948.[101]

NINE

A New Frontier

Cold War

During World War II, the United Nations established international criminal tribunals to prosecute high-level political officials and military authorities for crimes against humanity, planning and waging wars of aggression and conspiracy to violate world peace.

With horrific wartime casualties and destruction in mind, including the systematic extermination of six million innocent Jews and many others officially deemed undesirable by the defeated Nazi government, the International Military Tribunal (IMT) in Nuremberg, Germany, indicted twenty-two major Nazi political, judicial, industrial and military conspirators, finding nineteen guilty. The IMT sentenced them to punishments ranging from death by hanging to ten-years' imprisonment. Subsequent trials held until 1949 dealt with mid- to low-level officials. On October 19, 1946, the U.S. Army carried out the executions of ten top Nazi leaders.[1] The top-level trials received extensive media coverage, and a subsequent fictional trial of Nazi-era judges is the subject of the riveting 1961 motion picture *Judgement at Nuremburg*.

Among other charges, Karl Dönitz stood accused of conducting unrestricted submarine warfare. American Chief of Naval Operations Nimitz provided an affidavit, stating that under orders from Washington, his own submarine force had carried out the same kind of warfare. Although the IMT imposed a ten-year prison sentence on Dönitz, it did not impose the penalty for conducting unrestricted submarine warfare.[2]

In 1946 SCAP set up the International Military Tribunal for the

Far East in Tokyo and Manila, to preside over trials of senior Japanese leaders.[3] The Tokyo War Crimes Trials took place from May 1946 to November 1948. The IMTFE found twenty-eight defendants guilty and sentenced them to punishments ranging from death to seven years' imprisonment. The tribunal carried out seven executions, led by former prime minister Tojo.

Reality compelled the Truman administration to ditch the Morgenthau Plan, favored by the USSR, which envisioned the postwar partition and deindustrialization of Germany. Truman asked former president and political pariah Herbert Hoover for advice, and the renown humanitarian recommended immediate food and reconstruction assistance.[4] On September 6 Secretary of State Byrnes spoke at the Staatstheater in Stuttgart to announce that the United States renounced the Carthaginian peace envisioned by the Morgenthau Plan in favor of economic reconstruction of Germany. The speech was carefully prepared and vetted by John Kenneth Galbraith with the guidance of occupation commander Gen. Lucius Clay, who argued that communism could prevail unless the United States gave the German people hope.[5]

On September 24 presidential adviser Clark Clifford submitted a 100,000-word analysis of Soviet-American relations, mostly written by his assistant George Elsey, which described Stalin as being on a course toward eventual world domination.[6]

Byrnes believed he was going to be FDR's choice as running mate in 1944 and carried himself with an air of preeminence to Truman. It was therefore not a surprise when the president replaced Byrnes with Marshall when the general returned from China.[7] Byrnes became governor of South Carolina in 1951. He opposed school desegregation and later supported the migration of white Southern Democrats to the Republican Party.

Britain struggled in the immediate postwar years and began to shed the empire and global responsibilities that it could no longer afford. The Atlee government planned to withdraw forty thousand troops from Greece and cut economic aid on March 31, 1947. Marshall and Acheson told Truman and congressional leaders that Greece and Turkey would fall under Soviet control without expensive and prompt aid packages. Marshall advised that the Soviet Union "was playing one of the greatest gambles in history at minimal cost and they do not need to win all the possibilities." Vandenberg growled that Truman needed to get this before Congress and the American people right away and "scare the hell out of them."[8]

Truman flew to Mexico City, and it was the first time a sitting American president had set foot in Mexico. Receiving a warm welcome from large crowds, Truman told Mexican lawmakers that he wished to continue the Good Neighbor Policy. On March 5 Truman stopped his motorcade to visit the Los Niños Héroes monument in Chapultepec Park, which honors six teenage military cadets who died defending Chapultepec Castle from American troops on September 13, 1847. Walking past military cadets standing at attention, Truman laid a floral wreath at the monument and bowed his head. The kind gesture made a deep impression.[9]

Before a joint session of Congress on March 12 the president set forth the Truman Doctrine, which pledged the support of the United States to the "freedom of democratic choice and economic aid for nations and peoples pressured by outside forces." The United States was, in effect, stepping in to assume Britain's world responsibilities and to confront Soviet subversion. This was a clear shift in policy that the Soviets took note of.[10] On April 22, 1947, the Senate approved the aid package for Greece and Turkey by a 67–23 vote, and the House followed on May 9 by a 287–107 vote.[11]

Marshall attended a Council of Foreign Ministers meeting in Moscow from March 10 through April 24. Reparations, boundaries, and self-determination were all on the agenda. Meetings with Molotov were unproductive, and Stalin was indifferent. Marshall reluctantly concluded that there was no hope of negotiation with them.[12] Visiting Germany and France, he also concluded that time was of the essence in doing something to feed, heat, and rescue Western Europe. Marshall ordered Kennan to assemble a report about what to do, and as Kennan recalled, Marshall's admonition was "avoid trivia."[13]

Kennan saw the disruptive effect of the war as the cause of

Europe's helplessness, not communism per se, although the communists were *exploiting* the economic crisis. He recommended a recovery plan directed but not imposed by the United States and formally implemented by Europe as a responsible partner in its own recovery. Soviet satellites would be invited to participate, and there was only one nonnegotiable term, abandoning communist exclusivity of their economies.[14]

Under Secretary of State Will Clayton reported to Marshall that the economic crisis in Europe was worse than they thought because the United States had "grossly underestimated" the wartime destruction of Europe's economy. Millions of people were "slowly starving."[15]

President James B. Conant and the Harvard Governing Board offered Marshall honorary degrees in 1945 and 1946, but the general declined due to being in absentia overseas. Marshall agreed to come to accept the honor at the June 5, 1947, Cambridge commencement. Bohlen helped craft the final draft of a speech that Marshall did not clear with Truman and that would have an instantaneous effect in America and Europe. Marshall was intentionally calm and avoided dramatics. Issuing a "call to action," he said that Europe was in a state of economic crisis and needed America's help for three or four years. America would not direct this policy *at* any country, but it was *for* every country and "against hunger, poverty, despotism and chaos . . . its purpose shall be the revival of a working economy in the world so as to permit the emergence of political and social conditions in which free institutions can exist." Reminding Americans that the problems of Europe were in their best interest to help resolve, and that America had a special responsibility to help without politics or prejudice, Marshall concluded, "the whole world's future hangs on a proper judgment, hangs on the realization by the American people of what can best be done, *of what must be done.*[16]

Marshall thus defined what became the most intuitive foreign policy initiative in American and world history. Marshall subtly took FDR's vision of exceptionalism and elevated it to a purpose higher than stopping the comparatively selfish and simple-minded

Fig. 26. Gen. George C. Marshall, chief of staff of the Army of the United States, secretary of state, and secretary of defense. Portrait by James Anthony Wills, 1949. National Portrait Gallery, Smithsonian Institution, Washington DC (NPG.66.64).

Soviet communist juggernaut. Marshall's motivation was not belligerently anti-Soviet. The fact was that the United States had a moral obligation to act *despite the Soviets.*

British Foreign Minister Ernest Bevin held a conference in Paris to discuss Marshall's proposal. Five days into the conference, Molotov abruptly announced that the Soviet Union and its satellites were withdrawing because the Marshall Plan was "nothing but a vicious American scheme for using dollars to butt its way into the affairs of Europe."[17]

The Truman administration faced a stiff challenge with a Republican-controlled Congress intent on cutting expenditures and taxes. Vandenberg rallied Republican support, and the Marshall Plan, formally known as the Foreign Assistance Act and the Economic Cooperation Act of 1948, passed the House and Senate by overwhelming margins and became law on April 3, 1948.[18] The far-sighted legislation succeeded in restoring European agricultural and industrial productivity. Credited with preventing famine and political chaos, the historic initiative earned Marshall a Nobel Peace Prize in 1953.

The new world reality, or Cold War, confirmed the need for the voa. Congress passed the Smith-Mundt Act, permanently establishing international broadcasting, informational, and cultural exchange programs, in part to counter Soviet and Soviet-controlled activities.[19]

The Joint Chiefs of Staff Special Committee for the Reorganization of National Defense recommended April 11, 1945, that the armed forces of the United States organize into a single cabinet department, and three branches, the Army, Navy, and Air. Truman saw reorganization as a way of breaking up what he saw as Annapolis and West Point cliques and democratizing the military, which he also planned to fully desegregate. On July 26, 1947, the Department of Defense replaced the War and Navy Departments, and the Army Air Forces became the independent United States Air Force. The National Security Act also included the organization of a unified Central Intelligence Agency (cia).[20]

In 1917 Zionist Chaim Weizmann persuaded the British to issue

a statement known as the Balfour Declaration favoring the establishment of a Jewish nation in Palestine. The League of Nations
ratified the declaration in 1922 and appointed Britain to rule in
Palestine. Due to wartime exigencies, FDR did nothing to enable
Jewish migration or to create a Jewish homeland.

The buck passed to Truman in 1945 as pressure from American Jewish leaders mounted. The president believed that because
of the systematic Nazi extermination of at least six million Jews,
humanity owed the Jewish people a homeland. The United
Nations General Assembly set up a Special Committee on Palestine that recommended two states and British withdrawal. The
Arab League directed its members to move troops to Palestine.
Truman instructed the State Department to support the UN plan,
which the UN General Assembly passed it on November 29, 1947.

Secretary of Defense James Forrestal cautioned against the Zionist cause because of the strategic importance of Arab oil.[21] The State
Department opposed the partition; Marshall believed that accepting partition was a strategic error. On March 18, 1948, Truman privately assured Weizmann that the United States would support partition. The new state of Israel declared itself at midnight in Jerusalem
and 6:00 p.m. in Washington. Eleven minutes later, the United States
recognized Israel. Republicans Vandenberg, Dewey, and Dulles supported Truman's decision. At the State Department Marshall was taking steps to keep diplomats from resigning, and as he predicted, the
first Arab-Israeli war broke out, and the new state of Israel survived.[22]

In Hollywood, members of the Conference of Studio Unions
went on strike in March 1945. The CSU was a rival of the International Alliance of Theatrical Stage Employees, which advised its
members to cross the CSU picket lines. Violence erupted on October 5 outside Warner Brothers in Burbank. The American Federation of Labor sided with the IATSE and locked the CSU out of the
studios. This unrest led to the passage of the Taft-Hartley Act, or
Labor Management Relations Act of 1947, that limiting the ability
of labor to strike and radicals from assuming union leadership.
President Truman vetoed the bill, but Congress overrode him.[23]

In November 1946 the House Un-American Activities Committee resumed the prewar investigation of the motion picture industry and communism in Hollywood. The studios and conservative Motion Picture Alliance for the Preservation of American Ideals expressed their concerns about communist influence and recommended steps to counter it. In October 1947 HUAC subpoenaed many Hollywood figures. A group of industry professionals known as the "Hollywood Ten," including screenwriters Howard Koch and Dalton Trumbo, stood accused of communist sympathies and refused to testify.

Walt Disney testified that the threat of communists in the industry was real. Screen Actors Guild president Ronald Reagan said there was a small communist-like clique in his union but nothing out of control. Members of the liberal Committee for the First Amendment, including Humphrey Bogart, Lauren Bacall, John Huston, and Billy Wilder, protested the hearings. The Motion Picture Association of America and the Screen Actors Guild made anticommunist pledges, and the full House voted 346–17 to cite the uncooperative witnesses with contempt. The Supreme Court declined review of appeals, so the Hollywood Ten served one-year prison sentences starting in 1950.[24]

Hollywood had an even bigger challenge: television. As the owners of radio stations expanded into television and a government anti-trust action forced the studios to divest theater chains, wartime colleagues Paley and Sarnoff were dueling over which color television system, CBS or RCA, would become the national standard for transmission infrastructure and set production. CBS won FCC approval and the NTSC analog system remained until the implementation of digital technology in the early 2000s.[25]

On June 23, 1948, the Republican National Convention met in hot and humid Philadelphia and was brimming with confidence. Sen. Robert Taft of Ohio, son of a president and chief justice, was the traditionalist conservative candidate. Gov. Harold Stassen of Minnesota, a navy veteran, looked to ride a wave of popular support as a dark horse. The favorite was Gov. Thomas E. Dewey of New York, the 1944 candidate and leader of the internationalist wing of the party. While the media focused on the nomination and election of Dewey, events elsewhere intervened.

At 6:00 a.m. on June 24, the Soviet Union stopped all train, road, and barge traffic into Berlin, and electrical power to the western Berlin sectors went off. American proconsul Clay and the Western Allies had three options: retreat and abandon Berlin, stand firm as Berliners starved, or bring in food by force. In case of war, analysts predicted the Soviets could reach the English Channel in forty-eight hours, and the Americans would have to use nuclear weapons to stop them. The Soviets had boldly put before Clay what amounted to surrender terms.[26]

The Soviet blockade of Berlin was not precipitous. On March 20 the Soviets withdrew from the Allied Control Council for Germany, and on March 31 they limited access routes into Berlin to protest a plan by the Western Allies and German authorities to introduce currency reform. The plan was to devalue German currency by 90 percent, repudiate Reich debt, and make equalization payments to Germans. Economics Minister Ludwig Erhard went ahead with the directive for Germans to trade in Reichsmarks for new Deutsche Marks at a rate of 100 RM = 6.5 DM. This was the first step in the creation of a West German state. Clay began making contingency preparations for a blockade of Berlin.[27]

The Soviets walked out of the four-power Berlin Kommandatura meeting on June 16. When the currency reform took effect June 21, the Soviets did not recognize the new Deutsche Mark. On June 22 Clay's counterpart Marshal Vasily Sokolovsky announced a Soviet currency reform to begin June 24. Sokolovsky ordered that a Soviet-backed Reichsmark would be the only legal currency in Berlin starting June 26.

This amounted to the economic incorporation of all Berlin into the Soviet occupation zone and made it clear the Western Allies had no further role in the Berlin government. The western Kommandatura members, Clay, British Gen. Brian Robertson, and French Gen. Pierre Koenig refused to accept the Soviet order. The Berlin City Assembly courageously rejected the Soviet order and cast their lot with the West. It was at this precise moment the Soviets blockaded Berlin.

Clay expected the Soviets to order the Western Allies out of Berlin, but that never happened because they were not willing to escalate to war. This convinced Clay that the Soviets were bluffing.[28]

Ernst Reuter, the fearless socialist mayor of Berlin, agreed with Clay that the Soviets were bluffing. The Americans prepared to send an armed regimental combat team, engineer battalion, and a military supply convoy across the Autobahn from Helmstedt to Berlin. Clay instructed Maj. Gen. Curtis LeMay, commander of the U.S. Air Force in Europe, to be prepared for combat. Clay was willing to call the Soviets' bluff, but Washington vetoed his Autobahn challenge.

British proconsul Robertson suggested the idea of supplying Berlin by air. Clay was skeptical, although he had already ordered LeMay to direct some supply flights into Berlin. On June 26 the airlift started as ground crews loaded planes with food and coal. The Berliners, like all Germans, had enjoyed a high standard of comfortable living during the 1930s. Now they lived hand to mouth in rubble. The Soviets were inviting Berlin to join their Soviet *cordon sanitaire*, or communist protective zone. But a funny thing happened on the way to the workers' paradise. The irritating little capitalist enclave held out.[29]

Operation Vittles was the unofficial name of the supply mission. The Americans occupied Tempelhof airport, which was the old Nazi passenger terminal. The British occupied Gatow aerodrome, and the French occupied Tegel aerodrome. The AAF and RAF had to set up complicated air traffic procedures, radar and instrument landing equipment, ground approach control, radio ranges and beacons, crew schedules, ground transit times, and disembarkation procedures. Pilots had to stay within very tight air corridors or risk being shot down by Soviet fighters.[30] Stalin announced that he would lift the blockade if the Western Allies accepted the Soviet currency in Berlin. Walter Bedell Smith, the U.S. ambassador in Moscow, accepted the proposal without informing Clay, who strongly objected, because doing so would terminate any

Western control over Berlin's government. Experts believed that Berlin was indefensible and that it could not be indefinitely supplied by air. But as bipartisan Washington prepared to surrender, a determined Truman supported Clay.[31]

Gen. William Tunner, who directed wartime supply operations over the Hump between India and China, was sent to command the airlift. He calculated that Berlin needed 4,500 tons of cargo per day. There were three aerial autobahns into Berlin, each twenty miles wide. One plane arrived every three minutes. To avoid Soviet airspace, flights had to make very tight landings in generally poor visibility weather conditions.[32]

By the end of 1948, Tunner had 240 C-54s deployed for the airlift on any given day, with 100 more in the maintenance pipeline or repair depots. The USAF brought in air transport planes and crews to Germany from all over the world. American Overseas Airlines handled passenger traffic. The complicated organization of the airlift extended beyond Germany from across the Atlantic, as C-54s had to rotate to and from the United States for overhaul and reconditioning. Toward the end of the airlift, several new Boeing C-97 Stratofreighters arrived. Had the airlift continued, 52 C-97s could carry the same load as 240 C-54s. Poor weather was a constant problem, but only twenty-two accidents occurred in over three hundred thousand airlift flights.[33]

On July 20 Clay was aboard a plane leaving Tempelhof for Rhein-Main, when he saw a crowd of children waving handkerchiefs at the end of the runway. Asking why, he learned that they were waiting for the "candy bomber." A C-54 piloted by Lt. Gail Seymour "Hal" Halvorsen had started dropping candy using little homemade parachutes to children on the airport perimeter while landing at Tempelhof. The gesture turned into a public relations coup and a significant boost to local morale. Tunner approved the stunt and allowed more aircraft to participate. Here were the Americans, who recently dropped destruction, now bringing kindness to mobs of joyous *kinder*. The media got wind of the commotion. Reporters found hundreds of children and adults at the east end of the Tempelhof runway waiting for the *Rosinenbomber*—the raisin bomber.[34]

Fig. 27. Maj. Gen. Lucius D. Clay, March 31, 1945. Harris & Ewing Photographic Collection, LOC (39220-PPA).

The *Berliner Telegraf* said, "(American planes) are no longer a cause for anxiety. No, quite the contrary. Their roar is deep, good, and has a quieting effect." When a plane crashed near Tempelhof, Berliners put up a memorial that said, "Once we were your enemies, yet you now gave your lives for us. We are now doubly in your debt." They brought gifts to Tempelhof for American airmen and realized that the world was coming to see them as something other than people who had helped perpetrate wartime atrocities.

On September 9 the Berlin government voted to move from the historic Rathaus in the Soviet sector to temporary quarters in the British sector. Three hundred thousand Berliners rallied in front of the burnt-out Reichstag to denounce the USSR. The radio stations AFN Berlin and RIAS (Radio in the American Sector) became symbols of resilience and resistance, proof that America intended to remain in the divided city. The frustrated Soviets went ahead and formally divided Berlin on November 30 by installing a puppet city government in their sector.[35]

As expected, Dewey won the Republican presidential nomination and selected Gov. Earl Warren of California as his running mate. Their centrist and internationalist platform included fiscal responsibility, containment of the USSR, recognition of Israel, and a progressive civil rights agenda. On July 14 a contentious Democratic convention opened in Philadelphia, where both parties had convened to accommodate the new television networks. Truman had to compete with progressive favorite Henry Wallace and a southern segregationist "Dixiecrat" insurgency led by Sen. Strom Thurmond (D-SC). The Dixiecrats ended up walking out of the convention, and some FDR veterans wished for an Eisenhower favorite-son candidacy. But "Ike" said no, and Truman won the nomination with veteran Sen. Alben Barkley as his running mate. Although the media predicted Truman's certain defeat, the underdog enthusiastically embarked on a "whistle stop" tour and barnstormed the nation aboard the *Ferdinand Magellan*. To shouts of "give 'em hell, Harry," Truman campaigned against a "do nothing" Republican Congress. A restrained Dewey belatedly made his own national tour. The media almost unanimously praised Dewey as "statesmanlike" and criticized Truman as "competitive."

Dewey ran ahead in the polls and appeared presidential. He was well qualified but came across as cautious and distant. The final Gallup Poll showed a five-point national lead for Dewey, and the *New York Times* predicted a 345 electoral vote win. Surprising all the pundits, Truman upset Dewey with 49 percent of the popular vote and 303 electoral votes to Dewey's 45 percent and 189 electoral votes. Dixiecrat Thurmond siphoned off 6 percent and 39 southern electoral votes. The result could have easily been different and appeared so in the early returns. Truman narrowly carried California by less than one percent and won with extremely tight margins in several other key states. The Republicans lost both houses of Congress, but Grand Rapids, Michigan, elected navy veteran Gerald R. Ford to Vandenberg's old house seat.[36]

During the campaign the House Un-American Activities Committee, including freshman Richard M. Nixon (R-CA), heard testimony from former *Time* editor Whittaker Chambers that Alger Hiss, a veteran American diplomat who chaired the San Francisco Conference in 1945, was an accomplice in a communist intelligence network. Chambers admitted to being part of the network. Considered a smear by liberals for decades, the charges against Hiss turned out to be true, although some still deny the mountain of declassified American and Soviet evidence.[37]

The 1948 HUAC hearings were the first fissure within the wartime media and government alliance, as liberal public figures, intellectuals, and editorialists pushed back against hard-hitting anticommunist investigations. Along with tactics that he would use in a successful campaign against Sen. Helen Gahagan Douglas (D-CA) in 1950, the HUAC hearings established Nixon as a perennial villain in the eyes of the American Left.

On July 26, 1948, Truman signed Executive Order 9981, abolishing discrimination "on the basis of race, color, religion or national origin" in the United States Armed Forces.[38] The Department of Defense abolished the last all-black units in the armed forces in 1954.[39]

Marshall retired on January 7, 1949, and Acheson replaced him as secretary of state. The Western Allies signed the North Atlantic Treaty on April 4 and approved the establishment of the Bundesrepublik Deutschland (Federal Republic of Germany) on May 12. The formation of the North Atlantic Treaty Organization (NATO) joined the Marshall Plan as signature achievements and two of the most enduring examples of American exceptionalism. The Soviets replied by forming the Warsaw Pact, including a police state in East Germany. The Senate ratified the NATO Treaty on July 21 by a vote of 82–13.

The Berlin Airlift flew continuously until May 12, 1949, when the Soviets lifted the blockade the same day West Germany was founded. In the eyes of the German people, the army of occupation, or Besatzungsmacht, had become the army of protection, or Schutzmacht. On May 15 Gen. Lucius Dubignon Clay left Germany with great fanfare to return to the United States after serving four years as military governor of Germany and commander of American forces in Europe. When he left Rhein-Main an army band played "Dixie." In September 1949 John McCloy became American High Commissioner for Germany, a post he held until 1952.[40]

As Mao Zedong's forces pushed the Kuomintang out of China, Marshall and Acheson knew that the United States would not make any difference by intervening. On October 1, 1949, Mao declared the creation of the People's Republic of China. Chiang Kai-Shek, Soong May-ling, and the Kuomintang withdrew to Formosa. The United States would have no diplomatic ties with the PRC until 1972.[41]

The implication that the Truman administration had "lost" China launched militant Senator Joseph McCarthy (R-WI) on a jihad, smearing Marshall, Acheson, and numerous other officials as communists or communist sympathizers. In a three-hour tirade against Marshall, McCarthy spoke of "a conspiracy so immense and an infamy so black as to dwarf any previous venture in the history of man." McCarthy built a formidable national constituency, including Joseph P. Kennedy Sr.[42] As Republican leader Taft inexplicably gave McCarthy latitude, Vandenberg became ill with cancer. Speaking for her colleague and many Americans, Sen. Margaret Chase Smith (R-ME) called for McCarthy's censure with her "Declaration of Conscience" on June 1, 1950, but it would take the full Senate four painful years to follow her.[43]

On April 7, 1950, the Departments of Defense and State presented a National Security Council policy paper, NSC-68, which built upon Kennan's containment argument. It supported development of a hydrogen bomb, increased military spending, NATO, and a rollback of global communist expansion. Paul Nitze of State chaired the policy review group.[44]

On November 1, 1952, the United States detonated a 10.4 megaton hydrogen device, code-named Ivy Mike, at Eniwetok Atoll in the Marshall Islands. Oppenheimer and Fermi opposed development of the new and more powerful device, which was advocated by their Manhattan Project colleague Edward Teller.[45]

Hollywood produced thoughtful postwar films, including *Twelve O' Clock High, Battleground*, and *From Here to Eternity*. Billy Wilder put his stamp on *Stalag 17* and *A Foreign Affair*, filmed in Berlin. The wartime experience of navy supply operations described by James A. Michener became the musical *South Pacific*. To compete with television, the motion picture industry offered lavish spectacles. Hollywood developed new genres such as film noir, and socially responsible films with racial themes appeared. American and Japanese audiences met the nuclear age by flocking to science fiction thrillers, including *The Day the Earth Stood Still*, where thoughtful alien policeman Klaatu, played by Michael Rennie, lands his spaceship with his no-nonsense robot Gort on the mall in Washington and threatens Earth with destruction unless it renounces violence, and *Godzilla*, the first of a series of films where giant radiation-spawned monsters attack Tokyo.

But there was no escape from real-world horror. With stolen information provided by American collaborators, the Soviet Union detonated its first atomic weapon, First Lightning, based on Fat Man, on August 29, 1949, and its first hydrogen weapon on November 22, 1955, at the Semipalatinsk Test Site in Kazakhstan.[46]

Precipice

When the United States and USSR agreed to temporarily divide the Korean peninsula at the thirty-eighth parallel following Japan's surrender, Kim Il Sung organized a communist regime in the north and nationalist Syngman Rhee formed the Republic of Korea (ROK) in the south. Although it backed the ROK, the United States began to withdraw troops in 1948. In January 1950 Acheson implied that the Korean Peninsula lay outside the defense perimeter of the United States.[47]

On June 25, 1950, North Korea crossed the thirty-eighth parallel, invaded South Korea, and captured the capital of Seoul. On June 27 the UN Security Council declared a breach of the peace and authorized the dispatch of troops to stop it by a unanimous vote. The USSR did not veto the resolution because Stalin had left six months earlier to protest UN refusal to replace the Kuomintang with the PRC as the representative of China. Truman reversed policy and committed American forces to the multilateral UN intervention and named MacArthur commander of UN forces. The president did not seek a declaration of war from Congress and called the mission a "police action."[48]

Stalin believed that he had cleverly lured the United States into the war. He expected that the PRC would intervene to prevent a reunified Korea under ROK governance. The United States would overextend itself and give the USSR a global advantage with Asia torn apart by a war between America and China. After waiting for the UN to intervene in Korea, the USSR cynically returned to the Security Council.[49]

U.S. and ROK units held out in the Pusan Perimeter while the USAF and USN established control of the air and sea. On September 4, 1950, MacArthur launched a daring end run with an amphibious assault at Incheon. UN forces liberated Seoul and cut off retreating North Korean units. On September 27 the Joint Chiefs gave MacArthur an imprecise directive to "conduct military operations north of the 38th parallel" leading to "the destruction of North Korean forces." He was not to violate PRC or USSR airspace, and only ROK troops could approach the Yalu River bordering the PRC. New secretary of defense George Marshall, pressed back into service, told MacArthur, "We want you to feel unhampered tactically and strategically to proceed north of the 38th parallel," and MacArthur replied, "Unless and until the enemy capitulates, I regard all Korea as open for our military operations."[50]

The UN General Assembly, with the USSR present, voted to declare the UN objective was the establishment of a unified, independent, and democratic Korea. Zhou Enlai sent a message to UN Secretary General Trygve Lie of Norway and broadcast a warning that the PRC would not tolerate MacArthur moving north. MacArthur called upon Kim Il Sung to surrender. Zhou responded by threatening to attack, and Chinese People's Volunteer Army troops began quietly moving into North Korea. Zhou sent back-channel messages via New Delhi. Convinced the PRC was not bluffing, Indian prime minister Jawaharlal Nehru reported PVA troops massing on the Manchurian border.[51]

On October 15 Truman flew to remote Wake Island to meet MacArthur privately for two hours. Truman believed MacArthur assured him the Chinese would not intervene, and that he (Truman) would never have authorized any consolidation of North Korea if he had thought they would. But Washington did not consult MacArthur about the UN resolution to occupy North Korea. In truth, the decision to proceed north involved flawed intelligence and a lack of communication between SCAP and Washington.[52]

All the messages between SCAP and Washington went through the British Embassy in Washington to allied London. The embassy first secretary was H. A. R. "Kim" Philby. The second secretary was Guy Burgess, and Donald MacLean was the head of Britain's American Department. All three were communist agents who transmitted every secret that passed through them to the USSR. The enemy thus knew MacArthur's every move.[53]

On October 20 the Eighth Army captured Pyongyang. SCAP ordered the X Corps and Eighth Army ahead. At a press conference Truman said his understanding was that only ROK troops would advance northwest to the Yalu, but he then acceded to SCAP. Alarmed, Acheson did everything he could to reassure the PRC. He believed that holding a Pyongyang-Wonsan line and declaring territory north of it a neutral zone was a defensible strategy. The Security Council pledged full protection of the Manchurian frontier, and Truman announced the United States had no intention of hostilities with the PRC. But Mao and Zhou also heard the voices of Rhee and American conservatives, who argued, "Why stop at the Yalu?"[54]

By November 6 PVA troops began openly crossing the Yalu

and firing on UN units. Washington would not allow MacArthur to violate Chinese airspace, so the USAF could not destroy the Yalu bridges or pursue the enemy into Manchuria. As PVA units slammed into his forward units, the constrained MacArthur was furious. Then there was a pause as X Corps and Eighth Army pinchers moved to the Yalu in separate movements divided by the central Korean mountains. Moving by night, phantom Chinese forces had arrayed between and above them, invisible to aerial reconnaissance.

Suddenly, on November 26, along a three-hundred-mile front, 300,000 PVA troops came down from the mountains to the eerie echoes of bugles and attacked regiments of GIs that they often outnumbered ten to one. MacArthur ordered retreat. The withdrawal, while costly, was orderly. In subzero temperatures and mountainous terrain, 30,000 UN troops fought their way through 120,000 members of the PVA at the frozen Chosin Reservoir. Mao lost an estimated 50,000 soldiers, including his son, and would never again underestimate the Americans. But the stunning reversal panicked Truman and America's allies.

As Washington prepared to evacuate Korea, MacArthur's ground commander Gen. Matthew Ridgeway stabilized the front line along the prewar boundary, although Seoul fell for a second time on January 4, 1951. MacArthur replied to false media reports that he had disobeyed orders to stop at the thirty-eighth parallel. The Truman administration was leaking the stories to undermine SCAP. MacArthur's reply embarrassed Truman, who ordered Acheson and Marshall to issue directives that no officials could make any statements without clearance and officials must refrain from direct communication with the media. Truman's orders were clearly aimed at MacArthur.

Gen. Lawton Collins and Gen. Hoyt Vandenberg visited MacArthur, who gave them the gloomy assessment that evacuation of UN forces from Korea was inevitable unless they let him wage war without restrictions. Then they met Ridgeway, who believed the UN position was impregnable. MacArthur appeared to be out of touch with reality, and at that moment he lost the confidence of the Joint Chiefs.[55]

When Ridgeway recaptured Seoul on March 15, MacArthur seized upon the positive development to renew his push for escalation. He called for a radioactive corridor of atomic waste between Manchuria and Korea combined with dual amphibious assaults and airborne landings on both North Korean coasts. Just as Washington decided to propose a cease-fire with the communists, MacArthur inexplicably issued a quit-or-else ultimatum to the enemy. America appeared to be at the precipice of total war. In addition to torpedoing the diplomatic initiative, MacArthur's threat was insubordinate.

Even with Gallup Poll numbers hovering at only 26 percent approval, Truman had no choice but to relieve MacArthur of command. There were serious calls for Truman's impeachment. McCarthy crudely characterized the president as influenced by "bourbon and Bénédictine" and demanded, "the son of a bitch should be impeached."[56]

Tokyo reacted with shock to MacArthur's sudden departure. The Japanese deeply respected Makassar Genui. Japanese newspapers mourned his loss, and a quarter-million weeping people lined the route to Tokyo's Haneda airport at 6:30 a.m. on Tuesday, April 16, to wish him a heartfelt sayonara.[57]

On Thursday, April 18, MacArthur addressed a joint session of Congress. He defiantly recounted his decisions and beliefs, including that "in war, there can be no substitute for victory." Members interrupted him with applause thirty times in thirty-four minutes. He did not mention that he had threatened to use nuclear weapons. As thirty million people watched on television, MacArthur closed by saying, "Old soldiers never die, they just fade away." The next day over seven million people turned out in New York for a triumphant parade. Privately the president called MacArthur's speech "a bunch of damn bullshit."[58]

The tumult over MacArthur soon died out. Marshall appeared before Senate hearings about Korea following MacArthur, who admitted to no mistakes or errors of judgement. Marshall remarked,

"I am distressed to appear in opposition to my brother Army officer and a man for which I have tremendous respect."[59]

A cease-fire suspended hostilities in Korea on July 27, 1953. By then, 5 million people, including 54,246 Americans, were dead. Democratic South Korea became a phenomenally successful modern economic power. Dynastic North Korea became a medieval police state disaster.

Harry Truman never went to college but consistently learned from his mistakes. Acheson summed up Truman's postwar epiphany: "Released from the acceptance of a dogma that builders and wreckers of a new world order could and should work happily and successfully together, he was free to combine our power and coordinate our action with those who did have a common purpose. . . . Harry Truman and the United States saved the free world."[60]

The occupation of Japan officially ended April 28, 1952. The restorations of Germany and Japan were in America's self-interest but nonetheless remarkable. In victory the United States rose above prejudice and anger as had no nation before or since. The Americans did not seize territory, pillage, or subjugate. In this way America realized the principled exceptionalism envisioned by successive American moralists while faithful to the legitimate national security focus of former expansionists turned interventionists.

HUAC found no evidence of communist infiltration or propaganda in the film industry, but one of the Hollywood Ten, director Edward Dmytryk, announced he was once a communist and was prepared to give evidence against others. In 1950 a conservative pamphlet titled *Red Channels* accused 151 mostly broadcasting professionals of communist sympathies. The film and broadcasting industries banned most of them from employment.

In 1951 and under Democratic Party control, HUAC launched another series of hearings, maliciously pitting dozens of witnesses against each other. By 1957 the blacklists were dying out. Several hundred professionals lost work and had their reputations besmirched regardless of any evidence of subversive activities. Although communism had been valid issue, the high-profile Hollywood inquiry was unnecessary. Resentment percolated for decades and realigned Hollywood and the media exclusively to the political left.[61]

There was no question about the spies who subverted the Manhattan Project and gave or sold American nuclear weapons secrets to the Soviet Union. Prosecution of suspects was controversial among liberals and civil libertarians because the United States could not reveal Project Venona, the breaking of Soviet intelligence codes, and secret intercepts, in court. After the fall of the USSR, declassified Soviet and American documents confirmed the irrefutable evidence that led to the original prosecutions.[62]

Concerned scientists became traitors in misguided attempts to equalize nuclear development. The most infamous were Americans Julius and Ethel Rosenberg. Many continue to condemn the execution of the tragic but guilty couple. German physicist Klaus Fuchs passed key documentation to the Soviets and served jail time before emigrating to East Germany.[63] American physicist Theodore Alvin Hall (Holtzberg) gave the Soviets a detailed description of the Fat Man plutonium bomb. He escaped prosecution because the evidence against him was classified. In a sympathetic interview with CNN in 1998, Hall said, "I decided to give atomic secrets to the [Soviets] because it was important that there should be no monopoly, which could turn one nation into a menace and turn it loose on the world [like] Nazi Germany. The right thing to do was to act to break the American monopoly."[64]

Dwight D. Eisenhower defeated Sen. Robert Taft for the Republican nomination and breezed into the presidency with a landslide mandate in 1952 from Americans chanting "We like Ike." The popular general selected Sen. Richard M. Nixon as his running mate and defeated FDR disciple Gov. Adlai Stevenson of Illinois with 55 percent of the popular vote and 442 electoral votes. Two weeks before the 1952 election, Eisenhower vowed to go to Korea and end the war. He held over two hundred press conferences while in office, far more than his predecessors. Like Truman, Eisenhower found a bipartisan Senate ally, Lyndon B. Johnson (D-TX). In 1956, Eisenhower again defeated Stevenson with 57 percent of the popular vote and 457 electoral votes.[65]

Eisenhower's enduring domestic achievement was the Interstate Highway System, which the German autobahn system inspired him to build. He nominated Earl Warren as Chief Justice of the Supreme Court, Selecting Warren, whose term became very consequential, Eisenhower sought an experienced and centrist jurist.[66]

Implementation of Armed Forces desegregation had been slow, and Eisenhower would have none of it, remarking, "We have not taken, and we shall not take a single backward step. There must be no second-class citizens in this country." In the *Brown vs. Board of Education of Topeka* decision of May 17, 1954, the Supreme Court ruled in a unanimous 9–0 decision that "separate educational facilities are inherently unequal," and, as a result, de jure racial segregation was a violation of the Equal Protection Clause of the Fourteenth Amendment.[67] In 1957 the state of Arkansas refused to honor a federal court order to integrate their public school system. When Governor Orval Faubus rejected his order to comply, Eisenhower federalized the Arkansas National Guard and sent in the 101st Airborne Division. The paratroopers escorted nine black students into Little Rock Central High School. On December 1, 1955, in Montgomery, Alabama. Rosa Parks became a civil rights icon by refusing to give up her seat on a segregated bus. Parks organized with influential minister and activist Rev. Martin Luther King Jr., who went on to win the Nobel Peace Prize. The Eisenhower administration won approval of the Civil Rights Acts of 1957 and 1960 that foreshadowed the more decisive legislation in the 1960s but were the most significant reforms since Reconstruction.[68]

Sen. Joseph McCarthy continued to recklessly exploit concerns about communism. Eisenhower's preferred strategy of dealing with McCarthy was to ignore him. During a 1952 campaign speech in Wisconsin, Eisenhower said that he understood McCarthy's concerns but disagreed with his methods. William H. Laurence of the *New York Times* reported accurately that Eisenhower had deleted a defense of Marshall from the speech, and he received wide criticism. Pressured to publicly confront McCarthy, Eisenhower continued to refuse, saying privately that "nothing would please [McCarthy] more" and that he did not "want to get into the gutter with [McCarthy]."[69]

The twisted side of McCarthy was homophobic. Playing upon religious and other traditional taboos about homosexuality, McCarthy crudely tried to expose and destroy the lives of gays in Washington by linking communism to lifestyle preference. Public pressure caused the president to issue Executive Order 10450, Security Requirements for Government Employees, that detailed a range of security requirements for federal employment. The order included language that homosexuality was among the rationales for denying federal employment because it could expose officials and workers to blackmail and extortion and therefore was a national security threat.[70]

In the fall of 1953 McCarthy began his penultimate attack with an ill-fated inquiry into alleged communist infiltration of the army. The televised hearings put a spotlight on McCarthy's increasingly snarly demeanor. Army secretary Joseph Welch famously questioned McCarthy's lack of decency. Even Americans disposed to agree with his concerns had had enough.[71]

On March 9, 1954, Edward R. Murrow ran an episode of his CBS *See It Now* program titled "A Report on Senator Joseph R. McCarthy" that included a series of clips detailing McCarthy's claims and concluding with a damning Murrow commentary. CBS ran a follow-up piece on March 16. On the April 6 program McCarthy emotionally replied and impulsively accused Murrow, too, of being a communist.[72] Murrow's producers edited McCarthy's appearance to show the senator in a more unflattering light.[73]

On December 2, 1954, the Senate finally voted to censure McCarthy by a vote of 67–22.[74] Ruined, he continued to speak out as his drinking increased and health declined. McCarthy died of acute hepatitis at the age of forty-eight on May 2, 1957.[75]

As noted by Kennan, Soviet penetration of the American government "really existed" and assumed proportions that, "while never overwhelming, were also not trivial." Although there was reason to be concerned about Soviet infiltration, there was no justification for McCarthy's excessive zeal. America survived HUAC,

Hollywood blacklists, and McCarthy, but liberal intellectuals, disabused of faith in the ability of Americans to discern valid issues from hyperbola, bristled as families settled into what the elite considered to be superficial suburban lifestyles. There was a solution: taking control of higher education and guiding new generations of Americans in a more enlightened and progressive direction.[76]

Secretary of State John Foster Dulles attended the Geneva Conference of 1954, meant to wind up the Korean War and settle the French defeat in Indochina. Zhou Enlai, also in attendance, wanted to normalize relations with the United States. In a clear rebuke, Dulles refused to shake Zhou's hand when the Chinese leader offered it. The insult would not be corrected until 1972.[77]

Dulles was Eisenhower's secretary of state until diagnosed with colon cancer in 1959. He articulated a foreign policy that built upon containment but espoused a more active liberation strategy. He strengthened NATO, founded the Southeast Asia Treaty Organization (SEATO), and completed the ANZUS Treaty between Australia, New Zealand, and the United States. After the Viet Minh defeated the French at Dien Bien Phu, Vietnam was divided into two nations, and Ho Chi Minh was dedicated to unifying them. American policy became focused on stopping the spread of communism beyond Vietnam. With his brother Allen at the CIA, Dulles developed a strategy of using economic assets and covert action to counter opportunistic communist probes. Homeland defense relied on a massive nuclear deterrent supported by technological development to surpass Soviet capability.[78]

This was mutually assured destruction, or brinksmanship. In a *Life* article Dulles noted, "The ability to get to the verge without getting into the war is the necessary art." This posture alienated many non-aligned nations. One was India, which had won independence from the United Kingdom in 1947 and divided into the majority Hindu nation of India and Muslim nation of Pakistan. The newly independent third world sought to be neutral in the ideological showdown between liberal capitalism and communism.[79]

Eisenhower did not have to deal with an ailing and erratic Joseph Stalin, who mysteriously died on March 5, 1953, of a reported cerebral hemorrhage. Some historians believe that his Council of Ministers murdered him. His initial successor, Georgy Malenkov, proposed peaceful coexistence with the West. In an ensuing battle for leadership, the more militant Nikita Sergeyevich Khrushchev emerged in 1954 as Soviet premier.[80]

On April 16, 1953, Eisenhower delivered his *Chance for Peace* speech before the American Society of Newspaper Editors at the Staler Hotel. In it he called for a Korean armistice, free elections to reunify Germany, independence for Eastern European nations, and UN control of nuclear energy. In his *Atoms for Peace* speech before the UN General Assembly on December 8, Eisenhower called for the creation of the International Atomic Energy Agency (IAEA) and peaceful nuclear power plants around the world.

The president's *New Look* national security policy attempted to balance Cold War military requirements with a sound economy, relying on strategic nuclear weapons over more expensive conventional forces. NSC 162/2 articulated deterrence using a triad of intercontinental ballistic missiles (ICBM), long-range strategic bombers, and submarine-launched ballistic missiles (SLBM). The deterrence triad included a new nuclear-powered submarine fleet designed by Adm. Hyman G. Rickover. Nimitz had encouraged Rickover's plan to convert America's submarine fleet from diesel to nuclear propulsion. Eisenhower reduced reliance on large army divisions, promoting NATO and a new West German Bundeswehr. He sought to diminish Soviet influence and force the USSR to spend more than it could afford on weapons and technological development, where he knew the United States had an advantage.

Eisenhower also approved a stepped-up psy-ops campaign to nonviolently confront the USSR. He realized the United States had many nonmilitary advantages that could prove decisive in the asymmetrical and psychological competition with communism, including democratic values, capitalism, individual freedoms, diversity and, importantly, popular culture, including movies and music.[81]

The CIA under Allen Dulles became a more daring agency. When the air force rejected an innovative airplane designed to fly high and silently on reconnaissance missions, the CIA ordered the Lockheed U-2. What America gained from asymmetrical warfare was a nuclear deterrent and armed forces focused on obligatory strategic responsibilities. The CIA disrupted suspected potential communist governments or attempted takeovers. An early example was Operation Ajax in 1953. Shah Mohammed Pahlavi and pro-monarchy forces removed the elected prime minister of Iran, Mohammed Mosaddeq, in a successful coup d'état. In Guatemala the CIA instigated a 1954 military coup d'état against president Jacob Arbenz Guzmán. Revisionists condemn the American strategy that supported regime change or influenced elections in nations such as Iran and Guatemala as preventing self-determination and proof of American economic imperialism.[82]

Eisenhower's interest in effective international messaging led to establishment of the United States Information Agency on August 1, 1953. After creation of the USIA, the VOA had greater funding, autonomy, and journalistic integrity.[83]

Overt broadcast propaganda became the role of several quasi-government operations modeled after RIAS in Berlin. Conceived by Kennan and Frank Wisner of the OSS and CIA, Radio Free Europe and Radio Liberty transmitted uncensored news and information specifically behind the Iron Curtain using the talents of Soviet and Eastern European émigrés. RFE/RL, funded by the CIA until 1971, went on the air in 1950 from studios in Munich. Its editorial policies were more confrontational than the VOA or commercial broadcasters, although RFE/RL promoted evolutionary change rather than violent uprisings. RFE/RL offered programs not available from state-controlled media, including Western music, religion, and banned literature. Eastern European audiences came to trust RFE/RL.[84]

During November 1956 Britain and France supported Israel in a second Israeli-Arab War. The three allies secretly collaborated without the United States, following the action of Egyptian President Gamal Abdel Nassar to nationalize the Suez Canal. When Israeli forces captured Sinai and British and French paratroopers landed along the Suez Canal, Egypt blocked it to all shipping. The United States joined the Soviet Union in forcing the three allies to withdraw, for which Eisenhower won international praise. But Eisenhower's response may have emboldened the Soviets to brutally crack down on a revolution in Hungary, when, beginning with a student protest, the Warsaw Pact nation had bravely but futilely revolted against its Soviet occupiers.[85]

On October 4, 1957, the Soviet Union stunned the world by launching the *Sputnik* satellite into space and orbiting the capsule around the planet. *Sputnik* frightened Americans, and in response, on January 29, 1958, Eisenhower transformed the National Advisory Committee for Aeronautics (NACA) into the National Aeronautics and Space Administration (NASA).[86] NACA was already working on an American satellite program, *Vanguard*, as part of the International Geophysical Year (1957–1958). NASA combined, augmented, and sped up many missile and rocket programs, including the captured German v-2 ballistic missile program and scientists led by Dr. Werhner Von Braun.[87]

On January 1, 1959, Cuban revolutionaries captured the capital of Havana when dictator Fulgencio Batista fled the country. During the 1950s disaffected former Jesuit student Fidel Alejandro Castro Ruz and his brother Raul, the illegitimate sons of wealthy Oriente province Spanish farmer Angel Castro y Argiz and mistress Lina Ruz González, carried on a nearly quixotic revolutionary struggle in the isolated Sierra Maestra, joined by Cuban and Marxist-Leninist foreign fighters including Argentinian Ernesto "Che" Guevara.[88] Leftists in America and around the world came to idealize and worship them, including Herbert L. Matthews of the *New York Times*, who is credited with "creating" the problematic Castro mystique.[89]

On May 1, 1960, the Soviets shot down an American u-2 spy plane over their territory and captured the pilot, Francis Gary Powers, precipitating a major crisis. The u-2 incident was a major embarrassment for Eisenhower, and it scuttled a well-prepared and highly anticipated summit conference with Khrushchev.[90]

Eisenhower gave his televised farewell address to the nation on January 17, 1961. Summing up the Cold War, he observed, "We face a hostile ideology global in scope, atheistic in character, ruthless in purpose and insidious in method," but he also cautioned about unjustified government spending proposals and warned that "we must guard against the acquisition of unwarranted influence, whether sought or unsought, by the military-industrial complex."[91]

In 1956 the Department of State created the *Jazz Ambassadors* program, in which the government sent leading American jazz musicians on musical tours to improve the public image of the United States in the light of criticism from the Soviet Union around racial inequality and tension. The program coordinated with the USIA and VOA to emphasize jazz as a true American art form.[92]

When Dizzy Gillespie led the first tour in March 1956, an American ambassador reported back that "maybe we could have built a new tank for the cost of this tour, but you can't get as much goodwill out of a tank as you can out of Dizzy Gillespie's band."[93]

Benny Goodman toured the Far East in November 1956, Europe in May 1958, including the Brussel's World's Fair, and, famously, the USSR in July 1962, where he met packed houses and enthusiastic audiences. Goodman recalled that tape recorders were plainly visible.[94]

Between 1963 and 1973 Duke Ellington made more grueling tours than anyone. His 1971 tour of the USSR was his greatest international achievement. Jazz critic Leonard Feather remarked, "[The tour] is the greatest coup in the history of musical diplomacy."[95]

Louis Armstrong made his first unofficial ambassadorial visit to the African Gold Coast in 1956 with Edward R. Murrow of CBS. Scheduled for the Soviet Union in 1957, Armstrong canceled the plans due to the Little Rock school desegregation crisis. In October 1960 Armstrong made memorable a three-month African tour. In Leopoldville, Republic of Congo, admirers carried him on a throne. When he played in Elisabethville in Katanga Province, warring factions declared a truce in a long-standing civil war, so combatants on both sides could see him. The trip was so physically taxing that singer Velma Middleton suffered a stroke and did not survive, and the fatigued Armstrong's physician ordered him to suspend futher performances. Undeterred, Armstrong returned in January 1961 and completed the itinerary.[96]

The State Department worked with founder George Wein and the Newport Jazz Festival to sponsor musicians on tours behind the Iron Curtain, including the tours of Dizzy Gillespie, Quincy Jones, Dave Brubeck, Miles Davis, Gerry Mulligan, Earl "Fatha" Hines, Anita O'Day, Charles Mingus, Lionel Hampton, Thelonious Monk, Sonny Stitt, and Art Blakely.[97] Many other musicians made State Department tours, including Count Basie, Charley Byrd, Benny Carter, and Woody Herman, who visited Latin America in 1958 and Africa in 1966.

Willis Conover was the popular voice of American jazz heard worldwide over VOA. Conover's *Jazz Hour* and *Music USA* programs started on January 6, 1955. Conover reached thirty million people in eighty countries every week, and by 1965 the audience had grown to over one hundred million. He broke through the Iron Curtain, giving musicians and fans a vibrant link to jazz and popular music. Conover remained on the air with VOA for forty years until his death in 1996. He may have been the American that the Soviet Union feared the most.[98]

Millennium

On January 20, 1960, PT-boat skipper and senator John Fitzgerald Kennedy took the oath of office as president of the United States after defeating former vice president Richard M. Nixon in the closest election to that point in American history. The succeeding quarter century or more to 1993 would mark a detour for American exceptionalism despite moments of brilliance. As JFK emphasized in his inaugural address, the "torch was passing" from the generation that directed World War II to the younger generation that had fought the war. This was the first of two significant generational changes that had an important impact on postwar America. The second would be in 1993, when postwar baby boomers succeeded their parents. Media, liberals, intellectuals, and many conservatives embraced the young president and his attractive family. JFK campaigned on a "missile gap" with the USSR that really did not exist, but then he came to greatly value the private advice of his predecessor. Edward R. Murrow of CBS was among the talented and idealistic members of the new administration as heir to Davis and Sherwood as director of USIA and the VOA. "I do not mind being called a propagandist," he told the *Miami Herald*, "as long as that propaganda is based on the truth."[99]

The promise of America was asserted by JFK's daring vow to land Americans on the moon. With this sweeping declaration, America and NASA, exemplified by the irrepressible Dr. Werhner von Braun, would mount an effort resembling the scope of the Manhattan Project that dramatically outpaced Soviet resources and know-how to indeed land Americans on the moon on July 20, 1969. With the historic statement of astronaut Neil Armstrong, "That's one small step for man, one giant leap for mankind," as he stepped onto the lunar surface and planted the Stars and Stripes, America's ascendancy reached its zenith.

In his speech as Rice University on September 12, 1962, envisioning the Mercury, Gemini, and Apollo space programs, JFK summed up the vision of his wartime generation, if not the urge of philosophers and explorers throughout human history. He depicted space as the new frontier and invoked the American pioneer spirit. Prior to this speech, JFK's calls for a robust space program met with public and official skepticism.

With a sense of urgency and destiny, the president emphasized American freedom as a beacon and vehicle for humans to reach beyond Earth for the stars. JFK proposed making the moon landing a joint American-Soviet project, although cooperation between the competitors in space would not occur until after the successful moon landings by the United States. Written by Theodore Sorensen with changes by JFK, the speech noted that "we set sail on a new sea" and that "we choose to go to the moon and do other things . . . not because they are easy, but because they are hard . . . the challenge is one we are willing to accept" and *"we intend to win."*

The space program and the president's vow to put an American on the moon in a decade encapsulated the promise of the Kennedy presidency. Not only did JFK's initiative succeed, but it produced revolutionary developments in computing, engineering, and medicine rivaling the American-led inventions of communication, electrification, and transportation of the late nineteenth century. It appeared that there was nothing America could not achieve. JFK embodied American exceptionalism. But between JFK's inauguration and the lunar landing, decisions and developments would shake the exceptional nation, leading to a crisis of confidence and questions about the true nature of the American identity and purpose.[100]

It should have been obvious that the Castro brothers were Marxist-Leninist opportunists who had no intention of a liberal democratic Cuban revolution. Allen Dulles and the CIA had prepared a covert operation to depose the Cuban junta. Kennedy inherited the plan, watered it down, and launched it, but he hesitated to back up the American-trained Cuban volunteers of Brigada Asalto 2506, who suffered a humiliating defeat in April 1961 at the Bay of Pigs. This gave Khrushchev the confidence to place nuclear missiles in Cuba and bring the world to the brink of World War III. JFK recovered from his earlier mistake to resist calls for an attack during the tense October 1962 Cuban Missile Crisis. Quarantining Cuba, Kennedy gave the Soviet leader an opportunity to back down without losing face by privately withdrawing outdated American missiles from Turkey.[101]

On August 13, 1961, the USSR sealed the boundary between the Soviet sector and the Western sectors in Berlin to stop people from leaving communist East Germany. They erected a fortified wall to keep people in by force, and the melancholy barrier would stand until October 18, 1989.[102]

A self-described pro-Soviet and pro-Castro lunatic named Lee Harvey Oswald inconceivably assassinated JFK, ending the promise of his presidency on November 22, 1963. Many continue to believe that a government, international, or organized crime conspiracy was responsible. By then JFK had launched a historic initiative to bring full civil rights to all Americans, rectifying generations of discrimination and dealing honestly with the legacy of slavery. The president affirmed American support of NATO but desired to move away from nuclear brinksmanship. His interest in asymmetrical warfare led Kennedy to insert American special forces and advisers into South Vietnam to counter a North Vietnamese insurgency, and he sanctioned the assassination of South Vietnamese president Ngô Đình Diệm in a coup d'état on November 2, 1963.[103]

Vice President Lyndon Baines Johnson became president following JFK's death and easily won election in 1964 against conservative Republican Sen. Barry Goldwater (R-AZ). By then an escalating conflict in Vietnam had invaded American television screens. Goldwater's provocative platform included a dramatic policy that mirrored MacArthur's Korean "all-out war or withdrawal" posture. LBJ gradually increased American support for the South Vietnamese as Ho Chi Minh's Viet Cong guerilla force undermined the succession of military juntas that followed the ill-fated Diệm.

LBJ vowed to keep American commitments "from Vietnam to Berlin" with the help of many JFK advisers, including Secretary of Defense Robert McNamara. He implemented JFK's transformation of American civil rights with major legislation. The media remained steadfastly loyal to the JFK/LBJ civil rights program and the idea of American exceptionalism. But between 1964 and 1968, there were race riots at home, and Vietnam was an ever-deepening quagmire. LBJ steeply escalated American involvement on false evidence of North Vietnamese provocation in the Tonkin Gulf and flawed reasoning about the causes and ramifications of the Vietnamese conflict. He increased American troop levels to half a million, tied the hands of the military with restrictive rules of engagement, wavered back and forth about bombing the North, and squandered resources and equipment; before it was over, more than 58,000 Americans and an estimated 1.3 million Vietnamese were dead.[104]

"God almighty," LBJ said as he agonized over Vietnam, "what they said about us leaving China would just be warming up compared to what they'd say now." Conservative critics went a step further, calling Vietnam an opportunity to pursue a course that "should have been pursued" in China; namely, annihilating North Vietnam.[105]

LBJ lost the war not just by gradual escalation but by losing the trust of the American people as informed by their media. When he alienated CBS television anchor Walter Cronkite, the tragic

Vietnam adventure collapsed.[106] The detour divided the American people and caused a permanent government credibility gap. Correspondents such as Cronkite who had gone into battle alongside Americans in World War II—in Cronkite's case as a United Press International correspondent in North Africa and France and at the Arnhem airborne assault—were not anti-American or communistic. They reported the facts to the American people, and the United States government lied to them.[107]

North Vietnam did not win their war with the United States on the battlefield, but rather when the decisions of American leaders divided and disillusioned the American people. Americans of all races, regions, and backgrounds served with valor and distinction in Vietnam: soldiers and marines fighting and winning battles such as Hue and Da Nang and airmen surviving torture as POWs in squalid prisons such as the infamous "Hanoi Hilton."

The powerful and effective World War II and postwar media-government coalition appeared dead. Vietnam was not among America's vital interests, and the war squandered America's resources and reputation. Many Americans born after World War II would begrudge their country and cynically embrace revisionist condemnation of America for the rest of their lives. The baby boomers would come to memorialize their anger and guilt in a transformed educational system and judgmental media that emphasized American faults and contradictions and rejected American achievements and exceptionalism.

Disillusioned and divided America experienced the birth and bloom of a counterculture and social revolution. Two more lunatics murdered civil rights leader Dr. Martin Luther King and presidential candidate Sen. Robert F. Kennedy (D-NY). Race riots burned down swaths of entire cities from Detroit to Los Angeles, and American exceptionalism appeared dead or at least questionable.

While LBJ agonized over Vietnam, he sent troops to the Dominican Republic to intervene in a civil war. Israel overran Sinai and took the entire West Bank, humiliating Egypt, Jordan, and Syria in the lightning Six-Day War or Third Arab-Israeli War of 1967. The Soviet Union risked future détente with the United States by invading Czechoslovakia in 1968 and met no resistance. Vietnam emotionally and physically broke the proud president from the Hill Country of Texas, who had courageously stood up to his fellow segregationist Southern Democrats to join liberal Democrats and the Republicans in passing civil rights legislation. LBJ did not stand for election in 1968. A resurrected Richard M. Nixon won in another tight race, this time against Johnson's vice president, Hubert Horatio Humphrey.[108]

Nixon was America's political Lazarus, and most schizophrenic president, simultaneously projecting brilliance and spitefulness. He came back from a presidential defeat and loss in the 1962 California gubernatorial race, after which he famously told the media that "you won't have Dick Nixon to kick around anymore." He never got over a justified belief that the media and intelligentsia despised him, and his paranoia proved to be his ultimate downfall.

Emperor Hirohito was born into the Meiji dynasty in 1901. On September 25, 1971, he became the first reigning monarch of Japan to set foot on foreign soil as President Nixon welcomed His Majesty to Elemendorf Air Force Base in Anchorage, Alaska, with full honors. Hirohito had traveled to Europe as Crown Prince in 1921.[109] It was fitting that Hirohito's first overseas stop was in the United States, and symbolically halfway between Tokyo and Washington, in respect for the permanent American-Japanese bond developed by Douglas MacArthur and the emperor. Although MacArthur's decision not to prosecute Hirohito and the Royal Family for war crimes was provident, there is objective evidence that, had he been prosecuted, His Majesty may have been convicted, as he well realized in 1945 when MacArthur wisely protected him.

Nixon was a policy realist, convinced that power was the core dynamic of the international system. He promised to get America out of Vietnam, but the process was slow and deliberate while the war expanded to Cambodia and Laos. At home Nixon's governance was moderate and socially responsible, including creation of the Environmental Protection Agency. He made a historic decision to seek rapprochement with the People's Republic of China. Viewers worldwide were astonished when the Boeing 707 Air Force

One, *The Spirit of '76,* taxied to a stop at Beijing Capitol Airport. A beaming Nixon emerged to shake hands firmly with Zhou Enlai, symbolically respecting Zhou as an equal and pointedly correcting Dulles's 1954 rebuke. Then the president did the unthinkable, conferring with a visibly pleased Mao, trekking to the Great Wall and signing the Shanghai Communique with Zhou.[110] Nixon simultaneously and famously pursued *détente* with Khrushchev's successor Leonid Brezhnev, signing landmark Strategic Arms Treaties with the USSR. He ended direct American involvement in the Vietnam war with a furious bombing campaign.[111]

Nixon was reelected in a 1972 landslide, sealing an alliance with Southern Democrats that swung the conservative white South to the Republican party. But with all that going for him, Nixon's insecurity allowed illegal spying on his political opponents and a cover-up. During his second term the CIA and Secretary of State Henry Kissinger were involved in the overthrow and death of socialist Salvador Allende in polarized Chile. A military coup led by conservative Gen. Augusto Pinochet restored order and established what has evolved into a successful free-market democracy. While Nixon fought to survive the Watergate scandal, he had to grapple with a fourth Arab-Israeli War of October 1973 and an oil embargo and energy crisis precipitated by the Organization of the Petroleum Exporting Countries (OPEC). On August 7, 1974, Republican leaders told Nixon that he faced certain impeachment and conviction due to Watergate, which left him with no alternative but to resign in disgrace.[112]

Gerald R. Ford replaced Nixon's corrupt vice president Spiro Agnew months before Nixon resigned. Vandenberg's heir and the former University of Michigan All-American football star was a fortuitous president of equilibrium and moral clarity. Ford named Nelson Rockefeller as his vice president. He prudently did not seek congressional approval to intervene when Ho and the North unified Vietnam in 1975. In a far-sighted decision that probably cost him the 1976 election, Ford granted Nixon a full pardon. After surviving a nomination battle with California governor Ronald Reagan, Ford narrowly lost to Democratic governor James Earl "Jimmy"

Cater of Georgia, who won with 290 electoral votes and 50.1% of the popular vote. Kansas senator Bob Dole was Ford's running mate.[113]

Wilsonian Carter, the only Annapolis graduate to be president, moved the United States toward a multipolar outlook fully supportive of the developing world and social change. He was the first American president of the modern era to state as policy that the United States had a limited ability to find solutions to world issues. Carter mediated negotiations between Israeli prime minister Menachem Begin and Egyptian president Anwar Sadat, resulting in a formal peace agreement between Egypt and Israel in 1979. He also completed the normalization of relations with China in 1979 and transfer of the Panama Canal to Panama. Although Carter supported détente, he rejected the Nixon-Kissinger concept of "linkage." He promoted an end to apartheid and majority black rule in South Africa and scolded Americans about energy consumption. Carter abandoned ally Shah Reza Pahlavi of Iran for the exiled radical Islamic cleric Ruhollah Khomeini, who then swore death to America. A Soviet invasion of Afghanistan took place one month after Iranian militants stormed the U.S. Embassy in Tehran and took fifty-two Americans hostage. In addition to these crises, Carter faced mounting domestic economic issues, including increases in gasoline prices, inflation, and unemployment. He deregulated communications and airlines and boycotted the 1980 Summer Olympics in Moscow. The humiliating hostage crisis dragged on and worsened following a failed rescue attempt, only ending the day Carter's successor took the oath of office. After leaving the presidency Carter became widely admired for humanitarian initiatives and won the Nobel Peace Prize in 2002.[114]

In 1980 the stage was set for a change of direction. Former California governor Ronald Wilson Reagan and running mate George H. W. Bush of Texas won election with an overwhelming 489-electoral-vote mandate, if only 52 percent of the popular vote in a three-way race. Reagan set about a revival of assertive American world leadership coupled with supply-side conservative economics. He initially achieved mixed results but a palpable restoration of national confidence. Surviving an assassination attempt, Rea-

Fig. 28. Pres. Ronald W. Reagan. Photograph by Michael Evans, June 22, 1984. Ronald Reagan Presidential Library, Simi Valley, California, photo ME-1355–8.

gan objected to the implied moral equivalency of Soviet détente, instead insisting on the superiority of representative government, free-market capitalism, and freedom of conscience over what he viewed as godless and collectivist communism. This more confrontational approach was the Reagan Doctrine, which advocated opposition to communist-supported regimes and willingness to directly challenge the Soviet Union on a variety of fronts.

"The great communicator" framed the Cold War as a showdown between good and evil. In his inaugural address the new president contrasted the "enemies of freedom" as doomed to fail when faced with the "will and moral courage of free men and women." Later that year in an address at Notre Dame University he said that "the West won't *contain* Communism; it will *transcend* Communism." In 1983 he characterized the Soviet Union as an "evil empire," and in 1987, standing in front of the Berlin Wall, Reagan challenged the new and progressive Soviet leader Mikhail Gorbachev to "tear down this wall." British prime minister Margaret Thatcher was Reagan's staunch ally. Their close collaboration was reminiscent of FDR and Churchill. When Argentina moved to evict the UK from the Falkland (Malvinas) Islands, the United States supported the UK taking back the South Atlantic territory.[115]

A significant increase in American defense spending and technology put unbearable pressure on the Soviet Union. Facing Democratic opposition, Reagan insisted on placing intermediate-range Pershing II nuclear missiles in Europe, developing terrain-hugging cruise missiles, and the Strategic Defense Initiative, or "Star Wars" space-based defense system. While many pundits and politicians in the United States dismissed the practicality of the SDI, Gorbachev and the USSR viewed American development of the potentially game-changing technology with alarm. The Soviets knew that they could not afford to compete. Using asymmetrical warfare, ex-OSS officer and CIA director William Casey supported the Afghan resistance, anticommunist forces in Angola, and the Contras in Nicaragua. In 1983 American forces invaded Grenada to forestall installation of a Marxist regime. In a serious gaffe the administration launched Iran-Contra, an inexplicable scheme to fund Nicaraguan insurgents with prohibited arms sales to Iran.

Through his special ambassador, the multitalented and multilingual Gen. Vernon A. Walters, Reagan developed an alliance with Pope John Paul II, the former Cardinal Karol Wojtyla of Krakow, and, in turn, the Solidarity movement of workers in Poland led by Lech Walesa. The workers' movement for liberty spread to students and throughout the simmering Warsaw Pact.[116]

The United States increased spending for the USIA, VOA, and RFE/RL, signaling a reinvigorated importance placed on challenging Soviet ideology. In 1985 the administration launched Radio Martí, a broadcasting service separate from the VOA and akin to the RFE/RL. The service was named for the Apostle of Cuba, Jose Martí. A television service, TV Martí, went on the air in 1990.

Behind the scenes the Reagan administration began moving carefully to manage what intelligence services and the Department of State led by George Schultz perceived as an achievable opportunity to resolve the Cold War. In 1982 Reagan proposed decreasing nuclear weapon stockpiles, which resulted in the landmark Strategic Arms Reduction Treaty. Gorbachev, became a pragmatic partner willing to engage in substantive negotiations. A series of summit meetings reduced tensions and produced concrete results, such as the 1987 Intermediate-Range Nuclear Forces Treaty. Although Reagan won a resounding second election in 1986 with 525 electoral votes and 59 percent of the popular vote, the media remained skeptical. Apt to sarcastically dismiss Reagan as a lightweight former actor, many critics came to respect the president's manner if not his achievements. Reagan brought a positive and civil tone to political discourse that was disarming, His version of détente and the growing freedom movements in the Warsaw Pact satellites had a momentum that hesitant politicians could not prevent. The USSR had reached an ideological and economic crossroads, and Gorbachev realized it. Reagan transitioned with apparent ease from confrontation toward constructive collaboration.[117] Meanwhile, concerns arose about Reagan's health, and in 1994 the former president penned a poignant farewell letter to the American people, telling them that he had Alzheimer's disease.

The transformation put in motion by Reagan came to fruition during the term of his successor, George H. W. Bush. Patrician and self-effacing, Bush engaged foreign leaders with ease. The Berlin Wall fell on November 9, 1989, the Warsaw Pact dissolved, and the Soviet Union ceased to exist on December 25, 1991. The false and brutal legacy of Stalin passed quietly into history without America having to fire a shot in anger. The extraordinary change created a seismic shift in the international balance of power that left the United States as the sole remaining superpower. Bush and his team, including Secretary of State James Baker and National Security Advisor Brent Scowcroft, harmoniously enabled Chancellor Helmut Kohl to reunify Germany. Bush supported the reforms of Chairman Deng Xiaoping to move China toward economic capitalism but had to watch in horror as pro-democracy Chinese citizens were massacred by security forces in the 1989 Tiananmen Square protests.

Bush was gracious but not afraid of confrontation. He forcibly removed Panamanian strongman and drug lord Gen. Manuel Noreiga from power. Facing a crisis when strongman Sadaam Hussein of Iraq seized Kuwait and threatened Saudi Arabia, Bush patiently formed an unprecedented international coalition and sought approval from Congress; then in Operation Desert Storm his military team led by Chief of Staff Gen. Colin Powell and theater commander Gen. Norman Schwarzkopf forcefully evicted Hussein's forces from Kuwait. Working within his international mandate, Bush stopped short of capturing Baghdad and apprehending Hussein. The victorious but measured president told a joint session of Congress that America stood at the threshold of a "new world order . . . freer from the threat of terror, stronger in the pursuit of justice, and more secure in the quest for peace."[118]

The American foreign information services with OWI and OSS roots had played major roles in the disappearance of the Soviet Union and the Warsaw Pact. Many leaders including Vaclav Havel of the Czech Republic and Boris Yeltsin of Russia testified to the importance of the RFE/RL broadcasts in helping end the Cold War. Estonian president Lennart Meri nominated RFE/RL for the Nobel Peace prize in 1991. Nobel laureate Lech Walesa told an audience in 1989 that the role played by the RFE/RL in Poland's struggle for freedom "cannot even be described . . . would there be earth without the sun?"[119]

The progressive OWI intellectuals who resigned to protest Mike Cowles and advertising professionals had the answer to American exceptionalism only partially right. What presidents from FDR to JFK and Reagan realized was that Hollywood and Madison Avenue do make a difference. Messaging is as important as substance.

Not simply in how Americans see themselves, but in how they are seen by the world. Moreover, popular culture and advertising are key national assets of a republic with a free fourth estate enshrined in its founding principles and evident in its rough and tumble history. Substance and morality mattered and proved decisive in winning a world war, the peace that followed, and moving America toward the twenty-first century. But that national character and decency had to be communicated at home and abroad. Some dismiss American exceptionalism as propaganda or fiction. Others seek to erase the collective American memory by condemning prior generations and national leaders by judging their American ancestors by twenty-first-century standards. The United States cannot erase its rich history. If it does, then the republic becomes no better than the totalitarian and intolerant regimes that Americans have stood up against for generations. Americans should honestly discover and truly value their richly dynamic history without guilt or remorse. In so doing, they can come to embrace the real nature of their exceptionalism and thus better motivate humanity toward an enlightened future.

FDR brought national imperative and character together, and his media-government coalition defined and communicated that vision and promise to the world. This is not an imaginary America but a real nation that has never ceased to be the last best hope of humanity. And it often delivers on the promise.

America was inexorable from Hamilton through Roosevelt, and consistent from Truman through Bush. Americans, expansionist and moralist, despite their pride and prejudice or mistakes and imperfections, continue to fashion a better world. The audacious democratic experiment survived adversity, saved the world, and continued to shine a needed beacon of liberty for humanity.

At the dawn of the twenty-first century the liberal democratic republic that Alexander Hamilton envisioned, Franklin D. Roosevelt defined, John F. Kennedy challenged, and Ronald Reagan cherished had been realized by Americans and was poised to lead the world forward into a new millennium.

Americans are exceptional and America matters.

Epilogue

The succeeding quarter century since the end of the Soviet Union and Warsaw Pact has seen erratic swings between Democratic and Republican administrations as the World War II generation passed the torch to the postwar generation. First were eight years of a peace dividend and hi-tech growth with an era of relative tranquility accentuated by an impeachment without conviction. Reality returned in 2001 in the aftermath of a recount, when on September 11, in a diabolical feat of asymmetrical warfare never contemplated by the Soviets or attempted by their proxies, Osama bin Laden and the Al Qaeda Islamic activist group spectacularly attacked the United Stets by hijacking, murdering the pilots, and flying American Airlines and United Airlines flights from Boston, Newark, and Washington to Los Angeles and San Francisco into the World Trade Center Towers in New York and the Pentagon in Washington. A fourth plane crashed in rural Pennsylvania after the brave passengers revolted. The subsequent War on Terror, including invasions and arduous occupations of Afghanistan and Iraq, once again divided the nation.

In the wake of a precarious financial meltdown, America cleansed its guilt over slavery and inequality by electing a president of color, who advocated a comprehensive, socioeconomic rearrangement of American society. He apologized for the assertive history of American foreign policy, including the use of the atomic bomb by one of his predecessors, and pursued rapprochement with Cuba and Iran. The dramatic election upset of his overconfident secular progressive heir by an unorthodox candidate of the traditionist opposition continues to consume dismayed pundits and politicians, who characterize themselves as the resistance rather than the loyal opposition. Despite the subsequent political melodrama, the American economy is recovering from the financial downturn with its familiar resilience.

Among its inventions and achievements, exceptional America created the internet, or interconnected network, the global system of computer networks and devices now linking all private, corporate, and public computers worldwide with an incalculable amount of information, resources, and services. Though this ought to be democratizing, as Churchill observed, dictators are terrified of ideas. The PRC, Russian Federation, and others seek to censor and manipulate the internet and use it as a strategic avenue for disinformation, theft of intellectual property, and electronic warfare.

The great debates about the nature and destiny of the nation once strengthened America. With the media choice and audience fragmentation of the internet environment, Americans are increasingly separated by political outlook, region, race, gender, and special interests. The atmosphere has become uncivil.

The largely liberal news media is aligned with one political party and, increasingly, the leftist wing of that party. In opposition, a smaller but assertive traditionalist media thrives. The distinction between news and commentary has disappeared. The children of the third millennium have the choice to continue the blessings of civil political discourse and an enlightened capitalist system of individual rights and achievement, or they can descend into the chaos of uncivil discourse and the seductive trap of state socialism.

America's founders anticipated the impulses of extremes and designed three coequal branches of government, a Constitution and Bill of Rights, and a regionally balanced electoral college process to preserve and protect *equilibrium.*

Today's Americans live in the deliberative federal republic envisioned by Alexander Hamilton and realized by Franklin Delano Roosevelt. What all its leaders and the American people of their eras have had in common is *liberty.*

Liberty gave thirteen British North American colonies the intellectual and ideological foundation to expand into a continental nation and develop into a global superpower.

Liberty has been essential to the growth and development of the most successful liberal democratic and capitalist nation in history. The experiment in individual rights and religious freedom was extraordinary. Although its first hundred years were boisterous and uncertain, the republic came through stronger from every challenge, including a cataclysmic Civil War. Not without faults but always on an ascending trajectory, the United States reached its apex of development with the sweeping cultural changes of World War II and its immediate aftermath.

In 1941 Japan possessed the qualitatively best navy in the world, because the empire had the vision to build a fleet of modern aircraft carriers to project power. An aroused America then built fleets larger than all the navies of the world combined, including twenty-four modern *Essex* class aircraft carriers. Exceptional Americans of all races and creeds manufactured and deployed the army, navy, and air forces that destroyed fascism. Then the republic experienced its finest hour as its exceptional people supported the visionary restoration of former enemies and patiently prevailed over the challenge of Soviet communism. America has since led the advance of humanity in communications, technology, transportation, space exploration, environmental protection, civil rights, and racial and gender equality. Not always perfectly or immediately, but consistently and decisively.

What continues to be exceptional about America are the *Americans* . . . from all regions, races, religions, and ethnicities. No nation in human history has so effectively assimilated diverse racial and ethnic groups or offered more individual rights and opportunity enshrined in law. America is a sovereign nation with the duty to maintain secure borders that can at the same time welcome new generations of legal immigrants and refugees who seek liberty.

During the twentieth century, Americans learned that liberty was a more effective beacon of hope than military might or propaganda. Liberty continues to draw immigrants from around the world and particularly from Latin America. The United States must enact enlightened and rational immigration reform to both preserve its sovereignty and fulfill its promise. It must protect free expression, the internet, and intellectual property. This makes America stronger in competition with dynamic and dynastic China, the hybrid communist and nationalized capitalist power that cannot, by definition or practice, offer liberty to anyone.

Modern elites instinctively loath any assertion of American self-interest or traditional values as fundamentally racist, imperialist, and dishonest. In their cynical view the United States must be subservient to global technological and environmentalist dogmas that transcend national sovereignty and traditional religious ethics. This postmodern perspective argues that humanity does better to concede a new world order led by an emerging PRC. Traditionalist America must therefore offer and lead with a reasoned and compelling multilateral alternative encompassing the exceptional liberal democratic agenda of individual rights, competitive private sector capitalism, free markets, fair trade, technological innovation, invention, racial and gender equality, religious tolerance, responsible environmental stewardship and empowerment . . . in essence, *liberty*.

An argumentative and uncertain United States once found the courage to prevail in a global showdown with tyranny by building the most powerful armed forces ever known but then found the magnanimous wisdom to set forth an era of unprecedented human economic and social progress. The Americans who made it possible are the model for how millennial Americans can continue to lead the world. Twenty-first-century America can find within itself the common purpose discovered by Franklin Delano Roosevelt, as articulated in the Atlantic Charter, defined by his government-media coalition, and demonstrated by the sacrifices of a special generation.

Ascendant America reached its summit when Neil Armstrong of Ohio, once the frontier Northwest Territory, became the first human to set foot on the moon. *Assertive America* fulfilled its promise to preserve human progress by incinerating fascism, enabling peaceful reconciliation, and bridging an ideological chasm. *Adept America* can lead humanity forward beyond new frontiers to limitless horizons, including the stars, as John F. Kennedy once boldly proclaimed that his fellow Americans would do.

American exceptionalism lives in the hearts of the everyday champions of liberty, and America's most important days are before it. The planet is again at a crossroads that demands the enlightened leadership of a liberal democratic society of nations led by a deliberative republic with "liberty and justice for all."

If not America, who?

ACKNOWLEDGMENTS

Thank you to everyone who had confidence in *Glenn Miller Declassified* and helped make that important historical document a success. Many of the same sources and contributors have had an immeasurable impact on the conception and presentation of *America Ascendant*, including the media, government, and military figures who lived this true and exceptional American saga, most notably Maj. Gen. Vernon A. Walters, America's renaissance soldier-diplomat. *America Ascendant* is a sweeping history that those who lived it painted in vivid colors on a wide global landscape. It is time to tell the story of how a remarkable private and public sector coalition designed and delivered American exceptionalism in World War II, juxtaposed with the real human sacrifice and patriotism exemplified on the field of battle by Americans around the world. Furthermore, how America then went forward to build a new world order is just as important. This is an exceptional legacy that offers inspiration for today's Americans as they seek civil and productive political discourse.

I sincerely appreciate the patience and support of my literary agent Roger Williams, managing editor Tom Swanson, project editor Ann Baker, copyeditor Jane Curran, publisher Potomac Books and the University of Nebraska Press. It is also important to remember the late Claude Frederick "Alan" Cass, my mentor and colleague at the University of Colorado Boulder, who left us during the preparation of *America Ascendant*. The global perspective given to me by Catholic educators of American and Cuban heritage, with their mastery of history, the classics, and rational thinking is an indispensable gift. Thank you always to the late James A. Michener for his advice that I should write history . . . and for all the historians who have given me direction and insight. Most importantly, though, is the support and guidance of my wife Ann, without whom *America Ascendant* would not have been possible.

NOTES

1. From Sea to Shining Sea

1. The Declaration of Independence (1776): A History, NARA.
2. Ellis, *His Excellency*, 136.
3. "History of the Siege," Yorktown Battlefield, National Park Service, 2015, https://www.nps.gov/york/learn/historyculture/history-of-the-siege.htm.
4. *Constitution of the United States: Analysis and Interpretation.*
5. Maier, *Ratification*, 13–16, 30, 66.
6. Resolution of the Congress of September 13, 1788.
7. Issacson, *Benjamin Franklin*, 457–59.
8. Schweikart and Allen, *Patriot's History*, 96–135.
9. Haggard, "The Nicola Affair," 139–69.
10. Pasley, *Tyranny of Printers*, appendix 1, 43.
11. Thomas Jefferson to James Madison, November 26, 1795, in *Papers of Thomas Jefferson*, 28:540.
12. Washington, *Papers of George Washington*, 15:608.
13. George Washington to Alexander Hamilton, July 29, 1795, Alexander Hamilton Papers, LOC.
14. George Washington to Charles Carroll, May 1, 1796, in Washington, *Writings of George Washington*.
15. Burstein and Isenberg, *Madison and Jefferson*, 174–83.
16. Chernow, *Alexander Hamilton*, 6.
17. Kagan, *Dangerous Nation*, 37.
18. Burstein and Isenberg, *Madison and Jefferson*, 207–8.
19. Treaties of 1778 between the United States and France, Lillian Goldman Law Library, Yale Law School, New Haven CT.
20. French Alliance, French Assistance and European Diplomacy during the American Revolution, 1778–1782, STATE.
21. Chernow, *Alexander Hamilton*, 435–42.
22. Wheelan, *Jefferson's War*, 1–128.
23. Irwin and Sylla, *Founding Choices*, 287.
24. J. Miller, *Crisis in Freedom*, 187–93; Stone, *Perilous Times*, 63–64.

25. McCullough, *John Adams*, 538–96.

26. Chernow, *Alexander Hamilton*, 586–88.

27. November 9, 1799, was 18 Brumaire, Year 7, under the French Republican Calendar.

28. In 1915 the United States eventually compensated the heirs of claimants.

29. Meacham, *Thomas Jefferson*, 383–87; "The Louisiana Purchase: Jefferson's Constitutional Gamble," National Constitution Center, October 20, 2018, https://constitutioncenter.org/blog/the-louisiana-purchase-jeffersons-constitutional-gamble; "Louisiana Purchase," Primary Documents in American History, LOC; "The Louisiana Purchase Legislative Timeline," 8th Cong., 1st Sess., LOC; Thomas Jefferson to Robert Livingston, April 18, 1802, in Jefferson, *Papers of Thomas Jefferson*, 37:264, 266.

30. Meacham, *Thomas Jefferson*, 383–87; Purchase of Louisiana, July 5, 1803, NARA; James Madison Papers, LOC: "Thomas Jefferson to Pierre Samuel du Pont," April 25, 1802 in Jefferson, *Papers of Thomas Jefferson*, 37:332–34.

31. Schoultz, *Beneath the United States*, 15–16.

32. Chernow, *Alexander Hamilton*, 566.

33. Meacham, *Thomas Jefferson*, 389.

34. Constitution of the United States, Amendments 11–27, NARA.

35. Chernow, *Alexander Hamilton*, 695–740.

36. An Ordinance for the Government of the Territory of the United States North-West of the River Ohio, passed on July 13, 1787, LOC, NARA.

37. Beckert, *Empire of Cotton*, 109–10.

38. Hickey, *War of 1812*, 295.

39. The Monroe Doctrine (1823), Basic Readings in U.S. Democracy, STATE.

40. Finch, *Story of the New York State Canals*.

41. The Erie Canal crossed the ancestral lands of the Oneida, Onondaga, Cayuga, and Seneca.

42. Brands, *Andrew Jackson*, 62–65, 401–7.

43. Boller, *Presidential Campaigns*, 146.

44. Brands, *Andrew Jackson*, 71–73, 149–50, 556–60.

45. Brands, *Andrew Jackson*, 332–31.

46. Brands, *Andrew Jackson*, 309–21, 435–36, 489–93, 535–36.

47. Brands, *Andrew Jackson*, 508–9, 512–26, 544–47.

48. Fehrenbach, *Lone Star*, 205–15.

49. Fehrenbach, *Lone Star*, 291–346; Merck, *History of the Westward Movement*, 281–86; Crapol, *John Tyler*, 196–211.

50. Crapol, *John Tyler*, 15-20, 202–18.

51. Fehrenbach, *Lone Star*, 247–67; Merck, *History of the Westward Movement*, 281–86.

52. Heidler and Heidler, *Henry Clay*, 362–86.

53. Office of the Historian, Department of State, "The Oregon Territory, 1846," Milestones in the History of U.S. Foreign Relations, 1830–1860, STATE.

54. Office of the Historian, Department of State, "The Annexation of Texas, the Mexican-American War and the Treaty of Guadeloupe-Hidalgo, 1845–1848," Milestones in the History of U.S. Foreign Relations, 1830–1860, STATE.

55. Office of the Historian, Department of State, "The Gadsden Purchase, 1853–1854," Milestones in the History of U.S. Foreign Relations, 1830–1860, STATE.

56. R. J. Miller, *Native America, Discovered and Conquered*, 120.

57. Office of the Historian, Department of State, "United States Maritime Expansion across the Pacific during the 19th Century," Milestones in the History of U.S. Foreign Relations, 1830–1860, STATE.

58. Merck, *Manifest Destiny*, 215–16.

59. O'Sullivan, "Annexation."

60. McCrisken, "Exceptionalism," 68.

61. The Homestead Act of 1862, Primary Documents in American History, LOC.

62. Beckert, *Empire of Cotton*, 102–4.

63. Gates, "Slavery."

64. Susan Schulten, "Visualizing Slavery," opinion, *New York Times*, December 9, 2010.

65. Beckert, *Empire of Cotton*, 244, 259–60.

66. The Compromise of 1850, Primary Documents in American History, LOC.

67. Tocqueville, *Democracy in America*, chapter 18, "Future Conditions of the Three Races in the United States."

68. *Population of the United States in 1860; Compiled from Original Returns of the Eighth Census*, directed by Secretary of the Interior Joseph C. G. Kennedy, Washington DC, 1864, NARA.

69. Fehrenbacher, *Dred Scott Case*.

70. Col. Robert E. Lee, *Report to the Adjutant General concerning the Attack at Harper's Ferry, October 19, 1859*; RG 94, NARA; Finkelman, "John Brown"; Bernard Nalty, "United States Marines at Harper's Ferry and in the Civil War," History and Museums Division, USMC, 1983.

71. *Presidential Election of 1860: A Resource Guide*, LOC.

72. Beckert, *Empire of Cotton*, 242–44.

73. Office of the Historian, Department of State, "French Intervention in Mexico and the American Civil War, 1862–1867," Milestones in the History of U.S. Foreign Relations, 1861–1865, STATE.

74. Beckert, *Empire of Cotton*, 246.

75. *Constitution of the United States: Analysis and Interpretation*.

76. The Gettysburg Address, LOC.

77. Beckert, *Empire of Cotton*, 256–58.

78. Purchase of Alaska, 1867, STATE.

79. Executive Order of Abraham Lincoln, Fixing the Point of Commencement on the Union Pacific Railroad at Council Bluffs, Iowa, dated March 7, 1864 (38th Cong., Senate Ex. Doc. no. 277), NARA.

80. Ambrose, *Nothing Like It*, 23–24, 86–88, 270–71.

81. Donovan, *Terrible Glory*, chapter 12, "The Charge," 225–49.

82. Turner, "Significance of the Frontier."

83. Mayo-Smith, "Eleventh Census of the United States"; The Fate of the 1890 Census, NARA.

84. Government statistics estimated that 14.3% of 1890s immigrants were from Germany; 10.9% from Italy, 10.0% from Great Britain, 9.7% from Ireland, 8.9% from the Austro-Hungarian Empire (including many smaller states), 6.9% from Russia, 2.6% from Sweden. 1.8% from Norway, 1.5% from France, 1.3% from Greece, 4% from other countries.

85. Papke, *Pullman Case*, 35–37.

86. Brands, *Restless Decade*.

87. "Origins of Labor Day," *Newshour*, Public Broadcasting System, September 2, 2001, broadcast and online.

88. People's Party Candidate James B. Weaver carried Colorado, Idaho, Kansas, and Nevada.

89. Rove, *Triumph of William McKinley*, 365–83.

90. Mahan, *Influence of Sea Power*.

91. Mahan, "United States Looking Outward."

92. Mahan, *Influence of Sea Power*, 111.

93. Mahan, *Influence of Sea Power*, 118.

94. Louis Fisher, *Destruction of the USS Maine (1898)*, August 4, 2009, LOC.

95. Leeke, *Manila and Santiago*, 62–74, 214–22, including references from Dewey, *Autobiography of George Dewey*.

96. Leeke, *Manila and Santiago*, 83–89, 127–47, including references from Schley, *Forty-Five Years*.

97. Cashin, *Under Fire*, 207–8.

98. Thomas, "Race and the Spanish-American War."

99. Patrick Feng, "Maj. Walter Reed and the Eradication of Yellow Fever," U.S. Army History Museum, www.armyhistory.org, January 20, 2015.

100. Schweikart and Allen, *Patriot's History of the United States*, vii–xix.

2. Gospel of Americanism

1. Morris, *Theodore Rex*, 3–49.

2. Miller, *Theodore Roosevelt*, 276–312.

3. Miller, *Theodore Roosevelt*, 313–32.

4. Miller, *Theodore Roosevelt*, 353–58.

5. Morris, *Theodore Rex*, 52–58.

6. Brinkley, *Wilderness Warrior*, 396–430, 472–501, 631–72.

7. Morris, *Theodore Rex*, 201, 215–16, 318, 325–26.

8. McCullough, *Path between the Seas*, 361–86.

9. Morris, *Theodore Rex*, 468–70.

10. "The Real Teddy Bear Story," Theodore Roosevelt Association, www.theodore roosevelt.org).

11. Brands, *T. R.*, 513–14.

12. Morris, *Theodore Rex*, 473, 476.

13. "The Great White Fleet," Naval History and Heritage Command, USN, LOC.

14. Brands, *T. R.*, 633–34.

15. Morris, *Theodore Rex*, 482–85.

16. The 1908 Election: A Resource Guide, LOC.

17. The 1912 Election: A Resource Guide, LOC.

18. McCullough, *Path between the Seas*, 609–10.

19. Morris, *Colonel Roosevelt*, 358–60.

20. The 1916 Election: A Resource Guide, LOC.

21. Brody, "Worst Thing."

22. Berg, *Wilson*, 335–79.

23. Womack, "Mexican Revolution, 1910–1920," 125–200.

24. Francisco I. Madero, 38° Presidente de México, Todos los Presidentes de México, www.presidentes.mx.

25. Meyer, "Arms of the Ypiranga," 543–56.

26. Berg, *Wilson*, 322.

27. "Ypiranga and Bavaria Unload Cargoes at Puerto Mexico," *New York Times*, May 28, 1914.

28. Berg, *Wilson*, 323.

29. Berg, *Wilson*, 425.

30. Documents I–IV, Zimmerman telegram, (a) as received in code by German Ambassador in Mexico via Western Union; (b) Telegram with translation; (c) Decode worksheet, and (d) Telegram from Acting Secretary of State Frank L. Polk to the American Embassy in Mexico City, NARA.

31. Berg, *Wilson*, 425.

32. Berg, *Wilson*, 364.

33. "President Calls for War Declaration," *New York Times*, April 3, 1917, 1.

34. Joint Resolution Passed by the United States Senate and House of Representatives, 65th Cong., 1st Sess., April 4, 1917, NARA.

35. Garraty, *Henry Cabot Lodge*, 1–433.

36. Food and Duel Control Act, Executive Order 2679-A, August 10, 1917, establishing the United States Food Administration, 65th Cong., 1st Sess., Chs. 52, 53, 1917, NARA.

37. Berg, *Wilson*, 449.

38. Creel, *How We Advertised America*, foreword, xi–xv.

39. Creel, *How We Advertised America*, foreword, xi–xviii.

40. Creel, *How We Advertised America*, foreword, xi–xviii.

41. Berg, *Wilson*, 451.

42. Berg, *Wilson*, 451.

43. Creel, *How We Advertised America*, 84–98.

44. Berg, *Wilson*, 452.

45. Creel, *How We Advertised America*, 250–60.

46. Pub. L. 65–24, 40 Stat. 217: NARA; Moynihan, *Secrecy*, 89.

47. Moynihan, *Secrecy*, 92–96.

48. Pub. L. 65–150, 40 Stat. 553: NARA.

49. Berg, *Wilson*, 456.

50. Office of the Historian, Department of State, "Wilson's Fourteen Points, 1918," Milestones in the History of U.S. Foreign Relations, 1914–1920, STATE.

51. Badger, *Life in Ragtime*, 161–89.

52. Badger, *Life in Ragtime*, 190–212.

53. Badger, *Life in Ragtime*, 213–21.

54. Badger, *Life in Ragtime*, 222.

55. "Shot at Beast of Berlin," *Variety*, April 12, 1918, 47.

56. "President Wilson Calls upon Film Industry," *Moving Picture World*, July 14, 1917, 217.

57. "Industry in West to Back the Government," *Moving Picture World*, June 15, 1918, 1550.

58. NAMPI advertisement, *Variety*, October 12, 1917, 36–37; "Zukor Committee Announces Plan for Loan Drive," *Moving Picture World*, August 3, 1918, 665; "Great Array of Star Films to Boost Liberty Loan Drive," *Variety*, September 20, 1918; NAMPI advertisement, *Variety*, September 27, 1918, 44–45.

59. O'Toole, *Moralist*, 90.

60. "Treaty of Peace with Germany," Speech of Hon. Henry Cabot Lodge, U.S. Senate, Tuesday, August 12, 1919, U.S. Government Printing Office, 1–18, LOC.

61. Seventeenth Amendment to the Constitution, Joint Resolution of Congress, December 4, 1911, NARA.

62. Berg, *Wilson*, 504.

63. Keynes, *Economic Consequences of the Peace*, 32–34.

64. Berg, *Wilson*, 534.

65. MacMillan, *Paris 1919*, 78–79.

66. Berg, *Wilson*, 549.

67. Taft, *Collected Works*, 7:157–60, 194–96, 287–93.

68. Berg, *Wilson*, 582.

69. MacMillan, *Paris 1919*, 460–72.

70. MacMillan, *Paris 1919*, 476–78.

71. MacMillan, *Paris 1919*, 80, 467.

72. Berg, *Wilson*, 498–500.

73. J. E. Smith, *FDR*, 342–43.

74. Berg, *Wilson*, 591–92, 598, 626–27.

75. Tooze, *Deluge*, 46–47.

76. Wilson won 41.8 percent of the popular vote in 1912 and 49.2 percent in 1916.

77. Berg, *Wilson*, 612–16.

78. Berg, *Wilson*, 618–22.

79. Berg, *Wilson*, 682.

80. "The Great Pandemic: The United States in 1918–1919," U.S. Department of Health and Human Services, https://www.hsdl.org/?abstract&did=37153.

81. Cooper, *Woodrow Wilson*. 507–60.

82. Berg, *Wilson*, 677.

83. Northedge, *League of Nations*, 70–97, 278–92.

84. Berg, *Wilson*, 397.

3. Arsenal of Democracy

1. Edgar Eugene, Robinson, "The Presidential Vote, 1896–1932," American Leaders Speak: Recordings from World War I and the 1920 Election, LOC.

2. Nineteenth Amendment to the United States Constitution, LOC.

3. Evans and Peattie, *Kaigun*, 193–96.

4. Howarth, *Fighting Ships of the Rising Sun*, 167.

5. Howarth, *Fighting Ships of the Rising Sun*, 167: Admiral Isoroku Yamamoto argued that Japan should remain in the treaty. He believed the United States could easily outproduce the 5:3 ratio in any potential war. He commented, "anyone who has seen the auto factories of Detroit and the oil fields of Texas knows that Japan lacks the power for a naval race with the United States. The ratio works very well for Japan because it is a treaty to restrict the other parties." However, the antitreaty naval faction combined with the increasingly militant Japanese army won the argument.

6. Col. Philip S. Mellinger, *Bill Mitchell: United States Air Force*, American Airpower Biography Series, Air University, Maxwell-Gunter Air Force Base, Alabama.

7. Murray, *Harding Era*, 463–81.

8. Murray, *Harding Era*, 561.

9. Schiff, *Gershwin*, 51–61.

10. Berg, *Lindbergh*, 123–31, 156–77, 207–35, 236–41.

11. Goldman and Goldman, *Prisoners of Time*, 108–47.

12. Franklin D. Roosevelt, Presidential Address to Congress, March 1, 1945. Roosevelt did not publicly discuss his condition after 1925 until his "ten pounds of steel" comment that he made in an address to Congress on March 1, 1945, upon returning from the Yalta Conference.

13. U.S. Senate, *Biography of Robert Ferdinand Wagner* (1877–1953), https://www.senate.gov/.

14. Burlingame, *Don't Let Them Scare You*, 151.

15. Paine, *Wars for Asia*, 123–37.

16. WLS, Chicago (NBC Blue) radio broadcast, audio recording, collection of the author.

17. Berg, *Lindbergh*, 345–83.

18. K. Davis, *FDR: Into the Storm*, 503–4.

19. Marian Anderson, *New York Times*, April 9, 1993, 1; Biography: Marian Anderson, *American Experience*, PBS.

20. K. Davis, *FDR: Into the Storm*, 447–49.

21. *New York Times*, August 24, 1939, 1; *New York Herald-Tribune*, European ed., August 24, 1939, 1. The terms of the protocols between Nazi foreign minister Joachim von Ribbentrop and Soviet foreign secretary Vyacheslav Molotov called for "spheres of influence" and the division of Poland between the rivals.

22. *New York Times*, September 18, 1939, 1; *New York Herald-Tribune*, European ed., September 18, 1939, 1.

23. CBS rebroadcasts of Radio Warsaw, September 15, 1939, September 18, 1939, September 21, 1939, September 23, 1939, and September 28, 1939, audio recordings, GMA.

24. Clark, *Einstein*, 554; K. Davis, *FDR: Into the Storm*, 483–85. Leo Szilard felt that Einstein was the only physicist in American with enough fame and prestige to get a hearing from the American government. Furthermore, Szilard favored the approach of sending the letter directly to Roosevelt, and economist Alexander Sachs agreed. Einstein later said that the letter was "the one great mistake I made in my life." Clark and Davis credit this to a remark Einstein made to Linus Pauling. "But there was some justification," Einstein added, "the danger that the Germans would make atomic bombs."

25. K. Davis, *FDR: Into the Storm*, 483–85.

26. Churchill, *Their Finest Hour*, 118.

27. Churchill, *Churchill War Papers*, vols. 1–31. There are 1,700 extant wartime messages between FDR and Winston Churchill.

28. Stevenson, *Man Called Intrepid*, 155.

29. December 4, 1940, Department of State, Washington: Joseph P. Kennedy to the President, FDR. In his December 4, 1940, letter Kennedy cites his November 6, 1940, offer of resignation and Roosevelt's request that he (Kennedy) continue, and Kennedy's subsequent resignation on December 1, 1940, which Roosevelt accepted.

30. CBS broadcasts of December 29, 1940, and January 6, 1941, Presidential Addresses, audio recordings, GMA.

31. *Public Papers and Addresses of Franklin D. Roosevelt, 1940*, 663–72, FDR.

32. Lindbergh's bipartisan Senate allies included Bennett Champ Clark of Missouri, Ernest Lundeen and Henrik Shipstead of Minnesota, Burton K. Wheeler of Montana, Gerald P. Nye of North Dakota, Patrick McCarran of Nevada, and William Borah of Idaho.

33. Sherwood, *Roosevelt and Hopkins*, 2–3, 233–34.

34. Neal, *Dark Horse*, 188–90.

35. Kimball, *Churchill and Roosevelt*, 131.

36. Neal, *Dark Horse*, 203–6.

37. Walsh lost his Senate seat to Republican Henry Cabot Lodge II in 1946. Lodge defeated former Boston mayor James Michael Curley in the 1936 Senate race but resigned his seat to serve as a decorated army officer in Italy.

38. Churchill, *Grand Alliance*, 420–22.

39. Joseph Breen to Jack L. Warner, *Confessions of a Nazi Spy*, December 30, 1938, Production Code Administration Files, AMPAS.

40. *Confessions of a Nazi Spy*, Warner Brothers First National Pictures, 1939, DVD, collection of the author.

41. *Variety*, March 12, 1941, 4.

42. Lloyd Mellett to FDR, March 17, 1941, White House 1941 folder, Lowell Mellett Papers, FDR.

43. *Variety*, March 12, 1941, 4.

44. Executive Order 8802, *Prohibition of Discrimination in the Defense Industry*, FDR; "President Orders an Even Break for Minorities in Defense Jobs," *New York Times*, June 26, 1941, 1.

45. Winkler, *Politics of Propaganda*, 25.

46. Winkler, *Politics of Propaganda*, 20.

47. Mellett to FDR, May 5, 1941, Box 15, Mellett Papers, and March 17, 1941, Mellett Papers, FDR.

48. Churchill, *Grand Alliance*, 377–95.

49. The Atlantic Conference and Charter, 1941, STATE.

50. *Divini Redemptoris*, Pius XI, given at the Vatican on the feast of the venerable St. Joseph, March 19, 1937, Liberia Editrice Vaticano.

51. *Mit Brennender Sorge*, Pius XI, given at the Vatican on Passion Sunday, March 14, 1937, Liberia Editrice Vaticano.

52. Shirer, *Rise and Fall*, 234–35.

53. *Summi Pontificatus*, Pius XII, given at Castel Gandolfo on October 20, 1939, Liberia Editrice Vaticano.

54. K. Davis, *FDR: The War President*, 256–58.

55. *The Atlantic Conference and Charter*, 1941, STATE.

56. Churchill, *Grand Alliance*, 431–50.

57. K. Davis, *FDR: The War President*, 269–73.

58. Berg, *Lindbergh*, 426–28.

59. *New York Times*, September 15, 1940, 1.

60. *New York Times*, August 13, 1941, 1.

61. U.S. Senate, 77th Cong., 1st Sess., Propaganda in Motion Pictures, Hearing before a Subcommittee of the Committee on Interstate Commerce on S. Res. 152, September 9–26, 1941, LOC.

62. Propaganda in Motion Pictures, Hearings, 11–17.

63. Neal, *Dark Horse*, 216–18. Willkie received $100,000 from the studios to represent them. It was money well spent.

64. *Time*, September 22, 1941, 13.

65. Propaganda in Motion Pictures, Hearings, 19–20.

66. Propaganda in Motion Pictures, Hearings, 19–20.

67. McMillan, "McFarland and the Movies," 277–302.

68. Carrozza, *William D. Pawley*, 20–22, 69–71, 79–85, 103–5, 111–12.

69. Prange, Goldstein, and Dillon, *At Dawn We Slept*, 80–82, 84, 86, 118–19, 151, 276–77.

70. CBS *News*, broadcasts on December 7, 1941, 2:00 p.m.–11:00 p.m., audio recordings, GMA.

71. Churchill, *Grand Alliance*, 605–6.

72. Churchill, *Grand Alliance*, 618–20.

4. Why We Fight

1. Potter, *Nimitz*, 16–19.

2. CBS *News*, broadcast on December 26, 1941, Columbia Records C-85-1/2, CO 55010 A/B, GMA.

3. K. Davis, *FDR: The War President*, 366–96.

4. Joint Declaration of the United Nations, January 1–2, 1942, STATE.

5. Third Meeting of the Foreign Ministers of the American Republics held at Rio de Janeiro, January 15–28, 1942, Foreign Relations of the United States, Diplomatic Papers, 1942, The American Republics, vol. 5, STATE.

6. Gannon, *Operation Drumbeat*, 14–241, 345–57.

7. Churchill, *Hinge of Fate*, 111–18.

8. Gannon, *Operation Drumbeat*, 378–409.

9. *Broadcasting*, December 15, 1941, 7–11; December 22, 1941, 9–12; December 29, 1941, 10–12, 36–37; January 5, 1942, 10, 18; January 12, 1942, 12, 16.

10. Spragg, *Glenn Miller Declassified*, 18–19.

11. *Joint Army and Navy Basic War Plan—Rainbow No. 5*, November 3, 1941, M-1421, roll 11, RG 225, NARA.

12. Morton, *Fall of the Philippines*, 77–97.

13. *Bert Silen Reports from Manila, December 7–9, 1941*, NBC Red and NBC Blue networks, audio recordings, Glenn Miller Archives, University of Colorado Boulder.

14. Manchester, *American Caesar*, 206–7.

15. War Department BPR, A1/99, RG 107, NARA.

16. Wukovits, *Pacific Alamo*, 177–271.

17. *Broadcasting*, December 29, 1941, 9.

18. *Carnivale de Broadway* and *Camel Rumba Review*, NBC broadcasts, audio recordings, and radio scripts and logs, GMA and LOC.

19. Winkler, *Politics of Propaganda*, 26–28.

20. Office of War Information, Records of the Radio Bureau NC 148 6B, container 5, RG 208, OWI, NARA; 148 6B, RG 208, NARA.

21. Burlingame, *Don't Let Them Scare You*, 184.

22. *New York Herald Tribune*, October 9, 1941; Archibald MacLeish to Harry Hopkins, Harry Hopkins Papers, box 324, FDR.

23. *Variety*, December 24, 1941, 3.

24. *Variety*, January 14, 1942, 5, 7; January 21, 1942, 4, 13; January 28, 1942, 5.

25. Stevenson, *Man Called Intrepid*, 97.

26. M. E. Guilford to Lowell Mellett, July 15, 1942, Mellett Paper, box 3, FDR.

27. Burlingame, *Don't Let Them Scare You*, 186.

28. Burlingame, *Don't Let Them Scare You*, 185.

29. Lt. Col. William Donovan won the Medal of Honor for his service near Landres-et-St. Georges, France, October 14–15, 1918, while commanding the First Battalion, 165th Regiment, Forty-Second "Rainbow" Division (the famed Sixty-Ninth New York Volunteers).

30. Burlingame, *Don't Let Them Scare You*, 151.

31. Executive Order 9182, Consolidating Certain War Information Functions into an Office of War Information, June 13, 1942, *Federal Register*, June 16, 1942, 4468–69.

32. Burlingame, *Don't Let Them Scare You*, 189.

33. Office of the Director, Office of War Information, NC 148 6E, RG 208, NARA.

34. Morton, *Fall of the Philippines*, 442–54.

35. E. Davis, "War of Words," 7–9.

36. Prange, Goldstein, and Dillon, *Miracle at Midway*, 367.

37. OWI Bureau of Motion Pictures (BMP) Overseas Information Branch, San Francisco, Los Angeles Branch Office, Motion Picture Reviews and Analysis: *A Prisoner of Japan*, July 22, 1942, container 3512; *Remember Pearl Harbor*, May 11, 1942, container 3516; *Secret Agent of Japan*, April 1942, container 3518; *Danger in the Pacific*, July 12, 1942, and *Halfway to Shanghai*, June 29, 1942, container 3519, NC 148 576, OWI BMP, RG 208, NARA.

38. Dorothy Jones, War Features Inventory of July 15, 1942, OWI, Overseas Information Branch, San Francisco, Los Angeles Branch Office, container 1435, OWI BMP, NC 148 576, RG 208, NARA.

39. *Variety*, May 6, 1942, 5.

40. *Variety*, May 6, 1942, 5.

41. *Government Information Manual for the Motion Picture Industry*, 1942, Records of the Director, container 15, NC 148 1, 1/1-19. OWI, RG 208, NARA.

42. Willkie, *One World*, 1–206.

43. *Government Information Manual*.

44. Review of *Casablanca* by Lillian Bergquist, 1942, container 1432, NC 148 576, OWI BMP, RG 208, NARA.

45. *New York Times*, August 8, 1981, 44.

46. *Variety*, May 6, 1942, 31.

47. War Department BPR, A1/100, RG 107, NARA.

48. Spragg, *Glenn Miller Declassified*, 20.

49. *Broadcasting*, July 13, 1942, 20.

50. Bilby, *General*, 138.

51. Lyons, *David Sarnoff*, 216–24.

52. Lyons, *David Sarnoff*, 244–45.

53. *Down Beat*, August 1, 1941, 1.

54. DeLay, "Armed Forces Radio Service," 152–58.

55. Kirby and Harris, *Star Spangled Radio*, 46.

56. Osborn was provocative because he was a proponent of eugenics. At the Rockefeller Foundation and later in the military, he found, because African Americans scored lower than Caucasians on army intelligence tests and Caucasians from northern states scored higher than Caucasians from southern states, that education and other environmental factors, and not race or heredity, were the causes.

57. Capra, *Name above the Title*, 326.

58. Capra, Lewis Autobiography (unpublished).

59. Capra, Lewis Autobiography (unpublished).

60. Executive Order 9066, February 19, 1942, NARA.

61. *Los Angeles Times*, February 19, 1942, February 28, 1942, December 8, 1942, and April 22, 1943.

62. *Pearl Harbor Investigation, Japanese Diplomatic Traffic Logs,* Records of the Office of the Chief of Naval Operations, Containers 154–157, 5830/26-32, RG 38, NARA; MAGIC *Japanese Diplomatic Entries*, Records of the National Security Agency, Boxes 1–19. Record location: 190: 37/3/1–4, RG 457, NARA.

63. Robinson, *Tragedy of Democracy*, 44–47; Charles Mohr, "1941 Cables Boasted of Japanese-American Spying," *New York Times*, May 22, 1983, 18.

64. *Korematsu v. United States*, 323 U.S. 214, 1944, *Ex Parte Endo*, 323 U.S. 283, 1944, United States Reports.

65. McBride, *Searching for John Ford*, 123–24, 273–77, 362.

66. Gallagher, *John Ford*, 200–202.

67. Audrey Amidon, "John Ford and the First Battlefront of World War II," *Unwritten Record*, May 18, 2016, https://unwritten-record.blogs.archives.gov/2016/05/18/john-ford-and-the-first-battlefront-of-world-war-ii; NARA.

68. McBride, *Searching for John Ford*, 336–42.

69. McBride, *Searching for John Ford*, 356–57.

70. Prange, Goldstein, and Dillon, *Miracle at Midway*, 17–20, 45–46.

71. Oral History, *Battle of Midway*, Cmdr. John Ford, Chief, Field Photographic Unit, Office of Strategic Services, Box 10 of 11, Operations Archive Branch, USN.

72. Prange, Goldstein, and Dillon, *Miracle at Midway*, 363.

73. McBride, *Searching for John Ford*, 335–37, 358–66.

74. Gallagher, *John Ford*, 207.

75. Gallagher, *John Ford*, 208.

5. Good Neighbor

1. Banning and Davies, *Airlines of Latin America since 1919*, 224–39.

2. Banning and Davies, *Airlines of Latin America since 1919*, 359–73.

3. Banning and Davies, *Airlines of Latin America since 1919*, 374–75.

4. *Standard Oil Co. of New Jersey v. United States*, 221 U.S. 1 (1911): in the 1911 breakup, Standard Oil divided into Standard Oil of New Jersey (Esso, then Exxon), Standard Oil of New York (Mobil), Standard Oil of California (Chevron, which later acquired Texaco and Unocal), Standard Oil of Indiana (Amoco, later acquired by British Petroleum

or BP), and Standard Oil of Ohio (Sohio, later acquired by Amoco and thence BP). The breakup price of the assets exponentially increased the wealth of John D. Rockefeller.

5. R. N. Smith, *On His Own Terms*, 131–36.

6. Memorandum of Conversation between Cardenas and Rockefeller, October 14–15, 1939, Series 4A, Box 20, Folder 125, RAC.

7. Herring, *Good Neighbors*, 327.

8. *Nelson Rockefeller Oral Histories*, August 9, 1977, 4–5, RAC.

9. Executive Order 8840, July 30, 1941, Federal Register 6 FR 3857, August 2, 1941.

10. Stevenson, *Man Called Intrepid*.

11. William Donovan Memorandum to Nelson Rockefeller, October 9, 1941, RAC.

12. R. N. Smith, *On His Own Terms*, 159.

13. OCIAA Memorandum, Imogene Spencer, October 29, 1942, RAC.

14. R. N. Smith, *On His Own Terms*, 163–64.

15. "Communist Infiltration of Screen Cartoonists Guild," October 30, 1944, FBI, Screen Cartoonists Guild Folder, #10–22533, RG 85, NARA.

16. *Official Report of the Proceedings before the NLRB, In the Matter of Walt Disney Prods., Inc., and Arthur Babbitt*, Los Angeles, October 9, 1942. Babbitt Case, Inter-Office Correspondence, A-B, A1625, WDA.

17. The rumors about alleged Disney Nazi connections persist to the present day. There has never been any actual evidence to support such claims by conspiracy theorists and authors who wish to sensationalize and legitimize Babbitt's vicious yarn.

18. *Disney, Walt: Speeches: Talk to Studio Personnel*, May 27, 1941, TR 91–3, WDA.

19. NLRB, Babbitt Case, A1625, WDA.

20. These were terms to which Disney or Lessing had agreed with Willie Bioff in the event the strikers joined his IATSE union rather than remain represented by Herb Sorrell's Hollywood AFL-affiliated alliance of film studio unions.

21. *Variety*, July 2, 1941.

22. *Variety*, July 2, 1941, 6.

23. *Variety*, July 9, 1941, 22.

24. NLRB, Babbitt Case, A1625, WDA.

25. *Variety*, July 9, 1941, 22.

26. *Variety*, July 16, 1941, 23.

27. *Variety*, July 23, 1941, 7.

28. *Variety*, July 30, 1941, 6.

29. Roy Disney to Walt Disney, March 11, 1941, Inter-Office Correspondence, A3002, WDA.

30. Roy Disney to Walt Disney, August 20, 1941, Inter-Office Correspondence, D, A1627, WDA.

31. Roy Disney to Walt Disney, June 18, 1941, Inter-Office Correspondence, D, A1627, WDA.

32. Walt Disney to Jack Fugit, July 31, 1941, Walt Disney Correspondence, F, A1522, WDA.

33. Banning and Davies, *Airlines of Pan American since 1927*, 260–64.

34. *Interview (Video): Ken Anderson, Bill Cottrell and Herb Ryman*, September 15, 1983, WDA.

35. *South of the Border with Disney*, Walt Disney Studios for the Coordinator of Inter-American Affairs, 1942, DVD, collection of the author.

36. *Saludos Amigos*, Walt Disney Studios, 1942, DVD, collection of the author.

37. *South of the Border with Disney*.

38. *Der Fuhrer's Face*, Walt Disney Studios (short feature), 1942, DVD, collection of the author.

39. *Victory through Air Power*, Walt Disney Studios, 1943, DVD, collection of the author.

40. CAB, Docket SA-58, File 119–42, July 20, 1942, DOT.

41. Matzen, *Fireball*, 161, 164, 309, 330. There is evidence that Carole Lombard was in a rush to get home to save her marriage. According to numerous friends and acquaintances, Clark Gable was having an affair with *Somewhere I'll Find You* costar Lana Turner, who was ten years younger than Lombard. Turner denied this in her autobiography. If true, an intense sense of guilt mixed with grief could explain much of Gable's urgent desire to enlist. In any case, Lombard's death profoundly changed Gable.

42. Gen. H. H. Arnold, A1763, 168.65, AFHRA.

43. AAFTC, A2321, 225.01, AFHRA.

44. 351st BG (H), B0305, GP-351-SU, AFHRA.

45. Cronkite, *Reporter's Life*, 97.

46. Arnold, A1763, 168.65, AFHRA.

47. Spragg, *Glenn Miller Declassified*, 39–40.

48. 38th AAFBU, 235.231, A2527, AFHRA.

49. AAF FMPU, 65891–19369, RG 342, NARA.

50. Spragg, *Glenn Miller Declassified*, 170–71.

51. Harmetz, *Round Up the Usual Suspects*, 278.

52. Laurence Bergreen, "Prologue," vol. 28, no. 2, Summer 1996, NARA.

53. AAF Winged Victory Unit, A0501, AFHRA.

54. AAF Winged Victory Unit, A0501, AFHRA.

55. M/Sgt. Norman Leyden, Interview with Edward F. Polic (video), GMA.

56. Leyden, Interview with Edward F. Polic (video), GMA.

57. AAF Winged Victory Unit, A0501, AFHRA.

58. Services of Supply, A1 196-A, RG 160, NARA.

59. Spragg, *Glenn Miller Declassified*, 34–36.

60. *Broadcasting*, September 21, 1942, 12.

61. *Pittsburgh Post-Gazette*, December 8, 1941, 1.

62. *Broadcasting*, November 2, 1942, 51.

63. *Broadcasting*, December 1941–April 1942 weekly issues.

64. *Billboard*, *Down Beat*, and *Variety*, March 1942 issues.

65. *Broadcasting*, *Billboard*, *Down Beat*, and *Variety*, April 1943 issues.

66. Gallagher, *John Ford*, 213–14.

67. *December 7th*, uncut and edited versions (85 and 34 minutes), Office of Strategic Services, 1943, DVD, collection of the author.

68. War Department BPR, A 1 99, RG 107, NARA.

69. *The Pepsodent Show*, May 6, 1941, to May 27, 1941, NBC Production memoranda and program scripts, LOC.

70. Zoglin, *Hope: Entertainer of the Century*, 181–220.

71. Office of the Director, Radio, NC 148 1, 1/1-19, OWL, RG 208, NARA.

72. AFRS Progress Reports, 1942, DeLay Papers, USC.

73. Carroll, Interview with C. Schaeden, *Those Were the Days*, audio recording, GMA.

74. DeLay, "Armed Forces Radio Service," 144–58.

75. DeLay, "Armed Forces Radio Service," 212–62.

76. *Air Force*, Warner Brothers, 1943, DVD, collection of the author.

77. Script Review, *Air Force*, October 22, 1942, container 3515, NC 148 567, OWI, RG 208, NARA.

78. Elmer Davis to Lowell Mellett, September 7, 1942; Mellett to Davis, September 9, 1942, Office of the Director, NC 148 1, 1/1-19, container 890, OWI, RG 208, NARA.

79. *Minutes, OWI Board*, October 31, 1942, Office of the Director, container 41, NC 148 1/1-19, OWI, RG 208, NARA; *Variety*, November 4, 1942, 5; *Variety*, November 11, 1942, 4; *Variety*, November 4, 1942, 5; *Variety*, November 11, 1942, 4; *Variety*, November 18, 1942, 7.

80. Lowell Mellett to Hollywood Studios, letter, December 9, 1942, Lowell Mellett, container 1443, NC 148 264, OWI-BMP, RG 208, NARA.

81. Harry Warner to Lowell Mellett, December 16, 1942, Lowell Mellett, container 1443, NC 148 264, OWI BMP, RG 208, NARA.

82. Elmer Davis Press Conference, December 23, 1942, Lowell Mellett, container 1442, NC 148 264, OWI BMP, RG 208, NARA.

83. *Minutes, OWI Board*, December 26, 1942, Office of the Director, container 41, OWI, RG 208, NARA; Jean C. Herrick to Gardner Cowles, December 19, 1942, and December 22, 1942, Lowell Mellett, container 1443, NC 148 264, OWI BMP, RG 208, NARA.

6. Command Performance

1. Franklin Roosevelt, Daily Presidential Log, January 1941, FDR.

2. Roosevelt, Daily Presidential Log, January 1941, FDR.

3. CBS retransmission of BBC broadcast, November 10, 1942, Lord Mayor's Day Speech in London, audio recording, GMA.

4. Strodes, *Allen Dulles*, 251–53, 318–22.

5. *Mrs. Miniver*, Metro-Goldwyn-Mayer, 1942, DVD, collection of the author.

6. *Variety*, June 17, 1942, 1.

7. Fiona MacDonald, "Mrs. Miniver: The Film That Goebbels Feared," *BBC Culture*, February 9, 2015.

8. *Casablanca*, Warner Brothers, 1942, DVD, collection of the author.

9. Harmetz, *Round Up the Usual Suspects*, 208–25, 266–83.

10. D. D. Eisenhower, *Crusade in Europe*, 88–110.

11. Churchill, *Their Finest Hour*, 224–40.

12. *Casablanca*, Warner Brothers, 1942, DVD, collection of the author.

13. Memo, Robert Riskin to Ulric Bell, January 8, 1943, OWI: Motion Picture Bureau, Box 3510, RG 208, NARA.

14. Atkinson, *An Army at Dawn*, 339–59, 393–97.

15. Showell, *Enigma U-Boats*, chapter 16, "The Enigma Machine"; appendix1.

16. Allied freighter and tanker losses in the Caribbean dropped from 182 in 1942 to 45 in 1943 and 5 in 1944, a testimony to improved antisubmarine warfare tactics, the shallow water vulnerability of the U-boats, 100 percent coverage of coastal and Caribbean waters by patrol planes, and the German decision to downsize and withdraw American and Caribbean patrols.

17. C. A. Smith, "Martinique in World War II."

18. Morrison, *History of United States Naval Operations*, 10:190–91.

19. D. A. Davis, *Lightning Strike*, 216–62.

20. Churchill, *Hinge of Fate*, 782–831.

21. Winker, *Politics of Propaganda*, 65.

22. Burlingame, *Don't Let Them Scare You*, 192.

23. Winkler, *Politics of Propaganda*, 70; Cong. Rec., 78th Cong., 1st Sess., col. 89, part 5.

24. Burlingame, *Don't Let Them Scare You*, 214.

25. Burlingame, *Don't Let Them Scare You*, 259–60.

26. Owen Lattimore, FBI Records: The Vault: File 100-24628, 1–182, FBI; *Testimony of Alexander Barmine*, July 31, 1951, U.S. Congress, Senate Committee on the Judiciary, Internal Security Subcommittee, Institute of Pacific Relations, Hearings, 82nd Cong., 1st Sess., July 31, 1951, part 1, 199–200, LOC.

27. Burlingame, *Don't Let Them Scare You*, 217.

28. Winkler, *Politics of Propaganda*, 70–71.

29. OWI Overseas Branch: Radio Bureau, NC 148 6B, OWI, RG 208, NARA.

30. Alonso, *Sherwood In Peace and War*, 218.

31. OWI Overseas Branch: Radio Bureau, NC 148 6B, OWI, RG 208, NARA.

32. DeLay, "Armed Forces Radio Service," 388, 697.

33. Eisenhower, *Crusade in Europe*, 231.

34. OWI Overseas Branch: London, NC 148 6J, OWI, RG 208, NARA.

35. DeLay, "Armed Forces Radio Service," 403–12.

36. American Forces Network (AFN), R34/907/1, BBC.

37. Spragg, *Glenn Miller Declassified*, 84–85.

38. Lt. Col. Charles Gurney and Maj. John S. Hayes, *This Is AFN*, Memorandum to AFN Board: ETOUSA, OWI, services of Supply (SOS) and SSD, November 1, 1943, R34/907/1,1–8, BBC.

39. Atkinson, *Day of Battle*, 75–121.

40. Atkinson, *Day of Battle*, 161–71.

41. Dallek, *Unfinished Life*, 92–100.

42. R. B. Frank, *Guadalcanal*, 131, 153–54.

43. Sears, *V-Discs*, xxv–xxvii.

44. Sears, *V-Discs*, xxxv–xxxvii.

45. Sears, *V-Discs*, xliii–lxxxvii.

46. *Broadcasting*, August 9, 1943, 9.

47. DeLay, "Armed Forces Radio Service," 312, 402–42, 582–84.

48. DeLay, "Armed Forces Radio Service," 163–66, 222–32.

49. Robbins, "Tokyo Calling."

50. Atkinson, *Day of Battle*, 187–227.

51. Burlingame, *Don't Let Them Scare You*, 221–29.

52. *New York Times*, August 1, 1943.

53. *Chicago Daily Tribune*, July 30, 1943.

54. Burlingame, *Don't Let Them Scare You*, 222.

55. Burlingame, *Don't Let Them Scare You*, 231.

56. OWI Records of the Office of the Director, NC 148, OWI, RG 208, NARA.

57. OWI Records of the Office of the Director, NC 148, OWI, RG 208, NARA.

58. David Wilson, *South China Morning Post*, June 20, 2016, review of Robert Lyman, *Among the Headhunters: An Extraordinary World War II Story of Survival in the Burmese Jungle.*

59. Gallagher, *John Ford*, 216.

60. McBride, *Searching for John Ford*, 388–89.

61. Gallagher, *John Ford*, 216–17.

62. Phillips, *Steichen at War*, 8-56.

63. Neuschul and Neuschul, "With the Marines at Tarawa."

64. *With the Marines at Tarawa*, United States Marine Corps and Office of War Information, December 1943, with production assistance from Warner Brothers–First National Pictures and distributed by Universal Pictures, 1943, DVD, collection of the author.

65. Norman T. Hatch, "Marine Cinematographer, 96; Filmed World War II Combat," *New York Times*, May 2, 2017, B14A.

66. R. N. Smith, *On His Own Terms,* 165.

67. R. N. Smith, *On His Own Terms*, 167–71.

68. K. S. Davis, *FDR: The War President*, 303–12.

69. Bird and Sherwin, *American Prometheus*, 185–87.

70. Roosevelt, President's Daily Calendar, November 11–22, 1943, FDR.

71. Roosevelt, President's Daily Calendar, November 22, 1943, FDR.

72. Pakula, *Last Empress*, 469, remark by Lt. Gen. Joseph Stilwell, 1943.

73. Pakula, *Last Empress*, 470–76.

74. Pakula, *Last Empress*, 405–13.

75. Churchill, *Closing the Ring*, 325–41.

76. Roosevelt, President's Daily Calendar, November 23–27, 1943, FDR.

77. Churchill, *Closing the Ring*, 342–48.

78. Montefiore, *Stalin*, 467.

79. Montefiore, *Stalin*, 465.

80. Montefiore, *Stalin*, 466–69.

81. Roosevelt, President's Daily Calendar, November 28–December 17, 1943, FDR.

7. Road to Victory

1. *The Battle of China*, Records of the Office of the Chief Signal Officer, 111-of-6, RG 111, NARA.

2. Script review, *Charlie Chan in the Secret Service*, July 29, 1943, Script review, *Charlie Chan in the Mystery Mansion*, August 19, 1944, container 3539, OWI, RG 208, NARA.

3. Script review, *Dragon Seed*, September 10, 1942 and September 15, 1942; Feature review, *Dragon Seed*, July 3, 1944, container 3525, OWI, RG 208, NARA.

4. James Agee, *Nation*, August 5, 1944, 165; *Time*, July 24, 1944, *Chicago Tribune*, September 25, 1944, *New Republic*, August 7, 1944, 161.

5. Script review, *Keys of the Kingdom*, January 19, 1944, container 3518, OWI, RG 208, NARA.

6. Feature review, *Guadalcanal Diary*, October 25, 1943, container 3518, OWI, RG 208, NARA.

7. Script review, *Thirty Seconds over Tokyo*, November 11, 1943; Feature review, *Thirty Seconds over Tokyo*, September 12, 1944, container 3517, OWI, RG 208, NARA.

8. *The Purple Heart*, 20th Century Fox, 1944, DVD, collection of the author; *The Purple Heart*, 20th Century Fox, Story Conference Files, Doheny Library, USC.

9. *The Story of G. I. Joe*, United Artists, 1945, DVD, collection of the author.

10. "The CIAA Should Be Made Permanent: A Regional Structure for Hemispheric Unity, Memorandum," Nelson Rockefeller to Edward Stettinius, January 14, 1944, RAC.

11. Greg Bradsher, "The Z Plan Story, Parts 1–2," *Prologue Magazine* 37, no. 3 (Fall 2005), NARA.

12. SHAEF, SGS (Records of the Secretary, General Staff), 322.01, Organization, Publicity-Psychological Warfare, RG 331, NARA.

13. History of COSSAC, 314.8, SHAEF, RG 331, NARA.

14. SHAEF, SGS, 322.01, Organization, Publicity-Psychological Warfare, RG 331, NARA.

15. SHAEF, SGS, 091.412/3, Psychological Warfare against Germany, RG 331, NARA.

16. SHAEF, SGS, 000.7, Press Information and Censorship, RG 331, NARA.

17. SHAEF, SGS, 000.7, Press Policy, RG 331, NARA.

18. SHAEF, SGS, 381.9, Press Correspondents Plan for Overlord, RG 331, NARA.

19. Spragg, *Glenn Miller Declassified*, 77–89.

20. Spragg, *Glenn Miller Declassified*, 90–92.

21. Spragg, *Glenn Miller Declassified*, 68–75, 97–107.

22. SHAEF, SGS, 000.7, Press Policy, RG 331, NARA.

23. Spragg, *Glenn Miller Declassified*, 75.

24. Lyons, *David Sarnoff*, 247.

25. SHAEF, 000.77–0, Broadcast Engineering, RG 331, NARA.

26. Lyons, *David Sarnoff*, 250.

27. Lyons, *David Sarnoff*, 252.

28. Spragg, *Glenn Miller Declassified*, 77.

29. Spragg, *Glenn Miller Declassified*, 107–8.

30. SHAEF, Cables and Teleconference Transcripts, AGWAR, 311.22, SGS, 331.4, RG 331, NARA.

31. Gallagher, *John Ford*, 217.

32. Gallagher, *John Ford*, 218.

33. *D-Day to Berlin, The War in Color*, DVD, collection of the author.

34. Lyons, *David Sarnoff*, 257–58.

35. SHAEF, 000.77–9/, *Broadcasting*, 000.72–11, PRD, RG 331, NARA.

36. Atkinson, *Guns at Last Night*, 171–79.

37. Butler, *Field Marshal*, 469.

38. Nichols, *Ernie's War*, 351–54.

39. D'Este, *Eisenhower*, 576.

40. Spragg, *Glenn Miller Declassified*, 192–94, 199–203.

41. SHAEF, SGS, 000.74, Press Correspondents, RG 331, NARA.

42. D'Este, *Eisenhower*, 620–24.

43. *Overseas Branch*: ABSIE, *Summary*: NC 148 6B, container 7, OWI, RG 208, NARA.

44. *Overseas Branch, European Operations*: PWB: NC 148 6G, container 2, OWI, RG 208, NARA.

45. *Overseas Branch*, SHAEF PWD and *Radio Luxembourg*: PWB: NC 148 6G, container 10, OWI, RG 208, NARA.

46. *Overseas Branch*: ABSIE, *Summary*: NC 148 6B, container 7, OWI, RG 208, NARA.

47. *Overseas Branch*, ABSIE: *Guidances*, NC 148 363, container 830, OWI, RG 208, NARA.

48. *Overseas Branch*, ABSIE, *German Desk*, NC 148 6E, container 1, OWI, RG 208, NARA.

49. Spragg, *Glenn Miller Declassified*, 150–56.

50. *Overseas Branch*, ABSIE: *Schedules and Operations*, NC 148 362, container 130, OWI, RG 208, NARA.

51. Spragg, *Glenn Miller Declassified*, 150–56.

52. Kirby and Harris, *Star-Spangled Radio*, 126.

53. Spragg, *Glenn Miller Declassified*, 212–42.

54. Atkinson, *Guns at Last Light*, 421–39.

55. *Variety*, 1944 issues: October 4, 31; October 11, 1; October 18, 39; November 1, 35; November 15, 37.

56. M. H. Frank, *Arturo Toscanini*, 21–112.

57. Derewicz, "Songs as Bullets, Music as Bombs," University of North Carolina newsletter *Endeavors*, February 17, 2011.

58. *Office of the Director, Organization*, 1942–43, 1944–45, NC 148 1, container 3, OWI, RG 208, NARA.

59. Davies, *Mission to Moscow*, xi; Kennan, *Memoirs*, 85–86.

60. Davies, *Mission to Moscow*, 201–2, 270–80.

61. Cuthbert, *Mission to Moscow*, 57; Nelson Poynter to Robert Buckner, December 3, 1942, container 16, Mellett Papers, FDR.

62. *Mission to Moscow*, Warner Brothers, 1943, DVD, collection of the author.

63. James Agee, "Films," *Nation*, May 22, 1943, 749.

64. Koppes and Black, *Hollywood Goes to War*, 221.

65. Roosevelt, Presidential Daily Calendar, October 8–9, 1944, FDR.

66. *New York Times*, October 22, 1944, 1; Roosevelt, Presidential Daily Calendar, October 21, 1944, FDR.

67. Gallagher, *John Ford*, 218–24.

68. Le May and Kantor, *Mission with LeMay*, 323.

69. *Technical Reports Concerning B-29 Aircraft, June 5, 1944–November 3, 1944*, Twentieth Air Force, XX Bomber Command A7744, 760.3811, 1757-65, AFHRA.

70. *Summary of Combat Operations, June 5, 1944–August 14, 1944*, Twentieth Air Force, XX Bomber Command, A7737, 760.308-2. 1335-46, AFHRA.

71. LeMay and Kantor, *Mission with LeMay*, 336.

72. *Proceedings and Documents of the United Nations Monetary and Financial Conference, Bretton Woods, New Hampshire*, July 1–22, 1944, Department of State, Publication 2866, 1948, STATE.

73. International Monetary Fund, "IMF Chronology," https://www.imf.org/external/np/exr/chron/chron.asp.

74. Bohlen, *Witness to History*, 159.

75. Divine, *Second Chance*, 129–31.

76. Meijer, *Arthur Vandenberg*, chapter 16, "Hunting for the Middle Ground."

77. Meijer, *Arthur Vandenberg*, chapter 19, "The Speech."

78. Laurence Bergreen, "This Is the Army," *Prologue* 28, no. 2 (Summer 1996), NARA.

79. R. N. Smith, *On His Own Terms*, 173–77.

80. Signals Division: *Eclipse: Papers, Outline and Organization of Communications Section*, UD 69D, containers 6 and 7, SHAEF, RG 331, NARA.

81. Lyons, *David Sarnoff*, 263–64.

82. Croswell, *Beetle*, 786–96.

83. G-1 (Personnel): *Manpower, Establishment, Equipping, etc.*, 320/2, NM8 6, container 15, SHAEF, RG 331, NARA.

84. SHAEF, 000.73-2, Public Relations Div., RG 331, NARA.

85. SHAEF, 000.73-4, Psychological Warfare Div., RG 331, NARA.

86. Burlingame, *Don't Let Them Scare You*, 246–50.

87. Meacham, *Destiny and Power*, 58–67.

88. Kozak, *LeMay*, 178–79, 199–205.

89. R. B. Frank, *Downfall*, 60–62; 150, 155, 157.

90. Friedman, *U. S. Submarines through 1945*, 305–11.

91. Blair, *Silent Victory*, 439; Potter, *Nimitz*, 231–32.

92. Blair, *Silent Victory*, 876–78, and Japanese Naval and Merchant Shipping Losses during World War II by All Causes, Joint Army-Navy Assessment Committee (janac), iv–v, Appendix, U. S. Government Printing Office, Washington DC, February 1947.

8. United Nations

1. Robert A. Divine, *Second Chance: The Triumph of Internationalism*, The Issues, Box 1517, OWI, RG 208, NARA.

2. Leff and Simmons, "*Wilson*," 16–17.

3. Script review, *Wilson*, September 19, 1943, container 3518, OWI, RG 208, NARA.

4. Knock, "History with Lightning," 525–26, 542.

5. Roosevelt, Presidential Calendar, January 22–February 2, 1945, FDR.

6. Montefiore, *Stalin*, 465.

7. Roosevelt, Presidential Calendar, February 3–February 5, 1945, FDR.

8. Roosevelt, Presidential Calendar, February 6–February 14, 1945, FDR.

9. Roosevelt, Presidential Calendar, February 15–February 28, 1945, FDR.

10. LeMay and Kantor, *Mission with LeMay*, 379.

11. *Air Raid Protection and Allied Subjects Tokyo*, 1–3, 63, 72, 83, 155, Exhibit D, *Records of the United States Strategic Bomb Survey* (USSBS), RG 243, NARA.

12. *Fr. Joseph Flaujac, Tokyo Sous les Bombes*, JA 2802 0500 F 587, A1 147, container 84, SCAP, RG 554, NARA.

13. R. B. Frank, *Downfall*, 336–37.

14. Tuchman, *Stilwell and the American Experience in China*, 483–99.

15. Fenby, *Chiang Kai-Shek*, 414–22.

16. Pakula, *Last Empress*, 509–21.

17. *Nelson Rockefeller Oral Histories*, July 14, 1977, 36–38, RAC.

18. J. E. Smith, *FDR*, 634.

19. J. E. Smith, *FDR*, 636.

20. "Howard G. Bruenn, 90, Roosevelt's Doctor in Last Year of Life," *New York Times*, August 2, 1995, 20.

21. Katharine Q. Seelye, "An April Day, 51 Years Ago, War in Italy." *New York Times*, April 14, 1996, 22; Dole, *One Soldier's Story*, 144–62.

22. "Daniel Inouye: A Japanese American Soldier's Valor in World War II," National Park Service, Department of the Interior, https://www.nps.gov/articles/inouyeww2.htm.

23. *Nelson Rockefeller Oral Histories*, July 14, 1977, 39–44, RAC.

24. Office of the Historian, U.S. Department of State, "The United States and the Founding of the United Nations, August 1941–October 1945," 2016, STATE.

25. SHAEF PWD, OWI PWB and ABSIE, NC 148 6-G, container 1, *European Operations*, OWI, RG 208, NARA; *Psychological Warfare Division, An Account of Its Operations in the Western European Campaign, 1944–1945*, July 1945, 23–30; Appendices B-F, SHAEF, RG 331, NARA; ABSIE, *Operations*, NC 148 6-B, container 7; *German Operational Plans*, NC 148 6-E, container 1, OWI, RG 208, NARA.

26. Crosswell, *Beetle*, 916–24.

27. Edward M. Kennedy (AP), "The War in Europe Is Ended, Germany Surrenders," *New York Times*, May 7, 1945, 1; "First News of Surrender Given by AP, News Service's Staff Chief Barred from Dispatching as Result," *Los Angeles Times*, May 8, 1945, 1; PRD, *Correspondents: Accreditation*, 000.74-2, SHAEF, RG 331, NARA.

28. Edward Barrett, Overseas Branch Director, New York, cable to George Becker and Bernard Barnes, London, regarding ABSIE failure to follow VOA directive regarding surrender announcement, May 9, 1945, *Director of Overseas Operations*, ABSIE, NC 148 362, OWI, RG 208, NARA.

29. ABSIE, Closing Broadcast, July 4, 1945 (audio recording), GMA.

30. Baime, *Arsenal of Democracy*, 150–54.

31. Berg, *Lindbergh*, 443–67; *475th Fighter Group*, April 1944–March 1945, GP-457-HI, BO632, AFHRA.

32. *Nelson Rockefeller Oral Histories*, July 14, 1977, 45–50; September 27, 1977, 1–5, RAC.

33. Log of President Truman's Trip to Potsdam, July 6–July 15, 1945, compiled by Lt. William Rigdon, USN, HST.

34. McCullough, *Truman*, 405–7.

35. McCullough, *Truman*, 412.

36. Montefiore, *Stalin*, 498.

37. McCullough, *Truman*, 418–19.

38. Hershberg and Conant, *Harvard to Hiroshima*, 230–34, Appendix, 758–760, Conant's notes from Trinity Site, July 16, 1945.

39. Montefiore, *Stalin*, 498–99.

40. R. B. Frank, *Downfall*, 221–27.

41. McCullough, *Truman*, 424–32.

42. McCullough, *Truman*, 436–37.

43. Montefiore, *Stalin*. 498.

44. Log of President Truman's Trip to Potsdam: Potsdam Declaration to Japan, July 26, 1945, Appended, HST; Office of the Historian, Department of State, "The Potsdam Conference, 1945," Milestones in the History of U.S. Foreign Relations, STATE; *A Study of the Potsdam Declaration*, A 3165 0703 F 714, A1 147, container 4, SCAP, RG 554, NARA.

45. R. B. Frank, *Downfall*, 232–38.

46. *Strategic Plan for Operations in the Japanese Archipelago: Operation Downfall*, US 0810 0100 D; *Staff Study for Operation Olympic*, US 0810 0100 OL-A; *Staff Study for Operation Coronet*, US 0820 0100 C, A1 147, containers 128–29, SCAP, RG 554, NARA; Amendment No. 1 to G-2 Estimate of the Enemy Situation with respect to Kyushu, US 0810 0100 A 258 K: July 29, 1945, A1 147, container 126, SCAP, RG 554, NARA.

47. Manchester, *American Caesar*, 435–43; Potter, *Nimitz*, 385–87.

48. Log of President Truman's Trip to Potsdam, 80–88, HST.

49. *Central Pacific Operations*, container 1, NC 148 6G, OWI PWB, RG 208, NARA.

50. R. B. Frank, *Downfall*, 216–17.

51. *Psychological Warfare Operations*, Twentieth Air Force, A7720, 760.01 v.21, 903–1221, AFHRA.

52. *Central Pacific Operations*, container 1, NC 148 6G, OWI PWB, RG 208, NARA.

53. *PWB Pacific: Leaflets*, container 9, NC 148 6G, OWI PWB, RG 208, NARA.

54. Log of President Truman's Trip to Potsdam: July 27–August 7, 1945, HST.

55. R. B. Frank, *Downfall*, 268–72.

56. *Soviet Entry into War*, JA 0106 0004 W 261J, A1 147, container 60, SCAP, RG 554, NARA.

57. R. B. Frank, *Downfall*, 320–30.

58. Eisenhower, *Mandate for Change*, 312–13; Potter, *Nimitz*, 380–82.

59. Gaddis, *Cold War Statesmen Confront the Bomb*, 65.

60. *Japan's Struggle to End the War*, A6202 0000 U 82 P 25: USSBS, A1 147, container 6, SCAP, RG 554, NARA.

61. Sweeney, *War's End*, 206–21.

62. R. B. Frank, *Downfall*, 293–99.

63. McCullough, *Truman*, 469–71.

64. *Unpublished Memoirs of Foreign Minister Shigenori Tōgō*, JA 1000 1200 T 645J & E, A1 147, container 81, SCAP, RG 554, NARA.

65. R. B. Frank, *Downfall*, 308–12.

66. *PWB Pacific: Japan*, OWI, PWB, NC 148 6G, container 9, RG 208, NARA.

67. *Letter of Resignation of Prime Minister Suzuki*, August 15, 1945, JA 5407, 0000 S 968J, A1 147, container 91, SCAP, RG 554, NARA; *The Termination of the War as told by Kantoro Suzuki*, 1946, JA 0106 0500 R 695J, A1 147, container 63, SCAP, RG 554, NARA.

68. R. B. Frank, *Downfall*, 315–19.

69. *Requirements of the Supreme Commander for the Allied Powers Presented to Japanese Representatives at Manila, P. I.*, August 19–20, 1945, JA 0207 0400 S 285, A1 147, container 68, SCAP, RG 554, NARA.

70. *Time and Place of Formal Surrender of Japanese Armed Forces*, JA 106 0006 D 383, A1 147, container 61, SCAP, RG 554, NARA.

71. Kirby and Harris, *Star Spangled Radio*, 213–21.

72. Pham Van Dong served as prime minister of the Democratic Republic of Vietnam (North Vietnam) from 1955 to 1976 and, following unification, as prime minister of the Socialist Republic of Vietnam from 1976 until 1987.

73. Fenn, *At the Dragon's Gate*, 138–41.

74. The Comintern was the Communist International; an international organization devoted to communist conquest of the entire world by "all available means." Stalin dissolved the Comintern in 1943 to avoid antagonizing the United States and the United Kingdom.

75. Bartholomew-Feis, *OSS and Ho Chi Minh*, 145–46.

76. Fenn, *At the Dragon's Gate*, 78–81.

77. Bartholomew-Feis, *OSS and Ho Chi Minh*, 160.

78. Patti, *Why Vietnam?*, 58, 84-86.

79. Bartholomew-Feis, OSS *and Ho Chi Minh*, 209–18, 224–25, Fenn, *At the Dragon's Gate*, 188; Patti, *Why Vietnam?*, 172–73.

80. Bartholomew-Feis, OSS *and Ho Chi Minh*, 209–15.

81. Bob Bergin, "Old Man Ho: The OSS Role in Ho Chi Minh's Rise to Political Power," *Studies in Intelligence* 62, no. 2, excerpts from classified studies, June 2018, CIA.

82. *Kodo sempu* means dissemination of the Royal (Imperial) Way.

83. Mashbir, *I Was an American Spy*, 278–99.

84. *Life*, September 10, 1945.

85. Manchester, *American Caesar*, 439–440.

86. Manchester, *American Caesar*, 452.

87. Manchester, *American Caesar*, 454.

88. Potter, *Nimitz*, 397–98.

89. Manchester, *American Caesar*, 458.

90. *The Effects of Air Attack on Japanese Urban Economy*, A 6202 0000 U 82 P 55: USSBS, A1 147, container 6, SCAP, RG 554, NARA.

91. Manchester, *American Caesar*, 471–91.

92. McCullough, *Truman*, 475.

93. Fenby, *Chiang Kai-Shek*, 453–59; McCullough, *Truman*, 473.

94. Fenby, *Chiang Kai-Shek*, 453–59; McCullough, *Truman*, 474.

95. Fenby, *Chiang Kai-Shek*, 460–72.

96. Gilbert, *Churchill*, chapter 36, "An Iron Curtain," 844–67.

97. The "Long Telegram," Kennan to Byrnes via Marshall, Moscow to State Department via secure War Department cable, February 22, 1946, received 3:52 p.m., HST.

98. "Interview of George Kennan, May–June 1996," *Cold War* series, Cable News Network (CNN) video and transcript, collection of the author.

99. Delay, "Armed Forces Radio Service," 471–89; *History of AFRTS: The First Fifty Years, 1942–1992*, 63–77, AFRTS, DOD.

100. *Executive Orders of Harry S. Truman, 1945-1953*, Executive Order 9608, August 31, 1945, and Executive Order 9621, September 15, 1945, HST.

101. Pirsein, *Voice of America*, 107–8; Arthur MacMahon, *Memorandum on the Postwar International Information Program of the United States*, xi–xiii, 2–4, Publication 2438, STATE.

9. A New Frontier

1. *Press Releases and Trial Transcripts, 1945–1946*, IMT, P 17 container 1, RG 238, NARA; *Closing Addresses of the Prosecution, 1946*, IMT, PI-21 42, RG 238, NARA; *Final Statements of the Defendants, 1946*, IMT, A1 5667, container 13, RG 238, NARA.

2. Potter, *Nimitz*, 422–23.

3. *IMTFE Record*, A 5902 0000 W 253: A1 147, container 4, SCAP, RG 554, NARA; *IMTFE Affidavits*, JA 8025 0000 IMTFE, A1 147, container 93, SCAP, RG 554, NARA; *Transcriptions, IMTFE Proceedings*, JA 5902 0000 W 253, A1 147, container 91, SCAP, RG 554, NARA; *Judgements of the IMTFE*, NM1 334, containers 1–10, SCAP, RG 331, NARA.

4. McCullough, *Truman*, 389–90.

5. J. E. Smith, *Lucius D. Clay*, 414–16.

6. "Clark Clifford to the President: Containment of the Soviet Union, September 24, 1946," Clark Clifford Papers, HST.

7. Truman, *Memoirs*, 547–52.

8. McCullough, *Truman*, 540–42.

9. McCullough, *Truman*, 542.

10. Pogue, *George C. Marshall*, 4:161–65.

11. McCullough, *Truman*, 545–51.

12. Pogue, *George C. Marshall*, 4:183–96.

13. Kennan, *Memoirs*, 326.

14. Pogue, *George C. Marshall*, 4:204–5.

15. Pogue, *George C. Marshall*, 4:206–7.

16. Pogue, *George C. Marshall*, 4:213–15.

17. McCullough, *Truman*, 565.

18. Foreign Assistance Act of 1948 and Economic Cooperation Act of 1948, 80th Cong., 2nd Sess., chapter 169, April 3, 1948, NARA, STATE, CIA.

19. *United States Information and Education Exchange Act of 1948*, 80–402, 62 Stat 6, 22 U. S. C. ch. 18, Foreign Affairs, LOC.

20. McCullough, *Truman*, 476.

21. McCullough, *Truman*, 598–99.

22. R. N. Smith, *Thomas E. Dewey*, 512–14.

23. Statement, President to House of Representatives, Veto of Taft-Hartley Labor Bill, June 20, 1947, HST; Labor-Management Relations Act of 1947, 80 H. R. 3020, June 23, 1947, LOC.

24. *Committee on Un-American Activities, Exhibits, Evidence and Other Records, 1946–1947, Minutes of Full Committee and Sub-Committee Hearings, January–December 1947*, NWL 4780, container 1, HOUSE, RG 233, NARA.

25. Lyons, *David Sarnoff*, 83.

26. Cherney, *Candy Bombers*, 241–47.

27. J. E . Smith, *Lucius D. Clay*, 462–88.

28. J. E. Smith, *Lucius D. Clay*, 491–92.

29. J. E . Smith, *Lucius D. Clay*, 495–507.

30. *History of Rhein-Main Air Base*, A0072, Microfilm 0074, June 1948–June 1949, AFHRA; *History of Tempelhof Air Base*, A0082, Microfilm 0082, June 1948–June 1949, AFHRA; *History, 61st Communications Squadron, Rhein-Main Air Base* A0684, SQ-COM-61-HI, AFHRA.

31. McCullough, *Truman*, 630–31.

32. *Berlin Airlift (Operation Vittles) Crew and Route Procedures, William Tunner Papers*, Microfilm 34927, 168.7158, AFHRA; *Airways and Air Corridor Procedures—Rhein Main-Tempelhof/Gatow/Tegel*, SQ-1946-Air Communications Services, A3221, AFHRA.

33. *History, United States Air Forces Europe (USAFE), Berlin Airlift (Operation Vittles)*, William Tunner Papers, Microfilm 34927,168.7158, AFHRA.

34. Cherney, *Candy Bombers*, 297–300, 303–8.

35. Cherney, *Candy Bombers*, 343–45.

36. R. N. Smith, *Thomas E. Dewey*, 524–36.

37. Ehrman, *Alger Hiss Case*; U.S. Senate, "The Cold War," Moynihan Commission on Government Secrecy, 103rd Congress, 105-2, 1997, appendix A7.

38. Executive Order 9981, July 26, 1948, HST.

39. Nichols, *Matter of Justice*, 42–50.

40. McCullough, *Truman*, 739.

41. "The Office of the Historian, Department of State, "The Chinse Revolution of 1949," Milestones in U.S. Foreign Relations, 1945–1952, STATE.

42. Oshinsky, *Conspiracy So Immense*, 194; Crosby, *God, Church and Flag*, 200: Among the fellow lawmakers reluctant to oppose McCarthy was Joseph P. Kennedy's son John Fitzgerald Kennedy, who represented Massachusetts, a state with a sizable Catholic population. Another Kennedy son, Robert, worked on McCarthy's staff. In 1952 fellow Republican McCarthy did not support Massachusetts Sen. Henry Cabot Lodge Jr. for reelection because Lodge's opponent was Rep. John F. Kennedy.

43. Wallace, *Politics of Conscience*, 109: Six senators joined Smith's "Declaration of Conscience." McCarthy sarcastically called them "Snow White and the Six Dwarfs." Sen. Arthur Vandenberg died in 1954.

44. *United States Objectives and Programs for National Security*, NSC 68, April 14, 1950, STATE.

45. "Experiments for Hydrogen Bomb Held Successfully at Eniwetok," *New York Times*, November 16, 1952, 1; "Edward Teller," *New York Times*, September 11, 2003, 22.

46. Montefiore, *Stalin*, 599–601.

47. Brands, *General vs. the President*, 48–49.

48. Brands, *General vs. the President*, 76–77, 81.

49. Andrei Ledovskii, *"Stalin, Mao Tsedunh I Koreiskaia Voina 1950–1953* Godov," Novaya I Noveishaya Istoriia, no. 5 (September—October 2005), 79–113; *Letter from Filipov (Stalin) to Soviet Ambassador in Prague for cssr (Czech and Slovak Socialist Republic) Leader Klement Gottwald*, August 27, 1950, Russian State Archive of Socio-Political History (RGASPI), fond 558, Opis 11, Delo 62, Listy 71–72.

50. Manchester, *American Caesar*, 584.

51. Manchester, *American Caesar*, 587.

52. Brands, *General vs. the President*, 174–88.

53. Manchester, *American Caesar*, 596–98.

54. Brands, *General and vs. the President*, 188–89, 194–98.

55. Manchester, *American Caesar*, 624–27.

56. Crosby, *God, Church and Flag*, 194.

57. Manchester, *American Caesar*, 652–55.

58. McCullough, *Truman*, 852.

59. McCullough, *Truman*, 853.

60. McCullough, *Truman*, 554.

61. *Committee on Un-American Activities, Exhibits, Evidence and Other Records, 1950–1951, Minutes of Full Committee and Sub-Committee Hearings, January 1950–December, 1951,* NWL 4780, container 1, HOUSE, RG 233, NARA.

62. *Project Venona: Declassified Chronological Documents, 1940–1951* (complete set), released July 1995–September 1997, NSA.

63. U.S. Senate, "Experience of the Bomb," Moynihan Commission on Government Secrecy, 103rd Congress, 105-2, 1997, appendix A6.

64. Alan Cowell, "Theodore Hall, Prodigy and Atomic Spy, Dies at 74," *New York Times*. November 10, 1999.

65. Ambrose, *Eisenhower*, 13–35, 347–74.

66. Dwight D. Eisenhower to Milton Eisenhower, Dwight D. Eisenhower Papers, Document 460, October 9, 1953, DDE.

67. *Brown v. Board of Education of Topeka*, 347 U.S. 483, May 17, 1954, LOC.

68. Ambrose, *Eisenhower*, 411–35.

69. Oshinsky, *Conspiracy So Immense*, 226–46.

70. Executive Order 10450, April 27, 1953, Federal Register, NARA: There was gossip during the 1950s that McCarthy himself was gay, and some historians think this is plausible.

71. Oshinsky, *Conspiracy So Immense*, 457–71.

72. *See It Now*, CBS Television Network, March 9, 1954, DVD and transcript, collection of the author.

73. Herman, *Joseph McCarthy*, 253.

74. Censure of Joseph R. McCarthy, 83rd Cong., 2nd sess., S.R. 301, December 2, 1954, LOC.

75. John F. Kennedy was hospitalized with a back injury and did not vote for or against the censure of McCarthy. His brother Robert F. Kennedy, a former McCarthy staff member, attended McCarthy's funeral in Appleton, Wisconsin.

76. Herman, *Joseph McCarthy*, 5–6; Haynes and Klehr, *Venona*, 94–115, 165–90, 208–51; Dorothy Rabinowitz, "A Conspiracy So Vast," *Wall Street Journal*, July 7, 2003.

77. MacMillan, *Nixon and Mao*, 110–11.

78. Office of the Historian, Department of State, "Entrenchment of a Bipolar Foreign Policy," Milestones in U.S. Foreign Relations, 1953–1960, STATE.

79. Ambrose, *Eisenhower*, 172–73.

80. Montefiore, *Stalin*, 638–50.

81. Ambrose, *Eisenhower*, 94–96, 147–51, 171–72, 224–26; Potter, *Nimitz*, 424–25.

82. Kinzer, *Brothers*, 119–35, 147–69; Srodes, *Allen Dulles*, 418–19, 460–62.

83. *United States Information Agency, Reorganization Plan No. 8*, United States Statutes at Large, 83rd Cong., 1st sess., 1953, 67 Stat 642, 624–44, U.S. Government Printing Office.

84. Radio Free Europe / Radio Liberty Broadcast and Corporate Records, Hoover Institution, https://www.hoover.org/library-archives/collections/radio-free -europeradio-liberty-records.

85. Ambrose, *Eisenhower*, 354–56, 358–59.

86. National Aeronautics and Space Act of 1958, Public Law 85–568, 72 Stat., 426, signed by the president July 29, 1958, NASA, RG 255, NARA.

87. Neufeld, *Von Braun*, 333–53; National Aeronautics and Space Act, Pub. L. No. 111–314, Stat. 3328, December 18, 2010, NASA.

88. Quirk, *Fidel Castro*, 60–86, 119–39.

89. DePalma, *Man Who Invented Fidel*, 1–8.

90. Ambrose, *Eisenhower*, 571–79.

91. *Presidential Address of January 17, 1961*, DDE.

92. Von Eschen, *Satchmo Blows Up the World*, 27–57.

93. Kaplan, *1959, The Year Everything Changed*, 128.

94. Connor, *Benny Goodman*, 216–41.

95. "Duke Ellington: The Keys to Diplomacy," Jam Session, America's Jazz Ambassadors, Institute of Jazz Studies, Rutgers University, http://www.meridian .org/jazzambassadors/duke_ellington/duke_ellington.php.

96. "Louis Armstrong: Satchmo Blows Up the World," Jam Session, America's Jazz Ambassadors, Institute of Jazz Studies, Rutgers University, http://www.meridian .org/jazzambassadors/louis_armstrong/louis_armstrong.php.

97. "Enter the Newport Jazz Festival," Jam Session, America's Jazz Ambassadors, Institute of Jazz Studies, Rutgers University, http://www.meridian.org/jazzambassadors /newport/newport.php.

98. Ripmaster, *Willis Conover*; "Willis Conover, Jazz Icon," Voice of America, https:// www.insidevoa.com/a/willis-conover-international-icon-137984968/177542.html.

99. Tomlin, *Murrow's Cold War*, 27–33.

100. Cronkite, *Reporter's Life*, 271–88;.Dallek, *Unfinished Life*, 392–94, 585–86, 651–55.

101. Dallek, *Unfinished Life*, 535–75; Office of the Historian, Department of State, "The Cuban Missile Crisis, October 1962," Milestones in the History of U.S. Foreign Relations, 1945–1952, STATE.

102. Office of the Historian, Department of State, *The Berlin Crisis, 1958–1961*, STATE.

103. Dallek, *An Unfinished Life*, 418–35, 691–99.

104. Karnow, *Vietnam*, 387–426, 474–514.

105. *Foreign Relations of the United States, 1964–1968*, vol. 27, Mainland Southeast Asia; Regional Affairs, Washington DC, document no. 52, STATE; Recording and Transcripts, Telephone Conversations between President Johnson and Sen. J. William Fulbright (D-AR), December 2, 1963, and Sen. Richard Russell (D-GA), May 27, 1964 and July 26, 1965, LBJ.

106. Brinkley, *Cronkite*, 340–88.

107. Cronkite, *Reporter's Life*, 112–14, 264–70.

108. Dallek, *Lyndon B. Johnson*, 318–42.

109. "Nixon and Hirohito Pledge Amity in Anchorage Talks," *New York Times*, September 23, 1971, 1.

110. MacMillan, *Nixon and Mao*, 30, 104–5.

111. Kissinger, *White House Years*, 733–87, 1049–96, 1395–1471; MacMillan, *Nixon and Mao*, 71–75, 300–320; Office of the Historian, Department of State, "Rapprochement with China, 1972," Milestones in the History of U.S. Foreign Relations, 1969–

1976, STATE; Office of the Historian, Department of State, "Ending the Vietnam War, 1969–1973," Milestones in the History of U.S. Foreign Relations, 1969–1976, STATE.

112. Kissinger, *Years of Upheaval*, 374–413, 450–544, 854–95; Nixon, RN: *The Memoirs of Richard M. Nixon*, "The Presidency," 1973, 761–968; 1974, 969–1090; Office of the Historian, Department of State, "The 1973 Arab-Israeli War" and "Oil Embargo, 1973–1974," Milestones in the History of U.S. Foreign Relations, 1969–1976, STATE.

113. Brinkley, *Gerald R. Ford*, 53–80, 133–49; Kissinger, *Years of Renewal*, 17–42, 520–46.

114. Eizenstat, *President Carter*, 17–64, 498–530, 747–812, 863–92.

115. Brinkley, *Reagan Diaries*, 68, 80–87, 314–24, 369–71; Reagan, *American Life*, 233–308, 309–404.

116. Reagan, *Reagan Diaries*, 63, 72, 214, 226, 341, 440, 462, 529–30; Reagan, *American Life*, 405–68, 469–544.

117. Reagan, *Reagan Diaries*, 383–88, 441–44, 524, 555–57, 576; Reagan, *American Life*, 545–723.

118. Meacham, *Destiny and Power*, 379–83, 388–89, 400–408, 421–33, 450–57, 482–95.

119. Jay Nordlinger, "Still Broadcasting Freedom," *National Review*, April 16, 2018; "RFL/RL Mark Sixty Years of Fighting for Freedom," Radio Free Europe/Radio Liberty, press release, July 2, 2010.

BIBLIOGRAPHY

Manuscripts and Archives

AFHRA   U.S. Air Force Historic Research Agency, Maxwell-Gunter Air Force
        Base, Montgomery Alabama

AMPAS   Academy of Motion Picture Arts and Sciences, Los Angeles

BBC   British Broadcasting Corporation Written Archives Center, Caversham

BPR   Bureau of Public Affairs, War Department, Washington DC

CMH   U.S. Army Center for Military History, Fort McNair, Virginia

DDE   Dwight D. Eisenhower Presidential Library, Abilene, Kansas

DOD   Department of Defense, Washington DC

DOT   Department of Transportation, Washington DC

FDR   Franklin Delano Roosevelt Presidential Library, Hyde Park, New York

GHB   George H. W. Bush Presidential Library, College Station, Texas

GMA   Glenn Miller Archives, American Music Research Center, University of
        Colorado Boulder

HCH   Herbert C. Hoover Presidential Library, West Branch, Iowa

HST   Harry S. Truman Presidential Library, Independence, Missouri

IBRD   International Bank for Reconstruction and Development

IMF   International Monetary Fund

JFK   John F. Kennedy Presidential Library, Boston

LBJ   Lyndon B. Johnson Presidential Library, Austin, Texas

LOC   Library of Congress, Washington DC

NARA   National Archives and Records Administration, College Park, Maryland

NASA   National Aeronautics and Space Administration, Washington DC

NAUK   National Archives of the United Kingdom, Kew Gardens

OWI   Office of War Information, Washington DC

PRI   The Thomas Jefferson Papers, Princeton University, Princeton,
        New Jersey

RAC   Rockefeller Archive Center, Sleepy Hollow, New York

RMN   Richard M. Nixon Presidential Library, Simi Valley, California

RWR   Ronald W. Reagan Presidential Library, Yorba Linda, California

STATE   Department of State, Washington DC

UM   University of Maryland Library of American Broadcasting, College
         Park, Maryland
UCLA   University of California Los Angeles Libraries, Los Angeles
USMC   United States Marine Corps, Washington DC
USC   University of Southern California Libraries, Los Angeles
USN   Department of the Navy, Washington DC
WDA   Walt Disney Archives, Burbank, California

Published Works

Agee, James. *Agee on Film.* New York: McDowell, Obolensky, 1958.

Ambrose, Stephen E. *Eisenhower.* Vol. 2, *The President.* New York: Simon and
    Schuster, 1984.

———. *Nothing Like It in the World: The Men Who Built the Transcontinental
    Railroad, 1863–1869.* New York: Simon and Schuster, 2000.

Atkinson, Rick. *An Army at Dawn: The War in North Africa, 1942–1943.* New York:
    Henry Holt, 2002.

———. *The Day of Battle: The War in Sicily and Italy, 1943–1944.* New York: Henry
    Holt, 2007.

———. *The Guns at Last Light: The War in Western Europe, 1944–1945.* New York:
    Henry Holt, 2013.

Badger, Reid. *A Life in Ragtime: A Biography of James Reese Europe.* New York:
    Oxford University Press, 2007.

Baime, A. J. *The Arsenal of Democracy: FDR, Detroit and an Epic Quest to Arm an
    America at War.* New York: Houghton Mifflin Harcourt, 2014.

Banning, Gene, and R. E. G. Davies. *Airlines of Pan American since 1927.* McLean
    VA: Paladwr Press, 2001.

Bartholemew-Feis, Dixee. *The OSS and Ho Chi Minh: Unexpected Allies in the War
    against Japan.* Lawrence: University Press of Kansas, 2006.

Beckert, Sven. *Empire of Cotton,* A Global History. New York: Alfred A. Knopf, 2014.

Berg, A. Scott. *Lindbergh.* New York: G. P. Putnam's Sons, 1998.

———. *Wilson.* New York: G. P. Putnam's Sons, 2013.

Bergin, Bob. "The Operator: Ho Chi Minh as Political Activist in Europe and
    Asia." *Intelligencer: Journal of U.S. Intelligence Studies* 23, no. 2 (Fall 2017): 37.

Bergmeier, Horst, and Ranier Lotz. *Hitler's Airwaves: The Inside Story of Nazi Radio
    Broadcasting and Propaganda Swing.* New Haven CT: Yale University Press, 1997.

Bernard, Kenneth A. *Lincoln and the Music of the Civil War.* Caldwell ID: Cax-
    ton, 1966.

Bilby, Kenneth. *The General: David Sarnoff and the Rise of the Communications
    Industry.* New York: Harper and Row, 1986.

Bird, Kai, and Martin J. Sherwin. *American Prometheus: The Triumph and Tragedy
    of J. Robert Oppenheimer.* New York: Alfred A. Knopf, 2005.

Blair, Clay. *Silent Victory: The U. S. Submarine War against Japan.* Annapolis MD:
    Bluejacket, Naval Institute Press, 2001.

Bohlen, Charles Eustis. *Witness to History, 1929–1969.* New York: W. W. Norton, 1973.

Boller, Paul F., Jr. *Presidential Campaigns from George Washington to George W. Bush.* New York: Oxford University Press, 2004.

Bowen, H. V., Elizabeth Mancke, and John G. Reid. *Britain's Oceanic Empire: Atlantic and Indian Ocean Worlds, c. 1550–1850.* Cambridge: Cambridge University Press, 2012.

Brands, H. W. *Andrew Jackson: His Life and Times.* New York: Doubleday, 2005.

———. *The General vs. the President: MacArthur and Truman at the Brink of Nuclear War.* New York: Doubleday, 2016.

———. *The Restless Decade: America in the 1890s.* Chicago: University of Chicago Press, 2002.

———. *T. R.: The Last Romantic.* New York: Basic, 1997.

Brinkley, Douglas. *Cronkite.* New York: Harper Collins, 2012.

———. *Gerald R. Ford.* New York: Times, 2007.

———. *The Wilderness Warrior: Theodore Roosevelt and the Crusade for America.* New York: HarperCollins, 2009.

Brody, Richard. "The Worst Thing about 'Birth of a Nation' Is How Good It Is." *New Yorker,* May 20, 2014.

Burlingame, Roger. *Don't Let Them Scare You: The Life and Times of Elmer Davis.* New York: Cornwall, 1961.

Burstein, Andrew, and Nancy Isenberg. *Madison and Jefferson:* New York: Random House, 2010.

Capra, Frank. *The Name above the Title: An Autobiography.* New York: Macmillan, 1971.

Carrozza, Anthony. *William D. Pawley: The Extraordinary Life of the Adventurer, Entrepreneur and Diplomat Who Co-Founded the Flying Tigers.* Washington DC: Potomac, 2012.

Cashin, Herschel V. *Under Fire with the Tenth U.S. Cavalry.* Chicago: American, 1902.

Cherney, Andrei. *The Candy Bombers: The Untold Story of the Berlin Airlift and America's Finest Hour.* New York: G. P. Putnam's Sons, Penguin Group, 2008.

Chernow, Ron. *Alexander Hamilton.* New York: Penguin, 2004.

Churchill, Winston S. *At the Admiralty.* Vol. 1 of *The Churchill War Papers.* Edited by Martin Gilbert. New York: W. W. Norton, 1993.

———. *Never Surrender.* Vol. 2 of *The Churchill War Papers.* Edited by Martin Gilbert. New York: W. W. Norton, 1995.

———. *The Ever-Widening War.* Vol. 3 of *The Churchill War Papers.* Edited by Martin Gilbert. New York: W. W. Norton, 2001.

———. *Their Finest Hour.* Vol. 2 of *The Second World War.* Boston: Houghton Mifflin, 1949.

———. *The Grand Alliance.* Vol. 3 of *The Second World War.* Boston: Houghton Mifflin, 1949.

———. *The Hinge of Fate.* Vol. 4 of *The Second World War.* Boston: Houghton Mifflin, 1949.

———. *Closing the Ring.* Vol. 5 of *The Second World War.* Boston: Houghton Mifflin, 1949.Clark, Ronald. *Einstein: The Life and Times.* New York: Random House, 1995.

———. *The World Crisis.* Vol. 4 of *1918–1928: The Aftermath.* New York: Charles Scribner's Sons, 1929.

Clark, Ronald. *Einstein: The Life and Times.* New York: Random House, 1995.

Cole, Wayne S. *Charles A. Lindbergh and the Battle against American Intervention in World War II.* New York: Harcourt Brace Jovanovich, 1974.

Connor, D. Russell. *Benny Goodman: Listen to His Legacy.* Metuchen NJ: Scarecrow and Institute of Jazz Studies, 1988.

The Constitution of the United States: Analysis and Interpretation. U.S. Senate and Congressional Research Service, 1913–2013. Washington DC: Government Printing Office.

Coolidge, Calvin. *Foundations of the Republic, Speeches and Addresses.* Freeport NY: Books for Libraries Press, 1926.

Cooper, John Milton. *Woodrow Wilson: A Biography.* New York: Alfred A. Knopf, 2009.

Crackel, Theodore J., ed. *The Papers of George Washington, Presidential Series.* Charlottesville: University Press of Virginia, 2009.

Crapol, Edward P. *John Tyler: The Accidental President.* Chapel Hill: University of North Carolina Press, 2006.

Creel, George. *How We Advertised America: The First Telling of the Amazing Story of the Committee on Public Information That Carried the Gospel of Americanism to Every Corner of the Globe.* New York: Harper and Brothers, 1920.

Cronkite, Walter. *A Reporter's Life.* New York: Alfred A. Knopf, 1996.

Crosby, Donald F. *God, Church, and Flag: Senator Joseph R. McCarthy and the Catholic Church, 1950–1957.* Chapel Hill: University of North Carolina Press, 1976.

Croswell, D. K. R. *Beetle: The Life of General Walter Bedell Smith.* Lexington: University Press of Kentucky, 2010.

Cuthbert, David H. *Mission to Moscow.* Madison: University of Wisconsin Press, 1980.

Dallek, Robert. *An Unfinished Life: John F. Kennedy, 1917–1963.* New York: Little, Brown, 2003.

———. *Lyndon B. Johnson, Portrait of a President.* Oxford: Oxford University Press, 2004.

Davenport, Lisa. *Jazz Diplomacy: Promoting America in the Cold War Era.* Jackson: University Press of Mississippi, 2013.

Davies, Joseph. *Mission to Moscow.* New York: Simon and Schuster, 1941.

Davies, R. E. G. *Airlines of Latin America since 1919.* London: Putnam, 1984.

Davis, Donald A. *Lightning Strike: The Secret Mission to Kill Admiral Yamamoto and Avenge Pearl Harbor.* New York: St. Martin's, 2005.

Davis, Elmer. "War of Words: What the OWI Is Doing." *Saturday Review of Literature,* December 5, 1942, 7–9.

Davis, Kenneth S. *FDR: Into the Storm, 1937–1940.* New York: Random House, 2000.

———. *FDR: The War President, 1940–1943.* New York: Random House, 2000.

Dean, John W. *Warren Harding*. New York: Henry Holt, 2004.

DeLay, Theodore. "An Historical Study of the Armed Forces Radio Service to 1946." PhD diss., University of Southern California, 1951, RG 330, NARA and USC Libraries.

DePalma, Anthony. *The Man Who Invented Fidel: Castro, Cuba and Herbert L. Matthews of the New York Times*. Cambridge MA: PublicAffairs, 2006.

D'Este, Carlo. *Eisenhower: A Soldier's Life*. New York: Henry Holt, 2002.

Dewey, George. *The Autobiography of George Dewey, Admiral of the Navy*. New York: Charles Scribner's Sons, 1913.

Divine, Robert A. *Second Chance: The Triumph of Internationalism in America during World War II*. Garden City NY: Doubleday, 1967.

Dobbs, Michael. *Saboteurs: The Nazi Raid on America*. New York: Random House, 2007.

Doherty, Thomas. *Hollywood's Censor: Joseph I. Breen and the Production Code Administration*. New York: Columbia University Press, 2009.

Dole, Bob. *One Soldier's Story: A Memoir*. New York: HarperCollins, 2005.

Donovan, James. *A Terrible Glory: Custer and the Little Bighorn; The Last Great Battle of the American West*. New York: Little, Brown, 2008.

Ehrman, John. "A Half-Century of Controversy: The Alger Hiss Case." *Studies in Intelligence* 44, no. 10 (Winter-Spring 2001). Unclassified ed., https://www.cia.gov/library/center-for-the-study-of-intelligence/csi-publications/csi-studies/studies/winter_spring01/index.htm.

Eisenhower, Dwight D. *Crusade in Europe*. New York: Doubleday, 1948.

——— . *Mandate for Change, 1953–1956: The White House Years*. New York: Doubleday, 1963.

Eisenhower, John S. D. *Intervention: The United States and the Mexican Revolution, 1913–1917*. New York: W. W. Norton, 1995.

Eizenstat, Stuart. *President Carter: The White House Years*. New York: Thomas Dunne, St. Martin's, 2018.

Ellis, Joseph J. *His Excellency: George Washington*. New York: Alfred A. Knopf, 2011.

Evans, David, and Mark Peattie. *Kaigun: Strategy, Tactics and Technology in the Imperial Japanese Navy, 1887–1941*. Annapolis MD: Naval Institute Press, 1997.

Fehrenbacher, Don E. *The Dred Scott Case: Its Significance in American Law and Politics*. New York: Oxford University Press, 1978.

Fenby, Jonathan. *Chiang Kai-Shek: China's Generalissimo and the Nation He Lost*. New York: Carroll and Graf, 2004.

Fenn, Charles. *At the Dragon's Gate: With the OSS in the Far East*. Annapolis MD: Naval Institute Press, 2013.

Ferenbach. T. R. *Lone Star: A History of Texas and the Texans*. Rev. ed. Boston: De Capo, 2000. First published 1968.

Finch, Roy E. *The Story of the New York State Canals*. Albany: New York State Canal Corporation, 1998. First published 1925.

Finkelman, Paul. "John Brown: America's First Terrorist?" *Prologue Magazine* 43, no. 1 (Spring 2011).

Foote, Shelby. *The Civil War: A Narrative.* 3 vols. New York: Random House, 1958.

Frank, Mortimer H. *Arturo Toscanini: The NBC Years.* New York: Amadeus, 2002.

Frank, Richard B. *Downfall: The End of the Imperial Japanese Empire:* New York: Penguin, 1999.

———. *Guadalcanal: The Definitive Account of the Epic Battle.* New York: Random House, 1990.

Friedman, Norman. *U. S. Submarines through 1945: An Illustrated Design History.* Annapolis: Naval Institute Press, 1994.

Gaddis, John Lewis, Philip H. Gordon, Ernest R. May, and Jonathan Rosenberg, eds. *Cold War Statesmen Confront the Bomb: Nuclear Diplomacy since 1945.* Oxford: Oxford University Press, 1999.

Gallagher, Tag. *John Ford—A Man and His Films.* Berkeley: University of California Press, 1986.

Gannon, Michael. *Operation Drumbeat: The Dramatic True Story of Germany's U-Boat Attacks along the American Coast in World War II.* Annapolis MD: Naval Institute Press, 2009.

Garraty, John A. *Henry Cabot Lodge: A Biography.* New York: Alfred A. Knopf, 1953.

Gates, Henry Louis. "Slavery: By the Numbers." *Root,* February 10, 2014.

Gilbert, Martin. *Churchill: A Life.* New York: Henry Holt, 1991.

Goldman, Armond S., and Daniel A. Goldman. *Prisoners of Time: The Misdiagnosis of FDR's Illness.* Renton WA: EHDP, 2017.

Haggard, Robert. "The Nicola Affair: Lewis Nicola, George Washington, and American Military Discontent during the Revolutionary War." *Proceedings of the American Philosophical Society* 146, no. 2 (June 2002): 139–69.

Harmetz, Aljean. *Round Up the Usual Suspects: The Making of Casablanca, Bogart, Bergman, and World War II.* London: Orion, 1993.

Haynes, John Earl, and Harvey Klehr. *Verona: Decoding Soviet Espionage in America.* New Haven CT: Yale University Press, 1999.

Heidler, David Stephen, and Jeanne T. Heidler. *Henry Clay: The Essential American.* New York: Random House, 2011.

Heil, Alan L., Jr. *Voice of America: A History.* New York: Columbia University Press, 2003.

Herman, Arthur. *Joseph McCarthy: Reexamining the Life and Legacy of America's Most Hated Senator.* New York: Free Press, 2000.

Herring, Hubert. *Good Neighbors: Argentina, Brazil, Chile and Seventeen Other Countries.* New Haven CT: Yale University Press, 1941.

Hershberg, James, and James B. Conant. *Harvard to Hiroshima and the Making of the Nuclear Age.* New York: Alfred A. Knopf, 1993.

Hickey, Donald R. *The War of 1812: A Short History.* Urbana: University of Illinois Press, 2012.

Howarth, Stephen. *The Fighting Ships of the Rising Sun.* New York: Atheneum, 1983.

Irwin, Douglas, and Richard Sylla. *Founding Choices: American Economic Policy in the 1790s*. Chicago: University of Chicago Press, 2010.

Issacson, Walter. *Benjamin Franklin*. New York: Simon and Schuster, 2003.

Jefferson, Thomas. *The Papers of Thomas Jefferson*. Vol. 28, *January 1794 to February 1796*. Edited by John Catanzariti. Princeton NJ: Princeton University Press, 2000.

──── . *The Papers of Thomas Jefferson*. Vol. 37, *March to June 1802*. Edited by Barbara B. Oberg. Princeton NJ: Princeton University Press, 2011.

Jessup, Philip C. *Elihu Root*. Vol. 2, *1905–1937*. New York: Dodd Mead, 1938.

Kagan, Robert. *Dangerous Nation: America's Place in the World from Its Earliest Days to the Dawn of the Twentieth Century*. New York: Alfred A. Knopf, 2006.

Kaplan, Fred. *1959: The Year Everything Changed*. New York: John Wiley, 2009.

Karnow, Stanley. *Vietnam: A History*. New York: Viking, 1983.

Kennan, George C. *Memoirs: 1925–1950*. Boston: Little, Brown, 1967.

Keynes, John Maynard. *The Economic Consequences of the Peace*. New York: Penguin, 1995. First published 1919.

Kimball, Ward. *Churchill and Roosevelt: The Complete Correspondence*. 3 vols. Princeton NJ: Princeton University Press, 1984.

Kinzer, Stephen. *The Brothers: John Foster Dulles, Allen Dulles, and Their Secret World War*. New York: Henry Holt, 2013.

Kirby, Edward Montague, and Jack W. Harris. *Star-Spangled Radio*. New York: Ziff-Davis, 1948.

Kissinger, Henry. *White House Years*. Boston: Little, Brown, 1979.

──── . *Years of Renewal*. New York: Simon and Schuster, 1999.

──── . *Years of Upheaval*. New York: Boston: Little, Brown, 1982.

Knock, Thomas J. "'History with Lightning': The Forgotten Film *Wilson*." *American Quarterly* 28, no. 5 (Winter 1976): 523–43.

Koppes, Clayton R., and Gregory D. Black. *Hollywood Goes to War: How Politics, Profits and Propaganda Shaped World War II Movies*. Berkeley: University of California Press, 1987.

Kozak, Warren. *LeMay: The Life and Wars of Curtis LeMay*. Washington DC: Regnery, 2009.

Leeke, Jim. *Manila and Santiago: The New Steel Navy in the Spanish-American War*. Annapolis MD: Naval Institute Press, 2009.

Leff, Leonard J., and Jerold Simmons. "*Wilson*: Hollywood Propaganda for World Peace." *Historical Journal of Film, Radio and Television* 3, no. 1 (1983): 16–17.

LeMay, Curtis D. and MacKinlay Kantor. *Mission with LeMay: My Story*. New York: Doubleday, 1968.

Lyons, Eugene. *David Sarnoff: A Biography*. New York: Harper and Row, 1966.

MacMillan, Margaret. *Nixon and Mao: The Week That Changed the World*. New York: Random House, 2007.

──── . *Paris 1919: Six Months That Changed the World*: New York: Random House, 2002.

Mahan, Alfred Thayer. *The Influence of Sea Power upon History, 1660–1783*. Boston: Little, Brown, 1890.

———. "The United States Looking Outward." In *The Interest of America in Sea Power Present and Future*. Boston: Little Brown, 1897. First published 1890 in *Atlantic Monthly*.

Maier, Pauline. *Ratification: The People Debate the Constitution, 1787–1788*. New York: Simon and Schuster, 2010.

Manchester, William. *American Caesar: Douglas MacArthur, 1880–1964*. Boston: Little, Brown, 1978.

Mashbir, Sydney Forrester. *I Was an American Spy*. New York: Vantage, 1953.

Matzen, Robert. *Fireball: Carole Lombard and the Mystery of Flight 3*. Pittsburgh: Paladin Communications, 2013.

Mayo-Smith, Richmond. "The Eleventh Census of the United States." *Economic Journal* 1, no. 1 (1891).

McBride, Joseph. *Frank Capra: The Catastrophe of Success*. New York: Simon and Schuster, 1992.

———. *Searching for John Ford: A Life*. New York: St. Martin's, 2001.

McCrisken, Trevor B. "Exceptionalism: Manifest Destiny." *Encyclopedia of American Foreign Policy*, edited by Alexander Deconde, Richard Dean Burns, Fredrik Logeval, and Louise B. Ketz, 78. 2nd ed. Vol. 2. New York: Charles Scribner's Sons, 2001.

McCullough, David. *John Adams*. New York: Simon and Schuster, 2001.

———. *The Path between the Seas*. New York: Simon and Schuster, 1977.

———. *Truman*. New York: Simon and Schuster, 1992.

McMillan, James E. "McFarland and the Movies: The 1941 Senate Motion Picture Hearings." *Journal of Arizona History* 29, no. 3 (Autumn 1988): 277–302.

Meacham, Jon. *Destiny and Power: The American Odyssey of George Herbert Walker Bush*. New York: Random House, 2015.

———. *Thomas Jefferson: The Art of Power*. New York: Random House, 2012.

Meijer, Hendrik. *Arthur Vandenberg: The Man in the Middle of the American Century*. Chicago: University of Chicago Press, 2017.

Merck, Frederick. *History of the Westward Movement*. New York: Alfred A. Knopf, 1978.

Merck, Frederick, with the collaboration of Lois Bannister Merck. *Manifest Destiny and Mission in American History*. Cambridge MA: Harvard University Press, 1995. First published 1963 by Alfred A. Knopf.

Merry, Robert W. *A Country of Vast Designs: James K. Polk, the Mexican War and the Conquest of the American Continent*. New York: Simon and Schuster, 2009.

Merton, Robert K. Marjorie Fiske, and Alberta Curtis. *Mass Persuasion: The Social Psychology of a War Bond Drive*. New York: Harper and Brothers, 1946.

Meyer, Michael C. "The Arms of the Ypiranga." *Hispanic American Historical Review* 50, no. 3 (August 1970): 543–56.

Miller, John Chester. *Crisis in Freedom: The Alien and Sedition Acts*. Boston: Little, Brown, 1951.

Miller, Nathan. *Theodore Roosevelt: A Life*. New York: William Morrow, 1992.

Miller, Robert J. *Native America, Discovered and Conquered: Thomas Jefferson, Lewis & Clark and Manifest Destiny*. Lincoln: Bison Books, University of Nebraska Press, 2008.

Morley, Patrick. *This Is the American Forces Network*. Westport CT: Praeger, 2001.

Morris, Edmund. *Colonel Roosevelt*. New York: Random House, 2010.

———. *Theodore Rex*. New York: Random House, 2001.

Morrison, Samuel Elliott. *History of United States Naval Operations in World War II*. Vol 10, *The Atlantic Battle Won: May 1943–May 1945*. Boston: Little, Brown, 1956.

Morton, Louis. *The Fall of the Philippines*. Edited by Kent Roberts Greenfield. U.S. Army in World War II: The War in the Pacific. Washington DC: Center of Military History, 1953.

Moynihan, Daniel Patrick. *Secrecy: The American Experience*. New Haven CT: Yale University Press, 1999.

Murray, Robert K. *The Harding Era: Warren G. Harding and His Administration*. Minneapolis: University of Minnesota Press, 1969.

Neal, Steve. *Dark Horse: A Biography of Wendell Willkie*. New York: Doubleday, 1984.

Neufeld, Michael J. *Von Braun: Dreamer of Space, Engineer of War*. New York: Alfred A. Knopf, 2007.

Neuschul, Peter, and James Neuschul. "With the Marines at Tarawa." *U.S. Naval Institute Proceedings* 125/4/1 (April 1999), 154.

Nichols, David. *Ernie's War: The Best of Ernie Pyle's World War II Dispatches*. New York: Random House, 1986.

———. *A Matter of Justice: Eisenhower and the Beginning of the Civil Rights Revolution*. New York: Simon and Schuster, 2008.

Nixon, Richard M. *RN: The Memoirs of Richard M. Nixon*. New York: Simon and Schuster, 1990.

Northedge, F. S. *The League of Nations: Its Life and Times, 1920–1946*. Leicester UK: Leicester University Press, 1986.

Oshinsky, David M. *A Conspiracy So Immense: The World of Joe McCarthy*. Cambridge: Oxford University Press, 2005.

O'Sullivan, John L. "Annexation." *United States Magazine and Democratic Review* 17, no. 1 (1845): 5–10.

O'Toole, Patricia. *The Moralist: Woodrow Wilson and the World He Made*. New York: Simon and Schuster, 2018.

Paine, S. C. M. *The Wars for Asia, 1911–1949*. Cambridge: Cambridge University Press, 2015.

Pakula, Hannah. *The Last Empress: Madame Chiang Kai-Shek and the Birth of Modern China*. New York: Simon and Schuster, 2009.

Papke, David Ray. *The Pullman Case: The Clash of Labor and Capital in Industrial America*. Lawrence: University Press of Kansas, 1999.

Pasley, Jeffrey L. *The Tyranny of Printers: Newspaper Politics in the Early American Republic*. Charlottesville: University Press of Virginia, 2001.

Patti, Archimedes. *Why Viet Nam? Prelude to America's Albatross*. Berkeley: University of California Press, 1980.

Peress, Maurice. *Dvorak to Duke Ellington*. New York: Oxford University Press, 2004.

Persico, Joseph. *Casey: From the OSS to the CIA*: New York: Viking Penguin, 1990.

———. *Edward R. Murrow: An American Original*. New York: McGraw-Hill, 1988.

Phillips, Christopher. *Steichen at War*. New York: Henry N. Abrams, 1981.

Pirisein, Robert William. *The Voice of America: A History of the International Broadcasting Activities of the United States Government, 1940–1962*. New York: Arno, 1979.

Pogue, Forrest C. *George C. Marshall*.: Vol. 4, *Statesman, 1945–1959*. New York: Viking, 1987.

———. *The Supreme Command*. Washington DC: Office of the Chief of Military History, 1954.

Potter, E. B. *Nimitz*. Annapolis md: Naval Institute Press, 1979.

———. *Sea Power: A Naval History*. 2nd ed. Annapolis MD: Naval Institute Press, 1981.

Prange, Gordon, W., with Donald M. Goldstein and Katherine V. Dillion. *At Dawn We Slept: The Untold Story of Pearl Harbor*. New York: McGraw-Hill, 1981.

———. *Miracle at Midway*. New York: McGraw-Hill, 1982.

Quirk, Robert E. *Fidel Castro*. New York: W. W. Norton, 1993.

Rawson, Andrew. *Eyes Only: The Top-Secret Correspondence between Marshall and Eisenhower*. Spellmount, Glouchestershire UK: History Press, 2012.

Reagan, Ronald. *An American Life: The Autobiography of Ronald Reagan*. New York: Simon and Schuster, 1990.

———. *The Reagan Diaries*. Edited by Douglas Brinkley. New York: Harper Collins, 2007.

Resolution of the Congress, of September 13, 1788. *Journal of Congress*, 39, no. 1 (1788).

Ripmaster, Terrance. *Willis Conover: Broadcasting Jazz to the World*. New York: iUniverse, 2007.

Robbins, Jane M. "Tokyo Calling: Japanese Overseas Broadcasting, 1937–1945." Doctoral thesis, University of Sheffield, UK, August 1997.

Robinson, Greg. *A Tragedy of Democracy: Japanese Confinement in North America*. New York: Columbia University Press, 2009.

Roseman, Samuel. *Working with Roosevelt*. New York: Harper and Brothers, 1952.

Rove, Karl. *The Triumph of William McKinley: Why the Election of 1896 Still Matters*. New York: Simon and Schuster, 2016.

Schiff, David. *Gershwin: Rhapsody in Blue*. Cambridge: Cambridge University Press, 1997.

Schlaes, Amity. *Coolidge*. New York: HarperCollins, 2013.

Schley, Winfield Scott. *Forty-Five Years under the Flag*. New York: Appleton, 1903.

Schoultz, Lars. *Beneath the United States: A History of U.S. Policy toward Latin America*. Cambridge MA: Harvard University Press, 2009.

Schuller, Gunther. *The History of Jazz*. Vol. 2, *The Swing Era: The Development of Jazz, 1930–1945*. New York: Oxford University Press, 1989.

Schweikart, Larry, and Michael Allen. *A Patriot's History of the United States: From Columbus' Great Discovery to the Age of Entitlement*. New York: Sentinel, 2004; rev. ed., 2014.

Sears, Richard Sherwood. *V-Discs*. Westport CT: Greenwood, 1980.

Sherwood, Robert E. *Roosevelt and Hopkins: An Intimate History*. New York: Harper and Brothers, 1948.

Shirer, William L. *The Rise and Fall of the Third Reich*. New York: Simon and Schuster, 1960.

Showell, Jak P. Mallmann. *Enigma U-Boats: Breaking the Code; The True Story*. Annapolis MD: Naval Institute Press, 2000.

Smith, Arthur. *Hitler's Gold: The Story of Nazi War Loot*. Oxford: Berg, 1989.

Smith, Cmdr. C. Alphonso, USNR. "Martinique in World War II." *U.S. Naval Institute Proceedings* 81/2/624 (February 1955).

Smith, Jean Edward. *FDR*. New York: Random House, 2007.

———. *Lucius D. Clay: An American Life*: New York: Henry Holt, 1990.

Smith, Richard Norton. *On His Own Terms: A Life of Nelson Rockefeller*. New York: Random House, 2014.

———. *Thomas E. Dewey and His Times*. New York: Simon and Schuster, 1982.

Spragg, Dennis M. *Glenn Miller Declassified*. Lincoln: Potomac, 2017.

Srodes, James. *Allen Dulles: Master of Spies*. Washington DC: Regnery, 1999.

Stein, Burton. *A History of India*. 2nd ed. New York: John Wiley and Sons, 2010.

Stevenson, William. *A Man Called Intrepid: The Secret War*. New York: Harcourt Brace Jovanovich, 1976.

Stone, Geoffrey. *Perilous Times: Free Speech in Wartime, From the Sedition Acts to the War on Terrorism*. New York: W. W. Norton, 2005.

Suid, Lawrence, Michael Lee Lanning, M. S. Merrick, and Andreas Frederich. *History of AFRTS: The First 50 Years*. Washington DC: American Forces Information Service and Armed Forces Radio and Television Service, Department of Defense, 1992.

Sweeney, Charles W., James Antonucci, and Marion Antonucci. *War's End: An Eyewitness Account of America's Last Atomic Mission*. New York: Avon, 1997.

Taft, William Howard. *The Collected Works of William Howard Taft*. Vol. 7, *Taft Papers on the League of Nations*. Edited by Frank X. Garrity. Athens: Ohio University Press, 2003.

Thomas, Evan. "Race and the Spanish-American War." *Newsweek*, March 24, 2008.

Thompson, George Raynor, and Dixie Harris. *The Signal Corps: The Outcome (Mid-1943 through 1945)*. United States Army in World War II: The Technical Services. Washington DC: Office of the Chief Military Historian, 1946.

Tocqueville, Alexis de. *Democracy in America*: New York: Alfred A. Knopf, 1994. First published 1838 by George Dearborn.

Tomlin, Gregory M. *Murrow's Cold War: Public Diplomacy for the Kennedy Administration*. Lincoln: Potomac, 2016.

Tooze, Adam. *The Deluge: The Great War, America and the Remaking of Global Order, 1916–1931*. New York: Penguin, 2015.

Truman, Harry S. *Memoirs by Harry S. Truman*. Vol. 1, *Year of Decision*. New York: Doubleday, 1955.

Tuchman, Barbara. *Stillwell and the American Experience in China*. New York: Macmillan, 1970.

Turner, Frederick Jackson. "The Significance of the Frontier in American History." In *The Frontier in American History*. New York: Henry Holt, 1921, 1935. Originally presented at the World's Columbian Exposition, Chicago, 1893.

Von Eschen, Penny. *Satchmo Blows Up the World: Jazz Ambassadors Play the Cold War*. Cambridge MA: Harvard University Press, 2006.

Wallace, Patricia Ward. *Politics of Conscience: A Biography of Margaret Chase Smith*. Westport CT: Praeger, 1995.

Walters, Vernon A. *The Mighty and the Meek*. London: St. Ermin's, 2003.

——. *Silent Missions*. New York: Doubleday, 1978.

Washington, George. *The Papers of George Washington*. Presidential series, vol. 15, *1 January to 30 April 1794*. Edited by W. W. Abbot. Charlottesville: University of Virginia Press, 1988.

——. *The Writings of George Washington from the Original Manuscript Sources, 1745–1799*. Edited by John Clement Fitzpatrick and David Maydole Matteson. Washington DC: Government Printing Office, 1931.

Wheelan, Joseph. *Jefferson's War: The First War on Terror, 1801–1805*. New York: Carroll and Graf, 2003.

Willkie, Wendell. *One World*. New York. Simon and Schuster, 1943.

Winkler, Alan. *The Politics of Propaganda: The Office of War Information, 1942–1945*. New Haven CT: Yale University Press, 1978.

Womack, John. "The Mexican Revolution, 1910–1920." In *Mexico since Independence*, edited by Leslie Bethell, 125–200. Cambridge: Cambridge University Press, 1991.

Wukowitz, John. *Pacific Alamo: The Battle for Wake Island*. New York: Penguin, 2003.

Zoglin, Richard. *Hope: Entertainer of the Century*. New York: Simon and Schuster, 2014.

INDEX